Nietzsche and Jung

Nietzsche and Jung considers the thought and personalities of two icons of twentieth century philosophical and psychological thought, and reveals the extraordinary connections between them.

Through a thorough examination of their work, *Nietzsche & Jung* succeeds in illuminating complex areas of Nietzsche's thought and resolving ambiguities in Jung's reception of these theories. The location and analysis of the role played by opposites in the whole self according to Jung is considered, revealing the full extent of Nietzsche's influence. This rigorous and original analysis of Jungian theory and its philosophical roots, supported by Jung's seminars on Nietzsche's *Zarathustra*, leads to the development of a fresh interpretation of the theories of both. The shared model of selfhood is put into practice as the personalities of Nietzsche and Jung are evaluated according to the other's criteria for mental health, attempting to determine whether Nietzsche and Jung were themselves whole.

Nietzsche and Jung demonstrates how our understanding of analytical psychology can be enriched by investigating its philosophical roots, and considers whether the whole self is a realistic possibility for each of us. This book will prove fascinating reading for students in psychology, philosophy and religion as well as practicing Jungian analysts.

Lucy Huskinson is a fellow of the Centre for Psychoanalytic Studies, University of Essex. She has contributed articles for the *Journal of Analytical Psychology* and *Harvest Journal for Jungian Studies*.

Nietzsche and Jung

The Whole Self in the Union of Opposites

Lucy Huskinson

Brunner-Routledge
Taylor & Francis Group

HOVE AND NEW YORK

First published 2004 by Brunner-Routledge
27 Church Road, Hove, East Sussex BN3 2FA

Simultaneously published in the USA and Canada
by Brunner-Routledge
29 West 35th Street, New York, NY 10001

Brunner-Routledge is an imprint of the Taylor & Francis Group

© 2004 Lucy Huskinson

Typeset in Times by Keystroke, Jacaranda Lodge, Wolverhampton
Printed and bound in Great Britain by TJ International Ltd, Padstow, Cornwall
Cover design by Hybert Design

This publication has been produced with paper manufactured to strict
environmental standards and with pulp derived from sustainable forests.

British Library Cataloguing in Publication Data
A catalogue record for this book is available from the British Library

Library of Congress Cataloging in Publication Data
Huskinson, Lucy, 1976–
    Nietzsche and Jung : the whole self in the union of opposites / Lucy Huskinson.
        p. cm.
    Includes bibliographical references and index.
    ISBN 1-58391-832-9 (hardback : alk. paper) — ISBN 1-58391-833-7
(pbk. : alk. paper)
    1. Nietzsche, Friedrich Wilhelm, 1844–1900. 2. Jung, C. G. (Carl Gustav),
1875–1961. I. Title.
    B3317.H87 2004
    193—dc22

                                                    2004003889

ISBN 1-58391-832-9 (Hbk)
ISBN 1-58391-833-7 (Pbk)

For David
My other half
With love

Contents

Preface

I have left the writing of this preface to the end, and it has proved very tricky to write, as I have found it surprisingly difficult to detach myself from the content of this work and regard it as a finished product. This book is based on my doctoral thesis, and the greater part of it was written immediately after my doctoral examination. I therefore feel that I have been living and breathing its pages for an exceptionally long time, and with its completion comes the personal acknowledgement that my lively time as a university student is over. This book has found its way through countless revisions, supervisory boards, conference papers and sessions of 'liquid compensation' in the university bar. Indeed, I am not certain at what point I decided to start writing it. Its conception had been developing gradually through the different stages of my studies at the University of Essex. And it is to the people who have contributed most to my learning during this period (both academic and otherwise) that I wish to acknowledge my debt and gratitude.

I came to the University of Essex in October 1995 to read Philosophy. The two highlights of my studies were Freud and Nietzsche. At the time my enthusiasm for Freud was impressive (more so than for Nietzsche, which had been somewhat compromised by the fact that my undergraduate course was restricted to his 'middle period' – to *Daybreak, Human, All Too Human* and *The Gay Science*). My studies on Freud led to a master's degree in Psychoanalytic Studies in September 1998. It was here that I first came across Jungian theory. The more I read of Jung, the more I thought back to Nietzsche, and I was surprised that I was quite alone in making the connection. For me, the Jungian Self was clearly a reformulation of the Nietzschean *Übermensch*. Under the supervision of Roderick Main I wrote my dissertation on their similarities, which I soon discovered were vaster than I had anticipated. I decided then to focus on the role of opposites in their projects, with the greater focus on Jung.

In October 1999 I began my doctoral dissertation, *Nietzsche and Jung: The Whole Self in the Union of Opposites*, back in the Philosophy Department, under the joint supervision of Simon Critchley and Roderick Main. Near the beginning of my research I became interested in the ambivalent usage of philosophical criticism when applied to Jungian thought – how it can at once elucidate and distort

Jungian theory. This led me to write 'The Self as Violent Other: The Problem of Defining the Self', *Journal of Analytical Psychology*, 2002. I think the writing of this article displaced the general frustrations I would have otherwise felt when writing the doctoral thesis – it was excruciating, while my doctoral thesis seemed to flow.

My doctoral thesis was examined in 2003 by Stephen Houlgate (University of Warwick) and Renos Papadopoulous (University of Essex), and I thank them both for their constructive comments and invaluable insights, most of which I have incorporated within this work. Most importantly, I want to thank Roderick Main, who has been a scrupulous supervisor of my work throughout; I thank him for his meticulous concern for detail, his encouragement and general top-notch conversation. I also want to record a special thank you to Paul Bishop for his correspondence when writing my doctoral thesis, and for his all-round good sense of humour. The following people deserve a special mention for their indirect contributions to the realization of this book: Janet and Rachel Huskinson, Angus Bain, Nick Joll, Robbo Mossop, Andy McGee, Clive Zammit, Barbara Brickman, Marilyn Ward and, of course, Charmaine Coyle, my evil influence.

This work is dedicated to my husband, A. D. Smith, from whom I have learnt, and continue to learn, the most valuable lessons. I also thank him for taking on the unenviable task of reading through the 'final' drafts of this work (which was impressively executed, with only three (audible) sighs). I would also like to dedicate this work to those other characters of the Department of Philosophy at the University of Essex at the time I read for my first degree, in particular to Peter Dews, Mark Sacks, Tom Sorell, Simon Critchley, Mike Weston, Fiona Hughes, Will Cartwright and Barbara Crawshaw at the helm.

Acknowledgements

In this book I have made particular reference to the following works:

The Will to Power by Friedrich Nietzsche, edited by W. Kaufmann, translated by W. Kaufmann and R. J. Hollingdale, copyright © 1967 Vintage Books, New York. Permission applied for from Vintage Books, New York. *Human, All Too Human* by Friedrich Nietzsche, translated by R. J. Hollingdale, copyright © R. J. Hollingdale 1996, Cambridge University Press. Used by permission of Cambridge University Press. *Beyond Good and Evil* by Friedrich Nietzsche, translated by R. J. Hollingdale, copyright © R. J. Hollingdale 1973, Penguin Classics. Used by permission of Penguin Books Ltd. *Ecce Homo* by Friedrich Nietzsche, translated by R. J. Hollingdale, new introduction by Michael Tanner, copyright © R. J. Hollingdale 1992, introduction copyright © Michael Tanner, 1992, Penguin Classics. Used by permission of Penguin Books Ltd. *Thus Spoke Zarathustra* by Friedrich Nietzsche, translated by R. J. Hollingdale, copyright © R. J. Hollingdale 1961, 1969, Penguin Classics. Used by permission of Penguin Books Ltd. *Twilight of the Idols* by Friedrich Nietzsche, translated by R. J. Hollingdale, copyright © R. J. Hollingdale 1968, Penguin Classics. Used by permission of Penguin Books

Ltd. *Memories, Dreams, Reflections* by C. G. Jung, edited by Aniela Jaffé, translated by Richard and Clara Winston, copyright © 1961, 1962, 1963 and renewed 1989, 1990, 1991 by Random House, Inc. Used by permission of Pantheon Books, a division of Random House. Extracts from Jung's *Collected Works*, copyright © 1959, 1969, 1971, 1977 by Princeton University Press, published in the UK by Routledge. Used by permission of Princeton University Press and Routledge. *Nietzsche's Zarathustra: Notes of the Seminar Given in 1934–1939 by C. G. Jung*, edited by James Jarrett, two volumes, copyright © 1989 by Princeton University Press, published in the UK by Routledge. Used by permission of Princeton University Press and Routledge.

I wish to thank the *Journal of Analytical Psychology* for allowing me to reproduce material from my article 'The Self as Violent Other: The Problem of Defining the Self', *Journal of Analytical Psychology*, 2002. I also thank The British Academy (The Arts and Humanities Research Board) for their financial assistance when undertaking my doctoral research, which is incorporated within this work.

Book cover: *Untitled (for Francis)* by Antony Gormley. Courtesy of the artist and Jay Jopling/White Cube (London), copyright © Tate, London 2004.

Abbreviations

Nietzsche

Quotations are cited with reference to the following abbreviations.

AC   *The Anti-Christ (Der Antichrist*, 1888), translated by R. J. Hollingdale, Harmondsworth: Penguin, 1990.

AOM   *Assorted Opinions and Maxims (Vermischte Meinungen und Sprüche, HAH* II, 1879), translated by R. J. Hollingdale, Cambridge University Press, 1996.

BGE   *Beyond Good and Evil (Jenseits von Gut und Böse*, 1886), translated by R. J. Hollingdale, Harmondsworth: Penguin, 1990.

BT   *The Birth of Tragedy (Die Geburt der Tragödie*, 1872), edited by Michael Tanner, translated by Shaun Whiteside, Harmondsworth: Penguin, 1993.

D   *Daybreak (Morgenröte*, 1881), edited by Maudmarie Clark and Brian Leiter, translated by R. J. Hollingdale, Cambridge University Press, 1997.

EH   *Ecce Homo (Ecce Hommo*, 1888), translated by R. J. Hollingdale, Harmondsworth: Penguin, 1990.

GM I–IV   *The Genealogy of Morals (Zur Genealogie der Moral*, 1887), translated by Walter Kaufmann, New York: Random House, 1968.

GS   *The Gay Science (Die Fröhliche Wissenschaft*, 1882), translated by Walter Kaufmann, New York: Vintage, 1974.

HAH (I)   *Human, All Too Human (Menschliches, Allzumenschliches*, 1878), translated by R. J. Hollingdale, Cambridge University Press, 1996.

PTAG   *Philosophy in the Tragic Age of the Greeks (Die Philosophie im tragischen Zeitalter der Griechen*, 1873; unpublished by Nietzsche), translated by M. Cowan, Washington, DC: Regnery, Gateway, 1962.

TI   *Twilight of the Idols (Götzen-Dämmerung*, 1888), translated by R. J. Hollingdale, Harmondsworth: Penguin, 1990.

TL   *On Truth and Lie in the Extra-Moral Sense* (Über Wahrheit und Lüge im aussermoralischen Sinne, 1873, unpublished by Nietzsche), edited and translated by Daniel Breazeale, Atlantic Highlands, NJ: Humanities Press, 1979.

TSZ (I–IV)   *Thus Spoke Zarathustra* (*Also sprach Zarathustra* 1883–1885), translated by R. J. Hollingdale, Harmondsworth: Penguin, 1969.

UM (I-IV)   *Untimely Meditations* (*Unzeitgemässe Betrachtungen*, 1873–1876), translated by R. J. Hollingdale, Cambridge University Press, 1983.

WP   *The Will to Power* (*Der Wille zur Macht*), edited by Walter Kaufmann, translated by Walter Kaufmann and R. J. Hollingdale, New York: Vintage, 1967. This edition follows the 1911 German edition.

WS   *The Wanderer and his Shadow* (*Der Wanderer und sein Schatten*, *HAH* II, 1880), translated by R. J. Hollingdale, Cambridge University Press, 1996.

Jung

Quotations are cited with reference to the following abbreviations.

AP   *Analytical Psychology: Notes of the Seminar Given in 1925*, edited by William McGuire, London, 1984. Cited in the text with page reference.

CW   *Collected Works*, edited by Sir Herbert Read, Michael Fordham, Gergard Adler and William McGuire, translated by R. F. C. Hull, 20 volumes, London: Routledge and Kegan Paul, 1953–1983. Cited in the text with volume number. Essays from the *Collected Works* are cited in the text separately with date and paragraph number, their relevant volume number is indicated in the bibliography.

JS   *Jung Speaking: Interviews and Encounters*, edited by William McGuire and R. F. C. Hull, Princeton, NJ: Princeton University Press, 1977. Cited in the text with page reference.

MDR   *Memories, Dreams, Reflections*, recorded and edited by Aniela Jaffé, translated by Richard and Clara Winston, London: Fontana Press, 1983. Cited in the text with page reference.

MHS   *Man and his Symbols*, written with M. L. von Franz, Joseph Henderson, Jolande Jacobi and Aniela Jaffé. New York, edited by C. G. Jung, London: Arkana, 1990. Cited in the text with page reference.

MMSS   *Modern Man in Search of a Soul*, translated by W. S. Dell and Cary Baynes, London: Harcourt Brace Jovanovich, 1933.

SNZ   *Nietzsche's Zarathustra: Notes of the Seminar Given in 1934–1939*, edited by James Jarrett, two volumes, London: Routledge, 1989. Cited in the text with volume number and page reference.

Chapter 1

Introduction

This book concerns C. G. Jung's peculiar relation to the work and personality of Friedrich Nietzsche. Although the ambiguity that surrounds Sigmund Freud's reception of Nietzschean thought has been widely reported and to some degree explained,[1] the sense that one cannot but have of the even greater confusion and contradiction that envelops Jung's reception of Nietzsche has barely been investigated. Indeed, while Nietzsche's anticipation of central themes of Freudian psychoanalytic theory – including psychological drives, the unconscious, guilt, repression, dreaming, wishing, projection and sublimation – has been extensively reported, and is generally agreed to be beyond doubt, Nietzsche's influence on Jungian analytical psychology has received little attention, and even less by way of thorough evaluation.[2] This is surprising, almost embarrassing, as the similarities between the thought of Nietzsche and Jung are obvious. Indeed, Jung's affinity with the German philosopher, and his acceptance of philosophical speculation in general, is used by him to criticize and dissociate his theory from that of Freud.[3] For example, although Freud borrowed the Nietzschean term 'das Es' (translated in the English editions of Freud's works as the 'Id') to refer to an unconscious source of energy, the *nature* of this energy is significantly different for the two thinkers. Jung, on the other hand, endorses Nietzsche's conception, and for Jung this constitutes a fundamental difference between his theory and that of Freud.

Freud maintains that the unconscious consists of nothing but residues of the conscious mind that have become repressed. Simply put, this means that the value of the psyche is identified with consciousness or the ego. Nietzsche disagrees with this claim. Unlike Freud, Nietzsche recognizes that the unconscious exhibits contents that are wholly unlike those of consciousness and are ungraspable by the ego. A significant implication of this difference is that in Freud's model the unconscious has no autonomy, for it is simply a *product* of consciousness, or a container of its remnants. In Nietzsche's model, on the other hand, the unconscious is an autonomous entity that can function in opposition to consciousness. The Freudian understanding of the unconscious reveals a rigid framework of rationalism that gives primacy to the ego, which is in contrast to Nietzsche's richer framework that recognizes other sources of knowledge considered irrational, such as emotion, imagination and intuition.

The difference between Nietzschean psychology and Freudian psychoanalysis is more profound than is often realized and, as we shall see in the course of this inquiry, it is unwise to regard Nietzsche simply as a forerunner to *psychoanalysis*. Nietzsche's conception of the unconscious is not the 'classical' one adopted by Freud, among others, but is more like that particular notion of an *autonomous* and *collective* unconscious that marks the very separation of Jungian 'analytical psychology' from traditional 'psychoanalysis'.[4]

By enlarging the boundaries of the 'productive' psyche to include non-rational sources of knowledge, Nietzsche and Jung have effectively enlarged the capacity for personal growth and creativity. Thus, while Freud's understanding of the personality is essentially 'reductive', with its motivation being exclusively sexual, and with the communication of the unconscious having been filtered through *signs*, Nietzsche and Jung's understanding of the personality is 'constructive', with the focus being on its potential – specifically, its potential for becoming whole – and so encourages unconscious communication through *symbolic* language. The difference between the sign and the symbol is significant in that the former is a conscious construct – a fixed reference that conceals something knowable – whereas the latter is in part conscious and in part unconscious – a dynamic living entity that expresses something that is not fully graspable. In the Freudian model, the interpretation of the sign simply leads to the unmasking of a repressed conflict or wish; by contrast, the symbol in the Nietzschean and Jungian model facilitates psychic growth by naturally *uniting* consciousness with the unconscious.

Nietzsche and Jung place the symbol at the heart of their interpretation of psychic development. However, to leave Nietzsche and Jung coupled together in this way would be inadequate, for the very meaning of the symbol, and its subsequent implications for psychic development, are different for the two thinkers. And this is where our inquiry begins. For we shall see that the contradiction and confusion that penetrate Jung's reception of Nietzsche are rooted in his misunderstanding of Nietzsche's conception of the symbol. It is Jung's misinterpretation of the Nietzschean symbol as a mere conscious construct – a sign – that confuses Jung's subsequent reading of Nietzsche. Perhaps more significantly, this misinterpretation allows Jung, who was personally troubled by the prospect of his own mental illness, to distance himself from the insane personality of Nietzsche – for Jung regarded Nietzsche's madness (diagnosed by Jung as ego-inflation) as an inevitable consequence of Nietzsche having denied the creativity of the symbol.

Jung's reception of Nietzsche's work and personality is peculiar because, on the one hand, Jung readily acknowledges his debt to Nietzsche's influence and the similarity of their ideas, but, on the other hand, he wildly misinterprets Nietzsche's ideas. Now, it is not simply the case that Jung is a bad philosopher and so makes excusable mistakes in reasoning or interpretation; rather Jung overlooks obvious passages in Nietzsche's work that immediately overturn Jung's criticism of it. One has an overwhelming sense that Jung is purposely selective in his reading of Nietzsche. It is true that Nietzsche's aphoristic style of writing, together with his

avoidance of presenting one systematic viewpoint, easily lead to misinterpretation. It is relatively simple to find passages in Nietzsche that support or reject
most philosophical outlooks.[5] Yet in Jung's interpretation of Nietzsche (which
depends principally on *Thus Spoke Zarathustra*, a work that is not aphoristic
but a continuous text) one has a distinct sense of Jung 'cutting and pasting'
according to his needs, and of his own personal unease with some of the material
presented in Nietzsche – material that Jung often skates over at an alarming rate.
Furthermore, Jung's denigration of Nietzsche's personality and of his personal
life in general is laboured and unnecessary, and often diverts the reader from
Jung's own argument. There is thus an interesting taint and ambivalence in Jung's
reception of Nietzsche. Consciously he can be seen to endorse Nietzsche's views;
here there is a sense of affinity, of wanting to get close to Nietzsche. And yet there
is also a sense of rejection at an unconscious level, which expresses itself as an
enforced difference in his misrepresentation and misinterpretation of Nietzschean
theory.

Our inquiry will analyse in detail Jung's ambivalent relationship with
Nietzsche's work and personality, and it will attempt to explain the reasons that
lie behind the ambivalence. It will do this through a close examination and
evaluation of what I consider to be their similar models of psychological health
and illness. By first identifying aspects of affinity in their models, we shall be in
a better position to see where Jung's favourable reception of Nietzsche begins to
waver.

I shall argue that, for Nietzsche and Jung, the goal or height of human health
and potential is the realization of the whole self, which they refer to as the
'*Übermensch*' and 'Self' respectively.[6] This achievement is marked by creativity,
which is achieved by the cultivation and balance of all antithetical psychological
impulses – both rational and irrational – within the personality, and it is in this
sense that I shall refer to the whole self as a *union of opposites*. Specifically, the
whole self comprises the dynamic syntheses of Apollinian and Dionysian impulses
in the Nietzschean *Übermensch*, and consciousness and the unconscious in the
Jungian Self. When the opposites fail to synthesize, or when only one opposite
in the pair is present, Nietzsche and Jung warn of impending psychological
damage.

A few paragraphs earlier I noted that, for Nietzsche and Jung, the symbol is a
source of creativity; as we shall see in the course of our inquiry, they also regard
it as that which mediates between the opposites, thereby enabling their synthesis.
The symbol is therefore integral to mental health. Earlier I also mentioned that the
meaning of the symbol is different for either thinker; later our inquiry will evaluate
the implications of this difference for their models of the whole self. In particular,
we shall see that the conceptions of the *Übermensch* and the Self diverge most
profoundly by virtue of the different conceptions that Nietzsche and Jung have
of where the symbol stands in relation to the interplay of opposites, and thus, how
the personality should attempt to harness the energy generated by the symbol.
According to Jung, the symbol is 'a third thing' that lies outside of the opposites;

creativity must come from outside the individual, so that the whole self is a matter of *discovery*. For Nietzsche, however, the symbol is inherent within the opposites themselves, so that creativity is found within the individual, and the whole self is a matter of *creation*.[7] It is precisely because Jung could not find a symbol operating outside Nietzsche's opposites that he believed the opposites were incapable of synthesis, and that Nietzsche's psychological breakdown or stagnation was inevitable.

The structure of our inquiry

We shall begin our inquiry with the location and analysis of opposites in the whole self according to Nietzsche and Jung. Part I will engage with the controversial issue of the meaning and constitution of the Nietzschean *Übermensch* and the Jungian Self.[8] In Chapters 2 and 3 I analyse the development in Nietzsche's thought concerning the validity of the concept of opposites, and try to explain why Nietzsche first accepts opposites that are metaphysical, aesthetic and psychological, but eventually recognizes only psychological opposites. Chapter 4 argues that the *Übermensch* is a whole self that seeks to configure (psychological) opposites into a union. In Chapter 5 I turn to Jung's model of the psyche, and analyse the compensatory function of opposites, with reference to the alchemical *coniunctio oppositorum*. Chapter 6 argues that the Self is a whole self that seeks a configuration of opposites into a balanced union.

Part II examines the Nietzschean *Übermensch* and Jungian Self according to their similarities and differences. Here I shall begin to expose the ambiguous relation between the two models and the potentiality of a Jungian critique of Nietzsche's model. Chapter 7 identifies the differences between the two models by examining the respective *processes* through which the opposites are united. I shall try to account for these differences by relating them to the avowed philosophical influences on Nietzsche and Jung. We shall examine the theories of opposites proposed by Plato, Kant, Schopenhauer, Heraclitus and Aristotle and contrast them with those of Nietzsche and Jung. In Chapter 8 I identify seven similarities between the two models according to the *end-product* of the process, that is, what results from the union of opposites.[9] We shall consider the quality of the relationship between opposites; the value of completion over perfection, and its moral implications; the privilege and exclusivity of the union, and its political implications; the dangerous implications of the union for the personality; the particular opposites that are united; and the notion of the Dionysian. Also, not explicit in Nietzsche's model of opposites but beneath its surface is Nietzsche's anticipation of the fundamental tenets of Jung's 'individuation process' and analytical psychology in general. In this chapter I shall ask whether these similarities reflect Nietzsche's influence on Jung.

In order to expose fully the similarities and differences in the Nietzschean and Jungian models of the whole self, it is profitable to evaluate them from each other's perspective. Thus in Part III I assess Jung's critique of Nietzsche's model and offer a Nietzschean critique of Jung's model. Chapter 9 examines Jung's criticisms of Nietzsche's model and his subsequent diagnosis of Nietzsche's madness, through an examination of his seminars on Nietzsche's *Thus Spoke Zarathustra*. In Chapter 10 I argue that Jung's interpretation of Nietzsche's thought and his diagnosis of Nietzsche's personality is flawed and based upon wild misinterpretations. Chapter 11 tries to explain why Jung might want to deny Nietzsche's influence upon his own model despite their significant affinities. In keeping with Jung's and Nietzsche's insistence that the author is identified with his work,[10] I put forward an argument about Jung's psychological disposition, which I derive from an examination of *SNZ*,[11] focusing on those passages of *TSZ* he analyses and, principally, those he chooses to omit. In Chapter 12 I continue to enlarge upon the differences between Nietzsche and Jung by criticizing the Jungian model from a Nietzschean perspective. Part III, as a whole, will put their models of selfhood to the test by actively evaluating or 'diagnosing' the personalities of Nietzsche and Jung according to each other's criteria for mental health and illness. In other words, we shall determine whether or not Nietzsche and Jung are themselves *whole* – whether the former can aspire to Selfhood and the latter to *Übermenschlichkeit*. This will enable us to consider in the concluding Chapter 13 whether the whole self is a realistic possibility, for Nietzsche, for Jung and for us. In Chapter 13 we shall also look to the future of analytical psychology and ask how Nietzschean philosophy might enrich its further development.

Before we embark on our inquiry, however, I think it is worth turning to a problematic issue that is central to it, but that will find resolution in the pages that follow. This is the notion of a *union of opposites*.[12]

Opposites as incommensurable

To help us in our examination of the interplay of opposites in the models of Nietzsche and Jung, I here sketch a view embodying commonly held conceptions of opposites, which has, as one of its consequences, the view that opposites are incommensurable and incapable of uniting to form a whole – a view that I shall employ as a comparison in the discussion of the two models. I term the view in question the 'proto-theory'.

For Nietzsche and Jung, a self becomes whole when it dynamically synthesizes its antithetical psychological material. But in abstract terms opposites cannot be reconciled or united to form a coherent whole. Opposites are defined as such because they are incommensurable.[13] To say they can merge is to introduce compatibility between them and to deny their essential contrast and conflict.[14] We can thus put forward a theory of opposites, *contra* Nietzsche and Jung, in which a *union* of opposites is a chimera.

Opposites are required in the definition and identification of all things. Something is determined as what it is in relation to what it is not.[15] Opposing elements define one another. Opposites are inextricably linked and cannot be separated, because they entail one another. Although opposing forces must be intimately connected in this way, they remain, at all times, at an incommensurable distance from one another in a relationship defined by contradiction. Moreover, there is no primary member in a pair of opposites. Since opposition is a symmetrical relation, to regard one side as primary would remove the notion of 'opposition' itself. In other words, for one side to be accorded primacy over the other implies that the two sides are not equally balanced in opposition to one another after all. Furthermore, a third point of reference is required to validate the two sides, creating not a dyadic relationship of opposites but a triadic relationship consisting of one member that enables the comparison of the other two members.[16] Opposites, by definition, remain in a relationship of conflict and total difference; the one exists because it is essentially not the other; to reduce them to commensurable terms and to attribute greater qualitative value to one side is absurd.

Our proto-theory is therefore divided into four elements: opposites are incommensurable; opposites are related only by contradiction; there is no primary member in the binary pair; and a third point of reference is required to define opposites as 'opposite'. These are the four elements of the proto-theory that I shall utilize in my evaluation of the models of Nietzsche and Jung.

A word of warning should perhaps be given to the reader of the following pages. The inquiry that follows is a philosophical critique of Jungian thought; as with any method of inquiry, it has both positive and negative attributes. As a method of elucidation, philosophical criticism is both a help and a hindrance to Jungian thought. While it can substantiate claims and expose their flaws, it can also distort them, for Jungian psychology is reliant upon symbolic imagery to convey that which cannot be expressed by philosophical explanation and abstraction.[17] An attempt to apply intellectual judgement here would reduce the symbol to a sign and thereby forfeit its essential numinous quality.[18] Thus, philosophical criticism can enrich Jungian thought only in so far as it can inform us of its meaning and logical coherence; and it can suggest further developments of Jungian theory only by intellectually reflecting on its present status and then explicating its implications. In other words, the method of our inquiry is principally rational and evaluative; as such it loses the sense of the irrational and the experiential when it translates psychological language to that of philosophy. An example of such distortion occurs in my discussion of the opposites. In order to elucidate and evaluate the arguments of Nietzsche and Jung on opposites, the opposites are often presented as if they constituted an abstract philosophical theory, or even a mere mechanism. In other words, they are given a status that is too precise, too intellectual and too reductive of what Nietzsche and Jung had in mind. To them the opposites were living, and their affects experienced. The proto-theory that I have presented here is intended to be abstract and reductive, in that it attempts to define opposition in general, beyond the psychological arena. The proto-theory is used to contrast the conception of opposites held by Nietzsche and

Jung. This runs the danger of making the theories of Nietzsche and Jung appear abstract. However, as we shall see, because the theories of Nietzsche and Jung run counter to elements of the proto-theory, their sense of dynamism, creativity and spontaneity is retained.

Part I

Opposites in the whole self

Chapter 2

Opposites in early Nietzsche

Metaphysical, aesthetic and psychological opposites

Nietzsche regarded life and its experiences as a dynamic interplay of opposites in which thesis and antithesis are drawn together in energy-creating conflict. This fundamental condition is a reflection of 'the primordial contradiction that is concealed in things' (*BT*, 9). Nietzsche says that all reality – that is 'our empirical existence, and that of the world in general' – is a 'representation of the primary unity' (*BT*, 4).[1] This primal unity is a dynamic interplay of the separation and reunification of opposites, which reflects the Heraclitean notion of polarity, where 'polarity [is] the diverging of a force into two qualitatively different opposed activities that seek to reunite' (*PTAG*, 5). According to Nietzsche, opposites have an equal inherent value, so that one polar element cannot dominate and annihilate its counterpart. Nietzsche does not regard opposites as static values that remain antagonistic and incapable of equilibrium. They are, rather, experienced as relative and complementary to one another:

> Everlastingly, a given quality contends against itself and separates into opposites; everlastingly these opposites seek to reunite. Ordinary people fancy they see something rigid, complete and permanent; in truth, however, light and dark, bitter and sweet are attached to each other and interlocked at any given moment like wrestlers of whom sometimes the one, sometimes the other is on top.
>
> (*PTAG*, 5)

The wrestling of opposite forces exhibits the strife that is necessary for all existence: for 'everything that happens, happens in accordance with this strife' (ibid.). Reality is therefore a flux of contradictions, and the authentic individual, as an inhabitant of this reality, must not only acknowledge its nature but also seek to promote similar opposition within himself. According to Nietzsche, 'Each one of us . . . must organize the chaos within him' (*UM*, II, 10); and again, 'One is *fruitful* only at the cost of being rich in contradictions; one remains *young* only on condition the soul does not relax, does not long for peace' (*TI*, 'Morality as Anti-Nature', 3). Individuals who do not seek opposition might be satisfied, but they will 'become nothing' (*HAH*, 626); their experience of 'happiness' will merely contribute to Nietzsche's later concept of the 'herd ideal' (*WP*, 696). To overcome the self-satisfaction of the all-too-human masses, individuals must cease to be content with being a mere 'creature' and take on the role of 'creator'. They must seek growth through the energy of conflict, and 'and thus master the tremendous abundance of an apparently chaotic wilderness and . . . bring together in unity that which was formerly thought to be set irreconcilably asunder' (*UM*, IV, 5). According to Nietzsche, growth is enhanced through inner conflict that is engendered by opposition. This is because opposites create in their conflict not merely 'energy', but a 'mutual energy' that does not seek to establish a superior element but maintains the existence of both polar extremes. The value of the individual as creator is determined by the intensity of oppositions contained within him.[2]

The ideas that strife leads 'to new and more powerful births' (*BT*, 1) and that the greatest human achievements arise from the fullest tension of opposites is the underlying theme of *The Birth of Tragedy* (1872). Here Nietzsche argues that existence is justified only as an aesthetic phenomenon. In the absence of this aesthetic conception of reality, the individual is forced to acknowledge 'the impermanence of everything actual, which constantly acts and comes-to-be but never is', and this is a 'terrible, paralyzing thought' (*PTAG*, 5). Life appears as if it were an amoral game, ready to deceive (*PTAG*, 6); it forever seeks the destruction of the individual and all that seeks identity, form and shape. Incredibly, Nietzsche says that the individual should not respond to this state of affairs with an attitude that is 'gloomy, melancholy, tearful, sombre, atrabilarious, pessimistic, and altogether hateful' (ibid.). Instead he should adopt a response similar to that held by the early Greeks and joyfully affirm the horror of life in its devastation. In Greek tragedy suffering is transcended by an affirmation of the life force behind it; an affirmation that despite every phenomenological change, life is at bottom joyful and powerful, so that in its very expression

> nature cries to us with its true, undissembled voice: 'Be as I am! Amid the ceaseless flux of phenomena I am the eternally creative primordial mother, eternally impelling to existence, eternally finding satisfaction in this change of phenomena!'
>
> (*BT*, 16)

Nietzsche's analysis of Greek tragedy argues that aesthetic phenomena are central to the meaning of life. Nietzsche views art as the vehicle through which individuals can accept the temporality of their existence; art moves individuals to a psychological attitude that awakens and reinforces the sense that life is intrinsically valuable and meaningful despite the pains involved. Such an aesthetic experience, or 'tragic world view' (ibid.),[3] is crucial in enabling individuals to regard both their own existence and the existence of the world in general as joyous and wonderful. The Greeks had come face to face with the horrors and absurdities of life; such horror induces inaction because nothing can be done about it; action therefore requires illusion. The salvation and solace for this state of mind is art, which converts ideas of loathing into ideas that are acceptable. In art horror is tamed and made sublime; what was disgusting is made humorous.

Greek tragedy itself, in its attempt to transform the horror of the meaning-lessness of oppositional interplay into joyful experience, generates further experience of opposites. For example, the spectator of tragedy experiences a satisfying sense of illumination, even of 'omniscience' (*BT*, 22), and yet has the impulse to find satisfaction with something deeper:

> He beholds the transfigured world of the stage and nevertheless denies it. He sees the tragic hero before him, in epic clearness and beauty, and nevertheless rejoices in his annihilation. He comprehends the action deep down, and yet likes to flee into the incomprehensible. He feels the actions of the hero to be justified, and is nevertheless still more elated when these actions annihilate their agent. He shudders at the sufferings which will befall the hero, and yet anticipates in them a higher, much more overpowering joy. He sees more extensively and profoundly than ever, and yet wishes he were blind.
>
> (*BT*, 22)

These opposite feelings are experienced not only by the spectator of tragedy but also by the tragic artist. Artists find pleasure in the appearances they are creating, and yet they negate this pleasure for the higher satisfaction of their destruction. The experience of tragedy therefore generates opposition in the psychological make-up of the individual. The individual experiences a contradictory hybrid of fear and pleasure in the tragic performance, and it is in terms of this opposition that tragedy arises and is able to transfigure what would otherwise be an experience of pure fear at the meaningless flux of life. In other words, the tragic performance neutralizes fear by introducing its binary opposite, pleasure, into the experience, thereby enabling the individual to affirm life as both joyful and powerful.

I contend that, in Nietzsche's reading, Greek tragedy generates opposition within the individual to enable the individual to affirm the interplay of opposite forces that constitutes the flux of life around him. However, Nietzsche's view of tragedy does not correlate with the notion of opposites only according to its effects and ultimate aim. Indeed, the very 'essence' (*BT*, 12) or internal structure of tragedy is itself composed of two opposing principles – the Apollinian and the Dionysian. And it is because tragedy contains within it the complete integration of these opposing perspectives that Nietzsche considers it to be the highest of art forms.

Apollo and Dionysus as opposites

The Apollinian and the Dionysian are diametrically opposed tendencies or impulses of art, man, and life. The nature of any art varies according to the level at which the two impulses are functioning: often the two 'run parallel to each other, for the most part at variance; and they continually incite each other to new and more powerful births, which perpetuate an antagonism', and it is in these variable degrees of antagonism that art offers a 'superficial reconciliation' (*BT*, 1). When the two impulses are at total variance and are operating singularly they constitute a pure form of art, the classic examples of which, according to Nietzsche, are sculpture and epic poetry (as pure Apollinian art) and fine music (as pure Dionysian art). But when the two opposing impulses unite in equal degree, through a 'metaphysical miracle of the Hellenic "will"', art in its *highest* form is created. The union of the Dionysian and Apollinian, as the essence of tragic art, represents the highest meaning for the individual, as it is only through this metaphysical union that mankind is able to affirm its existence.

Nietzsche derives the names of the two impulses from the Greek deities Apollo and Dionysus. In ancient Greek religion each divinity had a set of functions and identifiable characteristics. Apollo is in many instances a god of higher civilization (for example, of medicine, healing and law), while Dionysus is a god of more primitive civilization (of nature and natural fertility, wine, music and orgiastic worship). Nietzsche regarded these two gods as representative of two powerful extremes, the relation of which determines not only forms of art, but also fundamental levels of experience. On an elemental level, Nietzsche considered the Apollinian and Dionysian impulses to be present in dreams and intoxication respectively.

Dreams give an immediate apprehension of form. Nietzsche says that 'in my experience' dreams have one kind of reality and at the same time they induce the feeling that there is another deeper reality underlying it.[4] This is analogous to life itself, for life as we know and experience it can be considered an illusion, a world of appearance that lies between us and the very ground of being, a metaphysical world of primordial unity of all individual things. Apollo is the sun-god, a symbol of brightness and appearance; and the Apollinian is the sphere of *individuation*, restraint, form, beauty and illusion. Nietzsche states that Apollo is 'the soothsaying god' (*BT*, 1), the god of the Delphic oracle; but although Apollinian images seem to offer higher truth, they remain at the level of mere appearance.

In contrast to the Apollinian 'dream-image', the Dionysian impulse expresses itself in intoxication. In this formless state individuals lose themselves and the structure of individuation collapses in favour of a rediscovered universal harmony that is at one with nature. Nietzsche demands that man becomes reunited with nature – we must begin 'to "naturalize" humanity in terms of a pure, newly discovered, newly redeemed nature' (*GS*, 109), in such a way that 'nature which has become alienated, hostile, or subjugated, celebrates once more her reconciliation with her lost son, man' (*BT*, 1). In its fullest sense this Dionysian reunion with nature is an ecstatic experience with mystical implications, an experience of supreme intensity and savagery – 'that horrible mixture of sensuality and cruelty which has always seemed to me the real "witches" brew' (*BT*, 2). Dionysian impulses can be aroused directly by intoxicants and by the approach of spring with its promise of rebirth, and they find collective expression in orgiastic festivities with their song, dance and sexual licence.

The Dionysian experience is antithetical to that of the Apollinian in that it runs contrary to all distinction and particularity: to limit, form, contrast and convention. The Dionysian impulse is an expression of the 'real' world that admits of no illusion and appearance. It is that sea of contradiction, or 'mixed drink which must be constantly stirred' (*PTAG*, 5). The Dionysian is the meaningless world from which man requires aesthetic salvation; it is therefore intolerable to the individual in its pure form. Apollinian form is required to stabilize the horror of the Dionysian and prevent the dissolution of individuality. The Apollinian, manifest both in its unconscious form in dreams and in its consciously artistic form, serves to conceal the horrific character of life by transforming it into images that are joyful and idealized. Nietzsche praises the Apollinian impulse because it protects the individual from the terrors of nature by using illusion to creatively falsify reality without denying its true nature; it does not try to convince us that life is rational and subject to critical improvements as Socrates had done. The Dionysian impulse similarly does not try to conceal or deny life but expresses its irrational and chaotic energy. The Dionysian impulse helps the individual to confront life, but instead of removing the immediate terror of life, it clothes this terror in a sense of bliss. This is achieved through the Dionysian capacity to reveal a further dimension of reality that would otherwise remain inaccessible to us: it is in the realm of *collectivity* (where individuality forms a cosmic unity with nature) that we feel bliss. This realm, or 'primal unity' as Nietzsche calls it, is equivalent to the Schopenhauerian 'Will' or Kantian 'thing-in-itself', in that it constitutes mankind's true and real nature. And it is through the Dionysian impulse that man blends with the authentic nature of reality. This is an experience of transcendence through intoxication, which can be only temporary; a temporary experience of becoming a higher being, one that is able to withstand, and even exalt, the terror of life.[5]

Nietzsche uses Apollo and Dionysus to elaborate his theory of two opposing impulses in art, man, and life, but he does so without any consistent historical justification. These impulses are 'reinterpretations', 'inventions' and 'two new composites which carry the Greek gods' names as symbols' (Silk and Stern, 1981, p. 167). Indeed, Nietzsche adds three new aspects to the function of Apollo. Nietzsche's Apollo is (1) god of dreams, (2) god of appearance and illusion, and (3) god of visual art form; these three combine in what Nietzsche calls the Apollinian 'world of visual imagery'. But these three aspects are not generally acknowledged or supported by historical evidence. Apollo is the god of prophecy but his prophecy is not characteristically mediated through dreams;[6] Nietzsche's claim for (2) depends solely upon a semantic ambiguity where 'Der Schein' refers to both 'a glimmer of light' and 'illusion' or 'appearance'. In contrast to Nietzsche's claim for (3), there was no ancient Greek god of visual art, and if Apollo were to be associated with art it would be with music.[7] He also fails to recognize Apollo's well-attested ecstatic character, and instead attributes this and the title 'god of music' to Dionysus, the deity that Nietzsche believes to be opposite to Apollo. However, 'Dionysus was no more of a god of music than Apollo was god of the visual arts' (Silk and Stern, 1981, p. 175). Nietzsche acknowledges that 'Dionysus possesses the dual nature of a cruel, depraved demon and a mild, gentle ruler', but he does not expand upon this duality; he is too preoccupied with Dionysus' orgiastic aspect to develop his connection with fertility. Overall, Nietzsche is more content to elaborate the paradoxical combination of horror and rapture. It might seem that Nietzsche's lack of fidelity to Greek tradition is irrelevant for our purpose. However, I believe Nietzsche's misrepresentation of the deities is significant. Untouched by Nietzsche's manipulations the deities and their characteristics are distinct from one another; so that, as expounded in Plato's *Laws*, Apollo would be a proponent of the Olympian (or 'Uranian') religion, the religion of heaven, and Dionysus would be a proponent of the chthonic religion, the religion of the earth (828C).[8] Yet, in Nietzsche's hands, the deities appear in greater contrast: the irrational impulses that were once in Apollo are now extracted and attributed to Dionysus, whose original penchant for irrationality is now magnified to a greater degree. It would seem that Nietzsche wants to channel the symbolism of the two deities towards abstract notions of the rational (the Apollinian impulse) and the irrational or instinctual (the Dionysian impulse).[9]

The nature of the opposites that feature in Nietzsche's early work fall within the categories of metaphysics, psychology and aesthetics. Nietzsche makes a claim in metaphysics when he argues that the fundamental condition of the universe is one of eternal flux and conflict between opposites (*BT*, 9). These metaphysical opposites are later made analogous to opposites of a psychological nature when Nietzsche asks the individual to reflect the condition of the universe and promote opposition within himself (*TI*, 'Morality as Anti-Nature', 3; *WP*, 966). Psychological opposition is again introduced through the effects of the tragic performance upon the spectator and tragic artist alike; it is also linked with metaphysics and aesthetics through the Apollinian and Dionysian, which are at the very core of tragedy.

As we have seen, the Apollinian and Dionysian are diametrically opposed tendencies of art, man, and life in general. There is an overlap between the aesthetic, psychological and metaphysical aspects of these impulses:[10] the Apollinian and Dionysian have a complex significance that simultaneously covers all three fields. On the aesthetic level, the two terms refer to any artistic or cultural tendencies and manifestations that are the outcome of those impulses. On the psychological level they are creative human impulses, which comprise modes of perceiving, experiencing, expressing and responding to reality. As modes of self-consciousness, the Apollinian impulse corresponds to feeling oneself to be distinct from one's environment, while the Dionysian impulse corresponds to the mental state of feeling conjoined to the rest of reality. On the metaphysical level, they denote the conditions of existence apprehended through the operation of the impulses, or the impulses themselves as universal principles of the eternal cosmos.

The Apollinian designates a specific consciousness of the world, an orientation or principle of individuation, that enables the individual to identify and relate to objects by establishing the a priori determinations of space, time and causality that make experience possible. The object that is experienced is an illusion that is created by the subjective perception of the individual; the Apollinian conscious orientation is therefore subjective. The subject–object relationship is based on subjectivity, so that the perceived object is not the thing-in-itself, but merely the individual's interpretation of it. The thing-in-itself is the 'primary unity' (*BT*, 4), that sea of contradictory impulses with no agency behind it. This metaphysical unity is beyond experience and blindly acts upon the individual in a horrific way. As an aesthetic impulse, the Apollinian consciousness interprets an object as beautiful. Nietzsche's understanding of beauty is taken from Schopenhauer and concerns an appearance of the ideal. Thus, when the Apollinian interprets an object as beautiful, it perceives the object's spirit appearing through matter; the object is beautiful because it expresses its essence. In contrast, the Dionysian is not dependent on such subjective interpretation. According to Nietzsche, its art form is music and, for Schopenhauer, music is the direct copy of the *Will* (*BT*, 16). The Dionysian therefore takes the individual to the very essence of reality, and it metaphysically transmutes him into the collective realm of unity with nature. Art for Nietzsche is religious. Nietzsche says that artists transcend themselves: 'In art, man takes delight in himself as perfection' (*TI*, 'Expeditions of an Untimely Man', 9); authentic art involves a transcendence that enriches and transforms: 'This *compulsion* to transform into the perfect is – art' (ibid.).

The Apollinian and Dionysian are a priori structures that determine reality. However, as objective structures, the Apollinian and Dionysian go against Nietzsche's insistence that opposites are not 'rigid, complete and permanent' but are relative, so that 'light and dark, bitter and sweet are attached to each other and interlocked at any given moment like wrestlers of whom sometimes the one, sometimes the other is on top' (*PTAG*, 5).[11] The Apollinian and Dionysian impulses are diametrically opposed, 'rigid and permanent' structures that determine very different realities from one another; but as we have seen with Greek tragedy, they are not so 'detached' from one another that they cannot relate and 'interlock' with each other. Nietzsche writes: 'Polarity [is] the diverging of a force into two qualitatively different opposed activities that seek to reunite' (*PTAG*, 5). The opposites of the Apollinian and Dionysian are therefore dependent upon one another. The Dionysian on its own is dangerous: it is barbaric and shatters subjectivity; it therefore needs the Apollinian.[12] Likewise Nietzsche argues that the Apollinian achievement cannot be appreciated fully until its source of nourishment, the Dionysian, is recognized. Dionysian music activates Apollinian drama to the highest degree – the drama acquires a supreme vividness and an intense metaphysical significance that is unattainable through words and actions alone. Indeed, the Dionysian and Apollinian are dependent upon one another more determinately. Only so much Dionysian experience is available to individual consciousness as can be controlled by the Apollinian: 'Where the Dionysian powers rise up as impetuously as we experience them now, Apollo, too, must already have descended among us' (*BT*, 25).

As psychological and aesthetic realities the Apollinian and the Dionysian are of equal value (even if the Dionysian is more powerful once its effects are felt): 'The two art drives must unfold their powers in a strict proportion, according to the law of eternal justice' (ibid.). Or, in other words, in both creative and intellectual undertakings, reason depends on the instincts for continuous renewal, and the instincts depend on reason as a vehicle for their expression. On a metaphysical level, however, they are not of equal value.[13] Ontologically the Dionysian is primary: it is the ground of the world and of all existence, and it is the original power that calls into being the entire world of phenomena (*BT*, 25). In this respect the Apollinian is secondary; it is the individuated response of the Dionysian, the source of the illusion through which the Dionysian world must be transformed. It is secondary even if mundane existence almost submerges the Dionysian and allows the everyday experience of particularity and distinctions to proceed unchallenged (*BT*, 1). As we saw at the beginning of this chapter, Nietzsche believes that the 'synthesis' of opposites and 'contrary drives' generates the energy necessary for the individual to grow and develop towards his full potential as 'master of the earth' (*WP*, 966). The correct synthesis of the Apollinian and Dionysian is vital to the growth of the individual, and this synthesis is determined by the law of 'eternal justice' (*BT*, 25) which corresponds to the 'mysterious primordial unity' manifested in the world and in the human psyche (*BT*, 1) and also to 'the discipline of self-mastery' (*D*, 109). Both justice and self-mastery are founded upon the principle of equilibrium (*WS*, 22), which, in turn, is maintained by the observance of measure, or the law of 'strict proportion' (*BT*, 25). 'Measure and moderation', Nietzsche says, are 'two very exalted things' (*AOM*, 230), which are critical in maintaining the appropriate interaction of opposites (*HAH*, 276). The failure to adopt them will lead to an exaggeration of one opposite at the expense of the other, which Nietzsche considers to be an unhealthy weakness. In response to the question 'who will prove to be the strongest?' Nietzsche answers: 'The most moderate; those who do not require any extreme articles of faith' (*WP*, 55).[14] The greatest self-mastery would culminate in the maintenance of the Apollinian and Dionysian at their most antagonistic: the most Dionysian energy that the Apollinian can control. Likewise, the weak individual would fail to unite the two impulses and would experience a lack of limit and proportion. Nietzsche regarded Socratism as having created this weakness; with the advent of Socratism came the dissolution of the powerful union of the Apollinian and the Dionysian and the promotion of an Apollinian one-sidedness.

The rationality of Socrates created the downfall of Greek tragedy, for tragedy became diverted from its course by a new insatiable desire for knowledge (*BT*, 11–15). Socrates thought that only the knowledgeable can be virtuous, and this thought was reflected in the tragedies of Euripides, which demanded intelligibility as a prerequisite of beauty.[15] Greek drama had thereby alienated itself from instinctive and unconscious Dionysian wisdom. Socrates had contempt for tragedy and the instincts (*BT*, 13) as he thought they had no concern for truth; instead Socrates introduced a dialectical tendency (the Platonic dialogue), which was inherently optimistic, for it presupposed that problems of existence could be solved by the active, rational mind. When tragedy came to an end at the end of the fifth century, it was replaced by the 'New Comedy' (*BT*, 11) that introduced a mundane naturalism. Comedy staged the mediocrity of ordinary life, where characters were able to 'speak', to debate and philosophize; the hero, became the cheerful slave with no responsibility or aspiration, an attitude that aspires towards simple satisfaction in the trivialities of the passing moment.

According to Nietzsche, since Socrates Western culture has become increasingly drawn to a one-sided Apollinian tendency. In *Twilight of the Idols* (1888) Nietzsche says that through the 'tyranny of reason' Socrates repressed 'the instincts' and 'the unconscious' and thereby created a division within the psyche (*TI*, 'The Problem of Socrates'). This destruction of psychic integrity is the origin of 'bad conscience' (*GM*, II). The elevation and separation of consciousness ('thinking, inferring, reckoning') from the instincts (the 'regulating, unconscious and infallible drives') induced 'the gravest and uncanniest illness, from which humanity has not yet recovered' (*GM*, II, 16). This event is described by Nietzsche as 'an abrupt break' and 'sudden leap and fall' into a new condition of existence (ibid.), a condition of 'decadence' and nihilism. The problem of decadence is essentially a problem of fragmentation and one-sidedness. In a letter to Carl Fuchs (winter 1884–1885), Nietzsche defines it as 'a change in perspective: the particular is seen too sharply, the whole is seen too dully' (Middleton, in Nietzsche, 1969, p. 233). Socrates, in seeking to promote the Apollinian above the Dionysian, is therefore described by Nietzsche as 'a typical *décadent*' (*EH*, 'BT', 1). Further-more, the faith in reason over instinct leads to nihilism (*BGE*, 1; *GM*, III, 24, 25, 27), for the exaggeration of theoretical abstraction and rationality diminishes creative vitality and takes away meaning and value from life:

> The fundamental mistake is simply that, instead of understanding con-sciousness as a tool and particular aspect of the total life, we posit it as the standard and the condition of life that is of supreme value: it is the erroneous perspective of *a parte ad totum* [from a part to the whole].
>
> (*WP*, 707; see also *BGE*, 205; *UM*, IV, 8)

Nietzsche therefore seeks the 'whole' individual, that is, a moderated collaboration of the Apollinian and Dionysian instincts, with as much Dionysian energy as the Apollinian can harness. He therefore does not value the irrational over the rational, but seeks a unification of the two.

Chapter 3

Opposites in Nietzsche post-1878

The denial of metaphysical opposites

In Chapter 2 we saw that opposites play a fundamental role in Nietzsche's early philosophy; Nietzsche upholds opposites that are aesthetic, metaphysical and psychological in nature. However, from *Human, All Too Human* (1878) Nietzsche's attitude towards opposites changes dramatically; he no longer insists on their promotion but emphatically denies their value for life. Nietzsche's attitude towards opposites from his 'middle' period onwards is ambiguous for, in direct contrast with his early works, Nietzsche repudiates opposites because they presuppose a metaphysical reality; and yet it is my assertion that he still values psychological opposites. Nietzsche rejects his previously held notion that opposites are an inextricable blend of the aesthetic, metaphysical and psychological, in favour of one that is purely psychological.[1] In this chapter I shall address the apparent contradictions found within Nietzsche's view of opposites. We shall decide whether Nietzsche's argument for psychological opposites is coherent and valid when viewed from the wider context of his dismissal of metaphysics, or if his argument is itself trapped within the very metaphysical confines of which he is critical. We shall also re-examine Nietzsche's earlier conception of opposites in light of this later conception to determine what, if anything, can be recovered from it in the wake of his rejection of metaphysics.

In *Human, All Too Human* (1878) and *Beyond Good and Evil* (1886), Nietzsche equates belief in opposites with metaphysics: 'The fundamental faith of the metaphysicians is *the faith in antithetical values*' (*BGE*, 2). Nietzsche argues that philosophical problems still take the same form as they did two thousand years ago: that is, 'How can something originate from its opposite' (*HAH*, 1). Nietzsche claims that metaphysics answers this question by denying that 'the one originates from the other',[2] and thereby assumes 'for the more highly valued thing, a miraculous source in the very kernel and essence of the thing-in-itself' (ibid.), and for the unconnected lower-valued things, an uninspiring source in 'this' world of mere appearance and illusion. Nietzsche regards this antithesis, which sets up a 'true' ideal world in opposition to 'this' empirically determined world, as the principal example of what goes wrong when opposites are affirmed.[3] In other words, Nietzsche thinks the value-judgements held by metaphysicians devalue life, for the things that they value are denied any connection with life. If their valued things were connected with this world they would consequently lose their value. Metaphysicians' faith in values defined by opposition is a faith in the ascetic ideal, a faith that things of the highest value are negations of things in this world; human existence is deprived of value, for value resides in that which negates this world. Likewise, knowledge for the metaphysicians is a priori, and therefore cannot be determined empirically or be dependent upon human experience, for this would result in a knowledge that is mistaken and illusory. This point is made explicit by the ascetic priest who, when induced to philosophize, will vent his 'innermost contrariness' upon what is felt to be most real, and will therefore 'look for error precisely where the instinct of life most unconditionally posits truth' (*GM*, I, 11). To believe in a metaphysical world, according to Nietzsche, is to believe that our best empirical theory is radically false, and that a priori knowledge is essentially different from that which satisfies our cognitive interests. Knowledge of the metaphysical world would be 'the most useless of all knowledge: more useless even than knowledge of the chemical composition of water must be to the sailor in danger of shipwreck' (*HAH*, 9).

Nietzsche wants to separate himself from the asceticism of opposites and the metaphysical tradition from which they arise. To confirm his intention he names his thought 'historical philosophy' as a foil for 'metaphysical philosophy' (*HAH*, 1). This 'historical philosophy', Nietzsche writes,

> which can no longer be separated from natural science, the youngest of all philosophical methods, has discovered . . . that there are no opposites, except in the customary exaggeration of popular or metaphysical interpretations, and . . . a mistake in reasoning lies at the bottom of this antithesis.
>
> (*HAH*, 1)

Nietzsche claims that opposites, the problem which gives rise to metaphysics, is simply a cognitive error: metaphysical oppositions are posited in order to explain the origin of things that are highly valued. Nietzsche attempts to undermine the metaphysical project by demonstrating it to be cognitively superfluous. He does this by dismissing metaphysics in favour of a more naturalistic interpretation of things of the highest value, an explanation that reunites these things with their apparent opposite, thereby demonstrating what was hitherto considered a highly-valued metaphysical ideal to be 'human, alas all too human' (*EH*, 'HAH', 1). Nietzsche claims that, according to his 'historical philosophy', 'there exists, strictly speaking, neither an unegoistic action nor completely disinterested contemplation; both are only sublimations' (*HAH*, 1). What appear to be opposites are in fact simply different modes of the same thing, thus '"warm and cold" . . . are not opposites, but differences of degree [or] transitions' (*WS*, 67). Nietzsche rejects the inference to a metaphysical world by arguing that there are no opposites, and that things come from their apparent opposite simply through a process of sublimation. He thereby provides an alternative answer to the metaphysician's original question ('How can something originate in its opposite?') and understands metaphysics to be founded by a 'mistake in reasoning' – the belief that something that is only the sublimation of another thing is really its opposite or negation. *Human, All Too Human* therefore regards metaphysics as based on a simple cognitive error: the metaphysician fails to solve the problem concerning the origin of opposites due to mistaken observations.

Nietzsche's refutation of opposites turns from a declaration in *Human, All Too Human* to critical engagement in *Beyond Good and Evil*.[4] While in *HAH* Nietzsche is content with exposing the metaphysical world as cognitively superfluous (*HAH* does not discard the metaphysical world completely),[5] *BGE* sees him attempt to abolish the existence of the metaphysical world altogether. In *BGE*, Nietzsche no longer needs to argue that there are no opposites, or that apparent opposites are interconnected, in order to deny a metaphysical world, for the focus is no longer on the cognitive error of the metaphysician. Indeed, the metaphysician does not seek a 'true' metaphysical world; what he seeks, according to Nietzsche, is to keep the things he most values free from the corruption of being connected to the things he does not value. Nietzsche writes:

> It has gradually become clear to me what every great philosopher has hitherto been: a confession on the part of its author and a kind of involuntary and unconscious memoir; moreover, that the moral (or immoral) intentions in every philosophy have every time constituted the real germ of life out of which the entire plant has grown. To explain how a philosopher's most remote metaphysical assertions have actually been arrived at, it is always well (and wise) to ask oneself first: what morality does this (does *he* –) aim at? I accordingly do not believe a 'drive to knowledge' to be the father of philosophy, but that another drive has, here as elsewhere, only employed knowledge (and false knowledge!) as a tool
>
> (*BGE*, 6)

The basis of a great philosophy for Nietzsche, therefore, can never be an innocent cognitive error. Philosophers seek truth and knowledge not for their intrinsic value but as instruments for what they consider to be a higher purpose. Nietzsche claims that in the case of great philosophy, knowledge, mistakes and cognitive problems are employed in the process of constructing the world so that it reflects the philosopher's values and ideals. Philosophical 'truth' is merely a vehicle through which the philosopher can express his subjective interpretation and perspective on the world; likewise, the reality of opposites,

> on which the metaphysicians have set their seal, are . . . merely foreground valuations, merely provisional perspectives, perhaps moreover the perspectives of a hole-and-corner [clandestine and underhand].
>
> (*BGE*, 2)

In *HAH* Nietzsche argues that the metaphysician's fundamental concern is to explain the origin of his highly valued things, and in *BGE* he argues that the metaphysician's fundamental concern is to keep these valued things uncorrupted, and thus unconnected to things of a lower value. The role of opposites changes in these two accounts. In *HAH* the metaphysician's belief in opposites is an innocent, intellectual mistake based on insufficient observation; but in *BGE* it is an attempt to express certain disputable value judgements. Things of the highest value are supposed to be contaminated by things of a lower value; the metaphysical world keeps the higher and lower values apart.

Nietzsche wants to be rid of the notions of the metaphysical world and of objective, rigid opposites, for they promote a conception of the world that is both false and ascetic. These notions, according to Nietzsche, are hostile to his interpretation of life as a painful, fleeting world of becoming, for they overemphasize objectivity and stability and that which has become. While the metaphysician regards temporality as inferior to permanence, Nietzsche holds the inverse view. For Nietzsche, all things are finite; they will be destroyed and replaced by other things again and again; and the metaphysical unchanging world is a mere fiction designed to protect the individual from the suffering that this continual destruction brings. According to Nietzsche, it is individuals' sense-experience that leads them to believe that things in life are regular and stable; their language then goes beyond this experience and strengthens the impression of regularity and stability by abstracting from individual circumstances and describing them in terms of universal qualities and properties. Language therefore falsifies life by simplifying its complexities and distorting its unique character. Language, for Nietzsche, is unable to express the instability of life: 'Linguistic means of expression are useless for expressing "becoming"; it accords with our inevitable need to preserve ourselves to posit a crude world of stability, of "things", etc.' (*WP*, 715). Language creates the illusion that there is a stable distinction between a subject and its properties or activities; but for Nietzsche there exists only the chaotic array of complex and unstable relations and activities, and these cannot be made into a coherent structured whole. Truth therefore becomes a contentious issue for Nietzsche, since life cannot be accurately represented by linguistic consciousness. 'Truth' must be interpreted as a hoard of metaphors, anthropomorphisms and relative perceptions that over time have come to be seen as objective and binding. According to Nietzsche, we must not seek knowledge of life that is a priori and metaphysical; rather, we must seek experience of life and our own interpretation of the world. We arrive at an interpretation through our feelings, sensations and intuitions, and these constitute what is fundamentally 'real'. If we are attentive enough, we can sense these instincts to be more authentic and fundamental to life than structured language.

Nietzsche's ontology is intended to be non-metaphysical. While the metaphysician's language is literal and truth-seeking, Nietzsche's is metaphorical; and while the metaphysician's conception of reality is static, unified and concerned with being, Nietzsche's is dynamic, pluralistic and concerned with becoming.

However, by making a distinction such as that between being and becoming, can we not consider Nietzsche to be a metaphysician himself? Both Adorno and Derrida claim that Nietzsche failed to recognize that, by operating with such oppositional terms, he has retained metaphysical structures of thought. Adorno writes: 'By positing chaos in opposition to stability, Nietzsche's critique fails to reflect upon the metaphysical grounding of such an opposition' (cited in Bauer, 1999, p. 83). Derrida writes:

> There is no sense in doing without the concepts of metaphysics in order to attack metaphysics. We have no language – no syntax and no lexicon – which is alien to that history [of metaphysics]; we cannot utter a single destructive proposition which has not already slipped into the forum, the logic, and the implicit postulation of precisely what it seeks to contest.
>
> (Derrida, 1978, p. 280)[6]

Furthermore, the very style of language that Nietzsche employs expresses the opposites that we see it reject. Nietzsche's use of aphorisms present arguments that are contradicted time and time again; it is as if Nietzsche adopts opposition in order to reject the confinement of committing himself to one fixed interpretation of the world. By shifting from one perspective or interpretation to another, and undermining positions he held elsewhere, Nietzsche is preserving the 'fascination of the opposing point of view' (*WP*, 470).[7] It would seem that Nietzsche cannot reject metaphysical opposites without falling into contradiction and inconsistency.[8]

Nietzsche's thought seems to be incoherent and contradictory, for he promotes opposites at the same time as explicitly rejecting them. For example, he tells us that great men develop through the 'feelings' that the 'presence of opposites' occasion (*WP*, 967); yet to see opposites in nature is 'the imprecise way of observing' nature (*WS*, 67). However, incoherence is avoided when different notions of oppositional thought are identified. I believe that Nietzsche is not attempting in *HAH* and *BGE* to destroy opposites altogether. (If he tried to do so he would be setting up a value or system of thought in opposition to his own.) He is concerned, rather, with the destruction of a *particular* notion of opposites. Nietzsche wants to reject opposites that have an a priori, objective, static structure that exists independently of the human being. These express the ascetic ideal and dictate standards of value to the human being independently of his will; they inform him that a certain thing is good but its opposite is not, and then insist that he choose the former at the expense of the latter. Not all opposites presuppose a metaphysical world that is beyond man, however. Nietzsche does not reject those opposites that are essentially 'anti-ascetic', that value the human being as the source of meaning. Indeed, opposites are promoted by Nietzsche if they represent the human being as intrinsically valuable, and both elements in the opposition can be experienced and actively affirmed: if only one element in the binary pair is experienced and affirmed, then Nietzsche will reject the opposition.

Nietzsche's refutation of metaphysics and its oppositions in favour of experienceable, life-affirming opposition represents his 'revaluation of values'. Meaning is no longer sought as objective a priori truth, but is subjectively determined, derived from a posteriori experience. According to Nietzsche, the only source of authentic meaning is that of the instincts: 'Nothing is "given" as real except our world of desires and passions, that we can rise or sink to no other 'reality' than the reality of our drives' (*BGE*, 36; cf. *WP*, 619). We are nothing more than this natural 'inner occurrence' of primitive and sublimated bodily desires. We can never fully know the content and character of these sensations. When we believe we are following the logic of our interpretations, by the inherent rational connections between ideas, we are merely the victim of our anonymous conflicting instincts, each of which is trying to assert its authority over the other, so that our most valuable convictions are merely the 'judgements of our muscles' (*WP*, 314).

To be an individual is continually to wage the battle for supremacy as Will to Power. Multitudes of opposing instincts in their dynamic conflict generate energy to enforce unstable relationships of domination and subordination. These shifting relations form the tenuous 'hierarchy' (Deleuze, 1983, p. 40) of values that determine the characteristics of our individuality. The individual is essentially taking 'sides against himself' (*AOM*, preface 4) and is 'torn back and forth by conflicting motives' (*HAH*, 107). In the establishment of the most powerful motive, we each have the potential to exhibit an almost infinite number of characteristics, depending on the number of opposing instincts within our psychological make-up and their hierarchical configuration. In contrast to the metaphysician's promotion of unity, Nietzsche prefers the multiple dynamic self. He is 'happy to harbour in himself not an "immortal soul", which is a fixed unity without change and without diversity, but many souls' (*AOM*, 17). Individuals are not determined by a metaphysical identity within or beyond them, but by physical drives; any desire they may entertain for an immortal world of eternal truth is the result of sublimated 'spiritual' drives, which ultimately express an all-too-human phobia of death and destruction. Likewise,

> Between good and evil actions there is no difference in kind, but at the most one of degree. Good actions are sublimated evil ones; evil actions are coarsened brutalized good ones.
>
> (*HAH*, 107)

In renouncing the concrete antithesis of good and evil Nietzsche embraced the subjectively determined opposition of good and bad, thereby rejecting metaphysical value for the instinctual.

If individuals depend upon fixed values and a single interpretation of the world, believing this to be the only permanent and unequivocal reality, they will relinquish the need to look for new interpretations, and their creative instincts will atrophy. To avoid such deterioration Nietzsche seeks an affirmation of the greatest multiplicity of conflicting views and interpretations, for the highest man would have the greatest multiplicity of drives, in the relatively greatest strength that can be endured. Indeed, where the plant 'man' shows himself strongest one finds instincts that conflict powerfully . . . but are controlled.

(*WP*, 966)

A rich diversity of interpretations will be achieved when individuals promote the Will to Power of conflicting instincts within them, for 'the definite and to us seemingly persistent qualities express only the momentary predominance of the one fighter, but with that the war is not at an end; the wrestling continues to all eternity', continually producing more and more interpretations (*PTAG*, 5).

The change in Nietzsche's thought about opposites is great. Perhaps the most significant change is that the individual replaces the metaphysical world as the standard for all meaning and value. This radical alteration in Nietzsche's thought is reflected in a variety of departures from his early account of opposites. The tragic attitude, for example, is reinterpreted; the individual should no longer seek to flee into a transcendent realm to escape confrontation with terrible reality, but must now learn to find joy in that confrontation itself. The tragic attitude is now equated with the heroism that revels in its own strength, which is powerful enough to endure its confrontation with Dionysus. This attitude is a 'pessimism of strength' that boldly confronts the inevitability of destruction and affirms this destruction as a means to further heroic activity; suffering becomes valuable, for it proves the worth of the tragic individual who endures it. The revised tragic attitude does not make aestheticism necessary for the individual's salvation from terrible reality. According to early Nietzsche, art enables individuals to accept the temporality of their existence by moving them to a psychological attitude that regards life as intrinsically valuable despite the pains involved. According to Nietzsche's revised model, the psyche does not require art – in its capacity to veil the harshness of reality – for its affirmation, as it is reliant only on its own energetic strength.[9] When they are at their most antagonistic, psychological opposites provide individuals with the strength to relate to the world around them and ultimately to affirm their temporal existence. We could therefore say that psychological opposition replaces aestheticism as mankind's salvation. Psychological opposition unites man with nature, not in terms of a 'metaphysical comfort' (*BT*, 17) that enables him to transcend humanity and become 'primordial being itself', but by their common composition, of contradictory elements that are in continual flux.

In accordance with the revision of the tragic attitude, the 'internal structure' of tragedy – its Apollinian and Dionysian make-up – must also be revised. As psychological impulses, the Apollinian and Dionysian require no further revision: the Apollinian conscious feeling of being distinct from one's environment, and the Dionysian conscious feeling of being conjoined with the rest of reality, can stand. But since psychology is now the only acceptable mode in which the Apollinian and Dionysian impulses can be manifest, as metaphysical conditions of existence they must be rejected. The Apollinian cannot establish the a priori determinations of space, time and causality that make experience possible; neither can the Dionysian be equivalent to the very essence of reality and the means by which the individual can be conjoined to it. The Apollinian and Dionysian are diametrically opposed psychological impulses: they do not determine different objective realities outside the individual; they determine different subjective 'feelings' within the individual.

Nietzsche is not guilty of contradiction when he simultaneously rejects and endorses opposites because, as we have seen, his rejection applies only to those opposites that are static and ascetic in their presupposition of an objective world above and beyond the individual. Psychological opposites are not in this category: they are relative and in continual flux. Psychological opposites compete for conscious expression; one will dominate, but this is only temporary, for their battle is ongoing; the hierarchy is not static, it will change as the individual's intuitions and feelings change.

In Chapters 2 and 3 we have seen that opposites are significant to Nietzsche's thought. We have seen that Nietzsche values the creative tension that is generated in the competition between opposites. Implicit within our discussion has been the beginnings of a Nietzschean project or vision of human authenticity. For Nietzsche praises powerful individuals who are able to harness the greatest tensions, for they are able not only to endure, but also to rejoice in the suffering and terror of the fleeting temporality of life. In Chapter 4 I shall describe Nietzsche's vision of human greatness. In particular we shall see how greatness is equated with *wholeness*, and how competing opposites are celebrated in Nietzsche's notion of the whole self, the *Übermensch*.

Chapter 4

The *Übermensch* as a union of opposites

Nietzsche does not explain in detail what he means by the *Übermensch*. This scarcity of explanation, and wanton vagueness, has led to multiple interpretations of what he might have had in mind, some of which are fanciful and even absurd.[1] It is therefore essential that any attempt at an explanation be kept in check and correspond appropriately to such meagre and piecemeal textual evidence as there is. The fragments that Nietzsche provides imply a submerged richness of thought, but we are denied any further insight into this thought, which is frustrating. Keith May takes the sense of frustration further by maintaining that Nietzsche himself does not know what the *Übermensch* means (May, 1990, pp. 167–168). Kurt Rudolph Fischer, however, claims that this frustration and lack of definition are necessary aspects of the *Übermensch*, for 'it is part of the determination of the "Übermensch" not to be determined' (cited in Aschheim, 1992, p. 8).

It is in *Thus Spoke Zarathustra* (1883) that the fragmentary description of the *Übermensch* appears. After this work, the term *Übermensch* does not appear again in Nietzsche's works except in *Ecce Homo* (1888), where he writes more about *TSZ* than any of his other books. In his allusion to *TSZ* Nietzsche writes: 'Here man is overcome at every moment, the concept "superman" here becomes the greatest reality' (*EH*, 'TSZ', 6). Nietzsche chooses 'Zarathustra' as the prophet of the *Übermensch* because he

> was the first to see in the struggle between good and evil the essential wheel in the working of things . . . Zarathustra created the most portentous error, morality. Consequently he should also be the first to perceive that error.
>
> (*SNZ*, I, p. 5n)

Zarathustra is thus seen by Nietzsche as having invented the opposites of good and evil and then as having come back to try to unite them. Zarathustra returns to improve on his former invention; in particular, to resolve the conflict between good and evil because Christianity cannot do it. In *TSZ*, we see the Christian point of view represented by the old man in the forest, who has no contact with the world and with humanity (*TSZ*, prologue, 2). Because Christianity is no longer in touch with the world, Zarathustra must be reborn; he must come back to show that

God is dead and that there is no difference between good and evil. His aspiration is, therefore, to overcome the opposites of good and evil from a standpoint that is beyond the opposites: he seeks a unification of opposites. Nietzsche saw in Zarathustra the first one to make mankind conscious of itself. For, as we saw in Chapters 2 and 3, it is Nietzsche's claim that the individual needs to promote conflict and opposition within himself if he is to aspire to greatness and fruition (*TI*, 'Morality as Anti-nature', 3); and now Zarathustra explicitly proclaims that 'one must have chaos in one' (*TSZ*, prologue, 5). Zarathustra is going to teach the opposites; he will teach both wise and poor men 'until the wise among men have again become happy in their folly and the poor happy in their wealth' (*TSZ*, prologue, 1). He is going to redress the balance; he is going to destroy a one-sided outright dominance and replace it with a competitive opposition, a creative tension that seeks strength in growth and productivity over that which seeks strength in sheer magnitude. Zarathustra is going to turn one element into two opposing elements, not in order to separate the two, but in order that they may be complementary to one another and seek unification – a unification that, as we saw in Chapter 2, following Heraclitus' model of polarity, is 'the diverging of a force into two qualitatively different opposed activities that seek to reunite' (*PTAG*, 5). Christianity failed, therefore, because it promoted the metaphysical model of static opposites, so that 'good' and 'evil' never sought unification. The thought of Zarathustra and Christianity are in direct opposition. Zarathustra is the 'dancing star' (*TSZ*, prologue, 5) who is fully conscious of his body and makes good use of the conflict of which it is composed, while the Christian is defined by rigidity and is taught to mortify and repress the flesh, so that he is divided and alienated from his very humanity. The *Übermensch* that Zarathustra proclaims is not like the Christian who promotes opposition and division *against* himself, thereby promoting one side of his humanity and alienating another; rather the *Übermensch* promotes opposition *within* himself (*WP* 966), thereby promoting every conflicting aspect of his humanity.

The *Übermensch* is anticipated in the thought of early Nietzsche, for it is the Dionysian impulse that enables 'nature which has become alienated, hostile, or subjugated' to celebrate 'once more her reconciliation with her lost son, man' (*BT*, 1). In complete contrast to Christianity, with its need to alienate man from nature, the *Übermensch* proclaims: 'Learn to become nature again yourselves and then with and in nature let yourselves be transformed' (*UM*, IV, 6). The *Übermensch* is identified with nature itself, a 'Dionysian' nature. The *Übermensch* is the one who has identified with primary unity, its pain and contradiction and thereby 'suffers in his own person the primordial contradiction that is concealed in things' (*BT*, 9). He is a tragic figure, or a tragic 'artist', who expresses nature's 'exuberant fertility' and 'creative joy' and uses such power to substantiate his own perfection.[2]

Nietzsche hoped that the future would be characterized by a 'supra-national and nomadic type of man' who would possess 'as its typical distinction a maximum of the art and power of adaptation' (*BGE*, 242). The *Übermensch* will draw upon his creative capacities in order to unite the opposites within him; he will 'educate himself' and 'draw forth and nourish all the forces which exist . . . and [will] bring them to a harmonious relationship with one another' (*UM*, III, 2). The *Übermensch*, like his prophet Zarathustra, is conscious of his psychological make-up, of how his instincts conflict, and of which ones are currently dominating others. He is therefore in a position to recognize which weaker instincts should be exaggerated in order to promote further conflict and strife, and a stronger capacity for creation. By drawing upon his artistic 'power of adaptation', the *Übermensch* increases opposition within him and thereby increases his capacity for creativity.[3] This process never ends; overcoming the instincts is never an end in itself, but is a means toward the higher goal of self-perfecting. Nietzsche writes:

> The man who has overcome his passions has entered into possession of the most fertile ground . . . to *sow* the seeds of good spiritual works in the soil of the subdued passions is then the immediate urgent task. The overcoming itself is only a *means*, not a goal; if it is not so viewed, all kinds of weeds and devilish nonsense will quickly spring up in this rich soil now unoccupied, and soon there will be more rank confusion than there ever was before.
>
> (*WS*, 53)

Nietzsche says: 'I believe that from the presence of opposites and from the feelings they occasion that the great man, *the bow with the greatest tension*, develops' (*WP*, 967). The greatest being is the one who unites the most antagonistic traits (*WP*, 881, 966). Nietzsche observes that commonplace beings 'perish when the multiplicity of elements and the tension of opposites, i.e., the preconditions for greatness in man, increases' (*WP*, 881). The *Übermensch* must therefore be preconditioned to be able to endure such inner tensions. In the commonplace being 'the tension, the range between the extremes . . . [is] less . . . the extremes themselves are . . . obliterated to the point of similarity' (*TI*, 'Expeditions of an Untimely Man', 37). It is different for the *Übermensch*: 'It is in precisely this compass of space, in this access to opposites that Zarathustra feels himself to be the *highest species of all existing things*' (*EH*, 'TSZ', 6). The *Übermensch*, however, does not merely represent opposites in their multitude; rather, he symbolizes the unification and synthesis of opposites that is appropriate to the further promotion of creativity. In other words, the *Übermensch* does not seek a mere accumulation of antithetical elements, but an 'increased co-ordination, of a harmonizing of all the strong desires' (*WP*, 800). Thus, 'Greatness of character does not consist in not possessing these affects – on the contrary, one possesses them to the highest degree – but in having them under control' (*WP*, 928). As we saw in Chapter 2, Nietzsche's notion of control is expressed in his concept of self-mastery, which is itself explained in terms of equilibrium (*WS*, 22) and moderation (*BT*, 25). He maintains that the most moderate will prove to be the strongest (*WP*, 55). We also saw in that chapter that the Apollinian and Dionysian impulses have to be balanced by one another if either is to be activated to its highest degree.

The notion of complementary opposites is continued throughout Nietzsche's thought, including his idea of the *Übermensch*. The *Übermensch* must promote both opposites in the binary pair, unlike the 'typical man', who

> does not understand the necessity for the reverse side of things: that he combats evils as if one could dispense with them; that he will not take the one with the other . . . approving only of one part of [a thing's] qualities and wishing to abolish the others . . . the ideal conceived as something in which nothing harmful, evil, dangerous, questionable, destructive would remain.
>
> (*WP*, 881)

The *Übermensch* stands apart from this ideal. In Nietzsche's words:

> With every increase of greatness and height in man, there is also an increase in depth and terribleness: one ought not to desire the one without the other – or rather: the more radically one desires the one, the more radically one achieves precisely the other.
>
> (*WP*, 1027)

The tension between opposites must be maintained to generate dynamic creativity; the victory of one element over its opposite, as with the superiority of good over evil in Christianity, will lead to stagnation and decay. The *Übermensch*, accordingly, is beyond good and evil; he will unite good and evil and will embody Zarathustra's teaching that 'the highest evil belongs to the highest goodness' (*TSZ*, II, 'Of Self-Overcoming'). Nietzsche writes:

> One cannot be one without being the other . . . with every growth of man, his other side must grow too . . . That man must grow better *and* more evil is my formula for this inevitability.
>
> (*WP*, 881)

If the tension of opposites is the formula of human growth, then the *Übermensch*, the master of humanity, would have the greatest concentration and tension of contrary instincts. Nietzsche writes:

> Most men represent pieces and fragments of man: one has to add them up for a complete man to appear. Whole ages, whole peoples are in this sense somewhat fragmentary; it is perhaps part of the economy of human evolution that man should evolve piece by piece. But that should not make one forget for a moment that the real issue is the production of the synthetic man.
>
> (*WP*, 881)

The *Übermensch* is not the disorganized totality of unconnected fragments of the mediocre man. He has synthesized every aspect of himself into a productive whole; he is 'a full, rich, great, whole human being in relation to countless incomplete fragmentary men' (*WP*, 997).[4] The *Übermensch* encompasses the fullest range of human capacities; he is synthetic because he must artificially exaggerate weaker instincts so that a greater conflict of drives can be promoted within him. Unlike the typical man who merely arranges the 'pieces of mankind', the *Übermensch* possesses

> the mighty capacity to draw together and unite, to reach the remotest threads and to preserve the web from being blown away . . . who unites what he has brought together into a living structure.
>
> (*UM*, IV, 4)

Patricia Dixon (1999), in her discussion of the importance of harmonizing the instincts for Nietzsche, traces the notion of 'living structure' to *On the Genealogy of Morals* (1887), where Nietzsche describes

> a ruling structure that *lives*, in which parts and functions are delimited and co-ordinated, in which nothing whatever finds a place that has not first been assigned a 'meaning' in relation to the whole.
>
> (*GM*, II, 17)

Speaking through Nietzsche, Dixon asks: 'Where . . . do we discover a harmonious whole at all, a simultaneous sounding of many voices in one nature?' Nietzsche replies:

> [In] men in whom everything, knowledge, desire, love, hate strives towards a central point, a root force, and where a harmonious system is constructed through the compelling domination of this living centre.
>
> (*UM*, III, 2; cited in Dixon, 1999, p. 332)

In *The Gay Science* (1882) Nietzsche further notes that

> Many hecatombs of human beings were sacrificed before these impulses learned to comprehend their coexistence and to feel that they were all functions of one organizing force within one human being.
>
> (*GS*, 113)

The 'living structure' of the *Übermensch* thus exhibits a unity dictated by a central organizing power that gives the opposite instincts 'their way and measure' (*WP*, 84) and 'precision and clarity of . . . direction' (*WP*, 64), so that they can develop and work for the whole. In other words, the *Übermensch* possesses '*all* the strong, seemingly contradictory gifts and desires – but in such a way that they go together beneath one yoke' (*WP*, 848). As a 'unifying principle' Nietzsche must promote one instinct above all others, one that can be justified as having static dominance, one that destroys the ascetic ideal and expresses the individual's life as inherently valuable. In my reading of Nietzsche, this 'central organizing power' is the 'power of adaptation' (*BGE*, 242), or the 'Will to Power' (which is described by Nietzsche as 'the strongest instinct': *TI*, 'What I Owe to the Ancients', 3): that power that increases the capacity for creation through the union of opposites.

Creation is precisely that which is required in Nietzsche's 'revaluation of values'. Creation is the process and principle that enables the individual to travel across the tightrope from the 'mediocre, typical man' to the noble *Übermensch* and safely cross the abyss of nihilism.[5] The effective expulsion of God from nature has motivated individuals to *recreate* themselves, to get rid of 'the shadow of God' and the idealistic dependency that God decreed, and to return to the earth (*TSZ*, prologue, 3), to become the first 'natural' man, the 'Dionysian' man.

The myth of Dionysus tells how he was born of an incestuous coupling between Zeus and his daughter, Persephone. In her jealousy, Hera (the wife of Zeus) aroused the Titans to attack the infant. These monstrous beings enticed Dionysus with toys and cut him to pieces with knives.[6] After the murder the Titans devoured the dismembered corpse. But the heart of Dionysus was saved and brought to Zeus by Athena. Dionysus was born again, for Zeus swallowed the heart and gave birth to him with Semele. In his anger at the Titans, Zeus destroyed them with thunder and lightning; but from their ashes humankind was born.[7] Dionysus is thus a man of 'creation', an embodiment of death and rebirth, and of those conditions necessary for creation – pain and great suffering. Nietzsche continues the depiction of Dionysian man:[8]

> The word '*Dionysian*' means: an urge to unity, a reaching out beyond personality, the everyday, society, reality, across the abyss of transitoriness: a passionate-painful overflowing into darker, fuller, more floating states; an ecstatic affirmation of the total character of life as that which remains the same, just as powerful, just as blissful, through all change; the great pantheistic sharing of joy and sorrow that sanctifies and calls good even the most terrible and questionable qualities of life; the eternal will to procreation, to fruitfulness, to recurrence; the feeling of the necessary unity of creation and destruction.
>
> (*WP*, 1050)

Dionysus calls on mankind to unite with nature and to unite the good with 'the most terrible'. The Dionysian man is reunited with humanity and all that is passionate, chaotic and irrational within him. He must joyfully and tragically restore himself to nature and experience 'an ascent – up into a high, free, even terrible nature and naturalness' (*WP*, 120). This terrible experience must be 'blissfully' endured over and over again, for Dionysus affirms nothing more than the tragedy of the eternal recurrence. There can be no self-overcoming without struggle and suffering; there will always be obstacles within the individual's path, for self-overcoming is a process without end and without reward. The eternal recurrence is, therefore, ultimately a teaching of strength through despair. The *Übermensch* is thus the

> ideal of the most exuberant, most living and most world-affirming man, who has not only learned to get on and treat with all that was and is but who wants to have it again *as it was and is* to all eternity.
>
> (*BGE*, 56)

The *Übermensch* is the being who promotes the 'Yes-saying instinct' as his unifying principle (*AC*, 57; *EH*, 'TSZ', 6), which gives him the strength for *amor fati*, to endure the unification of good and evil, to live a cursed existence, and to transmute this into the Dionysian intoxication of tragic acceptance.

Nietzsche regarded Goethe as the exemplar of the Dionysian, 'higher man' (*TI*, 'Expeditions of an Untimely Man', 49). What Goethe 'aspired to was *totality*; he strove against the separation of reason, sensuality, feeling, will . . . he disciplined himself to a whole, he *created* himself'. Nietzsche awards him the highest of all his honours:

> A spirit thus *emancipated* stands in the midst of the universe with a joyful and trusting fatalism, in the *faith* that only what is separate and individual may be rejected, that in the totality everything is redeemed and affirmed – *he no longer denies* . . . But such a faith is the highest of all possible faiths: I have baptized it with the name of *Dionysos*.
>
> (ibid.)

Goethe, according to Nietzsche, achieved humanity in its highest form: he exhibits a unification of the greatest contrary instincts (that is, reason, sensuality, feeling, and will) in the realization of *Übermenschlichkeit*. The *Übermensch* is the symbol of human totality, the unification of opposite instincts in the pursuit of creation. The individual who has realized such totality and unification of his human faculties is no longer all-too-human; he is indeed the *Übermensch*.

Chapter 5

Opposites in the Jungian model of the psyche

The interplay of opposites is crucial to Jungian psychology. Jung maintains: 'Life is born only of the spark of opposites' (Jung, 1917/1926/1943, par. 78). In accordance with the notion that 'there can be no reality without polarity' (Jung, 1951, par. 423), the psyche is construed by Jung to be a living system of opposites. Opposition is a necessary condition for the psyche as the very conflict and tension initiated by antithetical forces creates the energy needed by the psyche to generate its momentum and dynamism. Thus, the psyche 'like any other energetic system is dependent on the tension of opposites' (Jung, 1954, par. 483).

According to Jung, personality is a manifestation of 'definiteness, wholeness and ripeness' (Jung, 1934a, par. 288), and fundamental to its constitution are two principal opposites: the conscious and the unconscious, those 'real psychic facts that determine . . . whole being' (Jung, 1927, par. 491). The conscious represents what we can know and experience, and the unconscious refers to all that remains beyond our cognitive reach, that which is unknowable. The unconscious is, by definition, irreducible to conscious terms; if an unconscious element is accessible from a conscious perspective, then it is ultimately reduced to the level of consciousness and is no longer unconscious. Although the unconscious constitutes a vast part of our psyche, we are alienated from it: it is wholly other.[1] Conscious and unconscious are antithetical to one another; the nature of either is defined as opposite to the other. The former is familiar and the latter is unfamiliar. Although consciousness and the unconscious are diametrically opposed, they are, according to Jung, able to complement one another. Because the psyche is a self-regulating system, and, as such, cannot function without opposition (Jung, 1917/1926/1943, par. 92), it follows that the attitudes of consciousness and unconsciousness compensate one another to achieve psychic balance. Since energy is generated only through the tension of opposites, psychological growth necessitates the discovery of the opposite attitude to that of the conscious mind:

> The repressed content must be made conscious so as to produce a tension of opposites, without which no forward movement is possible. The conscious mind is on top, the shadow underneath, and just as high always longs for low

and hot for cold, so all consciousness, perhaps without being aware of it, seeks its unconscious opposite, lacking which it is doomed to stagnation, congestion and ossification.

(Jung, 1917/1926/1943, pars. 77–78)

Jung maintains that the attitude of the unconscious, and also its compensatory function, is discovered through the interpretation of the conscious recollection of the dream. The dream provides an active backdrop against which the interplay of opposites can be examined.

Although Jung would be the first to agree with Freud's famous dictum that dream interpretation is the 'royal road to the unconscious' (Freud, 1900/1991, p. 766; cf. Jung, 1916/1957, par. 152), he disagrees with Freud's account of the nature of the dream. While Freud regarded the dream as a repressed wish designed so as to find a way into expression, Jung regarded the dream as a statement of fact, of the way things are in the psyche. For Jung, the dream brings to consciousness an image of the psychological state that has been neglected and made unconscious; it is therefore an invaluable tool for understanding and diagnosing the personality. The dream compensates the conscious attitude as it unites the one-sided conscious orientation with its opposite, the unconscious attitude.[2] According to Jung, the dream achieves this reconciliation in one of three ways:

> If the conscious attitude to the life situation is in large degree one-sided, then the dream takes the opposite side. If the conscious has a position fairly near the 'middle', the dream is satisfied with variations. If the conscious attitude is 'correct' (adequate), then the dream coincides with and emphasizes this tendency, though without forfeiting its peculiar autonomy.
>
> (Jung, 1945/1948, par. 546)

Dreams therefore provide what is missing in the psychic wholeness of the individual, and help to re-establish relations between consciousness and unconsciousness, and secure overall psychic equilibrium.[3] The dream is the mediator of opposites; it controls the unconscious element in the binary pair, and through its manipulation, the dream either reinforces the existing bond between the two opposites or seeks its reconfiguration.

The compensatory relation itself – that which makes possible the stability and cooperation of the opposites – depends upon what Jung calls the 'transcendent function' (Jung, 1916/1957, par. 132). This is 'a natural process, a manifestation of the energy that springs from the tension of opposites, and it consists in a series of fantasy-occurrences which appear spontaneously in dreams and visions' (Jung, 1917/1926/1943, par. 121). It forms a basis for

> a process not of dissolution but of construction, in which thesis and antithesis both play their part. In this way it becomes a new content that governs the whole attitude, putting an end to the division and forcing the energy of the

opposite into a common channel. The standstill is overcome and life can flow on with renewed power towards new goals.

(Jung, 1921, par. 827)

The transcendent function is a twofold process: the spontaneous emergence of a unifying symbol unites opposing elements; and from this union, it establishes a new conscious attitude, one that is more integrated and enriched with those elements that were hitherto unconscious. Ego-consciousness tends to focus exclusively on adaptation to circumstances in its immediate environment, and fails to integrate the unconscious material that is not relevant to its adaptation. The ego can thus easily develop a one-sidedness that does not correspond to the overall instinctive wholeness of the personality. The transcendent function enables the personality to move from a one-sided attitude to a new, more complete, one (ibid., par. 145). By symbolically sketching new possibilities of life (in 'dreams and visions') it facilitates this transition and opens the way for further development.

The development of the personality is therefore advanced when the opposites of conscious and unconscious complement one another. The conscious attitude requires compensation from the unconscious attitude if it is to flourish, but this does not mean that the unconscious attitude is privileged over consciousness. Jung writes: 'Unconscious compensation is only effective when it co-operates with an integral consciousness; assimilation is never a question of "this *or* that", but always of "this *and* that"' (Jung, 1934b, par. 338). Both opposites must be regarded as having equal importance and must be integrally connected and move on parallel lines if the personality is to remain mentally stable; if they split apart or become dissociated, the personality will suffer from psychological disturbance (cf. *MHS*, p. 52). If either reason or unconscious instinct is exaggerated, this one-sidedness will lead to a pathological state: 'Too much of the animal distorts the civilized man, too much civilization makes sick animals' (Jung, 1917/1926/1943, par. 32).

According to Jung, Western civilization is guilty of exaggerating one opposite over and above its counterpart. Jung sees the civilized individual as a 'sick animal'.[4] Jung explains:

> Serene and tragic at once, it was just this archaic man who, having started to think, invented the dichotomy which Nietzsche laid at the door of Zarathustra: the discovery of the pairs of opposites, the division into odd and even, above and below, good and evil.
>
> (Jung, 1921, par. 963)

Thereafter, 'Western man became someone divided between his conscious and unconscious personality . . . [and as a result] we in the West have come to be highly disciplined, organized and rational' (*JS*, p. 397), so that 'in our time . . . the intellect . . . is making darkness, because we've let it take too big a place' (ibid., p. 420). Modern man has exaggerated and overdeveloped his rational conscious side at the expense of his unconscious instinctual side and has thereby exposed himself to a dangerous disequilibrium of opposites (Jung, 1957, par. 544). Jung warns:

> No matter how beautiful and perfect man may believe his reason to be, he can always be certain that it is only one of the possible mental functions, and covers only that one side of the phenomenal world which corresponds to it. But the irrational, that which is not agreeable to reason, rings it about on all sides. And the irrational is likewise a psychological function.
>
> (Jung, 1917/1926/1943, par. 110; also see par. 201)

> It needs only an almost imperceptible disturbance of equilibrium in a few of our rulers' heads to plunge the world into blood, fire, and radioactivity.
>
> (Jung, 1957, par. 561)

Opposites within consciousness

The favouring of one opposite over its counterpart is not limited to the promotion of reason and consciousness over instinct and the unconscious. It is also experienced on a more fundamental level within the very structure of consciousness itself, thereby making the prospect of the 'sick animal' more probable. The possibility of a discordant relationship between the opposites of conscious and unconscious is greatly increased when we note that consciousness is itself composed of opposites, which can conflict with one another. According to Jung, consciousness is *structured* according to the configuration of opposite forces inherent within it, and this configuration determines the psychological 'type' of the individual's personality, and whether he is healthy with 'definiteness, wholeness and ripeness', or a 'sick animal'.

The configuration of opposites within consciousness is regulated by a basic attitude to external events, and certain properties or 'functions' of consciousness. The 'attitude-types' are 'distinguished by the direction of [the individual's] interest, or of the movement of libido' and the 'function-types' are 'those more special types whose peculiarities are due to the fact that the individual adapts and orientates himself chiefly by means of his most differentiated function' (Jung, 1921, par. 556). Jung identifies two opposite attitude-types – introversion and extraversion. The former refers to an abstracted attitude to the object whereby the individual 'is always intent on withdrawing libido from the object, as though he had to prevent the object from gaining power over him'. The latter, in complete contrast, refers to a positive attitude to the object; the extravert

> affirms its importance to such an extent that his subjective attitude is constantly related to and orientated by the object. The object can never have enough value for him, and its importance must always be increased.
>
> (ibid., par. 557)

Although one or the other of these opposite orientations determines individuals' responses to the objects of their conscious experience, it also determines the compensatory action of their unconscious. Where consciousness is extraverted the unconscious is introverted, and conversely: the opposites counterbalance one another. Jung therefore talks of an unconscious attitude as well as a conscious attitude (ibid., pars. 568–576). The unconscious attitude impinges upon the conscious attitude to such an extent that the opposite attitudes often get blurred into one; it is therefore often difficult to decide which character traits belong to the conscious personality and which belong to the unconscious personality (ibid., par. 576).

In addition to the two attitude-types, Jung identified four functions of consciousness: thinking, feeling, sensation, and intuition. Jung writes:

> The essential function of sensation is to establish that something exists, thinking tells us what it means, feeling what its value is, and intuition surmises whence it comes and whither it goes.
>
> (Jung, 1921, par. 983)

These four functions divide into two antithetical pairs. Thinking and feeling are both termed 'rational' because both work with evaluations and judgements; thinking evaluates through cognition with the criteria of 'true' and 'false', feeling evaluates through the emotions with the criteria of 'pleasant' and 'unpleasant'. Sensation and intuition are both termed 'irrational' because they operate according to perception, which is not evaluated or interpreted; sensations perceive things as they are and not otherwise, intuition also 'perceives' through its capacity for an unconscious 'inner perception' of things.

Each one of us has within our ego-consciousness all four functions in antithetical pairs and both opposing attitudes. No one attitude or function occurs in its pure form. This means that the extravert cannot be entirely free from the characteristics of introversion; in this case, the inferior introverted attitude is simply demoted to the unconscious sphere where it can either compensate for the dominant extraverted attitude or remain dormant and incapable of integration within the ego. Similarly, we shall have a dominant mode of functioning from one of the four functions outlined earlier. This dominant function will come from one of the two pairs of rational or irrational functions. We shall also utilize another function as an 'auxiliary' to serve the dominant function, though 'naturally only those functions can appear as auxiliary whose nature is not opposed to the dominant function' (Jung, 1921, par. 667). For example, the two basic functions of thinking and feeling are evaluative and cannot be employed at the same time, and cannot be simultaneously applied to the same object. The relatively unconscious auxiliary function must come from the opposite pair of rational or irrational functions, depending on which pair the superior function came from, so that if I had a superior sensation function (from the irrational pair) my auxiliary function would be from either thinking or feeling (the rational pair).[5]

The unconscious functions group themselves in a similar pattern, in correlation with the conscious orientation, so that the superior function pertains entirely to the conscious realm, while its opposite, the inferior function, is confined to the unconscious realm. The two other functions are partly conscious and partly unconscious: the auxiliary function is relatively directed while its opposite, though seldom available to consciousness, can be raised to consciousness (this is possible because the auxiliary functions are not so opposed to one another as the dominant and inferior functions).

The conscious attitude and function predominate over those of the unconscious. If, however, the conscious attitude becomes overemphasized, so that one conscious function is promoted over its opposite, this opposite function will set up a compensatory drive, and will compel individuals, often by seemingly incomprehensible acts, to take account of the reality which they have neglected. The indirect manifestation of the unconscious takes the form of a disturbance within conscious behaviour. If the functions fail to compensate one another, they will be in a direct conflict with one another, thereby causing the opposites to split apart. This conflict aims at mutual repression of the functions, and if one of the functions becomes repressed, dissociation and splitting of the whole personality ensues, leading to neurosis:

> The acts that follow from such a condition are unco-ordinated, sometimes pathological, having the appearance of symptomatic actions. Although in part normal, they are based partly on the repressed opposite, which, instead of working as an equilibrating force, has an obstructive effect, thus hindering the possibility of further progress.
>
> (Jung, 1928, para. 61)[6]

The healthy personality seeks a balance of opposites (comprising the two attitudes and four functions of consciousness). The extreme promotion of only one opposite will result in *enantiodromia*: a complete reversal of the dominant opposite, when the unconscious inferior element overcomes the conscious dominant element to become the dominant element itself. The dominant element, in either case, generates a low level of energy, a state of entropy, which denies the psyche the dynamism necessary for its capacity to create and develop further (Jung, 1930/ 1950, par. 157). The ideal state of affairs is a *union* of opposites: the promotion of both opposites. This union does not minimize the tension between opposite forces, but increases it so that the production of psychic energy is maximized (Jung, 1942, par. 154). A union of opposites is the envisioned goal of the Jungian psyche. But, this goal is not a universal goal that is to be sought from the very start of life; rather, Jung tells us, it is to be sought in the second half of life (at approximately 35 years: see note 10), with the focus of the first half of life surprisingly being that which defines the 'sick animal': namely, promoting only one opposite in the binary pair.

In the first half of life the essential task of the individual is to develop ego-consciousness and consolidate a one-sided conscious attitude and dominant function. This is a slow process of centring where individuals must differentiate and isolate the function and attitude that will enable them, with most ease, to adapt to the demands of their environment and establish their social position within the world (their *persona*). For a certain one-sidedness and sense of discrimination will be needed to fulfil certain conventional demands that are required in the establishment of the persona. Only the dominant function and attitude inherent within the individual's psychic constitution can help him or her in this task.[7] The other attitude and functions are not yet required, and are thus relegated to the unconscious (Jung, 1928a, par. 64).[8] The need to confront the unconscious attitude is periodic and arises only when the one-sidedness of the conscious attitude is unable to adapt to the demands of reality, and consequently causes the individual to feel that his life has become stale, unprofitable, and lacking in meaning.[9] Jung writes:

> Thus it may easily happen that an attitude can no longer satisfy the demands of adaptation because changes have occurred in the environmental conditions which require a different attitude . . . the attitude breaks down and the progression of libido also ceases . . . The longer the stoppage lasts, the more the value of the opposed positions increases . . . In proportion to the decrease in value of the conscious opposites there is an increase in the value of all psychic processes which are not concerned with outwards adaptation . . . these psychic factors are for the most part unconscious. As the value of the subliminal elements and of the unconscious increases, it is to be expected that they will gain influence over the conscious mind.
>
> (Jung, 1928a, pars. 61–62)

> About a third of my cases are not suffering from any clinically definable neurosis, but from the senselessness and aimlessness of their lives. I should not object if this were called the general neurosis of our age. Fully two thirds of my patients are in the second half of life . . . In the majority of my cases the resources of the conscious mind are exhausted (or, in ordinary English, they are 'stuck') . . . I only know one thing: when my conscious mind no longer sees any possible road ahead and consequently gets stuck, my unconscious psyche will react to the unbearable standstill.
>
> (Jung, 1931b, pars. 83–84; also see Jung, 1928/1931, par. 160)

The unconscious contents that were originally unnecessary in the orientation of the individual's life now become essential if any progression is to be made in the latter half of life. The notion of a human being as a 'sick animal' is therefore a relative concept, for humans have the potential to develop beyond this particular stage of life. If they fail to develop and continue to promote only one opposite at a time when they must identify with both, they will remain steeped in neurosis. This stage of 'sickness' is a necessary developmental stage in the individual's life, for it provides the incentive and trigger to start the process of psychic unification and the realization of 'wholeness and ripeness' (Jung, 1934a, par. 288).[10] The establishment of ego-consciousness (and thus the promotion of a dominant opposite) is a prerequisite in the development of the personality (Jung, 1957, par. 528); individuals who have not established a conscious orientation do not yet have the capacity of regulation and the stability to enable them to seek their potential. Sickness occurs not only when individuals fail to promote both opposites, but also when they fail to identify a dominant element in the early stage of personality development. Thus, we see Jung claim that the individual must seek first to separate the opposites, and to promote one over the other, and then, when such promotion leads to 'stagnation, congestion and ossification', to reunite the opposites in order to maintain productivity and dynamism within the psyche.

Individuation: the interplay of opposites

Jung called the process when material of the unconscious compensates, and is incorporated into consciousness, the process of *individuation*. The process of individuation is therefore the dynamic interplay of opposites, in which opposites are actively balanced to form a new unity. This unity is Jung's conception of the *whole* self, or 'Self':

> Individuation means becoming a single, homogeneous being, and, in so far as 'individuality' embraces our innermost, last, and incomparable uniqueness, it also implies becoming one's own self. We could therefore translate individuation as 'coming to selfhood' or 'self-realization'.
>
> (Jung, 1928b, par. 266)

Self-realization implies an understanding of the structures of opposites inherent within the psyche.

We have seen that consciousness is composed of a series of innate functions that are configured as pairs of opposites, and the structure of the unconscious, in its role as counterweight to consciousness, is itself experienced by the individual as a powerful antithetical force. As a force of compensation the unconscious, though itself unknowable, must channel its energy in accordance with those structures of consciousness that it will affect, and it is in this sense that I regard the unconscious as also having 'structure' and direction. Indeed, Jung effectively attributes a structure to the unconscious when he divides it into a personal and collective realm:

> [T]he personal unconscious . . . includes all those psychic contents which have been forgotten during the course of the individual's life . . . In addition it contains all subliminal impressions or perceptions which have too little energy to reach consciousness. To these we must add unconscious

combinations of ideas that are feeble and too indistinct to cross over the threshold . . . The other part of the unconscious is what I call the impersonal or collective unconscious. As the name indicates, its contents are not personal but collective; that is, they do not belong to one individual alone but to a whole group of individuals, and generally to a whole nation, or even to the whole of mankind . . . [I]t is the deposit of the psychic functioning of the whole human race.

(Jung, 1920/1948, pars. 588–589; cf. Jung, 1934/1954, par. 42)

The personal unconscious is made up of all the forgotten and repressed material unique to the individual, while the collective unconscious represents a deeper level of unconsciousness – a 'retreat farther and farther into darkness' (Jung, 1940, par. 291). This dark level of the psyche lacks individuality and uniqueness; it is irreducible and incomprehensible to consciousness, and thus wholly unassailable by the ego. While the contents of the personal unconscious are subjective, those of the collective unconscious are objective and autonomous. This is because the collective unconscious is related to the phylogenetic instinctual base of the human race. The contents of the collective unconscious are thus common to every individual, and, unlike the personal unconscious that generates compensatory activity according to the individual's specific needs, the collective unconscious provides undifferentiated compensation to every individual alike (as we shall see later). The contents of the collective unconscious have never been conscious; it operates independently of the ego and of all conscious processes. Its manifestations appear in symbolic form, in fantasies and metaphor that have a universal structure, applicable to every individual in every culture. For the process of individuation to be successful, the individual must confront, and, to some extent, understand, the collective realm together with its primordial images.[11] It is important for individuals to assert their individuality against the collective, to differentiate themselves from it, in order to escape the collective ideal of inflation and megalomania with its potential inflictions of grandiose delusions and psychoses. The collective realm is incapable of developing consciousness and individuality; if individuals fail to develop this side of their personality they will be effectively promoting the unconscious over and above consciousness, and will then have to endure an inevitable 'sickness' (of an over-inflated ego).[12]

Jung gave the name 'archetypes' to the primordial images of the collective unconscious. Archetypes are not inherent ideas as such but are 'typical forms of behaviour which, once they become conscious, naturally present themselves *as ideas and images*, like everything else that becomes a content of consciousness' (Jung, 1947/1954, par. 435). They are typical forms of behaviour in that they are 'deposits of the constantly repeated experiences of humanity' (Jung, 1917/1926/1943, par. 109). The archetype thus has the capacity and readiness to produce the same mythical ideas and images over and over again. Archetypes have an organizing influence on images and ideas; they are recurrent subjective fantasy-ideas that are aroused by physical processes and entities found in the external world. Though they themselves are not conscious, conscious images and ideas are variations on them.

The process of individuation usually involves encountering a series of archetypal visual 'personifications', which compensate consciousness and indicate to the individual how the opposites are relating within him and how much progress has been made toward their unification. Archetypes are symbolically translated from their unconscious roots to consciousness, so that archetypes appear within dreams and in other manifestations of the unconscious – in 'visions, fantasies, emotions, grotesque ideas, and so forth' (Jung, 1932, par. 509). The individuation process is a long and arduous process in which the opposites of consciousness and the unconscious merge into a unity. A series of archetypal figures and situations are encountered along the way, and are – if the conditions are appropriate – accepted and assimilated into consciousness. According to Jung, the individual's 'acceptance' of one archetype leads him to encounter others; this process culminates in the 'acceptance' of 'the archetype of archetypes', 'the archetype par excellence' (Samuels, 1994, p. 87), the 'Self'. The Self is the totality of the personality, where all opposites are united, and consciousness is enriched in its coordination with the personal and collective unconscious.

Jung does not explicitly define the *process* of individuation, so that we cannot be certain of the specific stages involved in the gradual unification of opposites. Jung makes it clear that he does not want to define each stage in terms of an objective teleological formulation that applies to every individual: 'How the harmonizing of conscious and unconscious data is to be undertaken cannot be indicated in the form of a recipe' (Jung, 1939b, par. 524). It is also apparent that the archetypal encounters do not necessarily form a linear sequence or process, but can also be thought of as circular. According to this circular scheme, it would seem that an encounter with a particular archetype could happen at any time. It is not localized or allotted a specific place in the psychic order of things; rather it spontaneously materializes at a time appropriate to the individual concerned. However, more often than not we see in Jung's writings allusion to a linear sequence of archetypal encounters. The individuation process often begins with the confrontation of the personal unconscious, where individuals assimilate their neglected tendencies personified by the 'shadow' archetype (cf. Jung, 1917/1926/1943, par. 103). After this, the collective unconscious must be confronted, where the contra-sexual side of the individual is encountered, personified by the anima/animus (thereby providing the undifferentiated compensation to every individual alike). Finally, the archetype of the 'Self' is encountered. When this is accepted, the individual accepts the totality of his being.[13] Furthermore, Jung's discussion of the individuation process in *Aion* (*CW* 9ii, 1951) examines the archetypal figures in this sequence, supporting the notion of a linear framework of experience. According to this scheme, it is conceivable for individuals to estimate how far they have progressed towards the Self, for it provides a teleological map to chart the progressive stages of the merger between consciousness and the unconscious. That is, by paying careful attention to the motifs of archetypal appearances within their dreams, individuals should be able to estimate which stage in the process of individuation they have reached.[14] Such clarity and accuracy would be unachievable with a circular process.

The shadow is the first archetypal figure to be encountered in the individuation process because it is the most accessible: 'Its nature can in large measure be inferred from the contents of the personal unconscious' (Jung, 1951, par. 13). The shadow is the most apparent archetype to the individual as it embodies the very opposite of his conscious one-sided attitude; it is the inferior function and attitude type within consciousness. To incorporate the shadow into consciousness is to reject the 'sick animal' with his propensity to promote one opposite in the binary pair, for its incorporation entails the acceptance of the neglected opposite, and thus a unification of opposites. 'With insight and good will', Jung writes, 'The shadow can to some extent be assimilated into the conscious personality' (ibid., par. 16). However, Jung also notes that there can be resistance to this assimilation – notably 'projection', where some traits peculiar to the individual's shadow are projected outside of that individual and appear as traits within another person. The shadow is often rejected because it is of a contrary nature and often appears alien or even morally reprehensible. Projection works as a defence mechanism to remove the shadow-elements out of consciousness and into the external world. Jung writes: 'He must be convinced that he throws a very long shadow before he is willing to withdraw his emotionally-toned projections from their object' (ibid.). Jung continues to say that these projections are

> assumed to belong to the realm of the shadow, that is, to the negative side of the personality. This assumption becomes untenable after a certain point, because the symbols that then appear no longer refer to the same but to the opposite sex, in a man's case to a woman and vice versa. The source of the projections is no longer the shadow – which is always the same sex as the subject – but a contra-sexual figure.
>
> (Jung, 1951, par. 19; cf. par. 422)

In the linear process of individuation, it is, therefore, through experiencing a *resistance* in the shadow's assimilation into consciousness that the archetype of the anima (of a man) and the animus (of a woman) is encountered.

If the shadow is experienced first – as the antithesis of the conscious orientation – the archetype of anima/animus is the second set of opposites to be experienced. The incorporation of this archetype into consciousness signifies the union of genders: the anima is the feminine component of the unconscious male psyche, while the animus is the male component of the unconscious female psyche. The former personifies 'eros' or love, while the latter is a personification of 'spirit' and 'intellect' (Jung, 1951, par. 29). The archetypal image of the anima is usually singular to compensate the fundamental masculine tendency to discriminate, while the image of the animus is usually plural to compensate the fundamental female tendency to unify and synthesize (*SNZ*, II, pp. 1152–1153). The anima/animus therefore, like the shadow, compensates the *persona* of the individual – his (one-sided) conscious orientation. Jung writes:

> The persona, the ideal picture of a man as he should be, is inwardly compensated by feminine weakness and as the individual outwardly plays the strong man, so he becomes inwardly a woman, i.e., the anima, for it is the anima that reacts to the persona.
>
> (Jung, 1928b, par. 309)

The persona and anima/animus are opposites; while the persona represents the outer conscious attitude, the anima/animus represents the inner unconscious attitude. The anima/animus contains within it all those human qualities that the persona lacks. Thus, 'If the persona is intellectual, the anima will quite certainly be sentimental'; therefore

> the character of the anima can be deduced from that of the persona. Everything that should normally be in the outer attitude, but is conspicuously absent, will invariably be found in the inner attitude.
>
> (Jung, 1921, par. 806)

The anima/animus does not contain only negative attributes, as the shadow usually does; it can have characteristics of a positive or negative nature depending on those of the persona. The realization of the anima/animus together with the shadow is essential to the dissolution of the one-sided persona and to the process of the unification of opposites.

In this scheme it would seem that the process of uniting opposites begins with a discovery of the personal unconscious, of which the shadow is part. This is discovered by a matter of will: the individual must determine its content by recognizing all aspects (attitudes and functions) of his or her *whole* personality, and then by noting which are absent from the conscious orientation – something that is indicated by those unfavourable feelings that the individual might unconsciously project on to others. The process continues with the discovery of the collective unconscious, of which the anima/animus is part. This second stage is triggered by the first. This happens, according to Jung, when the first stage 'becomes untenable after a certain point' (Jung, 1951, par. 19). The details of how the transformation is made from the first stage to the second (from incorporating the personal unconscious into consciousness to the incorporation of the collective unconscious into consciousness) is not made clear by Jung. The implication is that the resistance experienced in the first stage, caused by trying to incorporate the shadow, somehow initiates archetypal activity from the anima/animus. However, this implies that the shadow has not yet been successfully accepted into consciousness, thereby making further progress in individuation unlikely.[15] Likewise, Jung tells us that once the anima/animus has been successfully incorporated into consciousness 'the unconscious again changes its dominant character and appears again in a new symbolic form, representing the Self, the innermost nucleus of the psyche' (*MHS*, p. 196). It would therefore seem that the progressive stages in the process of uniting opposites are not a matter for intellectual examination; rather, the process is an unconscious one that is marked only by spontaneous symbolic images that are linked by no definable causal relationship. The three stages in the individuation process can thus be discussed as one. Once the inferior unconscious traits (symbolized by *both* stages one and two: the archetypes of the shadow and anima/animus) are made conscious, the psyche is no longer expressed in one-sided terms as promoting one opposite, but is expressed as promoting an equal balance between the opposites. The psyche's oppositions are no longer related by conflict but by compensation and unification, and this psychic state of equilibrium is itself symbolized by stage three, the Self – the very centre of totality, which embraces both consciousness and unconsciousness just as the ego is the centre of the conscious mind (Jung, 1936a, par. 44).

It is not easy to decipher the movement between the stages (or even the stages themselves) of the individuation process. I understand this movement as the gradual unification of opposites, and I believe that a more thorough understanding of this process can be found in Jung's alchemical texts. Jung draws a parallel between his individuation process and the alchemical process; although Jung's interpretation of the latter is riddled with obscure and often incomprehensible symbols, I believe an overall scheme and structured stages, in which opposites are progressively united, can be identified. Once we have established this, we should be in a better position to understand the movement between the stages of the individuation process.

The unification of opposites in alchemy

In alchemy Jung found a wealth of symbolism that he recognized to be parallel to the process of individuation. As we saw earlier, the unconscious communicates its material to consciousness via the transcendent function, which spontaneously produces symbols in dreams, fantasies and visions. We cannot rely solely upon Jung's 'systematic' discourse to understand the process of uniting opposites. Indeed Jung points out many times that the psyche cannot be adequately described in 'scientific' and 'rational' terms. An attempt at examining Jung's difficult texts on alchemy and its symbols may compensate for the structured exposition of his thought.

The ancient art of alchemy was concerned with the complexities of change, of the transformation from one state to another. Alchemists worked with metals, and within their laboratories they tried to transform an ore of little value into silver or gold (or the 'Philosopher's Stone'). But this 'external work' with matter was, in many cases, intimately linked to an 'inner work' on the human personality. For example, we often read of the 'alchemical fire' that is the 'secret of the *opus*'. This is clearly a physical fire that was controlled within a vessel as part of the 'outer' process; but it is also the heat-producing quality of meditation and imagination that is linked with the 'inner' individuation process. Thus,

> alchemy had a double face: on the one hand the practical chemical work in the laboratory, on the other a psychological process, in part consciously psychic, in part unconsciously projected and seen in the various transformations of matter.
>
> (Jung, 1937a, par. 380)

As a method of understanding physical process, it is fair to say that alchemy is now redundant: it inevitably gave way to modern chemistry due to its inferior methodology (which lacked quantitative measurements), understanding and lack of success in the transformation of matter. However, alchemy is still relevant in its use as a tool for reflecting upon psychological change. Indeed, in *Psychology and Alchemy* (*CW* 12, 1944a) Jung discusses how certain archetypal images that are common in alchemy appear in the dreams of modern individuals who have no knowledge of alchemical literature:

> The world of alchemical symbols definitely does not belong to the rubbish heap of the past, but stands in a very real and living relationship to our most recent discoveries concerning the psychology of the unconscious.
>
> (Jung, 1955–1956, p. xiii)

The 'most recent discovery', according to Jung, is of course his individuation process.

The often cited saying 'solve et coagula' in alchemical texts describes the process of uniting opposites that is common to alchemy and the individuation process. Both the alchemist and the Jungian analyst see the essence of his art in terms of separation, on the one hand, and synthesis and consolidation on the other:

> There was first of all an initial state in which opposite tendencies or forces were in conflict . . . [and then] the great question of a procedure which would be capable of bringing the hostile elements and qualities, once they were separated, back to a unity again.
>
> (ibid., p. xiv)

This procedure in alchemy is, unfortunately, highly confused and complex, so that 'hardly two authors are of the same opinion regarding the exact course of the process and the sequence of its stages' (Jung, 1937a, par. 333) and 'It is quite hopeless to try to establish any kind of order' (Jung, 1937a, par. 401). It thus seems that our quest for arriving at a definite structure to the process of uniting the opposites by referring to the alchemical literature will fail. However, Jung maintains that 'the majority [of authors] are agreed on the principal points at issue' (ibid.). Thus, alchemists in general distinguish four stages to their work, which correspond, Jung notes, to

> the original colours mentioned in Heraclitus: *melanosis* (blackening), *leukosis* (whitening), *xanthosis* (yellowing) and *iosis* (reddening) . . . [But] later, about the fifteenth or sixteenth century, the colours were reduced to three, and the *xanthosis* . . . gradually fell into disuse or was seldom mentioned.
>
> (ibid.)

'Colours', Jung informs us, 'are feeling-values' (Jung, 1955–1956, par. 333). For evidence he cites the fact that when patients sketch their dream images they use colour at 'the moment when merely intellectual interest gives way to emotional participation' (ibid.). Likewise, it is often the case that significant emotional moments in the dream itself insist upon a specific colour for their expression. We could thus say that the use of colour to denote stages in the alchemical process indicates the transformation of the conscious mood or attitude in the individuation process, with its gradual incorporation of unconscious material. Jung seems to agree with this view:

> Psychologically it means that during the assimilation of the unconscious the personality passes through many transformations, which show it in different lights and are followed by ever-changing moods.
>
> (Jung, 1955–1956, par. 430)

The unconscious is gradually 'illuminated' in the developing personality, which is characterized by a change in mood from black to white (or yellow) to red:

> This dawning light corresponds to the *albedo*, the moonlight which in the opinion of some alchemists heralds the rising sun, the growing redness (*rubedo*) which now denotes an increase of warmth and light.
>
> (ibid., par. 307)

The first 'mood' or stage of the alchemical process is black, which corresponds to the lack of unconscious incorporation (the shadow of the individuation process or the alchemical *nigredo*). The final stage is red, which corresponds to the fullest expression or illumination. We can think of the red stage of enlightenment as the Nietzschean 'Daybreak', when authentic values, which were once hidden, are at last expressed, or in terms of the 'blood' that gives life to the *whole* individual, the Self (cf. Jung, 1947/1954, par. 384).

In order to ascertain a more detailed explanation of the stages in the alchemical process and their associated colours, we shall examine the external, chemical method of transforming a base metal into a nobler metal. This is clearly described by the historian Jack Lindsay, who is worth quoting at length.

Lead, a primary common metal, had to be broken up, changed, driven up the scale, towards silver or gold; it had to change its colour. So fire was invoked; and under its action the lead was reduced to a fluid state. The fluidity thus brought about was what constituted the primary level, in which new potentialities were actively present . . . Also the liquefaction of lead involved its blackening. So the blackness of the liquid condition above all expressed the attainment of a primary level, a state of chaos . . . Somehow the Primary Black had to be transformed into White or Yellow, which expressed the nobler metals. This could be done, it was believed, if one could find a metal which had certain affinities with both the lower and higher substances, which sympathized with both of them and which exerted its attractive power in both directions (downwards and upwards).

By using the right kind of metal, in the right kind of proportions, one could swing the balance towards the upper levels and thus transform the material into the higher . . . The two materials, that of primary matter or liquid blackness and that of the alloying and transforming addition, must have something in common, some element of harmony . . . But if that were all, a state of equilibrium was created and nothing happened; the first level was not transcended. So one nature must conquer the other. The conquering act was the moment of transformation, when the equilibrium was broken and a new relationship established.

The new fused substance existed at a higher level and involved the creation of a new quality, which revealed itself in the colour-change. But that was not enough. The new state must be stabilized, so that it might provide the basis for yet another upward movement.

(Lindsay, 1970, pp. 116–117; cited in Schwartz-Salant, 1995, pp. 8–9)

In Lindsay's description of the alchemical process we can identify three prominent stages of transformation. This triadic formula is implicit within alchemical texts and, according to Lindsay, has been communicated within alchemical thinking from its earliest forms in Bolos-Demokrites (200 BC), who is regarded as the founder of alchemy (Lindsay, 1970, p. 103). This triadic principle is the *Axiom of Ostanes*, which is stated thus: *A nature is delighted by another nature, a nature conquers another nature, a nature dominates another nature*. If we transpose this formula into the process of uniting opposites, we see that the first stage entails the promotion of opposites. This is the 'primary chaos', which is a 'mixture' (ibid., p. 117) of the base black metal and its *potential* to be other (i.e. the nobler white or yellow metal). It is interesting to note that the opposites must be created; they exist from the beginning only *in potentia*. Jung supports this premise thus:

The division into two was necessary in order to bring the 'one' world out of the state of potential into reality. Reality consists of a multiplicity of things. But one is not a number, the first number is two, and with it multiplicity and reality begin.

(Jung, 1955–1956, par. 659)

Lindsay tells us that the second stage of the process is defined by the 'introduction of a dynamic factor which changes the original relations' (Lindsay, 1970, p. 117). A third element is thus introduced to unite the opposites. This third element corresponds to Jung's *transcendent function* (Jung, 1921, par. 184), as it has affinities with both opposites, and thus enables the original element to unite with its potential. At this stage of the process we are told that the unification of opposites might result in a static condition where no energy is created. Earlier we saw that Jung regarded this condition as tantamount to the death of the psyche, for 'Like any other energetic system [the psyche] is dependent on the *tension* of opposites' (Jung, 1954, par. 483, italics mine). The unification of opposites in this case would entail their merger without maintaining their essential difference; the two opposites would merely blend into one. To counteract this, the notion of 'conquering' is introduced within this stage of the alchemical process. Here we see that the opposites are not equivalent, they share a common value with the 'third thing' that acts as a mediator between the two, but they themselves remain incommensurable. Thus, in this stage one opposite will conquer or overcome the other while maintaining their synthesis. The notion of domination of one opposite over the other in this union is not, however, equivalent to Jung's 'sick animal', for the latter entails complete domination to the extent that the inferior opposite is relegated to the unconscious when it should be consciously active. In the alchemical model the inferior opposite is acknowledged and plays a significant role; it is active in that it forges a tension with its superior counterpart, thereby allowing the process to continue. Indeed, Lindsay implies that the process continues so that the union of the opposites (the union of the base metal and its potential to be nobler) 'might provide the basis for yet another upward movement'. There is thus a more valued stage beyond the union of opposites. I believe this is yet another unification of opposites, triggered off by the previous one.[16] We saw a similar pattern of progression earlier when the union of consciousness and the personal unconscious (personified by the shadow) brought about the further union of consciousness and the collective unconscious (personified by the anima/animus). In this earlier case we were uncertain about how the second union of opposites might be initiated by the first; but now we can turn to the *Axiom of Ostanes* for a possible answer. Thus, the stabilization of the union of opposites (expressed by the colour white or yellow, and the chemical composition of silver or gold) provides the basis from which a further transformation can be made to a more valued stage (expressed by the colour red, and the 'Philosopher's Stone'). This process of transformation occurs as it did previously – the unvalued white/yellow element, now regarded as the synthesis of opposites, contains within it the potential to be other, the highly valued red stone, which is its opposite. And the 'third element' is again introduced to transform the 'mixture' by uniting its opposites.

The triadic formula of *Ostanes*, with its three-stage process of uniting opposites, can be traced in the alchemical symbolism that Jung interprets as paralleling his individuation process. Perhaps the simplest method to use to unravel the complex symbolism is the colour key. We have already recognized that the original black (lead) stage of the alchemical process corresponds to the shadow of the individuation process, the white or yellow (silver or gold) stage to the anima/animus, and the final red (philosopher's stone) stage to the Self. The symbols of alchemy, however, provide a more enriched explanation of this, which is summarized by Jung as follows:

> The *nigredo* or blackness is the initial state, either present from the beginning as a quality of the *prima materia*, the chaos or *massa confusa*, or else produced by the separation (*solutio, separatio, divisio, putrefactio*) of the elements. If the separated condition is assumed at the start, as sometimes happens, then a union of opposites is performed under the likeness of a union of male and female (called the *coniugium, matrimonium, coniunctio, coitus*), followed by the death of the product of the union (*mortificatio, calcinatio, putrfactio*) and a corresponding *nigredo*. From this the washing (*ablutio, baptisma*) either leads direct to the whitening (*albedo*), or else the soul (*anima*) released at the 'death' is reunited with the dead body and brings about its resurrection, or again the 'many colours' (*omnes colores*), or 'peacock's tail' (*cauda pavonis*), lead to the one white colour that contains all colours. At this point the first main goal of the process is reached, namely the *albedo, tinctura, alba, lapis albus* etc., highly prized by many alchemists as if it were the ultimate goal. It is the silver or moon condition. The *albedo* is, so to speak, the daybreak, but not until the *rubedo* is it sunrise . . . the *rubedo* then follows direct from the *albedo* as the result of raising the heat of the fire to its highest intensity. The red and the white are King and Queen, who may celebrate their 'chymical wedding' at this stage.
>
> (Jung, 1937a, par. 334)

The first stage of the process is evident in the black *prima materia* or *chaos*, where all elements are in total conflict so that the opposites repel one another and no connection or relation between them is possible (ibid., par. 381). This original state is symbolized in alchemy by many images. Perhaps the most common is that of water: it is 'a whirlpool in chaos', the 'material principle of all bodies' is 'eternal water', the 'water of life' (Jung, 1937a, pars. 433, 425). Water is construed by Jung to be 'an excellent symbol for the living power of the psyche', particularly its unconscious aspect (ibid., par. 94).

It is the role of the alchemical process to unite the opposites of the *prima material*, and this is embodied in the union of opposite genders – in the 'chymical wedding'. In alchemy the union of man and woman represents the highest union of opposites in which all other opposites become subsumed: 'The brother–sister pair stands allegorically for the whole conception of opposites' (Jung, 1955–1956, par. 436; Jung, 1944a, par. 43). Their 'wedding' is crucial to the process. It must be noted that in the above passage Jung speaks of this union immediately after the initial stage of *chaos* and again between the stages of *albedo* and *rubedo*. It would seem that either the initial union between the sexes is merely transitory and does not enjoy complete satisfaction or 'stability' until the end of the process, or that their 'wedding' occurs at each transformation. In support of the latter explanation, the wedding is often referred to as the *coniunctio*, which, Jung says, is equivalent to the transcendent function – that which enables the cooperation of opposites at *any* and *every* stage (Jung, 1955–1956, par. 261). However, the wedding of king and queen (Sol and Luna) is usually realized at the end of the process, culminating in the birth of their child, which represents the ultimate alchemical goal. If this is indeed the case, then the appearance of their wedding at the start (as the above passage indicates) is confusing. This confusion adds to our earlier uncertainty as to whether the individuation process is either a linear or circular process. Jung himself confirms the confusion:

> The displacement and overlapping of images are as great in alchemy as they are in mythology and folklore. As these archetypal images are produced directly by the unconscious, it is not surprising that they exhibit its contamination of content to a very high degree.
>
> (Jung, 1955–1956, par. 401)

We see that the chaotic, separated opposites find regulation and unity in the wedding of male and female. In terms of the *Axiom of Ostanes*, the first stage is in play, where *a nature is delighted by another nature*. In the wedding of male and female, the third element that is common to both opposites and implements their union, is the symbol of incest; we are thus informed that the king will marry his mother (Jung, 1955–1956, par. 410), that there will be a 'union of close blood-relatives' (Jung, 1946, par. 419), and a 'union with one's own being' (ibid.). After the wedding the union experiences 'death' and 'a corresponding *nigredo*'. This is because the king must die leaving the widowed queen in a transformed state of pregnancy. These events culminate in the second phase of the process, the white *albedo* stage, where *a nature conquers another nature*. Thus, in the union of male and female, the female is stronger than the male; she conquers him to avoid their complete merger into a static condition. The king is inferior, we are told, because he is intrinsically weak: 'The original imperfection of the king . . . becomes a problem' (Jung, 1955–1956, par. 368); 'The old king lacked something, on which account he grew senile' (Jung, 1945/1954, par. 427). Indeed, the king is suffering from the sickness of a one-sided conscious attitude:

> With increasing one-sidedness the power of the king decays . . . the more distinctly an idea emerges and the more consciousness gains in clarity, the more monarchic becomes its content, to which everything contradictory must submit . . . The king constantly needs the renewal that begins with a descent into his own darkness, an immersion in his own depths, and with a reminder that he is related by blood to his adversary.
>
> (Jung, 1955–1956, par. 471)

The king must die so that he can be reborn in a nobler form, as a *whole* being. He must suffer various fatalities at the hands of the queen, including 'immersion in the bath or sea' (of 'Luna unconsciousness'), 'dissolution and decomposition', 'extinction of his light (Sol) in the darkness (Luna)', and 'incineration in the fire'.[17] The death of the king 'signifies the overcoming of the old and obsolete as well as the dangerous preliminary stages [of the process of uniting opposites] which are characterized by animal symbols' (Jung, 1955–1956, par. 169). The king is represented by a dragon, which

> from inner necessity . . . destroyed itself and changed into the lion, and the adept, drawn involuntarily into the drama, then felt the need to cut off his paws . . . The dragon ate its own wings as the eagle did its feathers. These grotesque images reflect the conflict of opposites into which the researcher's curiosity had led him.
>
> (Jung, 1945/1954, par. 493; also see Jung, 1955–1956, par. 169)

The king's murder by the queen is principally described as a drowning in a bath, which is the return to the unconscious. The symbolic meaning of water is clearly conveyed here – for the king represents the conscious extreme, and the water is the (female) unconscious chaos that threatens to overcompensate. The king is destroyed, but all is not lost, because the waters are baptismal and enable the king to be reborn. The king is reborn as the child of the incestuous marriage between himself (in his original inferior form) and the queen. As the unborn child of the queen, the king experiences a 'return to the dark initial state', as he is again immersed in her waters and the 'amniotic fluid of the grave uterus' (Jung, 1946, par. 454).

The murder of the king by the superior queen describes the white *albedo* stage of the alchemical process. Returning to the above passage (Jung, 1937a, par. 334), we see that 'the washing . . . leads direct to the whitening . . . the one white colour that contains all colours'; and these 'many colours' are equivalent to the 'peacock's tail'. In order to encourage the transformation to the final stage of the alchemical process, in which the child is born, the queen consumes a special 'pregnancy diet' (Jung, 1955–1956, par. 388). This diet represents the third stage in the triadic formula of *Ostanes*, where *a nature dominates another nature*. The queen, by nourishing the unborn king inside her, expresses her dominance over him. This nourishment takes the form of 'peacock flesh' and the 'blood of the green lion' (ibid., par. 401).[18] Thus, the queen expresses her domination over the king by devouring that which represents all colours; that is, all the coloured stages in the alchemical process. The queen contains everything within her; she is what Jung refers to as the 'one white colour that contains all colours'. The final stage in the alchemical process occurs after the queen consumes the lion's blood and peacock's flesh,[19] when she gives birth to her son: the reborn king.

The king in his second birth is the *hermaphrodite*; he is both king and queen. In this state, the king is no longer inferior to the queen, so she cannot dominate him. This means the process of splitting and uniting opposites cannot continue: 'Because the lapis [the child of Sol and Luna] is both male and female there is no need for another coniunctio' (Jung, 1955–1956, par. 524). In the alchemical process the king passes through various stages of transformation characterized by the dragon, lion, eagle and hermaphrodite. Each stage represents a greater degree of insight as more of the unconscious is incorporated; the hermaphrodite king, as the final stage, represents complete unconscious integration.

The complexities of alchemical symbolism are evident in the exposition I have given. However, the triadic formula of *Ostanes* can be discerned within it, and this alchemical method gives us insight into how the opposites are united. The parallels between alchemical symbolism and the process of individuation are palpable, so that, an examination of the former can elucidate the latter. Thus, although the process of uniting opposites that underlies the progress of individuation is obscured, Jung's work on alchemy illuminates what he regarded as its essential aspects.

In this chapter we have seen that opposites are significant to Jung's thought. We have seen that Jung values the creativity that is generated when opposites balance and compensate one another. The development of the personality – the *individuation process* – depends on a complementary relationship between consciousness and the unconscious, where both opposites are given equal expression; a disequilibrium or one-sidedness will result in an unhealthy psychological disturbance.

We have seen that Jung does not explicitly define the stages of the individuation process. I presented it as a linear process that proceeds through stages that progressively reconcile opposites, culminating in the complete unification of opposites where both opposites are fully expressed. We saw that these stages are personified by particular archetypes in the individuation process and find their parallel in particular colours and symbols in the alchemical process. The process of individuation leads to the *whole* personality where consciousness is enriched in its coordination with the personal and collective unconscious. Jung calls the whole personality the Self, and in Chapter 6 we shall try to describe what Jung meant by this. Certain similarities between the Self and Nietzsche's *Übermensch* will emerge.

Chapter 6

The Self as a union of opposites

The achievement of the Self marks the telos of the psyche, where the opposites within the psyche are no longer related by conflict but by compensation. The Self is thus 'the container and the organizer of all opposites' (Jung, 1946, par. 536). It signifies the unification of opposites within the psyche, wherein the four functions, two attitude-types, shadow, anima/animus and persona are integrated within the wider unification of consciousness and the unconscious, thereby creating a new and richer focus within the personality to balance the ego with its tendency to prejudice.

It is generally thought that Jung primarily developed his concept of the Self primarily from his own concept of the 'transcendent function', and from Eastern Mysticism, which frequently refers to notions of totality (Jung, 1951, par. 350). As we saw in Chapter 5 , the transcendent function is part of the symbol-forming aspect of the unconscious that possesses a purposive tendency to hold both conscious and unconscious together. Its purpose is to enable the psyche to realize the Self – the ultimate psychic balance where all oppositions are resolved. In 1916 Jung wrote:

> The shuttling to and fro of arguments and affects represents the transcendent function of opposites. The confrontation of the two positions generates a tension charged with energy and creates a living third thing . . . a movement out of the suspension between opposites, a living birth that leads to a new level of being, a new situation.
>
> (Jung, 1916/1957, par. 189)

This 'third thing' and 'new level of being', which culminates in the unification of opposites, is virtually identical with the Self. In this sense the Self (as with the transcendent function) can be regarded as the mediator of opposites. It is equivalent to the 'third' element that is introduced in the second stage of the alchemical process of *Ostanes*, which, through its affinities with both opposites, enables their unification (cf. Jung, 1946, par. 474). The Self is both a crucial ingredient within the process of uniting opposites and the very end-product of this process, the union of opposites itself.

Jung did not develop a substantial theory of the Self; and thus the notion of the individuated personality, which has attained 'Selfhood', remains equally elusive. In 'The Undiscovered Self' (1957) he bluntly states: 'Since self-knowledge is a matter of getting to know the individual facts, theories are of very little help' (Jung, 1957, par. 493). We know that the Self is the ordering and unifying centre of the total psyche, and that while the ego is the centre of the conscious personality, the Self is the centre of both the conscious and unconscious personalities (Jung, 1936a, par. 44); but this description leads only to an inadequate and limited analysis of Selfhood. This is because the Self is only partly capable of being consciously perceived, as its totality encompasses every psychic manifestation – including those unconscious processes that remain ineffable and forever out of reach to ego comprehension and understanding:

> The self is a union of opposites *par excellence* . . . the self, however, is *absolutely paradoxical* in that it presents in every respect thesis and antithesis, and at the same time synthesis . . . it is itself both conflict and unity.
>
> (Jung, 1944a, par. 22, italics mine)

Thus, the Self as a paradoxical entity evades logical explanation.[1]

A rational theory based on empirical data is useless for the depiction of the Self, as it cannot be reduced to intellectual knowledge. Scientific discourse relies heavily on abstract theorizing about well-defined data and seeks to exclude the symbolic metaphors through which the unconscious finds expression. Indeed, Jung writes that the Self is experienced as having

> a value quality attached to it, namely its feeling-tone. This indicates the degree to which the subject is *affected* by the process or how much it means to him . . . In psychology one possesses nothing unless one has experienced it in reality. Hence a purely intellectual insight is not enough.
>
> (Jung, 1951, par. 61)

Trying to explain the Self is akin to explaining God. God, or the abstract idea of God, is not contained in rational thought or empirical sense-data. He is found through metaphors and symbols, as a force primarily *experienced* rather than *understood* on a reductive level of intellect.

The experience of the Self, as with all numinous experiences of Otherness, is an affective experience of immense proportion (Jung, 1951, par. 53). The Self is other to the ego; it is an experience of the 'not-me' in the 'me', a religious experience. Emmanuel Levinas takes up a similar idea in *Totality and Infinity* (1969) where the contradictory elements of 'Same' (ego) and 'Other' (Self) can never exist as a totality in union. The Same exists because the Other is irreconcilable with it, otherwise both Same and Other would be part of a greater totality or whole that would invade and invalidate their separateness. Levinas paradoxically says they are related as a 'relation without relation' (ibid., pp. 79–80). It is a relation because an encounter does take place, and it is 'without relation' because that encounter does not establish understanding: the Other remains resolutely Other. This does not invalidate the Jungian interpretation where the Self encompasses the ego in a totality, for the ego remains at all times an element separate to it. (If the ego were identified with the Self, ego-inflation would result: Jung, 1951, par. 44). The Levinasian discourse continues to parallel Jung's and offers insight into the nature of the Self. In his text Levinas proceeds by stating that the encounter between the Same and Other is essentially of a violent nature.[2] He writes: 'Violence consists in welcoming a being to which [the mind] is inadequate' (Levinas, 1969, p. 25). The encounter with the Other causes the Same to realize its impotence; it creates a surplus value of infinity within the Same, which disrupts the totality and self-containment of the Same.[3] The Same cannot integrate the Other and is reconditioned by it: 'The I loses its hold before the absolutely Other . . . [it] can no longer be powerful' (ibid., p. 17). Thus, the Other overturns the very egoism of the personality and puts consciousness into question; consciousness must answer to the Other and realize that it is not in total possession of the world (ibid., p. 173). Jung describes this encounter with the unconscious Other as a wounding:

> Whoever has suffered once from an intrusion of the unconscious has at least a scar if not an open wound. His wholeness, as he understood it, the wholeness of his ego personality, has been badly damaged, for it became obvious he was not alone; something which he did not control was in the same house with him, and that is of course wounding to the pride of the ego personality, a fatal blow to his own monarchy.
>
> (*SNZ*, II, p. 1233; also see *SNZ*, I, p. 449)

The individual must, therefore, acknowledge that he is a being of both consciousness and unconsciousness, of Same and Other. Experience of the unconscious directly affects the conscious ego; the ego is reformulated or damaged by the ethical demand placed on it in the presence of the Other. Jung warns of this potential danger many times. According to Jung, the individuation process is often experienced as dangerous and violent. Jung writes:

> The rediscovered unconscious often has a really dangerous effect on the ego . . . In the same way that the ego suppressed the unconscious before, a liberated unconscious can thrust the ego aside and overwhelm it. There is a danger of the ego losing its head, so to speak, that it will not be able to defend itself against the pressure of affective factors.
>
> (Jung, 1916/1957, par. 183; also see Jung, 1951, par. 33)

The danger and pressure arise when the conscious attitude is confronted by its shadow – those characteristics of a contrary nature that can appear alien and morally reprehensible. The realization of the whole personality is a powerful numinous experience that is dangerous and violent. As we saw in Chapter 5, the alchemical process describes the rebirth of the ego 'into' the Self as a painful experience, for the king (who represents ego-consciousness) must suffer an awful death if he is to be reborn into a complete form. The death of the ego, as with the death of the king, 'signifies the overcoming of the old and the obsolete' (Jung, 1955–1956, par. 169), and this entails a wounding from the might of the Self. The ego experiences the king's sufferings: of dissolution and decomposition, the extinction of its light (its power and domination over all), and incineration in the fire (in the greater power) (Jung, 1945/1954, par. 468). Within the individuation process the Self forces the ego to acknowledge its impotence, and through its affects it inflicts a radical change in the attitude of the ego. The ego is no longer in its petty personal world – believing itself to be in total possession of the world – as it was prior to individuation, but now participates freely in the wider world of objective interests (Jung, 1929, par. 68). It sheds its limited subjectivity for 'an attitude that is beyond the reach of emotional entanglements and violent shocks' (Jung, 1929, pars. 67–68). The king is thus reborn; his monarchy is revitalized so that his power can no longer be questioned, for he has attained the ultimate power: Selfhood.

The ego must try to accept its rebirth (Jung, 1951, par. 51) and try to ground its experience of the Other in a framework to which it can relate. The two opposing rational functions of thinking and feeling are required to secure this kind of understanding (ibid., par. 52); but this is difficult to achieve (ibid., par. 58) as it requires a personality that has already achieved a sufficient degree of individuation, where both functions have developed. If the ego does not try to accept its rebirth and tries instead to ignore the experience of the Other, or tries to explain it away as illusion, or reduce it to the level of the intellect, it will have to deal with the consequential onslaught of 'insanity' and 'destructive mass psychoses' (Jung, 1929, pars. 52, 53). Here the Other and the ego can be regarded as opposites; when the ego ignores the Other or reduces it to ego-consciousness it is equivalent to the domination of one opposite over its counterpart, and neurosis will inevitably follow. Likewise, the promotion of the Other over the ego will have similar results. Thus, although the Self, as the unknowable Other, appears as a violent entity to ego-consciousness, it cannot be wholly destructive. The Self does not seek to eradicate all ego-consciousness, for the opposites of ego and Self are of equal importance. As we saw in Chapter 5, 'Unconscious compensation is only effective when it co-operates with an integral consciousness. Assimilation is never a question of "this or that", but always of "this and that"' (Jung, 1934, par. 338). Therefore, the Self cannot kill the ego, for the ego is the Self's feet (*SNZ*, II, p. 978).

When the ego fails to accept its rebirth and is at a loss of understanding, the psyche spontaneously produces a compensatory symbol, a symbol that expresses totality (and thus the union of opposites). This symbolic framework enables the ego to relate to the unconscious experience and protects it from the onslaught of insanity that would otherwise overcome it.[4] When this symbol of unification is manifest, the balance between the ego and the unconscious is restored. The presence of these symbols provides an empirical grounding for Jung's 'theory' of the Self, for

> although 'wholeness' seems at first sight to be nothing but an abstract idea, it is nevertheless empirical in so far as it is anticipated by the psyche in the form of spontaneous or autonomous symbols.
>
> (ibid., par. 59)

An empirical grounding, however, does not mean that Jung is on his way to establishing an objective theory of the Self that can be tested and qualified, because these Self-symbols (or transcendent functions) remain numinous – they are conscious interpretations of unconscious communications, the archetypal images of the archetypal Self. These symbols are clothed with finite images that are accessible to the ego, images that are subjectively defined by the ego according to its response to the a priori archetype and its conscious attitude (Jung, 1951, par. 355);[5] but the archetype in itself, behind this subjective clothing, can never be attained. The Self remains elusive, concerned with individual facts that escape testable theory (Jung, 1957, par. 493). It is experienced by the individual and symbolically expressed in individual terms.

Symbols have a subjective power, and may thus be effective for one individual and appear as a mere sign for another. Likewise, from an objective standpoint, one symbol is only as appropriate as the next.[6] An intellectual classification of symbols will achieve little. Jung, however, is intent on making more of his 'empirical theory' (Jung, 1951, par. 59), to the extent that he is guilty of objectifying the subjective, by predetermining what is personal, in giving specific examples and an overall schematization of Self-imagery. Jung attempts the very thing he maintains should not be done: to establish a concrete theory of the Self, a theory of its objective symbolic form. He states that the Self will appear in dreams as an

> elephant, horse, bull, bear, white and black birds, fishes, and snakes ... tortoises, snails, spiders, and beetles. The principal plant symbols are the flower and the tree. Of the inorganic products, the commonest are the mountain and the lake.
>
> (Jung, 1951, par. 356)

Here Jung is limiting Self-symbols to rigid, personal examples, and consequently fails to acknowledge the subjective rule of symbolism, where a specific image may not express the Self and the unification of opposites to every individual. It would be more appropriate for Jung to express his 'theory' only with such abstract statements as: 'Anything that a man postulates as being a greater totality than himself can become a symbol of the self' (Jung, 1942/1948, par. 232). Or again: 'the self can appear in all shapes from the highest to the lowest, inasmuch as they transcend the scope of the ego personality in the manner of a daimonion' (Jung,

1951, par. 356). These statements are detailed and yet flexible enough to be applicable to every subjective symbolic formulation of the Self.

Jung is quite willing to give many examples of Self-symbols (most of which are found in *Aion*, *CW* 9ii, 1951). Edward Edinger dramatically summarizes these interchangeable images and themes of the Self as follows:

> Such themes as wholeness, totality, the union of opposites, the central generative point, the world navel, the axis of the universe, the creative point where God and man meet, the point where transpersonal energies flow into personal life, eternity as opposed to the temporal flux, incorruptibility, the inorganic united paradoxically with the organic, protective structures capable of bringing order out of chaos, the transformation of energy, the elixir of life – all refer to the Self, the central source of life energy, the fountain of our being which is most simply described as God.
>
> (Edinger, 1972, p. 4)

The God-image and the mandala sacred circle are the two Self-images that fascinate Jung the most. The former led Jung to his somewhat controversial response to the idea of theodicy by explaining God in terms of completion rather than perfection, and of therefore harbouring an evil shadow side (Jung, 1951, par. 123). Christ, as a Self-symbol, represents a personality greater than the average individual (Jung, 1942/1954, par. 414; Jung, 1951, par. 42); but to be a symbol of integration and unity Christ must be linked with His opposite – the Antichrist – to convey good and evil. And the latter led Jung to his experience and discovery of the Self, for in drawing mandalas every morning (in 1918–1919) he came to realize that they are 'cryptograms concerning the state of the Self' (*MDR*, p. 221), an illustration of his psychological disposition at that time. In these mandalas he saw his whole being actively at work, and through them he acquired a living conception of the Self. The mandala symbolizes a protective circle,[7] which would lessen the intensity of the violent experience of Otherness, and thus 'protect the unity of consciousness from being burst asunder by the unconscious' (Jung, 1929, par. 47).

Symbols are psychic images that, through the purposive tendency of the transcendent function, link opposites together: what is known to the unknown, the rational to the irrational, and consciousness to unconsciousness. These Self-images provide the ego with a subjective framework through which it can relate to the Self, and come to terms with its impinging unconscious forces. The images are not the actual Self; they are merely approximations representing states of relative wholeness or 'Self-ness'. It is impossible to arrive at the archetype-in-itself, we can experience its effects only in its corresponding symbol, and there are an infinite number of symbols that may apply. Such limitless conveyance of the Self suggests to me that the Self is not such an unbroken and coherent entity as is often thought. The images of the Self are not described theoretically, but metaphorically, as a finite expression of something infinite. The union of opposites, as a symbolic representative of the Self, is thus only one subjective interpretation from an infinite variety. In this sense it seems to have little prominence. However, if we regard the union of opposites as the process through which the Self is realized, then it assumes great significance. But this incurs a conceptual problem. For, if we attribute value to the union of opposites because it *produces* the Self as its 'end-product', then we imply that it is not equivalent to the Self; we presuppose that the process through which the 'product' is realized has an identity separate from it.[8] This problem can be avoided if we interpret the process as circular and not linear. In this case the Self is identified with the process and yet also beyond it; it is a synergy of the three elements of the process (the two opposites and the 'third' alchemical mediator). This means the Self is not identified with any of the three elements in isolation, neither is it identified with the sum of its parts; rather the Self surpasses its parts, thereby making its constitution beyond examination. Warren Colman adopts a similar approach to this in his analysis of the Self. Colman explicitly defines the Self as both the product realized by the process and the process of realization itself, as an organizing principle and that which is organized. Colman maintains that there is no principle or archetypal structure that is separate from that which it is organizing; the structure is inherent in itself. He regards the Self as both 'a tendency towards organization' (the process of uniting opposites) and 'the structure of that organization' (the Self). 'In other words, the psyche is self-structuring and the name for that process is the self' (Colman, 2000, p. 14). Colman does not regard the end-product of the process as separate from the process, but as the point at which the process ceases to continue. The process of uniting opposites is therefore inextricably linked with the Self; it is an expression of the Self's activity, its 'tendency towards organization'.[9]

The Self is Other and no complete explanation of it can be determined; only its partial representative elements can be examined, and if the Self is a 'synergy', the examination of its parts will not give an accurate representation of the Self. However, this has not deterred other commentators on Jung from attempting to do so; they offer definitions of the Self by regarding one of its different aspects as the principal aspect of the archetype. For example, Elie Humbert regards the Self primarily as an ethical postulate. He writes: 'If you were to ask what the other self signifies for me, I should reply that it is, above all, the inner voice which tells me frequently and precisely how I am to live' (Humbert, 1980, p. 240). Indeed, Jung himself describes the Self as 'the will of God' and an inner 'absolute which one must learn how to handle correctly' (Jung, 1951, par. 51). As a God-image, the Self provides an ethical challenge to confront one's projections and resolve the confrontational issues from within. Andrew Samuels also refers to the Self as a religious challenge:

> The self involves the potential to become whole or, experientially, to 'feel' whole – a part of feeling whole is feeling a sense of purpose, of sensing a goal. Part of wholeness is to feel that life makes sense and of having an

inclination to do something about it when it does not, thus, to have a religious capacity.

(Samuels, 1994, p. 91)

In support of his claim to a religious capacity he cites Jung as saying: 'The self, though on the one hand simple, is on the other hand an extremely composite thing, a "conglomerate soul"' (Jung, 1950, par. 634). Judith Hubback in 'The Dynamic Self' (1998) takes a different stance and suggests that the Self is principally associated not with its capacity to motivate, but with the movement it inspires. Hubback thus focuses on the Self's propensity to action and dynamism, an interpretation that takes us away from the structural interpretation of the Self as symbolic imagery. She notes that Jung's descriptions of the Self in *Aion* culminate in 'numerous nouns and verbs (powerful ones), containing the elements of energy and psychological action'. She proceeds to list these in their chronological order as follows:

'Integration' and 'assimilation' (par. 43), 'discrimination' (par. 44), 'energetic tension' (par. 53), 'confronts' (par. 59), 'affected' (par. 61), 'relate' (par. 65). In the later chapter 'The Structure and Dynamics of the Self' there are: the self 'a dynamic process' (par. 411), 'move' (par. 413) and 'Sooner or later nuclear physics and the psychology of the unconscious will *draw* closer together as both of them . . . *push forward* into transcendental territory' (par. 412).

(Hubback, 1998, p. 279)

The definitions of the Self, cited above as its principal (but incomplete) aspects, refer either directly to the process of uniting opposites or to its experienced effects. Thus, Humbert and Samuels refer to the sensing of a teleological purpose and movement towards a personal whole with ethical connotations, and Hubback refers to the process impersonally, in terms of its energetic movement and activity. Each of these commentators equates the Self with its process of realization; they do not attempt to define the Self as distinct from the process of uniting opposites. Although we noted that the process of uniting opposites, as a symbolic representative of the Self, is only one subjective interpretation from an infinite variety, it is significant that these commentators and I support Jung in raising it to a prominent position. Indeed, although there are an infinite number of symbols, the effectiveness of which are subjectively determined, some have greater significance than others. For example, the symbol of the cross does not endure solely because of one individual and his subjective determinations, but according to millions of people who all share in its symbolism as a power of collective validity. Similarly, the union of opposites is not 'just another symbol'; it has enormous influence; its connotations, unlike the particularity of the cross, range from the general to the specific as its potency incorporates such notions as difference, relationships, totality, unity, separateness, paradox, death, regeneration, dynamism and so on.

The symbol of the union of opposites, as Jung himself maintains, conveys the very meaning of life (cf. Jung, 1917/1926/1943, par. 78). I believe it is more applicable than other Self-symbols that Jung describes. It is certainly more pertinent than the 'elephant, horse, bull, bear, white and black birds, fishes, and snakes . . . tortoises, snails, spiders, and beetles . . . the flower and the tree . . . the mountain and the lake' (Jung, 1951, par. 356). It is perhaps also more powerful than that of the mandala and God Himself, which, although equally effective in the transformation of psychic energy, remain abstract images that are not immediately entertained in the individual's life. Thus, while the notion of opposition is empirically evident in life ('the sad truth is that man's real life consists of a complex of inexorable opposites – day and night, birth and death, happiness and misery, good and evil . . . life is a battle ground. It has always been, and always will be': *MHS*, p. 75), the notions of the 'sacred circle' and God remain obscure and perhaps less likely to be identified by ego-consciousness. Just as Nietzsche promoted the Will to Power over and above the other instincts as the 'unifying concept' that organizes the instincts into a 'hierarchy', the symbol of the union of opposites can be regarded as a more significant and powerful Self-symbol over and above other Self-symbols. However, we must remember that this attempt, as with any other attempt to rank symbols by value, can be justified only at a subjective level.

The Self is susceptible to potential inconsistency because it is not grounded within concrete theory, but within subjective interpretation. The Self is an elusive entity, one that is defined by infinity and irreducible to intellectual terms. It is effectively a transcendental postulate 'which, although justifiable psychologically, does not allow of scientific proof' (Jung, 1928b, par. 405). This postulate serves only to formulate and link together the psychic processes that have already been theoretically established.

If the Self were available for an intellectual encounter it could be understood without much difficulty, for its symbols are 'formulations that can easily be mastered by the philosophic intellect' (Jung, 1951, par. 60) – though, as we have seen, some can be mastered more easily than others. The intellect promotes the illusion that one can be in possession of the Self and can master and manipulate it accordingly,

> But actually one has acquired nothing more than its name, despite the age-old prejudice that the name magically represents the thing, and that it is sufficient to pronounce the name in order to posit the thing's existence . . . the intellectual 'grasp' of a psychological fact produces no more than a concept of it, and that concept is no more than a name, a *flatus vocis*.
>
> (Jung, 1951, par. 60)

In terms of an intellectual theory, the Self is simply the 'name' given to that which is unfathomable in the psyche, a metaphysical concept. But this is inappropriate for Jung. For, even though the Self cannot be known, the Self is a concept or postulate that is grounded neither in metaphysical speculation nor faith; rather, according to Jung, an adequate picture of the Self is formed on the basis of a thorough 'experience' of it: 'Just as the concept arose out of an experience of reality, so it can be elucidated only by further experience' (ibid., par. 63; cf. Jung, 1931c, par. 1292; Jung, 1932, par. 501).[10]

Part II

The potential influence of Nietzsche's model on that of Jung

Chapter 7

The disagreement between Nietzsche and Jung

The process of uniting opposites

In Part I of this book, I outlined the two models of opposites implicit in the works of Nietzsche and Jung. In this part, the two models will be compared and contrasted. In this chapter, I shall determine the differences between the two models by examining the processes through which the opposites are united. I shall also try to account for these differences by reference to the philosophical influences on the two models. Thus, the theories of opposites proposed by Plato, Kant, Schopenhauer, Heraclitus and Aristotle will be juxtaposed with Nietzsche's and Jung's. In Chapter 8, I shall focus on the similarities between the two models' conception of the telos of the process – that is, their similar conceptions of the union of opposites itself.

From Part I, it is evident that the models of opposites held by Nietzsche and Jung do not adhere completely to the theory of incommensurable opposites that I posed in Chapter 1 of this book. There the proto-theory held that (1) opposites are incommensurable; (2) opposites are related only by contradiction; (3) there is no primary member in the binary pair; and (4) a third point of reference is required to maintain the opposition. Both Nietzsche's and Jung's model adamantly deny (1) and (2) and agree with (3) in varying degrees. They are in disagreement over (4), where Jung's model is in favour but Nietzsche's model is not.

According to Nietzsche and Jung, opposites are not static elements that are incapable of any relationship other than contradiction and mutual difference. On the contrary, it is fundamental to our argument that both Nietzsche's and Jung's model of the whole self depend upon the *productive* and *dynamic* relationships maintained by opposites. Both the *Übermensch* and the Self seek the union of opposites and demand a relationship between opposites that generates the energy necessary to satisfy their vast creative capacities.

Both Nietzsche and Jung endorse (3), according to which opposing elements must be equally promoted. In Part I we saw that, according to Nietzsche, opposites are established by the division of a single force into two. As a consequence, the two opposites are of equal inherent value; they are dependent upon one another because they are simply different modes, transitions or sublimations of the same thing (*WS*, 67). Likewise, the presence of both the Apollinian and Dionysian impulses are required if either impulse is to be activated to its highest degree, without getting out of control and causing harm to the personality. Reason (the Apollinian) depends on instinct (the Dionysian) for its continuous renewal, and the instincts depend on reason as a vehicle for their expression. These opposing impulses are of equal inherent value even though the quantity of either impulse required for the growth of the personality may be unequal. In other words, although the opposites are dependent upon one another, only so much Dionysian experience is available to individual consciousness as can be controlled by the Apollinian; in this sense the Dionysian is the primary impulse, while the Apollinian is merely the vehicle through which it is attained.

Jung, for his part, valued his opposites equally as well. The relationship of compensation that Jung posits between psychological opposites means that if one opposite were to be accorded primacy over its counterpart, the psyche would set up a compensatory drive to restore equal value to the neglected opposite. Compensation is a process of equilibration. For Nietzsche and Jung, the presence of both opposites, equally valued, is essential for the health and continued development of the personality. To those individuals who value the opposites unequally, Nietzsche and Jung issue a warning of impending psychological damage. Nietzsche defines those who have too much of one thing as 'inverse cripples' (*TSZ*, II, 'Of Redemption'; 'the one-sided mediocrity': *WP*, 862). Jung equates such one-sidedness with the pathological (*MHS*, p. 52): 'Too much of the animal distorts the civilized man, too much civilization makes sick animals' (Jung, 1917/1926/1943, par. 32).

Coming now to (4), Jung's model, unlike Nietzsche's, explicitly supports the view that a third point of reference is required to maintain the opposites. Jung writes:

> If a union is to take place between opposites like . . . conscious and unconscious . . . it will happen in a *third thing*, which represents not a compromise but something new [and again] The confrontation of the two positions generates a tension charged with energy and creates a living *third thing* . . . a movement out of the suspension between opposites, a living birth that leads to a new level of being, a new situation.
>
> (Jung, 1916/1957, par. 189, italics mine)[1]

Jung never explains this 'third thing'.[2] These quotations obscure the nature of the 'third thing' further, as it is first described as an entity external to the opposites – in which their union can take place – and it is then described as a product of the opposites, as potentially inherent within them. We encountered similar obscurity in our discussion of Jung's notion of the Self, where we considered the Self as both external to the process that unites opposites and the end-product of their union (and thus potentially inherent within the opposites). Furthermore, in Chapter 6 we referred to the Self, and the transcendent function, in terms of the 'third thing' and the 'new level of being'. The 'third thing' is, I believe, any representation of the union of opposites: it is that which mediates between opposites and establishes their union. We saw, in the second stage of the triadic alchemical formula of *Ostanes*, the introduction of a mysterious third 'dynamic factor' that shares affinities with the two chemical materials, thereby causing them to unite and change their original properties. Likewise, dreams, the compensatory function, and the psyche itself are all potential candidates for Jung's elusive 'third thing'. Indeed, Jung writes:

> The unknown third thing . . . finds more or less adequate expression in all these similes, yet – to the perpetual vexation of the intellect – remains unknown and not to be fitted into a formula.
>
> (Jung, 1940, par. 267)

Nietzsche's model is not so explicit in its acceptance of a 'third thing'. Nietzsche's model is concerned only with the two opposites that neither originate in an external source (which could be construed as a 'third' element) nor create a 'third' and 'new level of being', for, according to Nietzsche, the opposites originate in each other as two elements that have become separated from one original source. Neither do Nietzsche's opposites require an external medium to encourage their unification, for we are told that once they have been formed from out of the one original element they will seek to regain this original state of oneness and achieve reunification (*PTAG*, 5). However, the process of opposites seeking unification is not so self-propelling that it can pursue the ultimate Nietzschean goal of *Übermenschlichkeit* on its own. Further encouragement and initiative is required if the energy generated by the oppositional interplay is to be appropriately harnessed. Nietzsche posits the Will to Power, the most life-affirming of instincts, as an ordering principle to assign the opposites their way and direction. Whether or not the Will to Power can be considered a 'third' mediating element in this model is, I think, unclear. In Chapter 3 we saw that Nietzsche describes the opposites as belonging 'together beneath one yoke' (*WP*, 848). This 'yoke', which I take to be the Will to Power, is not necessarily *separate* from the contrary instincts; rather, 'the *development* of one definite will into many forms' (*WP*, 692, italics mine). The Will to Power can be regarded as that original force that is divided into two opposing forces, seeking to reunite. The opposing instincts cannot be considered separate from the Will to Power, Nietzsche states: 'All driving force is the will to power . . . there is no other physical, dynamic or psychic force except this' (*WP*, 688).[3] The Will to Power is not a separate 'third thing' that mediates between the opposites; it is the quality inherent within them – their founding force.

It is evident that neither Nietzsche's nor Jung's models of opposites conform to the proto-theory that opposites are incommensurable. Out of its four principal elements, only one (that there is no inherently primary member in the binary pair) is accepted, in varying degree, by Nietzsche and Jung.

Opposites have been subject to much philosophical examination, and their union is a notion central to many works preceding Nietzsche and Jung. Thus, the potential philosophical influences on Nietzsche and Jung are likely to be many. Indeed, in his seminars on analytical psychology (1925), Jung points out that

> the idea of the pairs of opposites is as old as the world, and if we treated it properly, then we should have to go back to the earliest sources of Chinese philosophy.
>
> (Jung, 1925b/1991, p. 72)

However, both Nietzsche and Jung are conscious of specific influences on their thought, and these will now be examined.[4] By examining those works that have directly influenced Nietzsche and Jung, we shall be able to account for the differences between their models, specifically for the disagreement over elements (3) and (4) of the proto-theory.

We have seen that the models of Nietzsche and Jung insist on equal inherent value in the binary pair. For Jung, this equality is clearly expressed in the compensatory activity of the psyche, but for the early Nietzsche it is expressed rather ambiguously: rationality (as the Apollinian impulse) is given secondary status as the mere 'vehicle' through which irrationality (the Dionysian) can be harnessed and kept in check. I would argue that Nietzsche values rationality in terms of its 'necessity' rather than for its own sake. It is valued as that which 'dilutes' the Dionysian experience, thereby enabling Dionysian creativity to be experienced safely and in moderation. Nevertheless, rationality is valued as much as irrationality. Dionysian creativity is the goal of the Nietzschean project, but it must not be conceived as a goal in isolation or as the ultimate goal, for Apollinian rationality is required for its realization. The ultimate goal for Nietzsche is a union of both rational and irrational tendencies. Rationality is not a fixed value; it both initiates growth and development in the irrational realm of the Dionysian, and is itself prompted to grow and develop by that irrational realm. The Apollinian and Dionysian 'continually incite each other to new and more powerful births, which perpetuate an antagonism' (BT, 1). The Apollinian is as essential as the Dionysian; their union constitutes a rebirth of both elements, and the birth of the Übermensch.

If the opposite elements in the Nietzschean model have equal value, we need to establish the value of rationality in respect of the Dionysian (which is already justified as the goal of Nietzsche's project). The rational and irrational are equally valued in the Nietzschean model, but the value of rationality is questioned nonetheless.[5] By contrast, Jung, in arguing for equal value between the opposites, appeals to external 'rational' sources to ground and justify what, we assume, he considers to be an 'irrational' project. Thus, Nietzsche questions the authority of rationality within his model, and Jung seeks to ground his own model according to an external authority that is rational. Rationality for Nietzsche requires justification; whereas, for Jung, rationality is what provides justification. Both Nietzsche and Jung ultimately reject the notion that one opposite can have more value over and above its counterpart, but in arriving at this thesis, Jung appeals to external sources that contradict it. Although he rejects the primacy of rationality over the irrational, Jung appeals to philosophical theories that specifically promote this primacy, as direct influences in the development of his own archetypal theory and consequent theory of opposites. Thus, as we shall see, the Platonic doctrine of ideal Forms and the Kantian Idea of pure reason are contradictory to, and yet integral to, the epistemological consolidation of Jung's most fundamental pair of opposites – the (rational and known) conscious ego and (irrational and unknown) unconscious archetype. We shall also see that Nietzsche is vehemently opposed to these rational doctrines; he rejects these positive influences on Jung outright, as tools of asceticism and human degradation. Later in the chapter, we shall see that the positive influences on Nietzsche's model of opposites lie elsewhere.

Plato held the Heraclitean view of an eternally changing and unstable universe, but he maintained that the universe itself was founded upon and substantiated by unchanging objective and eternal Forms. Plato was concerned with establishing a moral basis for human life, so he wanted to show that there are absolute unmoving eternal factors that can secure it. Thus, according to Plato, essential knowledge is a priori (*Meno*, 81E–86B), and because there is knowledge before the fact of experience, it follows that, as with all 'true' knowledge, the moral law is eternal (87A–D). In the *Republic* Plato argues for the correlation of the existence of the eternal Forms with that of the immortal soul, so that true being is found in these eternal Forms and not in the images that characterize the soul (500B–521B). Thus, if human values are permanent and eternal, the mind must be construed as separate from the temporal body, just as objects of thought must be independent from the phenomenological objects in which they inhere. The mind and its *Ideas* are therefore primary to the phenomenal world of objects, which are mere representations or images of their eternal mental counterparts.

The concept that the ultimate structure of reality lies not in the materially observable realm of the world but at a non-material level, which only our minds can penetrate, is the crucial link between Plato's notion of transcendent causes and Jung's notion of the archetype. The objective Forms and archetypes determine all subsequent matter and ideas that can be directly experienced. The original Platonic Idea and the Jungian archetype cannot be directly experienced themselves; cognition must rely on the objects or images that clothe them and enable their communication. Jung explicitly recognizes Plato as a source for his archetypal theory:

In Plato, however, an extraordinarily high value is set on the archetypes as metaphysical ideas, as 'paradigms', or models, while real things are held to be only the copies of these model ideas. Medieval philosophy, from the time of St. Augustine[6] – from whom I have borrowed the idea of the archetype – . . . still stands on Platonic footing

(Jung, 1919, par. 275)[7]

Plato's doctrine is idealistic; he morally and epistemologically denies phenomenal experience in favour of a true reality of pure rationality. Plato therefore posits a dualistic world in which one opposite (the static world of Forms and Ideas) is valued over and above its counterpart (the phenomenal world of change). As we know, this contradicts the thesis of equality between opposites held by Jung and Nietzsche. Jung cannot, therefore, endorse the Platonic model completely. While Jung's concept of the archetype partakes of the innate or a priori quality of Plato's doctrine of the Forms, he does not accept the eternal, unmoving grounds of Plato's vision of true being. Affectivity and dynamism are crucial to Jung's concept of the archetype and to his model of opposites in general. While Plato's Idea is a model of perfection, Jung's archetype contains within it notions of positive and negative (that depend upon the characteristics of the contrasting ego-personality); although Jung regards the archetype as profoundly more creative than its opposite counterpart (the ego), he does not regard it as *more* valuable. Likewise, in Chapter 3 we saw Nietzsche reject the Platonic doctrine of the separation of true reality from phenomenal experience with reference to the ascetic metaphysician and his denial of the value inherent in 'this' world, and with reference to Socrates, the 'typical *décadent*' (*EH*, 'BT', 1), who according to Nietzsche, is guilty of promoting reason over and above the instincts. It would seem that both Nietzsche and Jung reject Plato's model of opposites because it seeks to uphold one opposite as absolute perfection, compared to which the other opposite must fall short.

However, contrary to my interpretation, Marilyn Nagy argues that Jung's psychology is similar to the Platonic view, because they both have perfection as its aim. Nagy argues that Jung's reasons for positing the archetypes are the same as Plato's:

> Jung wanted to save a place in the modern world for the human dream of eternal life, for the human sense of an ultimate meaningfulness in life, for human moral ideals.
>
> (Nagy, 1991, p. 161)[8]

However, as I shall argue in Chapter 8, the project of Jung (and also of Nietzsche) is defined in terms of *completion* rather than perfection. Also, while Plato places 'perfection' in a realm that is ultimately antithetical to humanity (it is, Plato maintains, accessible to the human mind, but only to its rational side; his instinctual side is repudiated), both Nietzsche and Jung place it not only in 'this' world (thereby dissolving the Platonic dualism) but within the human being as a whole – that which encompasses his rationality and irrationality. Both Nietzsche and Jung would therefore regard the Platonic Form as too selective and alienating. Furthermore, according to Plato, only the philosopher, with his extensive rational and intellectual capacities, can have access to the eternal forms and ultimate truths. Jung's archetypes, however, are grounded within the collective unconscious; they are thus typical patterns of behaviour that are grounded in a realm of irrationality that is inherent within *every* individual: *every* human being has access to the archetypes as they are 'deposits of the constantly repeated experiences of humanity' (Jung, 1917/1926/1943, par. 109). Likewise, for Nietzsche, the Will to Power is the ordering principle of life, and as such is 'the highest of all instincts'; as we saw in Chapter 2, Nietzsche insists that the instincts are acknowledged in every aspect of life, so that 'our most sacred convictions, the *unchanging elements in our supreme values*, are judgements of our muscles' (*WP*, 314, italics mine).

Plato's doctrine of the Forms, although recognized explicitly by Jung as influential on his archetypal theory, cannot provide solid foundation for his theory of opposites. Plato is an even more unlikely precursor of Nietzsche. However, Plato's doctrine is reformulated by Kant,[9] a thinker described by Jung as an even greater influence on his archetypal theory than Plato.[10]

In *The Critique of Pure Reason* (1781), Kant writes: 'What is an Idea to us, was to *Plato* an *idea in the divine understanding*' (A 568, B 569; cf. Jung, 1938/1954, par. 150.) It is not difficult to see how Kant's Idea might be equated with the Jungian archetype: they are both a priori regulative principles that order our experience, and 'principles of completeness' (Kant, 1790, 3). Eugen Bär in 'Archetypes and Ideas: Jung and Kant' (1976), argues for their similarity in terms of them being 'logically isomorphic' with one another. However, such correlation, I contend, is not warranted. Further analysis will reveal that Jung's archetype is in stark contrast to Kant's Idea, and Jung is wrong to appeal to Kant for justification of his own theory.

Kant's epistemology compounds both empiricism and rationalism, so that, for Kant, reality is merely perceptive experience that has been conditioned and structured by the a priori forms of intuitions of space and time, and by the categories of thought, a priori concepts including substance and causality. These forms of intuition and concepts do not exist in a world external to the individual, they are not attributes of the physical world as it is in itself, but are inherent within the individual as modes of perception and thought. Thus, knowledge is limited: we can have knowledge only of the world of appearance; we cannot know things-in-themselves as they are beyond sensory intuition and conceptualization. That is, all judgements require an a priori 'synthesis' of intuitions and concepts: 'Without sensibility no object would be given to us, without understanding no object would be thought. Thoughts without contents are empty; intuitions without concepts are blind' (Kant, 1781, A 51, B 75). Concepts that are isolated from their empirical conditions (i.e. unconditioned by the faculty of intuitions) are empty: 'The pure concepts of the understanding can *never* admit of *transcendental* but *always* only of *empirical* employment' (A 246, B 303). However, according to Kant, categories contain within themselves the tendency towards 'unconditioned' application; that is, reason operates beyond the limits of experience and inevitably leads us to search for the ultimate unconditioned premise. Thus, our own 'empirically limited' point of view on the world creates the *Idea* of a world in its totality, so that we always seek to know the world free from the limits of perspective: we strive 'to find for the conditioned knowledge of understanding, the unconditioned, whereby its unity might be brought to completion' (A 307, B 364). It is inevitable for 'pure reason' to treat such an idea of unconditioned completeness as a possible object of knowledge, and it thereby becomes the tool of illusion. Pure reason makes judgements using concepts that have no empirical conditions.

Ideas have no independent empirical reality; they supposedly give an absolute vantage point from which reality in its totality can be surveyed. But because the Ideas have no empirical basis, are not subject to perception and conceptualization, Kant rejects them as having *constitutive* status (as descriptions of reality). But he did not wholly dismiss their worth. Kant found a legitimate use for the Ideas as 'regulative principles' (A 644, B 672), which, if regarded as true descriptions of reality, could lead to the formulation of true hypotheses.[11] As constitutive, the Idea attempts to transcend experience into the illusory realm of reason; but as regulative function the Idea leads us to propose further laws through which the empirical world can become more intelligible:

> [The Idea] does not show us how an object is constituted, but how, under its guidance, we should *seek* to determine the constitution and connection of the objects of experience.
>
> (A 671, B 699)

Jung explicitly relates his own archetypal theory to Kantian philosophy: 'There are . . . innate possibilities of ideas, *a priori* conditions for fantasy-production, which are somewhat similar to the Kantian categories' (Jung, 1918, par. 14). For Jung, the archetype is the form or condition of the imagination, just as the Kantian categories govern the operation of the imagination in the synthesis of experience. Indeed, Jung speaks of the archetypes precisely as 'categories of the imagination':

> These are the universal dispositions of the mind, and they are to be understood as analogous to Plato's forms, in accordance with which the mind organizes its contents. One could also describe these forms as *categories* analogous to the logical categories, which are always and everywhere present as the basic postulates of reason. Only, in the case of our 'forms', we are not dealing with categories of reason but with categories of the *imagination*.
>
> (Jung, 1935/1953, par. 845)

Thus, for Jung, the archetype is equivalent to a Kantian category; it is a principle that is empirical and constitutive. However, Jung also attempts to explicitly correlate the archetype with Kant's Idea (Jung, 1921, par. 733), a dramatic move that would make the archetype a concept of pure reason – that which is not empirical and not constitutive but merely regulative. By correlating the archetype with the Kantian Idea Jung contradicts his above quotation, for the Idea is precisely that which 'deals with reason'. In *Psychological Types* (1921) Jung defines Kant's Idea as 'the 'archetype of all practical employment of reason', a transcendental concept which as such exceeds the bounds of the experienceable', and is 'a rational concept whose object is not to be found in experience'. Jung then proceeds to quote the following extract from the *Critique of Pure Reason*:

> Although we must say of the transcendental concepts of reason that *they are only ideas*, this is not by any means to be taken as signifying that they are superfluous and void. For even if they cannot determine any object, they may yet, in a fundamental and unobserved way, be of service to the understanding as a canon for its extended and consistent employment. The understanding does not thereby obtain more knowledge of any object than it would have by means of its own concepts, but for the acquiring of such knowledge it receives better and more extensive guidance. Further – what we need here no more than mention – concepts of reason may perhaps make a possible transition from the concepts of nature to the practical concepts, and in that way may give support to the moral ideas themselves
>
> (A329; cited in Jung, 1921, par. 733)

From this extract it is clear that the Jungian archetype is, in fact, *not* equivalent or, as Bär insists, 'Logically isomorphic', to the Kantian Idea. Jung's self-proclaimed allegiance to Kant is unfounded. As Jung notes four paragraphs later, 'The Idea is a psychological factor that not only determines thinking but, as a practical idea, also conditions feeling' (Jung, 1921, par. 737). Likewise, the archetypal *idea*, as a counterpart to the archetypal *image*, 'is the necessary counterpart of *instinct*' (ibid., par. 754). The Jungian archetype, with its instinctive and emotionally affective constitution, is therefore contrary to the Kantian Idea that constitutes merely intellectual and practical functioning. Thus, the rationality and intellectual functioning of the Kantian Idea is antithetical to the irrational feeling aspect of the Jungian archetype. And this irrationality is antithetical to the practical, and thus 'moral', functioning of the Kantian Idea. Indeed, Jung's archetypes have no direct moral implications as such (ibid., par. 356).[12] But it is not merely the absence of irrational affective tendencies within the Kantian Idea that sets it apart from that of Jung's archetype. Indeed, perhaps the most significant difference between Jung's archetype and Kant's Idea is that the latter has not a *constitutive* but a *regulative* function.[13] Kant argues in the 'paralogisms of pure reason', the 'antinomies of pure reason' and the 'ideal of pure reason', that to consider the Idea as an object leads to contradiction. Thus, as the above extract suggests, and as the *Critique of Practical Reason* (1788) argues at length, pure reason leads us to form the theological Idea, the cosmological Idea and the psychological Idea, but cannot itself prove their reality. The importance of these Ideas is merely practical: they have *moral* implications in their corresponding postulates of God, freedom and immortality. The Ideas in the first Critique are expounded in the second Critique as *postulates* of moral worth and not as objects defined empirically and intellectually. For Jung, however, the archetype *is* constitutive: '[The archetypal] is no conglomerate, however, but a homogeneous product with a meaning of its own' (Jung, 1921, par. 745).

Jung's argument is therefore not a (Kantian) argument about the conditions of experience, but an argument about what is beyond experience. The archetype is at once constitutive and beyond experience. Because it is constitutive, Jung is wrong to correlate it with Kant's 'Idea', and because it is beyond experience, Jung is wrong to correlate it with Kant's 'category'. I believe that Jung misunderstands Kant because he compounds Kant's Ideas (which are beyond experience and the limits of knowledge) with Plato's Ideas (which are constitutive and the objects of knowledge *par excellence*).[14] Our exposition is thus far from Bär's insistence on the archetype being logically isomorphic with Kant's Idea; instead it is in sceptical allegiance with Stephanie de Voogd who maintains that although 'Jung thought himself a Kantian . . . he was in fact a most un-Kantian Kantian' (Voogd, 1977, p. 176; see also J. J. Clark, 1992, p. 32; Bishop, 1995, p. 29).

It would seem that Jung is unjustified in appealing to the reductive doctrines of rationality posited by Plato and Kant for support of his own archetypal theory. Plato's original doctrine and its reformulation in Kant correlate with the Jungian archetype only in so far as they maintain that the ultimate structure of reality lies not in that which is materially observable but at a non-material level that is accessible only to our minds. However, to conclude from this that the 'Ideas' of Plato, Kant and Jung are interchangeable is a mistake. Jung, by referring to Plato and Kant for support and justification for his own theory, is in fact negating his own theory.[15] Jung is in effect trying to superimpose two doctrines that accord primacy to one opposite (rationality) in the binary pair (rationality–irrationality) on to his own contrasting doctrine that values the opposites equally. The archetype, as a *constitutive* concept that is both *beyond* experience and rooted within the collective realm of the *irrational* unconscious, cannot pertain to pure rationality; the archetype necessarily encompasses both of those oppositions posited by Plato and Kant because it values them both equally.

I believe that a more appropriate influence on Jung's archetype is Schopenhauer. Schopenhauer conflates the doctrines of Plato and Kant but arrives at an original doctrine of his own, one that admits irrationality and the equality of opposites, thereby justifying in part Jung's comment that 'the great find resulting from my researches was Schopenhauer' (*MDR*, p. 87). Jung correlates Schopenhauer's 'Idea' or 'intellect' (that which is 'not something absolutely *a priori* but . . . secondary and derived') with his archetypal image (Jung, 1921, par. 751).[16] Jung then proceeds to correlate Schopenhauer's 'Will' (the non-rational source of all phenomena) with the archetype in itself. Schopenhauer praised Kant for showing that we cannot have direct knowledge of thing in themselves and that reality is reduced to what can be experienced; but Schopenhauer believed that our individual experience of self-consciousness, of Will, leads us to the 'real nature of things'. Our motives spring from a psychological source, and the world is an expression of this Will. The Will is the Kantian thing-in-itself and grounds all life and the appearance of reality (Schopenhauer, 1818, vol. II, ch. XXXVIII, p. 443).

Schopenhauer alludes directly to the unconscious as a real affective realm equivalent to the Will (ibid., ch. XIX, pp. 238–239, ch. XIV, p. 136). Both the archetype and Will are therefore vehicles of the unconscious. Similarly, in both models the intellect with its capacity for reason and understanding carries the weight of consciousness. Schopenhauer does not posit the Will and intellect as direct opposites, but notes their essential contrast:

> The will is metaphysical, the intellect physical; the intellect, like its objects, is mere phenomenon, the will alone is thing-in-itself . . . the will is the substance of man, the intellect the accident; the will is the matter, the intellect is the form; the will is warmth, the intellect is light.
> (ibid., vol. 2, ch. XIX, p. 201; also see vol. 1, par. 39, p. 203)[17]

In accordance with Nietzsche and Jung's insistence on equality in opposites, Schopenhauer claims that his 'quasi-opposites' of Will and Idea/intellect/body do not try to overcome one another. The development of the intellect does not demand the demise of the will:

> The higher the consciousness has risen, the more distinct and connected are the thoughts, the clearer the perceptions, the deeper and profounder the sensations. In this way everything gains more depth: emotion, sadness, joy and sorrow.
> (ibid., vol. 2, ch. XXII, p. 281)

Likewise, 'The will manifests [the] *self-affirmation* of one's body' (ibid., vol. 1, par. 62, p. 334). Schopenhauer therefore employs compensation within his opposites, as Jung came to do later: as the intellect reaches a higher level of development, the feelings do also.

Jung's insistence on appealing to the rational doctrines of Plato and Kant to support his archetypal theory of opposites can be attributed to psychological insecurity on Jung's part. Jung was so determined to ground his theory in experience away from accusations of metaphysics and mysticism, that his theory makes repeated allusions to (what he considers to be) 'Kantian rationalism'. In contrast, for Nietzsche, a move towards Kant is a move towards metaphysics, a move of mistaken evaluation that ultimately rejects the union of opposites.

Jung's appeal to Plato and Kant is more persuasive if we regard their doctrines not in terms of the intrinsic value they place on either opposite in the binary pair, but in terms of their (and Schopenhauer's) general epistemological influence in consolidating the Jungian opposites: that is, the influence of the a priori unknown (the unconscious archetype in itself) and the empirically known (the conscious ego). However, Nietzsche would not recommend such appropriation; he would again condemn Jung's influences, for it is this abstract metaphysical and a priori basis, and consequent division into metaphysical and epistemological opposites, that Nietzsche refutes. By rejecting metaphysical truths and promoting empirical truths, Nietzsche redirects ultimate meaning from the transcendent world beyond humanity into the phenomenal world of representation and into humanity itself. The abolition of one opposite in the binary pair requires the abolition of both opposites, so that when Nietzsche abolishes the a priori, 'real' world-in-itself, he also abolishes the world of appearance – the metaphysical opposition therefore dissolves (*TI*, 'How the "Real World" At Last Became a Myth'). Thus, according to Nietzsche, Plato, Kant and Schopenhauer are guilty of making human reality meaningless by promoting a 'superior' metaphysical realm and consequent ascetic dualism.[18]

It must be noted that Nietzsche does not reject the a priori because it is an 'unknown' quality. Indeed, Nietzsche anticipates Jung in his promotion of an unknown unconscious agency:

> For the longest time, conscious thought was considered thought itself. Only now does the truth dawn on us that by far the greatest part of our spirit's activity remains unconscious.
>
> (*GS*, 333)

And again: 'What we call consciousness constitutes only one state of our spiritual and psychic world . . . *and not by any means the whole of it*' (*GS*, 357).[19] Both Nietzsche and Jung accept the existence of the unconscious as unknowable and boundless. What Nietzsche rejects in a priori metaphysical models is that which is more highly valued than the human being. The unknown unconscious (both personal and collective) that Jung posits is not rejected by Nietzsche in this context, for it is inherent within the individual; and the a priori archetypes, although autonomous things-in-themselves, are also inherent within the individual (as 'the ancestral heritage of possibilities of representation': Jung, 1928, par. 22).[20]

While Nietzsche, in his model of opposites, immediately rejects the 'metaphysical' philosophies of Plato, Kant and Schopenhauer, thereby developing his model outside a priori notions and giving *both* opposites in the binary pair an empirical grounding, Jung approached these philosophers with interest, and incorporated the a priori as a 'power unknown', into his model. We could thus say that Nietzsche turned away from these philosophers due to their insistence on the existence of an a priori *metaphysical world* that is of higher value than the individual, and Jung turned towards them due to their insistence on the a priori as an unknown *ordering quality*. However, both Nietzsche and Jung accept the existence of the unconscious, which is by nature an unknown and irrational quality, and both maintain that there cannot be a metaphysical world of higher value than the individual. Therefore, although Jung approached these 'metaphysical' philosophers as positive influences on his model, he developed it away from their thought, in a manner that would not displease Nietzsche. Jung sought to change the location of the unknown, a priori notion from an abstract realm beyond the individual to one that directly 'affects' the individual (*contra* Plato and

Kant) in a manner that is life enhancing (*contra* Schopenhauer). The Jungian archetype, as one opposite in the binary pair, correlates with the Platonic Form only so far as its a priori organizing aspect is concerned. As an *affective* principle of the collective unconscious, the archetype certainly does not correlate with the Form's purely rational and unchanging status. Neither does it lie in a world abstracted from the individual, and accessible only to a minority. Instead, the archetype is available to everybody through their collective ancestral heritage. Similarly, the Kantian thing-in-itself is the concern of pure rationality, but unlike the Platonic Form, the thing-in-itself can never be experienced – it has no constitution, it is a *regulative* function that cannot be empirically established, but is deduced as a transcendent postulate. The Schopenhauerian Will is a more appropriate model for the Jungian archetype. The Will is inherent within the individual as an a priori organizing force that is irrational, affective and dynamic. However, it does not exemplify all significant aspects of the Jungian model, for Schopenhauer tells us that the Will is blind and, as the reality underlying all phenomena, it is essentially pessimistic and self-negating. In contrast, the Jungian archetypes are teleological and optimistic as they encourage the individual towards greater self-integration. Jung therefore concedes that

> Schopenhauer made a . . . heroic attempt ['to try to solve the problem of opposites'], but he annihilates the whole world; he annuls all existence in order to settle the conflict of man, and that is going too far.
>
> (*SNZ*, I, p. 120; also see *MDR*, p. 88)

Both Nietzsche and Jung agree with aspect (3) of the proto-theory – that there is no primary member in the binary pair. While Jung ironically and inconsistently relies on the rationally reductive doctrines of Kant and Plato in the consolidation of his theory of equal opposites, Nietzsche rejects them outright because of this contradiction. We shall now examine the specific philosophical influences on Nietzsche's and Jung's model of opposites to try to account for their disagreement on element (4) of the proto-theory – whether or not a third point of reference is required to maintain the opposites.

Perhaps the most influential of theories explicitly acknowledged by both Nietzsche and Jung is that of Heraclitus (540–480/470 BC), whose doctrine of the tension of opposites as the basic life force is fundamental to their thought.[21] I believe that it is in Nietzsche and Jung's different reception of Heraclitus that we see their principal disagreement (on the need for a third thing to maintain the opposites) manifest.

Heraclitus' philosophy is concerned with the principle of change. Plato cites Heraclitus as saying: 'Everything gives way and nothing stands fast' (Plato, *Cratylus*, 402A). Heraclitus views the world as being in a state of permanent flux; he believes – something that Nietzsche himself was to enlarge upon – that everything supposedly permanent ('being') is simply change in slow motion ('becoming'). All structures undergo slow dissolution and alteration; they are 'coming-to-be and passing-away'. However, this flux is not a random series of events; rather, Heraclitus posits the existence of a hidden 'latent structure' in nature that 'masters' these events (*Fragments* 123, 54). This fundamental structure is the union of opposites, and as the fundamental force of life, it does not change; rather, it is what incites change in the world. According to Heraclitus, 'When one listens, not to me but to the *logos* [to 'reasonable proportion' or 'rationality'], it is wise to agree that all things are one' (*Fragment* 50). The union of opposites, as the fundamental structure of the world, substantiates this claim of monism. When Heraclitus states that 'all human laws are nourished [*trephontai*] by one divine law' (*Fragment* 114) he is expressing his idea that all things, all contradictions, are organized and fulfilled in one unity – the union of opposites – where plurality is nourished by a single source. The influence of Heraclitus upon Nietzsche is profound. In Chapter 2 we saw Nietzsche base his theory of opposites on what he regarded as a 'Heraclitean observation': that the world of 'coming-to-be and passing away' is a matter of polarity where 'the diverging of a force into two qualitatively different opposed activities . . . seek to re-unite' (*PTAG*, 5). I would even contend that Heraclitus' notion provides the grounding for the entire Nietzschean model, for in the rawest of terms Nietzsche's model is that of Heraclitus, with the name 'Will to Power' given to that 'one divine law that nourishes all human laws'. Thus, Nietzsche speaks of a 'multiplicity connected by a common mode of *nutrition* [*Ernährungs-Vorgang*], we call life' (*WP*, 641) and 'life *is* will to power' (*BGE*, 259). And again:

> Our entire instinctual life [is] the development and ramification of *one* basic form of will – as will to power . . . one [can] trace all organic functions back to this will to power and [can] also find in it the solution to the problem of procreation and nourishment.
>
> (*BGE*, 36)

The Heraclitean notion that everything is one was of great interest to Nietzsche, not only as a template for his own notion of the Will to Power, but also because it gave him a solution to counter the metaphysician's dualistic view of the world and the ensuing problem of asceticism: 'Heraclitus denied the duality of totally diverse worlds . . . He no longer distinguished a physical world from a metaphysical one, a realm of definite qualities from an undefinable "indefinite"' (*PTAG*, 5). Nietzsche's rejection of static and metaphysical opposites is a continuation of Heraclitus' insistence that all opposites are relative. On this matter Heraclitus writes:

> A road: uphill, downhill, one and the same (*Fragment* 60).
> Beginning is together with end [on a circle] (*Fragment* 103).
> Into rivers, the same ones, on those who step in, different and different waters flow (*Fragment* 12).

> The path of the carding rollers [cylindrical rollers used in carding felt], straight and crooked (*Fragment* 59).
>
> Physicians cut and burn people, and ask for a fee on top of that (*Fragment* 58).[22]

From these fragments it is evident that Heraclitus promotes opposites that are interdependent, coexistent, relative and liable to change into one another. (For example, the road can be either 'uphill' or 'downhill' relative to the direction one is travelling in; its unity supports both directions at the same time; they are both present as potentialities.) The agreement of Nietzsche and Jung on these points has already been discussed, though their agreement with Heraclitus on the latter point requires further elucidation.

Heraclitus' ancient commentators report Heraclitus as calling the occasion where one opposite suddenly reverses and assumes the character of its opposite counterpart *enantiodromia*. In the Jungian model, where opposites are related by compensation, we could expect enantiodromia to happen frequently (though of course the frequency would depend upon the psychic make-up of personality concerned). So, when consciousness becomes overwhelmed by a dominant function (for example the 'thinking function'), the psyche immediately sets up a compensatory drive to overturn the discrepancy and increase the value of the neglected unconscious opposite (the 'feeling function'). The value of the opposite functions has now reversed. Jung himself refers to enantiodromia, and defines it as 'running counter to' and 'the emergence of the unconscious opposite in the course of time' (Jung, 1921, pars. 708–709). Nietzsche does not refer to the concept explicitly, though its meaning did not escape him; he notes: 'The more one develops a drive, the more attractive does it become to plunge for once into its opposite' (*WP*, 92) and 'Extreme positions are not succeeded by moderate ones, but by extreme positions of the opposite kind' (*WP*, 55).

The fact that opposites can change into one another supports the idea that opposites are of inherent equal value. This is a significant aspect of Nietzsche's and Jung's model, and, according to ancient commentators, it also seems to have been significant to Heraclitus before them. For example, Simplicus, in his commentary on Aristotle's *Categories*, attributes to 'the Heracliteans' the view that 'if either of the opposites should fail, there would be complete and utter destruction of everything' (*Commentaria in Aristotelem Graea*, vol. VIII, p. 412; cited in Wheelwright, 1959, p. 140). Likewise, according to Aristotle, Heraclitus supports his repudiation of Homer's remark (in *Iliad*, xviii), by arguing that 'there could be no harmony without both low and high notes, nor could life exist without both male and female' (*Eudemian Ethics*, VII, 1235A).

According to Heraclitus, everything is one. All opposites are part of one original force or unity. The flux experienced around us is a process of change that occurs from one quality to its opposite, which is initiated by the original unity of which they are part. Heraclitus described this process as a 'turning back on itself': 'The diverging structure that agrees with itself, [must] turn back on itself, such as that of the bow or lyre' (*Fragment* 51). Philip Wheelwright (1959) interprets 'turning back on itself', in the case of the bow, as the movement of its parts – 'both relative to one another and to their own previous movements, when the bow is used' – and in the case of the lyre, with its 'vibrating strings or the up-and-down movements of [its] melody' (p. 96). In terms of a union of opposites in general, the original unity – that 'nourishing one divine law' – causes the opposites to interact in such a way that energy and movement is generated, most likely in a cyclical movement where either opposite comes to dominate. As Nietzsche describes the Heraclitean process: '[The opposites] at any given moment [are] like wrestlers of whom sometimes the one, sometimes the other is on top' (*PTAG*, 5). Change, for Heraclitus, is an alteration from one ontological opposite to another, so that 'cool things become warm, the warm grows cool; the moist dries, the parched becomes moist' (*Fragment* 126). However, as the proto-theory suggests, it is logically incorrect to say that 'the warm becomes cool'; a thing cannot turn into its own opposite, it is rather a matter of 'what was once warm becomes cool'.[23] In forming a conception of change, and a movement from one opposite to another, we must, as the proto-theory states, introduce the notion of a third element into the relationship: a third element in which both opposites inhere. While the Jungian model refers to this third thing (as that which compensates and mediates between the opposites), the Heraclitean and Nietzschean models do not. Both Heraclitus and Nietzsche simply rely upon the totality of the opposites to form a unity, and expect movement to occur from out of this isolated duality. Heraclitus posits a 'turning back on itself' motion inherent within the opposites themselves, and he describes the union of opposites as a 'divine nourishing force', which suggests an in-built teleology. Nietzsche's Will to Power, as we have argued, is merely a development of this nourishing force, which is the ordering force inherent in the contradictory instincts of the *übermenschlich* personality. In contrast, Jung's model has developed away from its Heraclitean 'roots', and has found influence elsewhere. Such influence, I believe, must include that of Aristotle, who anticipated Jung's criticism of the Heraclitean/Nietzschean model by claiming that opposites should not be thought dyadically, as two elements in isolation, but as a triadic arrangement. Aristotle writes:

> It is hard to conceive how density and rarity, for instance, each retaining its essential nature, could in anyway act upon each other. The same difficulties hold for every other pair of opposites: Love is not to be thought of as gathering up Strife and creating something out of it, nor can Strife do this to Love, but rather both of them must operate on a *third* something.[24]
>
> (*Physics* I, vi, 189a, italics mine)

But for Heraclitus and Nietzsche there is no need for 'a third something'; to them every change is a battle between two opposites without the referee that stands logically outside the process. The battle of conflict between *two* elements is all that is required; it is the ultimate condition of everything.

Nietzsche and Jung were influenced greatly by Heraclitus, though I believe his influence was more strongly felt by Nietzsche, as Jung was drawn elsewhere.[25] Though verging on supposition, this conjecture is supported by the difference in tone of their celebratory statements about Heraclitus (see note 21) (and also by the fact that Nietzsche refers to Heraclitus more often). One can sense the excitement that Nietzsche feels about Heraclitus, for 'the world really needs Heraclitus', and in his excitement Nietzsche even suggests that his own theories might have been taught by him (*EH*, 'BT', 3). (This can be construed as self-praise, as Nietzsche states that 'Heraclitus will always be right': *TI*, '"Reason" in Philosophy', 2.) Jung, on the other hand, is more methodical and impersonal in his praise of Heraclitus, heralding him as the discoverer of the regulative function of opposites (Jung, 1917/1926/1943, par. 111). In his autobiography *MDR*, when Jung cites those philosophers who have had most influence upon his thought, he mentions Heraclitus only in the company of other ancient Greek thinkers; he does not single him out: 'Above all I was attracted to the thought of Pythagoras, Heraclitus, Empedocles, and Plato, despite the longwindedness of Socratic dialogue'. Jung continues by saying that Heraclitus' ideas and the ideas of these other thinkers 'were beautiful and academic, like pictures in a gallery, *but somewhat remote*' (p. 87, italics mine). For Jung to regard Heraclitus' thought as remote implies that it is wholly unsuitable to his psychoanalysis, which is meant for *practical* application (for 'the psyche is a *living* system of opposites'). Heraclitus left Jung unsatisfied. Unlike Jung, Nietzsche found satisfaction in Heraclitus, and had no need to seek the elusive 'third thing'. Aristotle, we have seen, anticipates the 'third thing' necessary to Jung's model of opposites. Although Jung does not cite him as an explicit influence on his work, we can deduce from *MDR* (where he claims to have been, between the ages of 16 and 19, particularly attracted to ancient Greek philosophy), that he must certainly have been familiar with Aristotelian philosophy. Furthermore, the teleological movement that we have identified in Jung's model of opposites is distinctly Aristotelian.[26] Aristotle provides Jung with the support to develop his theory of opposites beyond Nietzsche and Heraclitus, and for introducing the notion of a third thing into the original duality

Let us now conclude the discussion thus far. The Nietzschean and Jungian models of opposites are not so far from one another. They both seek conflict and tension within opposites in order to create a *dynamic* dialectic that motivates, not just the rational capacity of the individual, but the *whole* individual in action (*contra* Plato and Kant). The tension is productive; that is, the antithetical forces of consciousness and unconsciousness do not work in *total* opposition to one another, but against one another, in a productive manner to reveal an energetic synthesis within the individual that affirms life as meaningful (*contra* Schopenhauer). Both Nietzsche and Jung found influence in Heraclitus; though Jung, unsatisfied with Heraclitus' notion of 'one force divided into two opposites that seek to reunite', sought to develop his theory of opposites further, by incorporating the notion of 'triadicy', which concerned Aristotle before him.

Jung relies on a third thing that is external to the opposites but has affinities with them, which enables it to act as their mediator and cause their eventual union. For Jung, the opposites can be united only through the 'third thing' – through their 'synthesis': an *already existing* union of opposites. For Jung, an a priori union of opposites must already be posited before any further unions can take place (cf. Jung, 1946, par. 378). 'As one alchemist says, one must start with a bit of the Philosopher's stone if one is to find it' (Edinger, 1994a, p. 6). Thus, the psyche 'has purposive orientation' and contains within it 'something like a preliminary exercise or sketch, or a plan roughed out in advance' (Jung, 1916/1948, par. 493; cf. par. 456), and it proceeds to work according to this pre-designated teleological scheme. The Self is the very telos of the psyche, it is the archetype of completeness and the union of opposites, and as such it is the required pre-designated union of opposites that enables all further unions to take place. By positing a pre-designated union of opposites, we are further encouraged to conceive the individuation process as circular rather than linear.

Nietzsche's model does not adopt this a priori, pre-designated union of opposites. For Nietzsche, as with Heraclitus before him, the union of opposites takes place *within* the opposites themselves; they do not appeal to an external mediator. The *Übermensch* is not predetermined. The *Übermensch* must be *created* (*TSZ*, prologue, 9; see Chapter 4) and not *discovered*, as Jung would have it (Jung, 1942/1954, par. 400). In the Nietzschean model, the 'union of opposites' is not an a priori starting point, but an (a posteriori) end-product of the two opposites acting alone. This implies that the opposites are more potent for Nietzsche than for Jung, for the energetic passage to *Übermenschlichkeit* is inherent in the opposites themselves; in the Jungian model the opposites depend on an external force for their energy.

In this chapter we have examined the differences between Nietzsche's and Jung's model of opposites in terms of the process through which the opposites are united. We have also examined their particular philosophical influences to account for these differences. What we have yet to consider is the profound influence that Nietzsche himself had upon Jung. The remaining pages of this book will, in effect, go some way toward explaining this. We have seen Jung reformulate the doctrines of Plato, Kant and Schopenhauer in his archetypal theory, thereby creating a more 'Nietzsche-friendly' model of opposites; in Chapter 8 we shall see Jung develop Nietzsche's model further, as he incorporates its essential aspects into his own model. Our analysis will focus on the explicit affinities between Nietzsche and Jung's concept of the union of opposites.

The similarities between Nietzsche and Jung

The whole self in the union of opposites

In Chapter 7 we examined the differences between Nietzsche's and Jung's models according to the *process* through which the opposites are united, and we accounted for these differences according to their different philosophical influences. In this chapter we shall consider one way in which Nietzsche and Jung converge in their treatment of the union of opposites, and the extent to which these similarities are a consequence of Nietzsche's influence on Jung.

For both Nietzsche and Jung the union of opposites represents the whole self – the *Übermensch* and Self respectively. Jung actually names Nietzsche as an authority on the notion of the union of opposites: 'Nietzsche . . . understands that the self consists in pairs of opposites and that it is in a way a reconciliation of opposites' (*SNZ*, I, p. 433; cf. 117, 1364). Further analysis of 'reconciliation' will, I believe, help to confirm that Nietzsche's influence on Jung is significant

Neither Nietzsche nor Jung provides a detailed description of the union of opposites; this is both frustrating and unfortunate. Jung at least acknowledges this problem and admits in detail that the Self cannot be examined because it is composed of unconscious and thus *unknowable* elements. Nietzsche, for his part, fails to explain why the *Übermensch* is addressed (principally in *TSZ*) only in ambiguous, scattered passages. In Chapters 4 and 6 we tried to arrive at a close interpretation of the *Übermensch* and Self based on the available texts. Although my interpretations elucidate the concepts further, they do not amount to a 'complete' and detailed account. Nevertheless, I believe we are in a position to identify the main affinities between the two philosophers. With reference principally to the notes of Jung's *Seminars on Nietzsche's Zarathustra* (1934–1939/1989), I shall identify apparent affinities between the *Übermensch* and Self, and ask whether Jung would acknowledge them.

Nietzsche's and Jung's notion of the union of opposites converge in six areas.[1] These are (1) the quality of the relationship between opposites (distinct from the *process* of their unification); (2) the value of completion over perfection, and the implications of this for morality; (3) the privilege and exclusivity of the union and its political implications; (4) the dangerous implications of the union; (5) the particular opposites that are united; and (6) the notion of the Dionysian.

Also, not explicit in Nietzsche's model of opposites but peripheral to its discussion, is (7) Nietzsche's anticipation of the fundamental tenets of Jung's individuation process and of analytical psychology in general.

The quality of the relationship between opposites and the value of completion over perfection

Although the actual processes through which the opposites are united are different in Nietzsche and Jung, the quality of the relationship between opposites is the same. Both Nietzsche and Jung seek a dynamic union that promotes competition and a 'controlled' tension between opposites (*WP*, 55, 881, 966; *TI*, 'Morality as Anti-Nature', 3; *TSZ*, prologue, 5; Jung, 1917/1926/1943, pars. 78, 80; cf. Jung, 1916/1957, par. 189). The union is highly creative, never static, and it continually seeks enrichment. Such creativity and enrichment are achievable through the continual interplay of opposites, as they battle for power over one another. The fact that both Nietzsche and Jung in general promote equality between opposites so that one element cannot completely dominate its opposite counterpart, and require all (psychological) opposites to be present (*WP*, 966, 976; cf. Jung, 1946, par. 536) guarantees that the competition between the opposites will be intense. The *Übermensch* and Self will therefore promote the strongest antagonism in the guise of multiple tensions that are 'directed' or 'harnessed' towards maximum creativity.[2] These two facts also indicate that the *Übermensch* and Self are not aspirations to human *perfection*. Perfection is an unsurpassable condition that is pure and unchanging, and excludes everything negative; the union of opposites, on the other hand, gives positive and negative equal value, and its aim, 'creativity', requires continual change. 'Perfection' is not only detrimental to the union of opposites but actually threatens it completely, as it seeks to promote only one opposite. The fact that neither the *Übermensch* nor the Self discriminates between values means that their actions are outside moral considerations; they are not moral entities, but are 'beyond good and evil'. They do not seek the *summum bonum* alone but also seek the greatest evil; their aspiration is therefore not 'perfection' but 'completion' – more specifically, a totality that promotes the greatest competition and creation within its elements.[3]

Jung's interpretation of Nietzsche runs contrary to mine. According to Jung, Nietzsche's *Übermensch* is merely an attempt to unite the opposites, an attempt that ultimately fails. It culminates not in an expression of wholeness and unity but in an 'unsatisfactory one-sidedness' (*SNZ*, I, p. 397; cf. II, pp. 1099, 1292). Jung's Self, on the other hand, is supposed to achieve wholeness and avoid one-sidedness. Jung is effectively charging Nietzsche's project with inner inconsistency and paradox, for he maintains that the *Übermensch* fails to exhibit those characteristics which its own teaching has explicitly deemed necessary – the promotion of both opposites in the binary pair.[4] If correct, this criticism is highly damaging to Nietzsche's project, for the promotion of only one opposite element not only limits (1) the quality of the relationship between opposites, by prohibiting the dynamic interplay between elements but also destroys (2) the possibility of completion in a union of opposites. In Chapter 7 I argued that Nietzsche's model lacks the mysterious 'third' thing that is essential to the process of unification in the Jungian model. This 'third' thing is the 'unifying symbol' or 'transcendent function' that makes possible the mediation and reconciliation of opposites.

In Jungian terms, Nietzsche's model identifies the opposites and recognizes the need for their reconciliation (ibid., I, pp. 120, 433), but fails to effect the reconciliation. The opposites can never form a productive relationship; they are not a dynamic and balanced binary pair but remain separated, so that only one opposite can be promoted at any one time. The lack of a mediating force also means that the opposites cannot be harnessed, controlled or directed; they will behave erratically or become static (cf. ibid., II, p. 1006). Jung writes:

> For those who have a symbol, the passing from one side to the other, the transmutation, is easier. In other words, those who have no symbol will find it very difficult to make the transition . . . Nietzsche . . . was without a symbol and so, naturally, to make the transition, to leave one condition and to enter another mental condition, would be exceedingly difficult, if not wholly impossible. In this case it was impossible.
>
> (*SNZ*, II, pp. 1248–1250; cf. Jung, 1934/1954, par. 61; also see Frey, 1971, p. 319)[5]

It is apparent, therefore, that Jung rejects my attribution of affinities (1) and (2) to his and Nietzsche's models. (As we shall see later, Jung's conviction that Nietzsche's project is one-sided has further implication for affinities (4), (5) and (6).)

The privilege and exclusivity of the union

Because the *Übermensch* and Self express 'evil' and 'negativity', individuals must actively confront such unpleasant feelings within themselves if they are to endure them and control them to their advantage.[6] Individuals are thus in a difficult and dangerous position, for they must assimilate what conventional morality has taught them to reject, without being seduced into an over-identification with it by its 'forbidden' power. Overcoming the negative element in the union of opposites is therefore a test of emotional strength, and forms, I believe, the first stage in the development of the *Übermensch* and Self. For Nietzsche it marks the moment where 'commonplace beings perish' (*WP*, 881); and for Jung it is manifest in the archetype of the shadow, the first archetype encountered in the individuation process. This stage filters out the 'commonplace beings' from those individuals who have the capacity for *Übermenschlichkeit* and Selfhood.

The *Übermensch* and Self are beyond the reach of the average person. They are realizable only by a select few (in the above argument of (1) and (2), those with extensive emotional strength). The union of opposites is thus privileged and exclusive (3).[7] The *Übermensch* and Self represent the elite – they are *individuals* separated from the 'herd' or 'aggregations of half-baked mass-men' (Jung, 1946, par. 539). The 'commonplace being' is *not* an individual per se; rather, according to Jung, an individual's own ego-consciousness is determined by the social group, so that his true self lies dormant and unconscious beneath the more powerful unconscious forces of the group: 'He is a mere particle that has forgotten what it is to be human and has lost its soul' (Jung, 1946, par. 539; 'a blind brute', Jung, 1944b, par. 563; cf. Freud, 1922, pp. 99–106). A movement towards individuality therefore involves a movement away from the unconscious affects of the group. As Jung writes:

> Every step towards fuller consciousness [to the Self] removes him from his original, purely animal *participation mystique* with the herd, from submersion in a common unconsciousness. Every step forward means tearing oneself loose from the maternal womb of unconsciousness in which the mass of men dwell.
>
> (Jung, 1928/1931, par. 150; also see Jung, 1947/1954, par. 410;
> Jung, 1933/1934, par. 326; Jung, 1943, par. 248)

But such forward steps are not taken easily, for only someone who is exceptionally 'creative', 'proficient in the highest degree', 'organized in his individuality' and 'capable of self reflection' can resist the unconscious of 'the organized mass' (Jung, 1928/1931, par. 153; Jung, 1957, par. 540).[8] According to Jung, 'Nature is aristocratic', so that the 'one person of value [who exhibits these traits] outweighs ten lesser ones' (Jung, 1928b, par. 236). Nietzsche's Zarathustra fits in with Jung's elitist claim for the individual over the herd. The prologue of *TSZ* ends with Zarathustra considering whether he should seek a minority audience of kindred spirits instead of the masses. Likewise, the teaching about the Will to Power in *TSZ* is not for everyone. Zarathustra addresses his discovery of the Will to Power only to 'you who are wisest' (*TSZ*, II, 'Of Self-Overcoming').

The political implications of this elitism must now be addressed. The *Übermensch* and Self are fully-fledged 'individuals', above the collective group; they are, Jung and Nietzsche argue, more conscious and more intelligent. One might think that such individuals are particularly well suited to govern society. Nietzsche succumbs to such a thought. Jung, however, does not. For Jung, the separation of the individual from the herd is the goal of individual completion. This is because the herd tends to repress the individual's instincts so that he is determined only by the totality of ego-consciousness – the social *persona*. Once the negative effects of society (as over-identification with the *persona*) are removed, individuals are free to explore their unrepressed individuality. Their social persona is still active, but it is no longer dominant. For Nietzsche, on the other hand, the individual, as *Übermenschlichkeit*, is separated from the herd so that he can overpower it. In Nietzsche's ideal vision, society is now dictated to, and (over-)identified with the *Übermensch*. Nietzsche has effectively transformed a not unrealistic project of individual completion into the exceptionally fanciful goal of 'social completion' and even world domination (*WP*, 960, 978; cf. *WP*, 862).

Both Nietzsche and Jung acknowledge that over-identification with the social group is detrimental to individual completion, but they differ in their treatment of the social group. In the Jungian model, the conscious social *persona* is not rejected outright in favour of an exploration of the unconscious depths of the individual. Rather, the opposites need to be rebalanced; the individual adheres to both his 'inner vocation' (Jung, 1934a, pars. 300–301, 318) and to his 'social instinct' (Jung, 1916b, par. 437–507) expressed by the 'external' ethics of society. In the Nietzschean model, the social group is denied, replaced and superseded by its opposite – the governing *Übermensch*. (Nietzsche therefore appears to promote one opposite over the other; for, in Jungian terms, the social *persona* is totally rejected and reformulated by its opposite – the hitherto asocial *Übermensch*.) The *Übermensch* is not at all limited by external social ethics, for he determines them; he follows his own self-created values, rooted within his Will to Power.[9]

Jung certainly recognizes the elitism of Nietzsche's works (cf. *SNZ*, I, p. 665), though to argue that Nietzsche was an influential source for elitism in his own model is naive. However, as Bishop notes, the ideas at the core of Jung's pre- and post-war essays, particularly 'Wotan' (1936) and 'After the Catastrophe' (1945), were discussed in and developed at the same time as his seminars on Nietzsche's *TSZ* (Bishop, 1995, p. 285; 1999a, p. 220). Furthermore, Bishop claims that Jung develops his understanding of Nietzsche's Dionysus by relating him to his analysis of the rise of Fascism, explicitly with reference to the political activity taking hold of Switzerland (Bishop, 1999a, p. 218). Jung associates Dionysus with the Teutonic war-god Wotan, the god of thunder.[10] In his examination of Nietzsche's *TSZ* Jung finds many Wotanic images,[11] which have political and psychological connotations for him (*SNZ*, I, p. 500; II, p. 868). In the figure of Wotan we see a direct connection between Nietzsche and Jung and the political (and psychological) ideology of elitism.

I have argued that both Nietzsche and Jung promote elitism, and while Nietzsche is not the only influence on Jung in this connection, he does leave his mark. There remains the question of the relationship of both figures to the ideology of National Socialism. This is a complex issue, which has generated much discussion, and it would take too long to consider it in depth here. However, it is interesting to note that while Jung is implicitly against the social elitism of Nietzsche, Jung hints at a possible explanation for Nietzsche's unrealistic claims and interestingly notes that although 'those occupying the highest positions in government' can make use of their 'individuality' by 'manipulating state doctrine to their own will in the name of state policy', such individuals (ones similar to the *Übermensch*, who dictates to society his own values and is therefore 'the state policy itself') are 'more likely to be the slaves of their own fictions'. The leader nearly always 'becomes the victim of his own inflated ego-consciousness' (Jung, 1957, par. 500). This means that the whole nation is by way of becoming a herd of sheep, constantly relying on a shepherd to drive them into good pastures. The shepherd's staff soon becomes a rod of iron, and the shepherds turn into wolves.

(ibid., par. 413)

Far from being the overtly 'more conscious and intelligent individual' ideally suited to ruling Nietzsche's aristocratic society, the *Übermensch* is here demoted to a 'slave' with an 'inflated ego-consciousness'.[12]

The dangerous implications of the union, the particular opposites that are united, and the notion of the Dionysian

Nietzsche's and Jung's notions of the union of opposites also converge in the idea of the Dionysian, which combines areas (4) and (5): the Dionysian is dangerous, and it exhibits pairs of opposites that are peculiar to both the *Übermensch* and Self.[13]

In Chapter 2 I analysed the concept of the Dionysian as the opposite of the Apollinian in early Nietzsche; together they formed 'tragic' being, anticipating Nietzsche's later formulation of the *Übermensch*. However, Nietzsche later revises his concept of the Dionysian to incorporate the Apollinian impulse within it (Dionysus promotes completion above perfection: *SNZ*, I, p. 480). So that 'Dionysus' versus Apollo in Nietzsche's first book and *Dionysus versus the Crucified* in the last line of Nietzsche's last book do not mean the same thing. The former is the deity of formless chaos that opposes Apollinian form and beauty, and the latter represents 'passion *controlled*' – as opposed to the extirpation of the passions (which Nietzsche associated with Christianity). The revised concept is a union of opposites, of both Dionysian and Apollinian impulses, and this later concept of the Dionysian is the sixth area of convergence between the *Übermensch* and Self.

According to (later) Nietzsche,

> the word '*Dionysian*' means: [i] an urge to unity, [ii] a reaching up beyond personality, the everyday, society, reality, across the abyss of transitoriness: [iii] a passionate-painful overflowing into darker, fuller, more floating states; [iv] an ecstatic affirmation of the total character of life as that which remains the same, just as powerful, just as blissful, through all change; [v] the great pantheistic sharing of joy and sorrow that sanctifies and calls good even the most terrible and questionable qualities of life; the eternal will to procreation, to fruitfulness, to recurrence; the feeling of the necessary unity of creation and destruction.

(*WP*, 1050)

The *Übermensch* and Self convey everything in this definition of the Dionysian according to Nietzsche. The significance of (i) for the *Übermensch* and Self has already been made apparent in their quest for wholeness, completion and unification of opposites; and they express (ii) in that they bring out the highest potential of individuals, and therefore elevate individuals beyond the 'commonplace beings' that identify solely with 'herd' mentality and the social *persona*.

The significance of definitions (iii), (iv) and (v) of Nietzsche's 'Dionysian' for the *Übermensch* and Self have yet to be brought out in detail. We shall see that the *Übermensch* and Self are both 'Dionysian' because they are both 'dangerous'. We shall see that definition (iv) of the 'Dionysian' refers to Nietzsche's notion of the Eternal Recurrence, a motif significant for both the *Übermensch* and Self. Lastly, we shall see that definition (v) exhibits particular opposites that are united in the *Übermensch* and Self.

Dionysian danger

The Dionysian is dangerous because it poses the threat of the loss of individuality. We see that it demands 'a reaching up *beyond* personality', which is described as a 'passionate-*painful* overflowing into *darker*, fuller, more floating states'. In Chapter 2 we saw that (the earlier Nietzschean notion of) the Dionysian impulse expresses itself in intoxication, so that the whole structure of individuation collapses to make room for a rediscovered universal harmony that is at one with nature (cf. Jung, 1936a, par. 118). I have argued that the *Übermensch* and Self are in a continual dynamic state of creation; they are defined by reformulation – by birth, death and rebirth. They must therefore find identity, 'unity' and 'rebirth' within chaos, for if they cannot, they will fail to 'ecstatically affirm life' and will effectively 'die'.[14] I have argued that the first stage in the passage to *Übermenschlichkeit* and Selfhood (that is, confronting evil and negativity) is marked with danger, for Nietzsche warns us the 'commonplace man' will 'perish' here. As Dionysian men of creation, the *Übermensch* and Self will also perish, but this does not mark their end; they perish so as to be born again and again (cf. the notion that strife leads 'to new and more powerful births': *BT*, 1).

Suffering, pain and death precede rebirth. Dionysus represents each of these things, which are illustrated in the mythological story of his birth from the incestuous coupling between Zeus and his daughter Persephone, his horrific mutilation and murder by the Titans, and his rebirth to Zeus and Semele (see Chapters 2 and 4). The *Übermensch* and Self are expressions of this continuous Dionysian cycle of destruction and creativity: the *Übermensch* is 'Dionysus *torn* into pieces . . . a *promise* of life: it will be eternally reborn and return again from destruction (*WP*, 1052; cf. *UM*, III, 1).[15] As we saw in Chapter 6, the rebirth of the ego as Self is a typical dangerous Dionysian experience:

The rediscovered unconscious often has a really dangerous effect on the ego. In the same way that the ego suppressed the unconscious before, a liberated unconscious can thrust the ego aside and overwhelm it. There is a danger of the ego losing its head, so to speak, that it will not be able to defend itself against the pressure of affective factors.

(Jung, 1916/1957, par. 183)[16]

The dangerous Dionysian experience is also manifest in the (psychological) alchemical parallel of the death of the ego and rebirth of the Self: in the various sufferings of the king (the ego) who must die so that he can be reborn in a complete form (and conceived, as Dionysus had been, from an incestuous coupling: cf. Jung, 1955–1956, par. 436; Jung, 1917/1926/1943, par. 43). The death of the ego/king 'signifies the overcoming of the old and the obsolete' (Jung, 1955–1956, par. 169), and thus the dynamics of creation; but before it/he dies it/he must experience a wounding from the might of the Self (represented by immersion in the bath or sea of the unconscious, dissolution and decomposition, extinction of light, and incineration in the fire).

Jung explicitly acknowledges the danger of Dionysus in Nietzsche's model, and we can regard this as the underlying theme of *SNZ*. Jung insists that Nietzsche over-identifies with Dionysus at the expense of Apollo because he believes Nietzsche's model promotes the irrational over the rational. Nietzsche's project is thereby identified with what he himself calls 'that horrible mixture of sensuality and cruelty which has always seemed to me the real "witches" brew' (*BT*, 2).[17]

Opposites in Dionysian affirmation

In Chapter 4 we saw that, according to Nietzsche, Dionysus is intimately linked with the notion of the Eternal Recurrence. The two concepts are connected with the affirmation of life even when it seems most terrible. The significance of (iv) in Nietzsche's definition of the 'Dionysian' is precisely this link with the Eternal Recurrence, and (v) describes some of those profound oppositions that are united in Dionysian affirmation.

Dionysus represents all that is natural; he seeks (*contra* Christianity) a union of mankind and nature so that 'nature which has become alienated, hostile, or subjugated, celebrates once more her reconciliation with her lost son, man' (*BT*, 1; cf. *GS*, 109). Dionysus is therefore the redeeming symbol that saves us from the asceticism of those metaphysical doctrines that Nietzsche rejects (see Chapter 3). As Dionysian individuals, the *Übermensch* and Self promote the 'natural body' as inherently valuable. The *Übermensch* is 'the meaning of the earth' (*TSZ*, prologue, 3); in connection with the Self, Jung comments:

> It is the head of earth which gives meaning to the earth. The body is the guarantee of consciousness, and consciousness is the instrument by which the meaning is created. There would be no meaning if there were no consciousness, and since there is no consciousness without body, there can be no meaning without the body.
>
> (*SNZ*, I, p. 350; see also *SNZ*, I, pp. 63–66; Jung, 1907, pars. 86–87)

Dionysus therefore calls for nature to be reunited with meaning, and spirit with body, for it is 'the mysterious truth that the spirit is the life of the body seen from within and the body the outward manifestation of the life of the spirit – the two being really one' (Jung, 1928/1931, par. 195; also see *TSZ*, I, 'Of the Despisers of the Body').[18] He also calls on us to affirm those profound psychological opposites in (v): to unite 'joy' with 'sorrow', that which is 'good' with 'the most terrible', and 'creation' with 'destruction'.

Dionysian individuals are those who are reunited with humanity and all that is passionate, chaotic and irrational within themselves. They must joyfully and tragically restore themselves to nature and experience 'an ascent-up into a high, free, even terrible nature and naturalness' (*WP*, 120). This terrible experience must be 'blissfully' endured over and over again, for Dionysus affirms nothing more than the tragedy of the Eternal Recurrence. There can be no 'reaching up beyond personality' without struggle and suffering. There will always be obstacles within the individual's path; the Eternal Recurrence is therefore a teaching of strength through despair. Nietzsche tells us that the *Übermensch* is the

> ideal of the most exuberant, most living and most world-affirming man, who has not only learned to get on and treat with all that was and is but who wants to have it again *as it was and is* to all eternity.
>
> (*BGE*, 56)

The *Übermensch* (as with the Self) is he who promotes the 'Yes-saying instinct' as his unifying principle (*AC*, 57; *EH*, 'TSZ', 6). This is what gives him the strength for *amor fati*: to endure the unification of good and evil, to live a cursed existence and to then transmute it into the Dionysian intoxication of tragic acceptance ('It is the man without *amor fati* who is the neurotic': Jung, 1934a, par. 312). Nietzsche therefore seeks the

> *Dionysian* world of the eternally self-creating, the eternally self-destroying, this mystery world of the twofold voluptuous delight, my 'beyond good and evil', without goal, unless the joy of the circle is itself a goal; without will, unless a ring feels good will toward itself.
>
> (*WP*, 1067; cf. *TI*, 'What I Owe to the Ancients', 4, 5)

Although Jung does not promote the anti-teleological doctrine behind Nietzsche's Eternal Recurrence,[19] its symbolism is central to the conveyance of his own Dionysian notion of totality.[20] Jung interprets the Eternal Recurrence as an effect accompanying Dionysian Rebirth (*SNZ*, I, pp. 191–192; cf. Jung, 1940/1950, par. 210), and he adopts its symbolic representation, the 'circle' or 'ring' (see Nietzsche's quote above), as an archetypal image of the Self. In Chapter 5 I alluded to the mandala sacred circle as a principal symbol of the Self; the Eternal Recurrence is another representation of this:

> Nietzsche's idea of the Eternal Recurrence . . . belongs with this symbolism of the ring, the ring of rings, the ring of Eternal Recurrence. Now this ring is the idea of totality and it is the idea of individuation naturally, an individuation symbol.
>
> (*SNZ*, II, p. 1044)

The affinities that I have posited between Nietzsche and Jung are extensive. Even the language and ideas used by Jung to express the totality of the Self are startlingly similar to those of Nietzsche (see note 20). This might lead one to conclude that Jung had found Nietzsche's argument convincing, and perhaps even appropriated it. Such an inference is not entirely correct. For I have interpreted the Eternal Recurrence as a unifying symbol; but in our discussion of affinities (1) and (2) we saw that, according to Jung, Nietzsche 'was without a symbol', which meant that it was 'impossible' for him to form a totality and unite the opposites (*SNZ*, II, pp. 1248–1250; cf. Jung, 1934/1954, par. 61; Frey, 1971, p. 319). According to Jung, there can be no correlation between Nietzsche's model, which lacks totality, and his own notion of the Self, which is totality. However, in the passage just quoted, we see Jung contradict himself and agree with my interpretation, for he allows Nietzsche the unifying symbol, thereby encouraging us to believe that he is convinced by Nietzsche's thought. This contradiction needs to be resolved.

In Chapter 6 we saw that the symbol is subjectively defined, so that it can be effective for the individual at one time, but have the status of a mere 'sign' at another. The demotion of symbol into sign occurs when it fails to promote growth and enrichment of the personality. Jung's apparent indecision over whether Nietzsche has or lacks a symbol is, I suggest, not a logical matter, but has to do with Jung's psychological disposition when he made his different interpretations: in his seminars of 5 May 1937 and 18 May 1938 respectively. Jung's reception of Nietzsche's project is ambiguous, and much hangs on this ambiguity; for if Jung does acknowledge Nietzsche as having a unifying symbol of totality, Nietzsche's project may not be doomed, as Jung claims. Nietzsche's one-sidedness could be overcome in a union of opposites after all.

However, there is more to Jung's criticism of one-sidedness than has so far emerged; Jung also denies that Nietzsche's project unites the particular opposites of spirit and body. I argued that while the *Übermensch* and Self promote the 'natural body' as inherently valuable, Jung maintains that the *Übermensch* promotes it too vigorously, so that it over-identifies with the body and does not adequately support its spiritual opposite, God. The fact that Nietzsche insists that God is dead, and that Jung rediscovered Him as a guiding principle of unity within the depths of the unconscious (for the Self is a God-image) crudely demonstrates their different outlooks. Jung, however, maintains that 'Nietzsche never gets rid of him [God] . . . Unnamed and not visible, he is still there' (*SNZ*, II, p. 843). To take his criticism of Nietzsche further, Jung names Nietzsche's God as Dionysus, the god of the *body* (cf. *SNZ*, II, p. 1129).

If this is right, Nietzsche never completely excludes the notion of spirit from his model; rather, he too readily conflates the spirit with the body, so that the body becomes deified (*SNZ*, II, p. 816).[21] In *TSZ* we see Zarathustra proclaim:

> The awakened, the enlightened man says: I am body entirely, and nothing beside; and soul is only a word for something in the body . . . Your little intelligence, my brother, which you call 'spirit', is also an instrument of your body, a little instrument and toy of your great intelligence. You say 'I' and you are proud of this word. But greater than this . . . is your body . . . [The Self] lives in your body, he is your body.
>
> (*TSZ*, I, 'Of the Despisers of the Body')

In response to this passage, in which the spirit is portrayed as a mere plaything of the body, Jung accuses Nietzsche of 'every unspeakable crime' (*SNZ*, I, p. 372). Indeed, such secondary identification – 'identifying the ego with the self and therefore with the Superman' – can only 'lead to an explosion' (ibid., p. 392).[22] Thus, according to Jung, Nietzsche's model self-destructs because of its one-sided orientation towards Dionysus at the expense of Apollinian control and spirit.

The 'Dionysian', then, connects Nietzsche's and Jung's models of the union of opposites, despite Jung's insistence that the value they each place upon it is significantly different. The connection is strengthened through the personality of Goethe, who represents their respective notions of a whole self, of 'Dionysian man'. According to Nietzsche, Goethe

> did not sever himself from life, he placed himself within it; nothing could discourage him and he took as much as possible upon himself, above himself, within himself. What he aspired to was *totality*.
>
> (*TI*, 'Expeditions of an Untimely Man', 49)

Goethe was a rare example, for Nietzsche, of the unification of 'reason, sensuality, feeling, will' (ibid.), which correspond almost exactly to the four Jungian functions of thinking, feeling, sensation and intuition. Goethe was someone who, exceptionally, 'strove against separation', 'affirmed the whole' and 'created his own Self' (ibid.). According to Jung, Goethe was an example of the 'great personality', of the individual who followed his 'inner vocation' and differentiated his ego from the 'voice of the group'; he thus sought 'individual wholeness' over the 'wholeness of the group' (Jung, 1934a, pars. 301–302). Similarly, Goethe's writings can be regarded as an outward manifestation of his inner totality; for, in parallel to that of Nietzsche and Jung, it explains the 'whole' personality in terms of a union of opposites.[23] Both the personality and works of Goethe were described by Nietzsche as exhibiting 'the highest of all possible faiths: I have baptized it with the name *Dionysos*' (*TI*, 'Expeditions of an Untimely Man', 49).

The 'Nietzschean Self'

In *The Dionysian Self* (1995), Paul Bishop offers two reasons why Jung should refer to Nietzsche as a predecessor to his own analytical psychology. First, Nietzsche and Jung agree on 'the preeminence of psychology, whatever the difference in their psychological outlooks'; and second, 'Nietzschean imagery . . . influenced the characterizations of two Jungian archetypes: the Old Wise Man and the Anima' (Bishop, 1995, pp. 192–193). This second point is certainly evident, but it understates the case. Roderick Peters is more realistic when he raises the stakes by claiming: 'The Superman . . . is to be understood as the Self, [and] the doctrine preached by Zarathustra is none other than the doctrine of individuation' (Peters, 1991, p. 125; cf. Casement, 2001, pp. 47–48; Storr, 1996, p. 10; Thatcher, 1977, p. 256; *SNZ*, I, pp. 60–61, 721; see also note 26). Nietzsche's influence on Jung's project is much greater than Bishop here intimates. In this chapter we have examined what I believe are six significant affinities between the models of Nietzsche and Jung, and I have tried to determine whether or not the incidence of these themes is the consequence of a direct influence Nietzsche had upon Jung. Now we shall examine Jung's model of the Self directly, to determine Nietzsche's influence in its formulation: that is, to determine exactly how Nietzsche 'understands that the Self . . . is a reconciliation of opposites' (*SNZ*, I, p. 433; cf. 117, 1364). I shall argue that, although Jung does not fully acknowledge it, Nietzsche anticipates the principal aspects of the Self's realization: its psychic foundation, the 'collective unconscious'; the process of 'individuation'; the typological arrangement of the Self; and the particular archetypes encountered in the individuation process (the shadow, the anima/animus and the Self).

The collective unconscious and the process of individuation

Nietzsche and Jung can both be regarded as philosophers and psychologists who acknowledge the existence and value of the unknowable unconscious mind. Nietzsche's conception of the unconscious is not, however, the 'traditional' notion adopted by Freud, among others, but is that particular notion of an *autonomous* and *collective* unconscious that marks the very separation of Jungian 'analytical psychology' from traditional 'psychoanalysis' (preface to the second edition of 'The Relations between the Ego and the Unconscious': Jung, 1917/1926/1943, pp. 121–123).[24]

In Chapter 5 we saw that, according to Jung, the autonomous and collective unconscious is related directly to the phylogenetic instinctual base of the human race; it is defined as 'the ancestral heritage of possibilities of representation . . . common to all men, and perhaps even to all animals' (Jung, 1928a, par. 22). However, before Jung, Nietzsche not only recognized the autonomy of the unconscious drives that 'command' the ego (*TSZ*, I, 'Of the Despisers of the Body'; *EH*, 'Why

I am So Wise', 9) and 'act contrary to our advantage, against the ego: and often *for* the ego' (*WP*, 372; also see *GS*, 8); he also anticipated Jung's notion of the unconscious as a collective ancestral store or 'an accumulated ancestral estate in which everyone has his share' (*TL*, 173; cf. *BGE*, 20; *WP*, 490). Thus, Jung starts with the premise, 'The autonomy of the unconscious . . . begins where emotions are generated' (Jung, 1939b, par. 497), and Nietzsche anticipates the conclusion: during such emotional 'outbursts of passion . . . a man rediscovers his own and mankind's prehistory' (*D*, 312). Furthermore, Nietzsche remarks personally: 'I have discovered for myself that the human and animal past, indeed the whole primal age and past of all sentient being continues in me to invent, to love, to hate, and to infer' (*GS*, 54). Indeed, Jung claims that it was the discovery of the collective unconscious that caused Nietzsche to exclaim, 'I am every name in history.' For Jung notes, 'Whoever speaks in primordial images speaks with a thousand voices' (Jung, 1922, par. 129; cited in Dixon, 1999, p. 205).[25] In his early work, *Psychology of the Unconscious* (1912), Jung explicitly refers to two passages in Nietzsche's *HAH* to explain his own notion of 'archaic images' (which he would later describe as the images or 'archetypes' of the 'collective unconscious'). Thus, in 'Dream and Culture', Nietzsche states: 'In sleep and dreams we repeat once again the curriculum of earlier mankind' (*HAH*, 12), and in 'Logic of the Dream', he writes: 'In my opinion, the conclusions man still draws in dreams to the present day for many millennia mankind also drew *when awake*' (*HAH*, 13).

In Chapter 5 we saw that the collective unconscious translates its material to consciousness through 'archetypes' (those primordial images and ideas that are 'deposits of the constantly repeated experiences of humanity') and the reception of these archetypal images marks the progressive development of the individuation process. I believe that there are intimations of this process and its archetypal representations in Nietzsche's work. They are not obvious, and few commentaries on Jung (and even fewer on Nietzsche) have acknowledged them. Fewer still have actually analysed these intimations in detail.[26] I shall now attempt a through examination of them.

Nietzsche alludes frequently to what he calls 'the fundamental law of your own true self', which is itself an unconscious project that must be developed and worked upon if it is to be realized. He refers to consciousness as our 'last and latest development', as 'what is most unfinished' (*GS*, 11), and in *WP*, 680 he writes: 'His highest interest, his highest expression of power [is] not judged from the consciousness but from the centre of the whole individuation.' Ironically, I have found that the anticipation of Jung's individuation process in Nietzsche's writings has been given most prominence by those Nietzschean commentators who have no apparent knowledge of Jung's model. For example, G. A. Morgan, in *What Nietzsche Means* (1943), writes:

To become himself the individual must find himself but not too soon. [Nietzsche's] recipe is: to live through a series of temporary 'selves' each of which is effective because it is believed permanent at the time, under the guidance of the ultimate self which finally makes itself known and uses the previous selves as functions.

(Morgan, 1943, pp. 202–203)

Alexander Nehamas, in *Nietzsche: Life as Literature* (1985), has this to say:

The unity [of the self] is a matter of incorporating more and more character traits under a constantly expanding and evolving rubric . . . Nietzsche does not think of unity as a state of being that follows and replaces an earlier process of becoming. Rather, he seems to think of it as a continual process of integrating one's character traits, habits, and patterns of action with one another. This process can also reach backward and integrate even a discarded characteristic into the personality by showing that it was necessary for one's subsequent development.

(Nehamas, 1985, pp. 183–185)

These two passages could sit comfortably within the text of a Jungian commentary. If we replace the name 'Nietzsche' for 'Jung' we have two descriptions of Jung's process of individuation.[27]

We do not, however, need to turn to secondary literature to situate Jung's individuation process in Nietzsche's writings, for Nietzsche himself does this particularly well in his autobiography (subtitled: 'How to Become What One Is'). Here Nietzsche talks about

the organizing 'idea' destined to rule [which] grows and grows in the depths – it begins to command, it slowly leads *back* from sidepaths and wrong turnings, it prepares *individual* qualities and abilities which will one day prove themselves indispensable as means to achieving the whole – it constructs the *ancillary* capacities one after the other before it gives any hint of the dominating task, of the 'goal', 'objective', 'meaning'.

(*EH*, 'Why I am so Clever', 9)

The process of individuation is that process of 'organizing', 'growing', 'commanding', 'preparing' and 'constructing' the 'goal', 'objective' and 'meaning' of the Self. The Self, Nietzsche tells us, is grown in the (unconscious) 'depths', and is a whole constructed from many parts: of 'individual qualities' and 'ancillary capacities'. According to Jung, the individual qualities of the Self comprise: the four functions of thinking, feeling, sensation and intuition (one of which will act, according to Nietzsche, as the 'dominant task': cf. the Jungian 'dominant function'), and another as an '*ancillary* capacity' (cf. the 'auxiliary function', which will 'serve the dominant function': Jung, 1921, par. 668), the two attitude types of introversion and extraversion, and the archetypes of the shadow and the anima/animus.

I shall now explain how these 'individual qualities' of the Jungian Self are anticipated in Nietzsche. We shall then be in a position to indicate how much influence Nietzsche exerted on the formulation of the Jungian Self, and how exactly 'Nietzsche: his *Zarathustra*, in particular, brings to light the contents of the collective unconscious of our time, and [how] in him we find the same distinguishing features' (Jung, 1921, par. 322).

The typological arrangement of the Self

According to Jung, the psyche is composed of two attitude-types and four functions that are configured in pairs of opposites. According to Nietzsche, the 'psyche' is composed of one principal pair of opposites – the Apollinian and Dionysian impulses. These can be regarded as the *prima materia* from which Jung creates his own opposing impulses.

In his essay 'A Contribution to the Study of Psychological Types' (1913), Jung equates the Dionysian and Apollinian impulses with his two attitude types. The Dionysian is equated with extraversion because Dionysus is the investment of libido in as many objects in the world outside the self as possible, or the 'plunging into the multiplicity of the objective world' (Jung, 1913, par. 876), and the Apollinian is equated with introversion because Apollo is a withdrawal of the libido into oneself or 'shut up within oneself' (ibid.). However, in 1921, in *Psychological Types* (*CW*, 6), Jung uses Nietzsche's distinction between the Dionysian and Apollinian to develop his model further. Jung devotes a whole, albeit brief, chapter to 'The Apollinian and the Dionysian' (pars. 223–242), and throughout he refers to passages in *The Birth of Tragedy* where Nietzsche specifically alludes to the relationship between Dionysus and Apollo. Jung's revision of both his 'typological' theory and his interpretation of Nietzsche's opposing impulses is announced when Jung claims that it is now necessary to go beyond the distinction between introversion and extraversion. He has in mind a new set of opposites that goes beyond 'logical and rational elaboration' (in other words, beyond 'thinking and feeling': the two functions which Jung had already adopted at this stage): namely, the so-called 'aesthetic' functions. This new set of psychological functions Jung claims to have derived directly from Nietzsche:

> Nietzsche's concepts [the Apollinian and Dionysian] thus lead us to the principles of a third and fourth psychological type, which one might call 'aesthetic' types as opposed to rational types (thinking and feeling). These are the intuitive and sensation types.
>
> (Jung, 1921, par. 240)

The two categories of intuition and sensation are associated with Apollo and Dionysus, respectively: 'The Apollinian mode is an inner perception, an intuition of ideas', and 'Dionysian feeling has the thoroughly archaic character of affective sensation' (ibid., par. 238). The Apollinian impulse represents order, measure and controlled proportion; it is thus a mode of inner perception and intuition of the world of ideas. In contrast, the Dionysian impulse is 'a flood of overpowering universal feeling which bursts forth irresistibly, intoxicating the senses' (ibid., par. 234).[28]

Jung appropriates the Apollinian and Dionysian impulses from Nietzsche to describe and determine the two attitude types and two functions of intuition and sensation, which, together with the functions of thinking and feeling, ground Jung's theory of typology. Nietzsche's influence therefore infiltrates the Jungian process of diagnosing both the individual's conscious orientation (his psychological 'type') and his unconscious orientation (those *shadow* aspects which he will incorporate in the process of individuation). Indeed, Nietzsche can be seen to perform a similar diagnosis of his own for, in an early essay of his, he claims that the pre-Socratic philosophers represent 'all the eternal types' (as well as 'the archetypes of all philosophical thought': *PTAG*, 1), and he singles out Heraclitus as an example of the eternal intuitive type (*PTAG*, 5).

The particular archetypes encountered in the individuation process (and within the Self)

Not only does Nietzsche anticipate Jung's typological framework, but also he seems to make use of archetypes that are specific to Jung's individuation process and to the constitution of the Self: the shadow and anima/animus. However, Jung insists that Nietzsche does not understand what these archetypes represent, and consequently fails to acknowledge them in his own psyche. I, on the contrary, disagree with Jung's claim; I believe that Nietzsche was aware of their meaning (perhaps only intuitively) and that he incorporated their message within his writings, admittedly without giving them the detailed examination that Jung provided.

The first archetype to be encountered in the Jungian journey to the Self is the shadow, the 'guilt-laden personality' that contains the negative and morally reprehensible tendencies of the individual. Nietzsche not only acknowledged this 'dark side' of the personality, but also called it the 'shadow'. In *TSZ*, part IV, Nietzsche makes the Jungian shadow speak:

> If you do not like me . . . I praise you in your good taste in that . . . I have striven with you into all that was forbidden, worst, most remote: and if anything in me be a virtue, it is that I have feared no prohibition . . . I have pursued the most dangerous desires – truly, I once went beyond every crime . . . 'Nothing is true, everything is permitted': thus I told myself.
>
> (*TSZ*, IV, 'The Shadow')[29]

Nietzsche first refers to the shadow in *The Wanderer and his Shadow* (1880), where he describes the intimate connection between light and dark:

> Close beside dark and gloomy men there is to be found, almost as a rule and as though tied to them, a soul of light. It is as if it were the negative shadow they cast . . . Men press towards the light, not so as to see better, but so as to shine better.
>
> (*WS*, 258; cf. 254)

Nietzsche pursues the link between shadow and that which 'shines', so that in *TSZ* its resonance is Jungian. He now regards the appearance of the shadow as denoting the arrival of the *Übermensch*: 'For a shadow came to me – the most silent, the lightest of all things once came to me! The beauty of the Superman came to me as a shadow' (*TSZ*, II, 'On the Blissful Islands'; *EH*, 'TSZ', 8; compare Jung: 'the shadow contains the self. Behind the shadow looms up the self': *SNZ*, I, p. 123).

Jung does not accept Nietzsche's use of the term 'shadow' as a source of his own (*SNZ*, I, p. 703). Jung claims that he 'cannot remember [this latter] passage' (ibid.). Such a claim is surprising when we consider how close it is to his own. Moreover, Jung not only considers Nietzsche's 'ugliest man' (described in the section of *TSZ* that immediately follows 'The Shadow') to be an early personification of his shadow (Jung, 1921, par. 906; *SNZ*, I, p. 702; cf. *SNZ*, I, p. 143: that 'sort of miserable Christian'), but he also believes that Nietzsche is the first thinker of 'our age' to have 'discovered' this notion (Jung, 1921, pars. 208, 322).[30]

The second archetype to be encountered in the individuation process is the anima/animus, the personality that is contra-sexual to the conscious personality. Jung writes:

> Every man carries within him the eternal image of a woman . . . a deposit, as it were, of all the impressions ever made by a woman . . . Since this image is unconscious, it is always unconsciously projected upon the person or the beloved, and is one of the chief reasons for passionate attraction or aversion.
>
> (Jung, 1925a, par. 338)

Nietzsche's description of this archetype is very similar:[31]

> Everyone bears within him a picture of woman derived from his mother: it is this which determines whether, in his dealings with women, he respects them or despises them or is in general indifferent to them.
>
> (*HAH*, 380; cf. *HAH*, 412; *AOM*, 272)

Nietzsche has Zarathustra tells us that we have within us 'the eternal-womanly' (*TSZ*, II, 'Of Poets'; cf. *BGE*, 231). Furthermore, both Nietzsche and Jung claim that the image of the eternal woman originates with the mother (cf. Jung, 1951, par. 24). Nietzsche further claims that women have a similar contra-sexual counterpart. After citing Goethe's phrase 'the eternal-womanly draws us *upward*',

Nietzsche adds: 'I do not doubt that every nobler woman will resist this belief, for *that* is precisely what she believes of the eternal manly' (*BGE*, 236; cited in Dixon, 1999, p. 216). However, Jung does not acknowledge these Nietzschean counterparts of his own ideas.[32]

Jung does explicitly acknowledge the influence of the following notions from Nietzsche: the *autonomous* and *collective* unconscious; the idea that an unconscious teleological process is at work within the individual to create the 'true self'; and Nietzsche's early theory of 'typology'. However, Jung is reluctant to acknowledge a debt to Nietzsche's early notions of the shadow (which Jung acknowledges only implicitly and ambiguously) and the anima/animus (which Jung does not acknowledge at all).[33] There is no doubt, however, that Jung endorses Nietzsche's early conception of the Self, which is grounded in all of these things.

Indeed, Nietzsche's prefigurations of Jung's Self are explicit throughout his writings. In addition to what I have already quoted, Nietzsche, early in his writings, speaks of

> 'I': of course, this self is not the same as that of the waking, empirically real man, but the only truly existent and eternal self resting at the basis of things.
>
> (*BT*, 5)

Later in his writings he describes the Self as a homecoming:

> It is returning, at last it is coming home to me – my own Self and those parts of it that have long been abroad and scattered among all things and accidents.
>
> (*TSZ*, III, 'the Wanderer')[34]

But perhaps the most explicit passage is to be found in *TSZ*, I, 'On the Despisers of the Body', where Zarathustra dismisses the body and soul dualism of the child in favour of the esoteric declarations of the mysterious 'one who knows'. Here Nietzsche writes:

> The Self is always listening and seeking: it compares, subdues, conquers, destroys. It rules and is also the Ego's ruler. Behind your thoughts and feelings, my brother, stands a mighty commander, an unknown sage – he is called Self. He lives in your body, he is your body. There is more reason in your body than in your best wisdom . . . Your Self laughs at your Ego and its proud leapings. 'What are these leapings and flights of thought to me?' it says to itself. 'A by-way to my goal. I am the Ego's leading-string and I prompt its conceptions!' The Self says to the Ego: 'Feel pain!' . . . The Self says to the Ego: 'Feel joy!' . . . The creative Self created for itself esteem and disesteem, it created for itself joy and sorrow. The creative body created spirit for itself, as a hand of its will. Even in your folly and contempt, you despisers of the body, you serve your Self. I tell you: your Self itself wants to die and turn

away from life . . . I do not go your way, you despisers of the body! You are not bridges to the Superman!

Here Nietzsche implicitly equates the Self with the *Übermensch*. The 'despisers of the body' are denied access to the *Übermensch* by Zarathustra because they themselves have denied the Self access to life. According to Jung, 'What [Nietzsche] says about the self here is absolutely to the point' (*SNZ*, 1, p. 397). Jung is quite willing to acknowledge Nietzsche as a specific influence for his concept of the Self. Thus, we have already noted that Jung believes that 'Nietzsche . . . understands that the Self consists in pairs of opposites and that it is in a way a reconciliation of opposites' (*SNZ*, I, p. 433). Furthermore, it was through reading Nietzsche, particularly *TSZ*, that Jung derived his concept of the Self:

> Of course I knew that Nietzsche had [the concept of the Self] because I read *Zarathustra* for the first time when I was only twenty-three . . . I was already interested in the concept of the self, but I was not clear how I should understand it . . . The concept of the self continued to recommend itself to me nevertheless. I thought Nietzsche meant a sort of thing-in-itself behind the psychological phenomenon.
>
> (*SNZ*, I, p. 391; cf. ibid., p. 120)

However, *TSZ* could not originally have brought Nietzsche's concept of the Self to Jung's attention, for in his autobiography Jung tells us '*Thoughts Out of Season* was the first volume that fell into my hands. I was carried away by its enthusiasms, and soon afterwards read *Thus Spoke Zarathustra*' (*MDR*, p. 123).

If we look at the *Untimely Meditations* we find Nietzsche's even earlier discussions of the character and cultivation of the 'true self'. It is the thesis of the third meditation, *Schopenhauer as Educator* (1874), that true education involves the liberation of the self from everything foreign to it, including those elements of it that one judges to be incompatible with one's true and future self. The third meditation certainly has Jungian resonances, for genuine selfhood is described as an infinite process of self-development and overcoming. The 'true' self is neither an externally given and unchangeable 'essence', nor a random and freely willed 'construct'; it is something that the individual has to 'become'; but, paradoxically, it is also what he already is. Nietzsche writes: 'Your true nature lies, not concealed deep within you, but immeasurably high above you, or at least above that which you usually take yourself to be' (*UM*, III, 1). One must 'seek with all [one's] might . . . a higher self as yet concealed' within one's 'deepest and innermost core' (*UM*, III, 6).

From our analysis of the seven affinities between Nietzsche and Jung only one is explicitly acknowledged by Jung, and then only in part. Jung tells us that his notion of the Self can be found in Nietzsche's work and, indeed, we have found that Nietzsche anticipates the features of its fundamental composition and structure.

However, at this level of analysis, Jung's reception of Nietzsche is surprisingly ambivalent. Jung recognizes the foundations of the collective unconscious, the individuation process and typological theory present in Nietzsche's work, but his recognition of the archetype of the shadow is most ambiguous, and he completely fails to acknowledge Nietzsche's anticipation of the anima. Jung's ambivalence and reluctance to draw certain parallels between his model and Nietzsche's is sustained in relation to the other six affinities that we examined. Thus, although Jung acknowledges that both he and Nietzsche promote elitism, Jung's model breaks sharply from Nietzsche's in its implications: Nietzsche's model promotes an elitism beyond the individual and into society, which Jung repudiates. Similarly, although Jung acknowledges that both models exhibit 'Dionysian' danger, Jung maintains that only his model can contain such danger, while Nietzsche's cannot. This last point helps to explain why Jung denies the remaining affinities that I have posited. For, according to Jung, the excessive danger of Nietzsche's model consists of its failure to promote both opposites in the binary pair, landing it in one-sidedness. Jung believes that Nietzsche's over-identification with the irrational Dionysian side prevents his model from realizing a *controlled* union of opposites, including that essential union of body and spirit.

Far from supporting my claim of a significant Nietzschean influence, Jung, it would seem, has tried to distance himself from Nietzsche. The two models are perhaps not easily reconciled, and it is indeed unfair to try to force their merger. Although Nietzsche contributes to Jung's concept of the Self (indeed perhaps more than Jung himself admits), he obviously does not anticipate it completely. Nietzsche's philosophy leads to analytical psychology, but cannot be reduced to it; both remain projects in their own right.[35]

So far, I have attempted to expound the models of opposites implicit within the works of Nietzsche and Jung by exposing their influences, differences and affinities. In this chapter I have proposed an explicit link between the two in the form of a significant Nietzschean influence on Jung. However, although similar in content and aim, the two models seem to be linked tenuously. In order to bring them closer together we must change our method of analysis from one of direct comparison to an assessment of each from the perspective of the other. That will put us in a position to evaluate the two more fully.

Jung's rejection of Nietzsche's model

Chapter 9

Nietzsche's madness

A Jungian critique of Nietzsche's model

Part III will attempt to test both Nietzsche's and Jung's model of opposites, and critically evaluate them from each other's perspective. In accordance with their common insistence that the author is to be identified with his work, each criticism will comment upon the thinker's model and the thinker himself. By evaluating each model by cross-examination we hope to arrive at a closer understanding of Nietzsche's influence on Jung's model and on Jung himself. We therefore hope to resolve the ambiguous relationship that was revealed by the method of direct comparison employed in Chapter 8. The first chapter in this part will focus upon a Jungian critique of Nietzsche's model and will offer a Jungian 'diagnosis' of Nietzsche's personality. We shall see that, according to Jung, Nietzsche's model fails to unite the opposites and is essentially one-sided, and that this failure is the cause of Nietzsche's eventual mental collapse. Nietzsche, far from attaining Selfhood in the union of opposites, is, in Jungian terms, an 'un-individuated' and neurotic personality. In Chapter 10 I shall criticize this Jungian interpretation and explain why I believe Jung misunderstands Nietzsche and his model. We shall see that Nietzsche's model does not fail for the reasons Jung puts forward and we shall therefore try, in Chapter 11, to understand why Jung is reluctant to acknowledge those affinities between his own model and Nietzsche's that I proposed in Chapter 8. Finally, Chapter 12 will focus upon a Nietzschean critique of Jung's model and will offer a Nietzschean 'diagnosis' of Jung's personality. I shall argue that Jung fails to adhere to the teaching of the Will to Power, so that, far from attaining *Übermenschlichkeit* in the union of opposites, Jung is, in Nietzschean terms, a 'commonplace being' or 'inverse cripple'.

Jungian critique of Nietzsche's model

In Chapter 8 we saw the beginnings of a Jungian attack on Nietzsche's model. Jung maintains that although Nietzsche 'is actually at grips with the problem [of the union of opposites]' (*SNZ*, I, p. 120), and 'understands that the Self . . . [is] a reconciliation of opposites' and thus a solution to the problem (ibid., p. 433), he believes that Nietzsche ultimately fails in its actualization (ibid., p. 117). I believe that according to Jung, the *Übermensch* fails to unite the opposites principally because it merely promotes one opposite element at the expense of the other, and it lacks the mysterious 'third' thing, the unifying symbol that would enable the appropriate balance. Jung thus charges Nietzsche's project with one-sidedness. The crux of Jung's critique rests on Nietzsche's insistence on, and response to, the death of God; it is this premise that compels Nietzsche's model into the two errors above.

According to Jung, 'God is a fact that has always happened' (*SNZ*, I, p. 335; Frey-Rohn, 1988, p. 85). God 'is a very definite psychological fact' (*SNZ*, II, p. 903). God's existence, therefore, cannot be determined in any way by the finite individual, and thus Jung cannot condone Nietzsche for proclaiming that God is dead and that He was merely a conjecture or 'invention' of mankind (ibid., pp. 329, 341). By eliminating God, Nietzsche promotes finitude and the human being as the source of all meaning; the 'definite psychological fact' of God, as Jung would have it, is now found within mankind, so that 'man is now responsible for all that God once was' (*SNZ*, I, p. 50). The 'meaning of the earth', as Zarathustra proclaims, becomes the assurance of genuine value, and this value is embodied within the *Übermensch*, Nietzsche's 'Dionysian' god, the deification of man (ibid., p. 333). It is Nietzsche's rejection of God and consequent need to replace Him with a deification of the body, with 'superhumanity', that Jung criticizes. By elevating the individual to the position of God, Nietzsche denies the possibility of anything beyond the individual, that which is 'unknown' and unconscious to him. Jung writes:

> One cannot feel a presence if one is God, because it is then one's own presence and there is no other. If all is conscious, one knows of no presence because one is everything, so long as one is identical with the deity there is no presence.
>
> (*SNZ*, II, p. 1174; cf. p. 67)

According to Jung, the deification of the body is merely the deification of consciousness: Nietzsche's *Übermensch* 'is the man with an absolutely superior consciousness'. He lacks unconscious insight (*SNZ*, I, p. 350; also see Jung, 1928b, par. 388), and consequently lacks 'real knowledge of the human soul' (*SNZ*, II, p. 903).

According to Jung, the notion of 'body' is not to be equated with 'soul', it is simply 'the guarantee of consciousness' (ibid., p. 350) and 'a biological function' (ibid., p. 397) that the Self directs to its own purpose (*SNZ*, I, p. 372; cf. p. 403). In Chapter 8 we saw Jung criticize Nietzsche for reversing the situation and making the Self a mere plaything of the body (*TSZ*, I, 'Of the Despisers of the Body'). According to Jung, the body can only enable the physical 'outward manifestation' of the Self (Jung, 1928/1931, par. 195; cf. *SNZ*, II, pp. 64, 65, 978). It is not the totality of the Self, for the Self is also identified with an 'inner spiritual manifestation' (ibid.). In other words, it is both conscious and unconscious. Jung criticizes Nietzsche for conflating the two and for endowing the body with a creative faculty or a meaningful faculty, which, even with a tremendous effort of imagination, cannot be put into it . . . it is not really the body which restores damaged tissues; it is a peculiar vital principle which does the job and it should not be put down to the chemistry of the body.

(*SNZ*, I, p. 397)

This 'vital principle' is that 'spiritual' faculty which is 'outwardly expressed' by the body, but is not identified with it. (If it is to be 'located' at all it would be found in the 'inner manifestation' or unconscious aspect of the Self.) By contrast, Nietzsche locates the vital principle and 'instinct of inwardness' (Frey-Rohn, 1988, pp. 93–94) in the body. According to Jung, there is no room for 'spirit' as an active and productive force in Nietzsche's model, for Nietzsche equates spirit with abstract thought and 'little reason', which has subordinate significance as a function of the mind and 'instrument of the body' (*TSZ*, I, 'Of the Despisers of the Body'). There is only 'body', which culminates in 'great reason' and 'instinctive wisdom' (ibid.). For Nietzsche, meaning and reality are identified with the definiteness of the bodily instincts. Nietzsche's model therefore 'determines *physiologically* "the inmost parts", "the entrails" of every soul' (Frey-Rohn, 1988, p. 97, italics mine; cf. *SNZ*, I, p. 393). According to Jung, by promoting the bodily instincts as the source of all meaning, Nietzsche's model is exposed to the chaos and tension of multiple conflicting values, which consciousness alone cannot harness. His 'physiological' model will inevitably fail to regulate and balance the opposites and will destruct under its own weight. For

the individual ego is much too small, its brain is much too feeble, to incorporate all the projections withdrawn from the world. Ego and brain burst asunder in the effort.

(Jung, 1938/1940, par. 145)[1]

According to Jung, Nietzsche's model is one-sided because he deifies the body so that nothing meaningful can exist outside of it; Nietzsche does not explicitly admit a spiritual realm outside of the body and thus 'unknowable' and 'unconscious' to the body.[2] Jung regards the body in Nietzsche's model as being both wholly conscious and irrational, which is a fateful and unproductive combination that sees consciousness fall apart under the tension of opposite impulses. Nietzsche's model fails to unite the opposites because it merely promotes one opposite element at the expense of the other – body above spirit and conscious above unconscious.

According to Jung, Nietzsche's model would have successfully united the opposites, if it had acknowledged God as a 'definite fact'. Jung is critical of Nietzsche because he believes that Nietzsche is concerned only with the aesthetic approach to things, and consciously ignores the religious meaning of the symbol of redemption – that is the 'psychological fact of God' (Jung, 1921, p. 141n; cf. Frey-Rohn, 1988, p. 28). In his analysis of *BT*, Jung claims that with Nietzsche 'the religious viewpoint is entirely overlooked and is replaced by the aesthetic'; 'Nietzsche quite forgets that in the struggle between Apollo and Dionysus and their ultimate reconciliation the problem for the Greeks was never an aesthetic one, but was essentially religious' (Jung, 1921, par. 231). Although

> aestheticism can, of course, take the place of the religious function . . . and may be a very noble substitute, it is nevertheless only a compensation for the real thing that is lacking. Moreover, Nietzsche's later 'conversion' to Dionysus best shows that the aesthetic substitute did not stand the test of time.
>
> (Jung, 1921, p. 141n)

It is thus only 'God' that is credited by Jung as the real 'unifying symbol', that mysterious 'third thing' of Chapter 5 that mediates between the opposites and enables the reconciliation between Apollo and Dionysus.

In Chapter 6 we saw that the symbol is a union of conscious and unconscious elements; thus if Nietzsche's model is entirely identified with the conscious body, it cannot begin to generate that which enables the union of opposites. According to Jung, Nietzsche's model is an attempt to build a conscious structure '*against* the unconscious' (*SNZ*, II, p. 1250) and its main constituents – the *Übermensch* and the teachings of the Will to Power and Eternal Recurrence – are merely 'inventions' or 'bold attempts' of consciousness to deny the unconscious its expression. Just as God is the unifying symbol in Jung's model but a mere 'conscious invention' in Nietzsche's model, the Will to Power (which I interpreted in Chapter 4 to be Nietzsche's 'unifying principle', and 'the central organizing power' and 'power of adaptation': *BGE*, 242; cf. *WP*, 848) is demoted to a mere 'conscious invention' by Jung. Jung is critical of Nietzsche for rejecting the power of symbol (God) in favour of a mere sign (exemplified by the 'Will to Power'), a move that inevitably leads to the separation of opposites. The *Übermensch*, Eternal Recurrence and Will to Power, like

> any structure built over against the unconscious . . . no matter how bold, will always collapse because it has no feet, no roots. Only something that is rooted in the unconscious can live, because that is its origin.
>
> (*SNZ*, II, p. 1250)

According to Jung, only a symbol can unite the opposites, and 'a symbol is never an invention. It *happens* to man' (ibid., p. 1251).

In Chapter 7 I argued that the Self, as the telos of Jung's model, is predetermined and must be *discovered*, whereas the *Übermensch*, as the telos of Nietzsche's model, is not predetermined and must be *created*. We can now appreciate the significance of this difference for Jung. Nietzsche defines the *Übermensch* as that which the individual heroically endeavours to create beyond himself (*TSZ*, prologue, 3), but according to Jung, such a definition must be rejected outright.

This is because creativity is a notion that is validated by God alone, for only God can 'create beyond' Himself (*SNZ*, I, pp. 55, 61). The individual cannot generate creative processes; rather they must originate outside of the individual:

> You cannot rule them; they create what they choose . . . so creating something beyond ourselves is only a formulation which comes from the idea that we are creating. We are not creating. We are only instrumental in the creative process: it creates in us, through us.
>
> (ibid., p. 61; cf. p. 723; p. 675: 'creative power is almost
> a metaphysical concept')

According to Jung, the 'creative person' – who aspires to *Übermenschlichkeit* – is a 'victim' (ibid., p. 720), his life is defined by 'self-destruction' (ibid., p. 57; cf. p. 116), for 'if you know you are creative and enjoy being creative, you will be crucified afterwards, because anybody identified with God will be dismembered' (ibid., p. 58). Creativity is an autonomous process of the collective unconscious that cannot be consciously willed: it is 'discovered' working within the individual.[3] Nietzsche, in identifying the *Übermensch* with the capacity to 'create beyond himself', is criticized by Jung for attempting to make consciousness the overriding source of meaning. His model lacks the essential unconscious compensation, which engenders the symbol and appropriates the balance of opposites.

Neurotic Nietzsche

Far from realizing self-completion in the union of opposites, we can interpret the *Übermensch* as a worthy candidate for Jung's one-sided 'sick animal' (Jung, 1917/1926/1943, par. 32) – a description that could also be used to describe its author. Indeed, Jung interprets the *Übermensch* as a projection of Nietzsche's own pathology. Nietzsche's model is thereby construed as a 'symptom' of his own neurosis.[4] Thus we see that Nietzsche's rejection of God as a 'definite psychological fact' has repercussions not only for his intellectual model but also for the psychological model of his own mind – the two simply being different expressions of the same thing:

> If you knew what reality that fact possesses which has been called God, you would know that you could not possibly get away from it. But you have lost sight of it; you don't know what that thing means and so it gets you unconsciously, and then without knowing it you are transformed into God almighty, as happened to Nietzsche. It got into him to such an extent that he went crazy and signed his letters 'the dismembered Zagreus' or 'Christ Dionysus', because he became identical with the God he had eliminated.
>
> (*SNZ*, II, p. 903)

> [I]f he does not know what he has done by saying that God is dead, he can
> have an inflation of his whole personality. Then his unconscious will get
> inflated; he will be hampered by the continuous presence of God in the
> unconscious, which is of course the most terrible thing.
>
> (*SNZ*, I, p. 51; cf. *SNZ*, II, p. 929; p. 1519)

Nietzsche, by explicitly denying one opposite in the binary pair, initiates its
overwhelming compensation. By consciously focusing too much on the body,
Nietzsche has relegated its spiritual counterpart to the unconscious where it has
become autonomous and seeks continual expression. *Enantiodromia* is certainly
at play here. However, this is not the full extent of the matter for, as I have argued,
Nietzsche, by proclaiming the death of God, is not simply rejecting one opposite
in the binary pair, he is also rejecting the 'unifying' symbol, which regulates the
opposites. God is a symbol of the Self; it is therefore an affective archetypal
experience of unequalled numinosity and power. Any attempt to deny its need
for expression will inevitably lead to profound psychological disturbance (see
Chapter 6): to the onslaught of 'insanity' and 'destructive mass psychoses' (Jung,
1929, pars. 52, 53). According to Frey-Rohn, a healthy psyche is acquired only
when the 'fact' of God is accepted 'both externally and internally' (Frey-Rohn,
1988, p. 85). She maintains that Nietzsche failed to do this on both accounts.
(In terms of the scheme I am presenting, Nietzsche rejects the fact of God in
both his 'external' intellectual model and in his own 'internal' psychological
make-up.) Such failure, she notes, is expressed either in 'deflation and despair' or
the divination of the ego ('inflation'); in Nietzsche's case it was the latter, so that
'he overestimates his own personality to a dangerous extent, losing his detachment
from things human and claiming for himself the power that belongs to God alone'
(ibid.). According to a Jungian diagnosis, Nietzsche went insane because he
identified himself with the autonomous complex of a god-like being, with his
Übermensch, and literally became that 'man with absolutely superior consciousness' (*SNZ*, I, p. 350) or inflated ego. By identifying himself with the 'unifying
symbol' Nietzsche had effectively cut himself off from the vital regulating powers
that it possessed; he removed the possibility of relating to a reality autonomous
and external to himself (*SNZ*, II, p. 1174; cf. *TSZ*, III, 'The Convalescent', 3: 'For
me – how could there be an outside-of-me. There is no outside!'), and thereby
rejected the capacity for creation that, according to Jung, must come from this
external source (*SNZ*, I, p. 61; cf. II, p. 723).

Jung criticized Nietzsche for not acknowledging the unconscious at work
within him and for not attributing it with the creative and regulative power that
it deserves. As we saw in Chapter 5, the conscious and unconscious must interact
and compensate each other if the personality is to aspire towards 'definiteness,
wholeness and ripeness' (Jung, 1934a, par. 288). Nietzsche, by having an inflated
consciousness – in which 'consciousness takes too many unconscious contents
upon itself' (Jung, 1945/1948, par. 563) – is effectively denying its essential
interaction and compensation. That is, 'inflated consciousness . . . loses the faculty

of discrimination' (ibid.). Conscious and unconscious merge in an unhealthy relationship that denies their essential difference and dynamic interaction.

Thus Spoke Zarathustra forms the basis of Jung's critique of Nietzsche's model and his diagnosis of Nietzsche's psychological disturbance. Jung regards *TSZ* as a philosophical text and an unconscious account of Nietzsche's psychological disposition. This is because it expounds the central tenets of Nietzsche's teachings in a manner that is not rigid and 'intellectual' but more 'poetical', and in a manner that grants expression to the unconscious: '*Zarathustra* is a most passionate confession from beginning to end, and moreover it is an experience: his life flows into these chapters' (*SNZ*, I, p. 461; cf. 483); in *TSZ* 'it will be shown clearly how the thing that was denied was working in Nietzsche' (*SNZ*, II, p. 931). According to Jung, *TSZ* will demonstrate the affective experience of the unconscious at work in its author, in both its personal manifestation (Nietzsche's 'shadow') and its collective archetypal manifestation, as the anima and Self or 'God-image'. In Chapter 8 we saw Nietzsche's model anticipate Jung's in terms of the collective unconscious and the individuation process. Now I shall describe how Nietzsche's own psychology can be diagnosed according to the Jungian model. The results of this diagnosis will go towards explaining Jung's reluctance to acknowledge Nietzsche as a serious influence on his model.

Nietzsche's rejection of his shadow and anima

In Chapter 8 we saw that Jung integrates Nietzsche's early formulations of the Apollinian and Dionysian impulses into his own typological theory that he uses to diagnose the individual's conscious orientation (psychological 'type') and unconscious orientation (*shadow*). We also saw that Nietzsche adopts a similar method of diagnosis in his examination of Heraclitus and the pre-Socratic philosophers. However, to suggest that Nietzsche therefore anticipated Jung's whole typological theory is excessive. According to Jung, Nietzsche was aware only of the conscious orientation and not its compensating unconscious counter-part. Thus, although we see Nietzsche refer to Heraclitus as an eternal intuitive type (*PTAG*, 5), he does not refer to the unconscious orientation – in particular, Heraclitus' need to promote a more 'sensationalist' disposition. More significantly, however, Jung believes that Nietzsche fails to acknowledge his own unconscious orientation working within him.

Jung deduces that Nietzsche was an introverted intuitive type: 'Nietzsche in the time when he wrote *Zarathustra* was absolutely identical with intuition, using only that function, to the very exhaustion of his brain' (*SNZ*, II, p. 1082; see also *SNZ*, II, cf. p. 1195; Jung, 1921, par. 146). In terms of his work

> Nietzsche as an intuitive simply touches upon a thing and off he goes. He does not dwell upon the subject, though in the long run one can say he really does dwell upon it by amplification. But he doesn't deal with things in a logical way, going into the intellectual process of elucidation; he just catches

such an intuition on the wing and leaves it, going round and round amplifying, so that in the end we get a complete picture but by intuitive means, not by logical means.

(*SNZ*, II, p. 1083; cf. p. 1047; I, p. 81)

Jung's interpretation provides an answer to why Nietzsche does not offer a thorough definition of the *Übermensch*: because Nietzsche is too dependent on his intuitive function, the central themes of his project escape thorough intellectual examination. I believe, it is Nietzsche's profound intuition and consequent lack of sensation (i.e. that which is concerned with factual detail, 'rational moderation and conciseness': Jung, 1921, par. 242) that allows us to regard him as anticipating Jungian theory at the same time as Jung rejects him as an explicit influence. In other words, Nietzsche's intuition enables him to have great insight into the themes of psychology, but his lack of sensation prevents him from consolidating his insights into convincing theory. Jung is therefore reluctant to endorse Nietzsche because he 'doesn't realize the full extent of what he is saying and moves on quickly' (*SNZ*, II, p. 1047).[5]

Jung gave the name 'shadow' to the unconscious orientation. Although, in Chapter 8, we saw Nietzsche intuit the existence of this aspect of the personality and even call it the 'shadow', Jung maintains that he does not realize its full implications, including the fact that it is actively working within him. This is because Nietzsche's inflated personality and consequent need to become 'something marvellous and great' (the *Übermensch*) forbids him from accepting that which is inferior and lowly, and thus from accepting both opposites in the binary pair (see *SNZ*, II, p. 1292). Jung equates human greatness with wholeness, and this is achieved only through the union of opposites. Jung reminds us:

> The superior thing can only be created if it is built upon the inferior thing. The inferior thing must be accepted in order to build the superior . . . You must not be afraid of the dirt; one has to accept the ugliest man if one wants to create.
>
> (*SNZ*, II, p. 1006; cf. I, p. 124)

Furthermore, Jung notes that when Nietzsche talks about the *Übermensch* (in terms of 'creative love'), he 'gets an intuition of imminent danger, of a thunder-cloud: namely, the possibility of the revolution of the inferior man or the impossibility of accepting the ugliest man' (ibid.; cf. *TSZ*, II, 'Of the Compassionate').[6]

As much as Nietzsche is identified with Zarathustra, his 'great man', he is also affected by the compensation of the shadow, the 'ugliest man'. The former overwhelms him in his inflation and the latter overwhelms him to the extent that

> Nietzsche used every imaginable trick ['and the most acrobatic feats', *SNZ*, II, p. 1504] to defend himself against the onslaught. He belittled the shadow and made light of him, he ridiculed him and projected the shadow into

everybody. [As a result . . .] he accuses and criticizes everybody, the mediocrity of the world and of all those qualities which adhere to Nietzsche himself.

(*SNZ*, II, p. 1361; cf. I, p. 120)

Nietzsche's critique of all that is mediocre in the world is therefore interpreted by Jung as a projection of all that Nietzsche unconsciously reviles as mediocre in himself (cf. ibid., p. 1343; p. 1457; p. 1113; pp. 989–990). To support this claim Jung, throughout *SNZ*, refers to passages in *TSZ* in which Nietzsche is particularly drawn to his shadow, which he would not have been had the world been genuinely mediocre and not made as such by his own projections. For example, in the chapter 'Of Passing By', we are told that Zarathustra comes to the gate of the great city 'unawares'. His reasons for entering the city are made all the more questionable when we note that in the preceding chapters he has been reviling the small people who live in small houses in the city where he has to stoop low to enter. Jung interprets Zarathustra's movements in terms of an unconscious draw or 'secret wish', 'fascination' and 'unholy attraction' to get in contact with the inferior man (*SNZ*, II, pp. 1389, 1390), for 'the city is the connection with all that rabble, the crowd of miserable non-entities that he has reviled, and yet he cannot let them go' (ibid.). Furthermore, this unusual need to visit the city is acknowledged by the 'foaming fool' whom Zarathustra meets at the gate to the city. The fool says to Zarathustra:

Oh Zarathustra, here is the great city: here you have nothing to seek and everything to lose. Why do you want to wade through this mire? Take pity on your feet! Spit rather upon the gate of the city – turn back!' Jung praises the fool, this 'shadow', for being 'very helpful in telling Zarathustra not to repeat the same nonsense, not to go into the city to revile those people because he is really reviling himself.

(*SNZ*, II, p. 1395)

By failing to accept his shadow-personality, Nietzsche has effectively fallen at the first stage in the development of the Self. Nietzsche fails to incorporate the negative element in the union of opposites; he promotes only that which is consciously strong and superior. He does not attempt to exercise his emotional strength, which would enable the overcoming of the inferior shadow, and because this capacity remains dormant within him, Nietzsche can also be accused of failing in his quest to become *übermenschlich*, for, as we saw earlier, the test of emotional strength marks that point where 'commonplace beings perish' (*WP*, 881). According to my interpretation of Jung's critique, therefore, the *Übermensch*, far from being the whole self, is merely a one-sided inflation that ignores its compensating opposite, the inferior shadow. There is no difference between the *Übermensch* and the commonplace being (cf. *SNZ*, I, p. 336; II, p. 1231); for the great man is he who unites both inferior and superior. Because the *Übermensch* promotes the superior at the expense of the inferior, it is an inferior entity itself – as is Nietzsche, for he is the inflated embodiment of the *Übermensch*. Likewise, the Will to Power, as the most fundamental teaching of the *Übermensch*, is merely a conscious power-attitude that Nietzsche constructs to conceal his unconscious inferior feelings within him – for 'the more one has feelings of inferiority, the more one has a power attitude, and the more one has a power attitude, the more one has feelings of inferiority' (*SNZ*, II, p. 1213). Indeed, Nietzsche's dependence on the power attitude may appear indisputable. He tells us that 'the world is will to power and nothing besides! And you yourselves are also this will to power – and nothing besides!' (*WP*, 1067). Indeed, Jung interprets Nietzsche's great dependence on 'the power aspect of things' as 'a great mistake', and the consequence of Nietzsche's being 'blindfolded by his own complex . . . he most beautiful inferiority complex you can imagine' (*SNZ*, II, p. 1213). He thus

> makes tremendous noise with his words . . . to make an impression, to show what he is and to make everybody believe it. So no one can conclude as to the abysmal intensity of his feelings of inferiority.
> (ibid., p. 1214; cf. I, pp. 28–30; II, p. 1255)

If Nietzsche had recognized the negative projections of his shadow as his own, he might have progressed significantly in his own process of individuation towards Selfhood and the union of opposites. Earlier I suggested that one encounters the anima in the individuation process after the shadow has been successfully incorporated into consciousness. If this is correct, then it is no surprise that Jung believes Nietzsche also fails to acknowledge his own anima. The reason behind Nietzsche's failure to incorporate and relate to his anima is no different from that in the case of his shadow. Nietzsche is utterly unconscious of his anima because he is completely identified with it (*SNZ*, I, p. 734; see also Jung, 1955–1956, par. 330) and 'if one identifies with the anima, one is in trouble, neurotic, a sack full of moods, a most unaccountable being, most unreliable – everything wrong under the sun' (*SNZ*, II, p. 1048). Jung does not examine Nietzsche's anima to the same extent as his shadow; instead he simply illustrates his point by citing analogous instances from *TSZ*.[7] Perhaps the most considered illustration from Jung is his response to the chapter 'The Dance Song', where Zarathustra comes across several girls dancing in a meadow. Jung interprets these girls as 'a plurality of anima figures' (*SNZ*, II, p. 1152), which he regards as 'a very particular condition of the anima', for 'the anima by definition is always one' (only the female animus is plural). Jung questions Nietzsche's unusual 'collective' disposition towards his anima, and confirms that his anima is in 'a very primitive condition, inferior' and 'very unconscious':

> A multiplicity of anima figures is only to be met with in cases where the individual is utterly unconscious of his anima. In a man who is completely identical with the anima, you might find that plurality, but the moment he

becomes conscious of that figure, she assumes a personality and is definitely one . . . you can conclude that Nietzsche/Zarathustra is profoundly unconscious of the fact of the anima.

(SNZ, II, pp. 1152–1153)

Insane Nietzsche

Nietzsche fails in the process of individuation (to acknowledge both the shadow and anima) and consequently cannot realize the Self within him. He is resigned to a neurotic life that is grounded in continual psychological disturbance, in imbalance and one-sidedness. Moreover, according to Jung's diagnosis of Nietzsche, this neurosis must inevitably lead to the onslaught of 'insanity' and 'destructive mass psychoses' (Jung, 1929, pars. 52, 53), as the unconscious threatens to overcompensate.

Just as Jung uses *TSZ* to formulate his diagnosis of Nietzsche's neurosis, he cites many passages in *TSZ* to demonstrate Nietzsche's encroaching insanity, the full realization of which was to occur three years after he wrote *TSZ*, in early 1889, when he wrote his last work, *EH*. One significant passage of *TSZ* cited by Jung is from the prologue where Zarathustra says to the dying tightrope walker, 'Thy soul will be dead even sooner than thy body' (*TSZ*, prologue, 6). According to Jung,

> This is the prophetic word [that] prophesizes Nietzsche's fate [for] his soul died in 1889 when his general paralysis began, but [his body] lived on for eleven years more. So the fate of that rope-dancer symbolically anticipates the fate that overcame Nietzsche – Nietzsche himself is the rope-dancer and the same fate will befall him.

(SNZ, I, p. 115; cf. p. 136)

Before the tightrope walker begins his fateful walk along the rope that 'was stretched between two towers' (*TSZ*, prologue, 6), Zarathustra tells us that the rope represents mankind's journey towards the *Übermensch*, for 'man is a rope, fastened between animal and Superman – a rope over an abyss. A dangerous going-across, a dangerous wayfaring' (ibid., 4). According to Jung, the tightrope walker's attempt to cross the rope is 'the reality test' of the *Übermensch*; it is 'Nietzsche's attempt to become the Superman' (*SNZ*, I, p. 112). So, when the walker falls and dies, Jung would have us construe the *Übermensch* as an impossible goal, one that will never be realized.[8]

But perhaps the most eloquent of prophecies that Jung cites occurs later in *TSZ*, in a chapter called 'The Prophet'. Here Zarathustra recounts a dream where he is in a hill-fortress of death. Nietzsche writes:

> Up there I guarded death's coffins: the musty vaults stood full of these symbols of death's victory. Life overcome regarded me from glass coffins. I

breathed the odour of dust-covered eternities: my soul lay sultry and dust-covered. And who could have ventilated his soul there? Brightness of midnight was all around me; solitude crouched beside it; and, as a third, the rasping silence of death, the worst of my companions. I carried keys, the rustiest of all keys; and I could open with them the most creaking of all doors . . . And I turned the key and tugged at the door and exerted myself. But it did not open by so much as a finger's breadth: Then a raging wind tore the door asunder: whistling, shrilling and piercing it threw me to a black coffin: And in the roaring and whistling and shrilling, the coffin burst asunder and vomited forth a thousand peals of laughter. And from a thousand masks of children, angels, owls, fools, and child-sized butterflies it laughed and mocked and roared at me.

(*TSZ*, II, 'The Prophet')

Nietzsche adds: 'Zarathustra did not yet know the interpretation of his dream.' Zarathustra is in hell itself, where he watches the graves in order to bring up a fearful secret hidden below. When the door flies open, we see that the secret is a merciless laughing wind. According to Jung, this wind is insanity itself (*SNZ*, II, p. 1226). Insanity is the secret, the utter destruction of his mind. Jung proceeds to tells us that Nietzsche, when he was about 15 years of age, already had such an experience (ibid., p. 1227). He tells us in his autobiography (though this is missed out in the English translation) that he had a dream about taking a walk in the night with his friend, Wilhelm Pindar (and Jung comments that something similar undoubtedly happened to him in reality). In the dream they were walking in a dark wood when they heard a terrible cry issuing from a nearby lunatic asylum. They then go astray in the wood and meet a wild hunter who suddenly picks up a whistle and blows the most awful whistling sound, causing Nietzsche to lose consciousness. Now, this shrieking and whistling from the *dream*-lunatic asylum and the hunter are prophetic cries that warn Nietzsche of the impending *reality* of the lunatic asylum. Jung interprets the hunter who approaches Nietzsche as Wotan, the old wind god breaking forth, the god of inspiration, of madness, intoxication and wildness. The shrieking and whistling of the wind in a nocturnal wood, that dark and impenetrable place, is symbolic of the unconscious. It is thus the unconscious itself that bursts forth and forces the doors to fly open with a thousand laughters. It is a horrible foreboding of his insanity, and Nietzsche admits that he does not know the interpretation of his experience. Instead, Nietzsche twists the meaning of Zarathustra's dream to sound favourable to him. He interprets Zarathustra himself as the wind, and concludes that he has dreamt of his enemies, but he does not acknowledge the enemy to be himself, his unconscious.

According to Jung, Nietzsche's insanity is fully realized in his last work *Ecce Homo*. Frey-Rohn notes that in *EH*

Nietzsche's identification with the symbol of the self reaches its climax . . . the entire piece is the expression of his self-advancement, his untimeliness and his corresponding withdrawal from contemporary events. Loathing for humanity alternates with glorification of his own greatness . . . [*EH*] demonstrates both the *strongest possible claims to power and the most hopeless feeling of impotence* . . . It was clearly the *suffering of an ego overpowered by the greater personality*.

(Frey-Rohn, 1988, pp. 255, 264)[9]

Nietzsche's insistence on self-glorification and his conviction that he had a mission to fulfil is most apparent in this work. Nietzsche, after all, comes 'from the heights that no bird ever reached in its flight, [he] knows abysses into which no foot ever strayed' ('Why I Write Such Good Books', 3). Aside from those chapters which address the content of Nietzsche's other main works, the remaining four chapters are arrogantly entitled 'Why I am So Wise', 'Why I am So Clever', 'Why I Write Such Good Books' and 'Why I am a Destiny'. Furthermore, in the final chapter, where he refers to his *world-historical importance*, Nietzsche proclaims that the arrogance he was fully aware of possessing should not be interpreted negatively, but rather as positive proof of his greatness.[10]

In *EH* Nietzsche equates his greatness with Dionysus. His neurotic delusions of self-importance are caused, according to Jung, by his complete identification with his god Dionysus.[11] At the start of *EH* Nietzsche describes himself as a 'disciple of the philosopher Dionysus', and the very end sees Dionysus declare war on the crucified Christ. Furthermore, at the time of writing *EH* Nietzsche began to sign his letters 'the dismembered Zagreus' or 'Christ Dionysus' (*SNZ*, II, p. 903). One letter in particular reveals his disturbing state of god-like delusion. On 6 January 1889, Nietzsche writes to Jakob Burckhardt:

Actually in the end I would much rather be a Basle professor than God; but I have not dared push my private egoism so far as to desist for its sake from the creation of the world. You see, one must make sacrifices, however and wherever one lives.

(Nietzsche, 1969, p. 346)

According to Jung's model of opposites and its critical 'diagnosis', Nietzsche's model fails to unite the opposites and, as a result, far from attaining Selfhood in the union of opposites, Nietzsche is an 'un-individuated' and neurotic person. In Chapter 10 I shall criticize Jung's interpretations and put forward reasons why, I believe, Jung misunderstands both Nietzsche and his model. We shall see that Nietzsche's model does not fail for the reasons Jung puts forward.

Nietzsche's absolution

A metacritique of Jung's critique of Nietzsche's model

Nietzsche: 'Do not, above all, confound me with what I am not!'

(*EH*, 'Foreword', 1)

According to Jung, Nietzsche's model fails to unite the opposites for two reasons: it is one-sided, as it promotes one opposite at the expense of the other (the conscious body over the unconscious spirit) and it lacks the essential unifying symbol (God), which would appropriate the balance between opposites. Jung's evaluation of Nietzsche's model is incorrect. I intend to show in this chapter that Nietzsche's model does acknowledge a spiritual, creative realm outside the body, and that this vital principle works symbolically to unite the opposites. We shall also see that Nietzsche's insanity was not, as Jung claims, the result of a one-sided ego-inflation. Our analysis of their affinities in Chapter 8 uncovered an ambivalence and resistance in Jung's reception of Nietzsche's model. In this chapter, we shall try to reunite their models in the face of an even more explicit resistance from Jung. I shall try to diagnose this resistance in Chapter 11, by hypothesizing an unconscious personal need on Jung's part to dissociate himself from Nietzsche in his work.

Jung praises Nietzsche for discovering the existence of the collective and autonomous unconscious, and criticizes him for not admitting a spiritual realm outside of the body, of which it was unconscious. Jung escapes contradiction here by maintaining that Nietzsche only 'intuits' the existence of the unconscious: he does not grasp its essential meaning, and therefore does not acknowledge its implications – in particular, the fact that it is active within himself, that he is identifiable with more than mere 'body' (*SNZ*, II, p. 1147). Although Jung's interpretation is at first sight sound, it is untenable. Nietzsche certainly intuits the autonomous unconscious of Jung's model, but his insight into the dynamics of the unconscious is more than intuitive. Nietzsche is aware of the essential meaning of the unconscious, and not only 'admits a spiritual realm outside of the body' but also critically applies his model to himself. Let us now consider these claims in turn.

The spiritual realm in Nietzsche's model

Jung is too hasty in denying the spiritual component of Nietzsche's model. Indeed, Nietzsche clearly acknowledges the value of the spiritual realm. More specifically, he gives it the same value as the physical body; he acknowledges the autonomous unconscious (which, in Jungian terms, correlates with the existence of God); and he is hospitable to the religious viewpoint.

Jung is exaggerating when he says that, for Nietzsche, spirit becomes a mere 'plaything of the body' and is not autonomous of it. The passage that he cites to support his claim is *TSZ*, I, 'On the Despisers of the Body', where Nietzsche writes:

> The enlightened man says: I am the body entirely, and nothing beside; and soul is only a word for something in the body . . . 'Spirit', is also an instrument of your body, a little instrument and toy of your great intelligence.

Admittedly, Nietzsche here makes the spirit subordinate to the body. However, Jung fails to acknowledge the particular context in which Nietzsche is writing this passage. Nietzsche is writing to those metaphysicians and 'despisers of the body' who wrongly promote the spirit over the body; he therefore purposely accentuates the value of the body and plays down that of the spirit in an act of compensation to redress the balance (something that Jung would have endorsed). Nietzsche in fact promotes spirit and body equally; so that, contrary to Jung's own argument, we see Jung cite this chapter again a mere two weeks/seminars later to demonstrate Nietzsche's anticipation of the Self. Jung is adamant that Nietzsche argues for a 'sort of thing-in-itself behind the psychological phenomenon' (*SNZ*, I, p. 391). Now, a thing-in-itself, by definition, cannot be identified with the body. Indeed, in the same chapter Nietzsche writes: 'The Self . . . rules and is also the Ego's ruler . . . it says to itself . . . I am the Ego's leading-string and I prompt its conceptions'. Nietzsche clearly postulates here something beyond the ego; something, indeed, that would seem to have a 'spiritual' status. So the Nietzschean Self is not, as Jung argues, identified with consciousness alone. When Nietzsche writes that the Self, as 'an unknown [unconscious] sage', 'lives in your body, he is your body', he is not referring to a body that is merely ego-conscious or 'physiological'; the body, for Nietzsche, is also unconscious, it contains a spiritual realm that acts upon consciousness.[1] Jung is wrong to claim that Nietzsche seeks to overvalue the body by elevating it to a spiritual level. Rather, Nietzsche's position is similar to Jung's: they both argue for a spiritual realm that is contained within the body and yet separate from it. In line with Nietzsche's claim that the Self 'lives in your body, he is your body' and that 'the Self seeks with the eyes of sense, it listens too with the ears of the spirit', Jung admits that 'the spirit is the life of the body seen from within and the body the outward manifestation of the life of the spirit – the two being really one' (Jung, 1928/1931, par. 195). For both Nietzsche and Jung, the body and the spirit are united in the realization of the Self; they are two different (and equal) ways of expressing the whole Self.

The spirit in the body is the unconscious, and in Chapter 8 we saw Nietzsche and Jung agree on the nature of this unconscious realm as collective and autonomous. According to Jung, 'We cannot tell whether God and the unconscious are two different entities' (Jung, 1952b, par. 757); God is that affective autonomous unconscious force within the individual that encourages personal growth and development. It is therefore not illogical to conclude that God is also at work within the depths of Nietzsche's model, within the autonomous unconscious realm of the 'body', within the *Übermensch* itself. If this is correct, then Nietzsche's model has the reconciliatory symbol that, according to Jung, makes possible the union of opposites. Against this view Jung cites Nietzsche as proclaiming the death of God. Jung argues that by eliminating God from his model, Nietzsche is without the unifying symbol and his project must inevitably fail. However, Jung fails to understand that in proclaiming the death of God, Nietzsche is only proclaiming the death of the Christian God, which he considers to be a false idea of God.

According to Nietzsche, Christianity has become disconnected from its authentic values: 'We see the religious community of Christianity shaken to its lowest foundations; the faith in God has collapsed' (GS, 358). Thus, the Christian God is dead because He is no longer feared. This means He can no longer spur the individual on to acts of spiritual strength and growth; the task of personal salvation thereby loses its significance. By adhering to the Christian God, we deny God's essential attributes, and thus worship a false god. Thus Nietzsche writes: 'What sets *us* apart is not that we recognize no God . . . but that we find that which has been reverenced as God not godlike' (*AC*, 47; cf. 16, 18). Dixon (1999) argues that, for Nietzsche, belief in God constitutes an existential affirmation, and not a matter of adherence to the central tenets of faith and ritual. Nietzsche is particularly appalled by the values promoted in the Christian faith, for he regards it as having degenerated into a superficial religion of sentimentality. Nietzsche is disgusted that

> anti-Christians through and through, still call themselves Christians today and go to Communion . . . Being a soldier, being a judge, being a patriot; defending oneself; preserving one's honour; desiring to seeks one's advantage; being *proud*. The practice of every hour, every instinct, every valuation which leads to *action* is today anti-Christian: what a *monster of falsity* modern man must be that he is none the less *not ashamed* to be called Christian!
>
> (*AC*, 38)

Nietzsche rejects the Christian ideal 'not with the aim of destroying it but only of putting an end to its tyranny and clearing the way for new ideals, for *more robust* ideals' (*WP*, 361). Nietzsche is an atheist only in so far as he rejects what he considers to be a false idea of God; such a rejection initiates in Nietzsche the need to find the true God. Nietzsche has not killed God; Christianity has killed Him. The true God will be found in the revaluation of values. The more robust ideal to which Nietzsche refers is a return to a noble religion, a noble spiritual strength, which is not a dogma but a way of life (Dixon, 1999, p. 118). Nietzsche is, of course, referring to the Will to Power. Nietzsche tells us that God is found in the Will to Power (cf. *WP*, 639, 1037). The Will to Power generates the energy for life; it is 'life at its highest potency' (*WP*, 639). For Nietzsche, God is equivalent to life, and God is not yet dead, for: 'Life is only lying hidden, in prison, it has not yet withered away and died' (*UM*, II, 10).

Jung is thus wrong to assert that Nietzsche lacks the unifying symbol because his God is dead. In fact the positions of Jung and Nietzsche are similar. Jung supports Nietzsche's view that Christianity's ideal is sentimental and weak. Jung writes:

> Christian civilization has proved hollow to a terrifying degree: it is all veneer, but the inner man has remained untouched and therefore unchanged. His soul is out of key with his external beliefs; in his soul the Christian has not kept pace with external developments. Yes, everything is to be found outside – . . . in Church and Bible – but never inside.
>
> (Jung, 1944, par. 12; cf. Jung, 1938/1940, par. 52)

In this sense Jung, by the same token, admits that God is dead; and he too turns to a revaluation of values grounded in psychology:

> I am not, however, addressing myself to the happy possessors of faith, but to those many people for whom the light has gone out, the mystery has faded, and God is dead . . . To gain an understanding of religious matters, probably all that is left us today is the psychological approach.
>
> (Jung, 1938/1940, par. 148; cited in Bishop, 1999a, p. 224)[2]

Jung's interpretation of Nietzsche is ill considered. First, he takes Nietzsche's argument out of context and wrongly concludes that the body is made superior to spirit. Then he admits a position contrary to his main thesis: that God and his 'contents' are present within Nietzsche's model. What is more, he does so in a manner that suggests he does not think this particularly relevant. That is, he mentions this position only briefly in response to a question raised by a member of his seminar; he does not offer the information spontaneously, and he does not argue through the significant (and potentially devastating) implications it has for his overall thesis and criticism of Nietzsche. Jung interprets Nietzsche's god as Dionysus, the god of the body, and in Chapter 8 we saw that Jung does not acknowledge Nietzsche's later usage of the term 'Dionysus' as 'passion controlled' (*WP*, 1050) – that is, a union of Apollo and Dionysus; Jung recognizes only his earlier formulation as 'impassioned dissolution' (Jung, 1936a, par. 118), that one-sided 'barbarian' (Jung, 1921, par. 346). This is relevant to the current argument, for it is Jung's interpretation of Nietzsche's Dionysus that causes him to find in Nietzsche's model a mere sign and not the required symbol. In other words, a symbol requires both conscious and unconscious elements. But this finds full expression not in the Dionysus of *BT* (1872) but in the Dionysus of *WP*, 1050 (1888). If Jung had acknowledged this later formulation, he might have also acknowledged Nietzsche's reconciliatory symbol.

Jung further misinterprets Nietzsche as failing to acknowledge the value of religion. Jung insists that in Nietzsche 'the religious viewpoint is entirely overlooked and is replaced by the aesthetic' (Jung, 1921, par. 231) so that (in *BT*) 'Nietzsche quite forgets that in the struggle between Apollo and Dionysus and their ultimate reconciliation the problem for the Greeks was never an aesthetic one, but was essentially religious'. Jung then attempts to correct Nietzsche by claiming that 'Greek tragedy arose out of an originally religious ceremony'. However, these comments are strongly at variance with the fact that Nietzsche recognized the religious origins of Greek tragedy. As M. S. Silk and J. P. Stern note: 'It is in the area of Greek religion, especially religious attitudes to life, that Nietzsche's reinterpretation of Greece has had the greatest impact on classical studies' (Silk and Stern, 1981, p. 159; cited in Dixon, 1999, p. 67). Moreover, they note that Nietzsche

> devotes as much space to Greek religion as to any other aspect of Greece, tragedy included. Above all, much of the discussion of tragedy itself is vitally concerned with religion . . . Nietzsche affirms the generic religious ground and the 'theological' significance of tragedy.
>
> (Silk and Stern, 1981, p. 265)[3]

Jung's claim that Nietzsche replaced the religious viewpoint with the aesthetic also fails to recognize the profound relationship between the two in Nietzsche's work. So that, when Nietzsche refers to 'art' in *BT*, he refers to 'art in the metaphysical, broadest and profoundest sense' (*BT*, 15). Art, for Nietzsche, has a religious context; it is a 'higher conception of art'.[4]

It should be apparent that Nietzsche does not fail to acknowledge the value of the spiritual realm; his model does not identify solely with the body, and he expresses the need for a noble religion, where God equates with life. This means that Nietzsche is not as far as Jung suggests he is from establishing the creative capacity or reconciliatory symbol required to unite the opposites. Indeed, it is my contention that the symbol is very much present in Nietzsche's model, though Jung is not ready to admit as much. However, Jung does quietly acknowledge that Nietzsche had not got rid of God completely – which, despite Jung's protests, means that the symbol is present yet hidden:

> It is a funny thing, however, that throughout the whole of *Zarathustra* you get a feeling as if this god whom he calls dead were not absolutely dead. He is somehow lurking in the background as the great unknowable one of whom you should not speak . . . he is taboo . . . Nietzsche's God exists somewhere and has contents but he must be careful not to mention them.
>
> (*SNZ*, I, p. 72; see also p. 843; cf. pp. 1515, 1013)

Jung further contradicts himself in his seminars on *TSZ* when he suggests that the symbol is indeed present within Nietzsche's work. Jung first maintains (on 18 May 1938) that the *Übermensch* and Eternal Recurrence are merely 'inventions' and 'bold attempts' of consciousness to deny the unconscious its expression, and they cannot constitute 'symbols' because 'a symbol is never a [conscious] invention' (*SNZ*, II, p. 1250) – it is unconscious and '*happens* to man'. But later (2 November 1938) Jung claims that the *Übermensch* and Eternal Recurrence have 'prevailed for many centuries . . . the idea of the eternal return is as old as mankind practically' (*SNZ*, II, p. 1388). This second passage gives Nietzsche's ideas archetypal status; they now constitute unconscious symbols. Furthermore, Jung interprets Zarathustra as an archetypal saving symbol, for 'Zarathustra appears [in *TSZ*] in the moment when something has happened which made his presence necessary . . . [he is] a new revelation, to give birth to a new truth' (*SNZ*, I, p. 24; cf. Jung's description of the 'third thing' as 'a new level of being, a new situation': Jung, 1916/1957, par. 189). And this archetypal 'birth' and 'new truth' can refer only to the *Übermensch*, Will to Power, and Eternal Recurrence – the teachings of Zarathustra the prophet.

If we are right about Nietzsche's promoting a spiritual realm, then Jung is wrong to charge his model with one-sidedness, and as lacking the principle necessary for uniting the opposites. By the same token, Jung cannot conclude that Nietzsche's insanity was the result of this disposition to one-sidedness. According to Jung, Nietzsche went mad because he could not recognize the unconscious as an autonomous realm within him; instead he identified directly with it, thereby elevating body to the level of spirit (inflation). We have found, however, that Nietzsche did distinguish between the body and spirit and attributed equal value to both of them. Moreover, as I shall now argue, Nietzsche critically applied his model to himself; that is, he did not have an ego-inflation, because he was able to differentiate himself (his ego) from the collective 'spiritual' realm.

Jung's misdiagnosis: Nietzsche critically applies his model to himself

According to Jung, Nietzsche had a 'pathological' case of ego-inflation that led to the 'splitting' of his mind.[5] This, Jung believes, is directly related to Nietzsche's 'innate weakness of personality' – that is, his having an ego so weak that is incapable of distinguishing what properly belongs to itself from what belongs to the objective transpersonal psyche (Jung, 1938/1940, pars. 144, 145). Jung argues that, when dealing with extreme cases of inflation such as Nietzsche's, 'it is far more necessary to strengthen and consolidate the ego than to understand and assimilate the products of the unconscious' (Jung, 1934/1950, par. 621) and this is possible only when a critical line of demarcation is drawn between the ego and the unconscious (Jung, 1951, par. 44; Jung, 1928b, par. 381). However, according to Jung, Nietzsche lacked an adequate capacity for critical discrimination, self-knowledge and self-criticism.

In his essay 'On the Psychology of the Unconscious' (1917/1926/1943), Jung observes that 'the only thing' that could have helped Nietzsche avoid his 'transformation into a superhuman entity' was 'cautious self-criticism' (Jung, 1917/1926/1943, par. 41). He continues to note that: 'Nietzsche, as a philologist, could have adduced a few obvious classical parallels which would certainly have calmed his mind'. Both of these comments are shallow, and demonstrate a serious lack of judgement on Jung's part – for Nietzsche demonstrates precisely those things that Jung claims he lacks. Not only was Nietzsche exceptionally self-critical,[6] but also he was aware of the dangers of ego-inflation, and even cites historical examples to warn the reader of such dangers! Patricia Dixon, in *Sailing a Deeper Night* (1999), cites sufficient evidence to clear Nietzsche of the Jungian charge of inflation and neurotic one-sidedness (pp. 263–266). Following her lead will, in effect, enable us to admit the possibility of Nietzsche's unhindered development towards Selfhood.

In *Ecce Homo*, Nietzsche insists that the journey toward self-realization should not proceed too quickly, in order to protect the integrity of ego consciousness:

> The entire surface of consciousness – consciousness *is* a surface – has to be kept clear of any of the great imperatives. Even the grand words, the grand attitudes must be guarded against! All of them represent a danger that the instinct will 'understand itself' too early.
>
> (*EH*, 'Why I Am So Clever', 9; cf. *WS*, 297)

This argument runs throughout Nietzsche's work, and can be seen as early as 1873, where Nietzsche insists on the need for self-possession in both the philosopher and dramatic artist (*PTAG*, 3). In *BT* Nietzsche warns of the dangers of promoting the Dionysus at the expense of Apollo. The strict balance between Apollo and Dionysus is particularly relevant to self-knowledge. For Nietzsche warns that excessive knowledge of the unconscious, which cannot be contained by consciousness (i.e. Dionysus without Apollo), will throw individuals into the destructive abyss of their own mental downfall:

> Wisdom, and particularly Dionysian wisdom, is an unnatural abomination; that he who by means of his knowledge plunges nature into the abyss of destruction must also suffer the dissolution of nature in his own person.
>
> (*BT*, 9)

Indeed, Nietzsche later insists that 'the god of Delos' (Apollo) is 'necessary to heal your dithyrambic madness!' (*BT*, 25). This is made all the more relevant to our argument when we note that over the doors of the temple of Apollo at Delphi two commandments were inscribed: 'Know Thyself' and 'Nothing in Excess'.

In *HAH*, Nietzsche's warnings against the dangers of ego-inflation are most explicit. The following passage alone is enough to put Jung's judgement in doubt:

It is in any event a dangerous sign when a man is assailed by awe of himself
. . . when the sacrificial incense which is properly rendered only to a god,
penetrates the brain of the genius, so that his head begins to swim and he
comes to regard himself as something supra-human. The consequences that
slowly result are: the feeling of irresponsibility, of exceptional rights,
the belief that he confers a favour by his mere presence, insane rage when
anyone attempts even to compare him with others, let alone to rate him
beneath them, or to draw attention to lapses in his work. Because he ceases to
practise criticism of himself, at last one pinion after the other falls out of his
plumage . . . in the case of every 'genius' who believes in his own divinity
the poison shows itself to the same degree that the 'genius' grows old: one
may recall, for example, the case of Napoleon, whose nature certainly grew
into the mighty unity that sets him apart from all men of modern times
precisely through his belief in himself and his star . . . until in the end,
however, this same belief went over into an almost insane fatalism, robbed
him of his acuteness and swiftness of perception, and became the cause of his
destruction.

(*HAH*, 164)

Here Nietzsche not only underlines the need for self-criticism in the avoidance of
ego-inflation, but also cites the historical example of Napoleon to support and
justify his argument.

Jung's judgement on Nietzsche's failure to refer to historical precedents is
further confounded when we note that Nietzsche explicitly promotes the study of
history as offering endless opportunities to explicate the workings and conclusions
of psychological theory:

Direct observation is not nearly sufficient for us to know ourselves: we require
history, for the past continues to flow within us in a hundred waves; we
ourselves are, indeed, nothing but that which at every moment we experience
of this continued flowing.

(*AOM*, 223; cf. *GS*, 357, 377, 83; *BGE*, 224)

Indeed, in addition to the example of Napoleon, which is the most significant
historical allusion he makes to ego-inflation, Nietzsche, in *BT*, addresses the
specific problem of ego-inflation with reference to the Greeks and Titans. After
exclaiming that individuation knows but one law – '*measure*', which demands
'self-knowledge' in order to maintain it – Nietzsche makes a distinction between,
on the one hand, the Greeks, who insist 'know thyself' and 'nothing in excess' and,
on the other hand, the 'overweening pride and excess' of the Titans and barbarians
who 'succumbed to the self-oblivion of the Dionysian states, forgetting the
precepts of Apollo' (*BT*, 4).[7]

Jung concludes his discussion of Nietzsche's ego-inflation by describing it in terms that do not accord with Nietzsche's often celebrated status as the 'untimely' critic of contemporary culture. Jung tells us that

> an inflated consciousness is always egocentric and conscious of nothing but its own existence. It is incapable of learning from the past, incapable of understanding contemporary events, and incapable of drawing right conclusions about the future.
>
> (Jung, 1944b, par. 563)

Nietzsche, however, was profoundly critical of this age, and did not seek to promote himself personally so much as the development of the 'future-individual' – the *Übermensch* – who would not fall victim to the degenerate decadence that Nietzsche associates with individuals of the past and his own day. These ideas come together in the chapter 'Of the Land of Culture' in part two of *TSZ*. Here he writes: 'The men of the present . . . are strange to me and a mockery; and I have been driven from fatherlands and motherlands. So now I love only my *children's land*.' This remark is particularly significant for our argument, for this chapter is one of six chapters that are explicitly omitted in Jung's commentary and analysis of *TSZ*, for no justifiable reason. Jung tells us he is 'bored' and 'lacks enthusiasm' and will only 'do what the Germans call *Die Rosinen aus dem Kuchen picken* ["to pick the plums out of the cake"]' (*SNZ*, II, p. 1209).

Jung goes on to note that the feeling of 'god-almightiness' that affected Nietzsche was, at a cultural level, also the cause of the Second World War:

> A war of monumental frightfulness on the stage of Europe – a war that *nobody* wanted – nobody dreamed of asking exactly who or what had caused the war and its continuation. Nobody realized that European man was possessed by something that robbed him of all free will. And this state of unconscious possession will continue undeterred until we Europeans become scared of our 'god-almightiness'.
>
> (Jung, 1944b, par. 563)

But this same charge against Nietzsche is precisely that which Nietzsche himself levels against humanity. According to Nietzsche,

> The most fatal kind of megalomania there has ever been on earth [occurred when] man began to reverse values according to his own image, as if *he* were the meaning, the salt, the measure, and the standard of all the rest.
>
> (*WP*, 202; cf. AC, 44)

Nietzsche and Jung are therefore in agreement with one another, although Jung does not realize it, and wrongly associates Nietzsche's *Übermensch* with the very notion of humanity that Nietzsche strongly rejects (Jung, 1945/1954, pars. 437, 439). The *Übermensch* does not represent a one-sided inflated state to compensate for Nietzsche's supposed feelings of inferiority; rather, it represents the realization and balance of both opposites, and is the product of a personal and cultural concern for unity and the whole self.

Nietzsche did not have an inflated consciousness, as Jung argues; such a diagnosis is unjustified.[8] There are other, more reasonable explanations for Nietzsche's mental breakdown.[9] These include paresis, a brain disease caused by syphilis, which induces dementia;[10] a paralytic stroke caused by a possible inherited mental disorder;[11] a manic-depressive disorder caused by his cyclotymic personality of great mood swings (Cybulska, 2000, pp. 571–575). Finally, Dixon interestingly argues that Nietzsche's extreme loneliness intensified during the last years of his sane life, and 'Nietzsche's mental collapse had to do with his inability to communicate his thoughts' (Dixon, 1999, pp. 255–258). Indeed, Dixon cites compelling evidence to support her argument in the form of many letters written by Nietzsche.[12]

Conclusion: the affinities between the models of Nietzsche and Jung revisited

According to Jung, Nietzsche's model is a failure for two reasons: it is one-sided, as it promotes one opposite at the expense of the other, in particular the conscious body over the unconscious spirit, and it lacks the essential unifying symbol that would enable the appropriate balance between opposites. In this chapter we have found Jung's argument to be inadequate on both counts. Nietzsche's model does not fail for the reasons Jung gives. Furthermore, Nietzsche is not guilty of neurotic one-sidedness.

In Chapter 8 we found that Jung is strangely reluctant to acknowledge what I believe are great affinities between his and Nietzsche's models of the union of opposites. In this chapter we have concluded that Jung's criticisms, and his reasons for separating his model from that of Nietzsche, are suspect, and can be dismissed with relative ease. Indeed, there seems to be a peculiar and almost *forced* ambiguity in Jung's reception of Nietzsche.

In Chapter 8 we tried to bring the models of Nietzsche and Jung together by positing certain affinities between them, but we noted a significant resistance preventing us from doing this. While we found that both models require the notion of 'Dionysian danger', Jung claims that Nietzsche's model is *too* dangerous, and this interpretation of Jung had significant consequences for the remaining affinities that we posited (for the one-sided exaggeration of Dionysus effectively nullified Nietzsche's project as the 'controlled' 'union' of opposites, and subsequently removed the potential for its parallel and comparison with that of Jung). In this chapter I have evaluated Jung's claim by analysing the extent to which Dionysian danger is crucial to Nietzsche's model; that is, whether or not it compromises the goal of a union of opposites. I have concluded that Nietzsche's model does not suffer from the level of danger that Jung claims, and consequently does not fail to unite the opposites (for Nietzsche does not extol the Dionysian at the expense of the Apollinian, but seeks a balance of both). There is, therefore, no apparent reason why Jung should deny the affinities that we originally posited in Chapter 8.

Nietzsche and Jung demonstrate in their models the same quality of relationship between opposites; the same value of completion over perfection; the same notion of privilege and exclusivity of the union; the same dangerous implications of the union; the same particular opposites that are united (i.e. unconscious and conscious, body and spirit); and the same notion of the Dionysian. Furthermore, not only did Nietzsche, contrary to Jung's interpretation, anticipate the fundamental tenets of Jung's individuation process and analytical psychology in general, but also, as we have found in this chapter, he was able to apply this process self-critically to himself, and he was aware of the need to differentiate himself from the collective unconscious. We can conclude that Jung and Nietzsche argue for the same thing, though Jung continually denies this fact by separating his theory from Nietzsche's. This latter claim is difficult to prove, though the many *surprising* errors of reasoning and outright exaggerations in Jung's interpretation and criticism of Nietzsche's thought give substance to my speculation. Jung was either incompetent or had something to hide! In the next chapter I attempt to expose what that something might be.

Chapter 11

Jung's shadow

The ambiguities of Jung's reception of Nietzsche resolved

> Jung: Now the time is up and I have told you a very great deal, but do not
> assume that I have told you all!
>
> (*AP*, p. 34; Lecture 4, 13 April 1925)

Jung's critique of Nietzsche's model and his diagnosis of Nietzsche's ego-inflation are derived from *Thus Spoke Zarathustra*. Jung focuses on this work because its poetic style gives him access to Nietzsche's unconscious, and the motivations for his philosophical ideas (*SNZ*, I, p. 461). I believe Jung's analysis of Nietzsche is inadequate on two counts. First, a thorough interpretation of Nietzsche's philosophical theories demands more than a close inspection of *TSZ*; his more 'theoretical' or 'philosophical' works should also be consulted. Second, I have found that Jung's inspection of *TSZ* is not as thorough as his seminar commentaries suggest, for he is selective in the passages of *TSZ* that he considers. An examination of the passages he chooses to omit supports my claim that Jung's presentation of Nietzsche is purposely exaggerated to cover up the fact that the theories and personalities of Nietzsche and Jung are similar. In other words, I believe that Jung sets out to present Nietzsche as the definitive neurotic, and to hide any evidence that his diagnosis of Nietzsche is really a self-diagnosis.

I shall argue that Nietzsche is, effectively, a shadow personality of Jung, and that the ambiguity in Jung's reception of Nietzsche can be explained in terms of a conscious need, on Jung's part, to reject that which he unconsciously identifies with. Jung would unconsciously accept those affinities between his model and Nietzsche's that I argue for in Chapter 8, but he consciously rejects them out of a fear of the implications. An explicit identification with Nietzsche's model would be nothing less than identification with (the insanity of) Nietzsche himself.

First we shall first focus on Jung's 'unconscious reception' of Nietzsche in *SNZ*, and then seek support for my claims in an early case-history of Jung's – the fantasies of Miss Frank Miller.

Jung's unconscious reception of Nietzsche in *SNZ*

My belief that Jung's *Seminars on Nietzsche's Zarathustra* harbour hidden psychological truths about their author is in keeping with the air of mystery that has surrounded this work since its publication in 1989.[1] Bishop comments on its 'occult status' (Bishop, 1994, p. 93),[2] and attributes this to the fact that the seminar notes were for the exclusive use of 'members of the Seminar with the understanding that [they were] not to be loaned and that no part of [them was] to be copied or quoted for publication without Professor Jung's written permission' (cited in Jarrett, introduction to *SNZ*, 1989, p. ix). Such restrictions lasted until 1957, and even then the seminar notes were available only to individuals undergoing Jungian analysis or training. Jung did not want these notes to fall into the hands of those who would interpret them in a non-Jungian way – that is, those that were not in awe of the 'great man',[3] and who might see his faults or anything he might wish to hide. My suggestion is lent credibility by Jarrett, who maintains that the seminar notes 'afforded an opportunity to get acquainted with Professor Jung . . . speaking extemporaneously and with considerable informality'. Just as Jung believed the poetic style of *TSZ* gave access to the unconscious mind of its author, Jung's seminars, written not in rigid and prepared prose but as free-flowing conversation, permit a potential Jungian analysis of Jung himself. In other words, just as *TSZ* lends itself to a Jungian diagnosis of Nietzsche the author, *SNZ* provokes a Jungian self-diagnosis in turn. The seminar notes were thus kept safe among Jung's disciples. Any potentially damaging revelation could be contained, for 'Jung directed the literary material down the interpretative paths *he* wished to follow, and one has the distinct sense that Jung never lost control over the discussion' (Bishop, 1994, p. 97, italics mine).[4]

Roderick Peters has also claimed that Jung's reception of Nietzsche is incoherent but, while I have found the incoherence surprising and often extreme, Peters does not, for

> anyone who says enough to fill 1,500 pages is going to contradict themselves [and] Jung certainly does. Ideas are approached now from this perspective, now from that; often they seem to be irreconcilable; in almost every seminar one at least of the members exclaims 'But I thought you said . . . ' Jung usually responds by reminding his listeners of the difference between seeing things from the point of view of the ego on the one hand, and from that of the self on the other.
>
> (Peters, 1991, p. 126–7)

Peters does note, however, that although Jung's approach is often illuminating, 'there are times when it feels as if he has to be the one who knows' (ibid.). I believe Jung's 'superior knowledge' (superior enough to override apparent contradictions) and tendency to 'control' the discussion can be read as an attempt on Jung's part to hide or divert the seminars away from what he did not want to talk about: his own psychological disposition.

Jung would have been most familiar with the fact of Nietzsche's neurotic behaviour and mental collapse, to the extent that one could argue that he was socially conditioned into thinking of Nietzsche as an object of hostility, aversion and ridicule. Jung tells us that he had 'hesitated' to read Nietzsche, not only because he felt he was 'insufficiently prepared', but also because Nietzsche had an unsavoury reputation. Jung tells us:

> At that time [Nietzsche] was much discussed, mostly in adverse terms, by the allegedly competent philosophy students, from which I was able to deduce the hostility he aroused in the higher echelons. The supreme authority, of course, was Jakob Burckhardt, whose various critical comments on Nietzsche were bandied about. Moreover, there were some persons at the university who had known Nietzsche personally and were able to retail all sorts of unflattering tidbits about him.
>
> (*MDR*, p. 122)

Nietzsche's reputation had a double effect on Jung; for while it attracted him to Nietzsche and became 'the strongest incentive' for him to study Nietzsche's works, it also kept him at a distance. Jung notes:

> But I was held back by a secret fear that I might perhaps be like him . . . he had had inner experiences, insights which he had unfortunately attempted to talk about, and had found that no one understood him. Obviously he was, or at least was considered to be, an eccentric, a sport of nature, which I did not want to be under any circumstances. I feared I might be forced to recognize that I too was another such strange bird . . . [Nietzsche] could well afford to be something of an eccentric, but I must not let myself find out how far I might be like him.
>
> (*MDR*, pp. 122–123)

Here we see the beginnings of Jung's ambiguous relationship with Nietzsche, and I believe it is in Jung's 'secret fear' of being like Nietzsche – of being 'forced to recognize' that he too was 'an eccentric' – that we find the explanation of Jung's reluctance to acknowledge the great affinities between their models of the whole self.

Jung was indeed similar to Nietzsche. He knew that, like himself, Nietzsche had rebelled against the religious ideas of his pastor father.[5] But perhaps their most significant similarity, which establishes their associations with madness, is the fact that they had not one but two personalities. Jung claims that

> I always knew that I was two persons. One was the son of my parents, who went to school and was less intelligent, attentive, hard-working, decent, and clean than many other boys. The other was grown up – old, in fact – sceptical, mistrustful, remote from the world of men, but close to nature, the earth, the

sun, the moon, the weather, all living creatures, and above all close to the night, to dreams, and whatever 'God' worked directly in him.

(*MDR*, p. 61)

It is significant that Jung associates his second personality with God, for it is the very identification of personality with God that, according to Jung, caused Nietzsche's ego-inflation and eventual mental demise. Jung tells us:

nature seemed, like myself . . . [to be] created by [God] as an expression of Himself . . . it seemed to me that the high mountains, the rivers, lakes, trees, flowers, and animals [i.e. all those things related to his second personality] . . . exemplified the essence of God.

(*MDR*, p. 62)

Jung goes on to note that

besides his [*sc.* Jung's number one personality's] world there existed another realm, like a temple in which anyone who entered was transformed and suddenly overpowered by a vision of the whole cosmos, so that he could only marvel and admire, forgetful of himself. Here lived the 'Other' . . . it was as though the human mind looked down upon Creation simultaneously with God.

(*MDR*, p. 62)

This realm of the Other is that Dionysian realm of the *Übermensch*; it is the 'transformation' of the human being into God.[6] According to Jung, Nietzsche has two personalities, the first being himself and the second being Zarathustra, the timeless, eternal counterpart that brought about Nietzsche's transformation and destruction with its all-too-powerful archetypal force. Jung notes that 'my No. 2 now corresponded to *Zarathustra*' and 'Zarathustra', he tells us, 'was morbid'. He asks himself: 'Was my No. 2 also morbid?'; and he writes that

this possibility filled me with a terror which for a long time I refused to admit but the idea cropped up again and again and in inopportune moments, throwing me into a cold sweat, so that in the end I was forced to reflect on myself.

It is clear that Jung suspected he might suffer the same fate as Nietzsche; but I believe his period of self-reflection did not extend to *SNZ* and his critique of Nietzsche's model of opposites. Although Jung's 'autobiography' (*MDR*) acknowledges the link between himself and the insane Nietzsche, there is no acknowledgement of it in *SNZ*. This is surprising, as the main argument and purpose of *SNZ* is to chart and explain Nietzsche's madness.[7] On the contrary, in *SNZ* Jung adopts a completely different stance towards Nietzsche: he criticizes

Nietzsche's model of opposites as one-sided, and promotes his own method and model as a successful attempt to do what Nietzsche failed to do. Thus, Jung insinuates that he is nothing like Nietzsche: that he is not a psychologically unbalanced person.

Jung did, however, have what can be considered a mental breakdown – his 'confrontation with the unconscious' – and when he came out of it he realized that his wife and family provided the 'guarantee' that he was in fact in a very different situation from Nietzsche, for his family

> were actualities which made demands upon me and proved to me again and again that I really existed, that I was not a blank page whirling about in the winds of spirit, like Nietzsche . . . my family and my profession always remained a joyful reality and a guarantee that I also had a normal existence.
>
> (*MDR*, p. 214)[8]

Jung insinuates that he could not be destroyed by the onslaught of the unconscious as Nietzsche had been, because he was not as isolated as Nietzsche. (Cf. Chapter 10, where Nietzsche's madness is understood as resulting from his extreme isolation and loneliness.)

Jung's secret fear revealed in *SNZ*

Although Jung does not comment on his 'fear' of being identified with Nietzsche's madness in *SNZ*, it can be located as hidden, almost unconscious, within his commentary, in terms of what Jung does and does not say. That is, it emerges in his unnecessary denigration of Nietzsche's character and in those passages of *TSZ* he chooses not to discuss.

What Jung does say

Throughout *SNZ* Jung attacks Nietzsche's personality and appearance.[9] Jung's comments are often exaggerated. They not only are unnecessary to his argument, but also threaten to invalidate it by exposing his own shadow side. That is, according to Jung, traits peculiar to the individual's shadow are always projected and appear to be traits within another individual (Jung, 1951, par. 16). Those shadow elements within Jung's own personality (those personal characteristics which he consciously rejects and 'fears' to acknowledge) are projected as a defence mechanism on to Nietzsche. We see Jung in his very first seminar introduce his audience to the personality of Nietzsche by focusing only on his negative attributes. Nietzsche was 'always alone' because

> he could not stand people. He was desirous of having friends, always seeking a friend, but when such a poor fellow turned up, he was never good enough and Nietzsche got impatient right away . . . he was absolutely unable to accept

people . . . He was terribly, recklessly impulsive . . . He liked to be invited to certain social gatherings, but if there was a piano, he played madly; he went at it till his fingers bled.

(*SNZ*, I, pp. 16–17; also see *MDR*, p. 122)

Jung appears to recognize one positive aspect of Nietzsche's personality: that 'he was quite funny'.[10] But Jung relates this to Nietzsche's physical appearance, and ridicules him: 'And with that moustache!' Jung continues his exaggerated, one-sided negative portrayal of Nietzsche, or '*Mr.* Friedrich Nietzsche' as he later refers to him (*SNZ*, I, p. 169, italics mine: Jung seems to be enforcing a common courtesy upon Nietzsche, thereby implying he is not worthy of it, of being a 'gentleman'). Nietzsche's life 'was as poor and miserable as possible, a sick neurotic existence' (*SNZ*, I, p. 60), one that could never achieve *Übermenschlichkeit*. Indeed, in his criticism of Zarathustra's inability to explain what the *Übermensch* actually entails, Jung suddenly refers back to Nietzsche and asks him directly:

How can you become the Superman? For it is expected of you . . . personally, Friedrich Nietzsche. How do you get beyond your migraines, your vomiting and sleeplessness and chloral and all the other narcotics, and your terrible sensitiveness and irritability?

(*SNZ*, I, p. 83)

The list of Nietzsche's physical and psychological disorders is laboured. It is as if Jung wants to jeer momentarily at Nietzsche – something that might be considered a projection from Jung. Indeed, Jung discusses the relationship between uncontrolled emotion and projection immediately before admitting his irritation at Nietzsche for being psychologically unaware. Thus:

Whatever arouses emotions has touched upon the unconscious. When you get an emotional impression on something, you can be sure that you have instantly made a projection; otherwise you would not have an emotion . . . It is very curious that Nietzsche, a highly intelligent man, had not a scientific mind. He could not accept psychological facts in a scientific way and take them for what they are . . . That is the most unspeakably foolish and irritating way in which he screws himself into his madness, an awful fatality . . . And the fatality does not consist of anything tragic or great; it consists of a lack of intelligence, the lack of a scientific and philosophical attitude.

(*SNZ*, II, p. 1237)

In addition to the personal taunts, Jung makes snide comments about *TSZ*. For example, he says that 'any damned nonsense can be justified by *Zarathustra*' (*SNZ*, I, p. 476). Such a remark clearly expresses Jung's personal frustration with Nietzsche's work. This frustration is associated with supposed feelings of boredom in Jung: 'And when I looked through the chapters we have dealt with and those we have still to deal with, I must tell you frankly, I got bored stiff' (*SNZ*, II, p. 1209). And again: '[Nietzsche] became so negative and sterile that it was even boring' (*SNZ*, II, p. 1424; cf. p. 626).[11] The control Jung tries to exert over Nietzsche in order to portray himself in a more favourable light is most evident. In addition to the put-downs of Nietzsche's personality and style of writing, Jung attempts to raise himself above Nietzsche. Jung claims to know exactly what and how Nietzsche feels; there is no admission of speculation, his insistence is categorical: he states time and again, 'That is the way Nietzsche felt' (*SNZ*, I, p. 59). A particularly interesting and perhaps revealing example of Jung's claim to authority over Nietzsche is found in an allusion he makes to the anima. Throughout *SNZ* Jung claims that Nietzsche was not conscious of his anima, and was therefore unconsciously possessed by it (*SNZ*, I, pp. 533, 597, 631) and in a late seminar Jung claims that he himself is aware of his anima and, in ironic tones, he implicitly concludes that he is, in contrast to Nietzsche, a 'real man':

> The effeminisation of men was not so obvious [in Nietzsche's time], but as a matter of fact there is something very peculiar about the men of today: *there are very few real men*. This comes from the fact . . . that most of them are possessed by the anima – practically all. *Of course I exclude myself*!
>
> (*SNZ*, II, p. 1349, italics mine)[12]

What Jung does not say

I believe that Jung's secret fear of being identified with Nietzsche's madness is expressed in those passages he chooses to omit from his analysis and seminar discussion. In these passages we find evidence to suggest his diagnosis of Nietzsche is a self-diagnosis.[13] Jung's seminars ended on 15 February 1939, due to the start of the Second World War in that same year. By then he had reached *TSZ*, III, chapter 56, 'Of Old and New Law Tables', section 12, leaving unanalysed eighteen sections of chapter 56, the four remaining chapters of part three, and the whole of part four.[14] Those chapters of *TSZ*, including the whole of part four, are not of concern to us.[15] Our argument is concerned only with those passages that Jung *chose* to omit. It is chapters 35–39 and 50, together with fragments of other chapters ignored, that I shall examine.[16]

Jung says that he got 'bored stiff' with the style of *TSZ*, and made the decision not to go 'further into the actual detail' of the text but 'to pick the plums out of the cake' (*SNZ*, II, p. 1209). So Jung leaves out most of chapter 34 ('Of Self-Overcoming') and notes that

> there is nothing very important in the next chapter, 'The Sublime Ones' [chapter 35] nor in the following one, 'The Land of Culture' [chapter 36], nor in that chapter called 'Immaculate Perception' [chapter 37] . . . Then, in

the chapter called 'Scholars' [chapter 38], he chiefly realizes professional resentments, and in the chapter called 'Poets' [chapter 39], he chiefly realizes all his resentments when he was called a poet. Of course it is all represented in a generalized form, but it is quite obvious that they are his personal resentments. So we [will go straight] to the fortieth chapter, 'Great Events'.

(SNZ, II, p. 1215)

It is interesting that in four of these five chapters that Jung omits (chapters 34–37), Nietzsche alludes to the 'mirror'. The notion of the mirror, along with the mask (also in chapter 36), is often incorporated in Nietzsche's writings in order to prevent the systematization of his argument and avoid commitment to a single perspective. Nietzsche does not, however, allude to the mirror often in *TSZ*. Apart from chapters 34–37, the mirror appears in only three other chapters ('Of the Friend', 'The Child with the Mirror' and 'Of the Virtuous'). The fact that it appears in four consecutive chapters is therefore significant, all the more so, when we note that these are the chapters Jung chose to omit (on the basis, as I shall argue, that he did not like what these mirrors reflected back at him).

In chapter 34, Nietzsche alludes to the mirror 'as the mind's mirror and reflection' and he refers to 'a hundred-fold mirror', which has obvious Jungian connotations of the collective unconscious, as a 'deeper' more penetrative reflection of the mind. This image crops up again in chapter 37, as the 'mirror with a hundred eyes'. In chapter 36, he puts 'men of the present' in front of 'fifty mirrors' and describes the reflection of the mind of the contemporary man as 'opalescent', something that merely 'flatters' and 'repeats' the 'fifty blotches painted on his face and limbs'. In chapter 35, Nietzsche refers to one mirror, and this time he sits the 'sublime man' in front of it; the reflection he describes is one that will 'one day (be) fair' and 'beautiful', and 'will shudder with divine desires'. I interpret this sublime man to be Nietzsche's shadow personality, and I believe its transformation into a beautiful reflection is an indication of the process of individuation, of Nietzsche's archetypal progression from the shadow to the divine Self: a theme Jung should not have omitted from his analysis.

Nietzsche starts chapter 35: 'Still is the bottom of my sea: who could guess that it hides sportive monsters! Imperturbable is my depth: but it glitters with swimming riddles and laughter'. According to Jung, the unconscious is often symbolized by the sea and deep waters (cf. *SNZ*, II, p. 887). Nietzsche here admits that his unconscious is more disturbed than it appears. One of the 'monsters' it harbours is the 'sublime man', a religious figure who repels Nietzsche. He describes him as

> a solemn man, a penitent of the spirit: oh, how my soul laughed at his ugliness! . . . Hung with ugly truths, the booty of his hunt, and rich in torn clothes; many thorns, too, hung on him – but I saw no rose . . . my taste is hostile towards all these withdrawn men.

That this is Nietzsche's shadow appears to be confirmed when we see Nietzsche relate this figure to his inferior function: sensation (cf. *SNZ*, II, p. 1195). Nietzsche notes:

> All life is dispute over taste and tasting! . . . If he grew weary of his sublimity, this wise man, only then would his beauty rise up – and only then will I taste him and find him tasty . . . the sense of his eyes, too, is overshadowed.

Nietzsche claims that only when the sublime man is overcome (i.e. when the shadow is integrated into consciousness) will he then be able to find him tasty (i.e. be able to promote his inferior sensation function). To confirm this interpretation Nietzsche himself writes: 'And only if he [the sublime man] turns away from himself will he jump over his own shadow – and jump, in truth, into his own sunlight' (according to Jung, light symbolizes consciousness: *SNZ*, II, p. 1381).

It is difficult to believe Jung thought there was 'nothing important' in this chapter. Not only does it reveal Nietzsche's shadow personality, but also it exposes his own evaluation of it. Surely Jung would have been interested in Nietzsche's acknowledgement that the shadow must 'grow weary' of himself if its 'beauty' is to 'rise up' and 'jump, in truth, into sunlight'. Moreover, he would have been interested in Nietzsche's interpretation of whether or not his shadow can in fact make the jump – that is, whether or not Nietzsche thinks he is capable of individuation. For his part, Nietzsche, in this chapter, emphasizes the weariness of his shadow: 'He has sat all too long in the shadows, the cheeks of the penitent spirit have grown pale; he has almost starved on his expectations'. Despite such weariness, Nietzsche's shadow is very much intact, for 'there is still contempt in his eye, and disgust lurks around his mouth'; his shadow also remains unconscious, for 'he rests now, to be sure, but he has never yet lain down in the sunlight'. Nietzsche, however, does not want the shadow to rest unconscious, instead

> he should behave like the ox; and his happiness should smell of the earth and not of contempt of the earth. I should like to see him as a white ox, snorting and bellowing as he goes before the plough: and his bellowing, too, should laud all earthly things![17]

In my interpretation, Nietzsche wants the shadow roused from its slumber, and wants to initiate the individuation process and progress towards the Self. Thus, Nietzsche loves

> the neck of the ox (i.e. the shadow): but now I want to see the eye of the angel too . . . [The shadow] has tamed monsters, he has solved riddles: but he should also redeem his monsters and riddles, he should transform them into heavenly children.

Nietzsche holds the mirror up to his shadow and claims that 'you too shall one day be fair . . . then your soul will shudder with divine desires'. Thus, one day, when Nietzsche's shadow is overcome, the mirror of his mind will reflect the divine Self. But this day has not yet arrived; he has yet to 'redeem his monsters and riddles'. Nietzsche's shadow is evident: he notes that 'his countenance is still dark . . . He has still not overcome his deed', and that 'his knowledge has not yet learned to smile and to be without jealousy; his gushing passion has not yet grown calm in beauty'. Nietzsche's ultimate 'desire' is to attain the 'beauty' of the divine Self, and he tells us that it will eventually come to him through the (psychoanalytic) medium of the 'dream', as 'the secret of the soul' – but only after the shadow has 'deserted the soul'.

Officially, Jung does not think these four chapters, with their allusions to the 'mirror of the mind', are significant; yet in his commentary on chapter 49, 'Of the Virtue that Makes Small', he finds it necessary to discuss the relevance of the mirror to the *Übermensch* and to 'knowledge' in general.[18] The timing and positioning of Jung's discussion is odd, for Nietzsche makes no allusion whatsoever to the mirror in chapter 49; it is also interesting to note that Jung's discussion on mirrors immediately precedes the last chapter of *TSZ* that he chooses to omit from his analysis, chapter 50, 'On the Mount of Olives'. In other words, Jung chooses to omit four consecutive chapters that allude to the mirror, and when he does come to discuss the relevance of this concept, he does so immediately prior to omitting another chapter. The link between Nietzsche's mirror and Jung's chosen omissions is notable.

When Jung comes to discuss the concept of the mirror, it is in relation to the intellect, which is the underlying theme of 'the fullest point of consciousness' (*SNZ*, II, p. 1381; also see Jung, 1928–1930/1995, p. 291) or '*the great noontide*' that Zarathustra preaches at the end of chapter 49, 'Of the Virtue that Makes Small'. Jung says:

> I am more or less convinced that [Nietzsche's] idea of the superman originated [in 'Schopenhauer as Educator' (1874), *UM*, III] in that idea of the one who is able to hold a mirror up to the blind will, so that the blind primordial will that has created the world may be able to see its own face in the mirror of the intellect. This is very much like the Indian idea really, like the psychological education Buddha tried to give to his time, the idea of looking into the mirror of knowledge or understanding in order to destroy the error and illusion of the world.
>
> (*SNZ*, II, p. 1382)

In Jung's understanding, the mirror must be looked into in order to destroy error and illusion and to arrive at genuine self-understanding and self-knowledge. In my interpretation Jung has failed to 'look into' the mirrors of the chapters he omits, and has not been able to destroy the error and illusion that surrounds his reception of Nietzsche. If only Jung could see that Nietzsche's mirror reflects himself, he would be able to withdraw his projections of inferiority on to Nietzsche and then begin to understand himself.[19]

My argument is merely speculative, but it is given more credence by Jung's analysis of the chapter 'The Child with the Mirror'. Before I discuss the relevance of this chapter I want to mention Jung's interpretation of those two other places in *TSZ* where Nietzsche alludes to the mirror: in chapter 14, 'Of the Friend' and chapter 27, 'Of the Virtuous'. The mirror in chapter 27 plays an insignificant role, and Jung does not allude to it further. (He refers to it not as a 'mirror', but as a 'buckler'.) Chapter 14 is more revealing, however. Here Nietzsche writes: 'Have you ever watched your friend asleep – to discover what he looked like? Yet your friend's face is something else beside. It is your own face, in a rough and imperfect mirror'. I would argue that Nietzsche's face is a rough and imperfect reflection of Jung's, and Jung's reaction to this passage does not refute my interpretation. Instead of examining Nietzsche's insights into psychological theory, as we should expect, Jung casually responds: 'Therefore one does better not to see him asleep, one would say' (*SNZ*, I, p. 630). Jung's reaction is simply to turn away from the mirror, even though he knows it is a source of 'psychological education' that will 'destroy error and illusion' (cf. *SNZ*, II, p. 1382). Jung would rather not discover what Nietzsche really 'looked like', perhaps so that he can avoid looking at his own rough and imperfect reflection.

In the chapter 'The Child with the Mirror' Zarathustra recounts a frightening dream in which a child came to him carrying a mirror. Nietzsche writes:

> 'O Zarathustra,' the child said to me, 'look at yourself in the mirror! But when I looked into the mirror I shrieked, and my heart throbbed: for I did not see myself there, but a devil's grimace and sneer. Truly I understand the dream's omen and warning all too well: my *doctrine* is in danger, weeds want to be called wheat! . . . My friends are lost to me; the hour has come to seek my lost ones!

Jung claims that only someone who was familiar with analytical psychology could understand this dream, and 'only an ordinary unsophisticated human being [i.e. Nietzsche] . . . would leap to the conclusion that somebody else must have painted him black' (*SNZ*, II, p. 845). I contend that Jung is guilty of the mistake he charges Nietzsche with: '[Nietzsche] makes the awful mistake . . . [H]e ought to see the devil in himself' (*SNZ*, II, p. 847)'. This may be so; but Jung also does not see the devil in himself, for Jung's neurotic devil is projected on to Nietzsche. Jung advises Nietzsche to regard the presence of the mirror as 'a very helpful hint from the unconscious that he might have a careful look at his other side where he really looks like a devil' (ibid.), but this is advice Jung himself fails to follow, for he ignores the four consecutive chapters of *TSZ* in which the mirror is mentioned. Jung claims Nietzsche has misinterpreted the dream. Jung contends that the dream does not show, as Nietzsche believes, that his *doctrine* is in danger, but that his psychological health is. I maintain, however, that Nietzsche's interpretation reflects a truth in Jung himself: it is Jung's psychological health (and doctrine) that is in danger. Jung wants to project his own 'weeds' on to Nietzsche so he can then consciously promote himself as 'wheat'.[20] Jung argues that

> if Zarathustra-Nietzsche could realize that his face is also black, it would help him to disidentify. He could then make a difference between himself and Zarathustra. Of course it would injure his effect, but the effect would be poisonous anyhow because he would not create conviction, but only persuasion and mental contagion; and then he would not have real disciples. He would have sucklings, bambinos.
>
> (*SNZ*, II, p. 851; cf. p. 1349)

This could easily be applied to Jung himself, for Jung's need to distance himself from the insane Nietzsche by exaggerating Nietzsche's neurosis at the same time as promoting his own psychological health undermines Jung's own authority and the conviction of his argument. The fact that Jung was always in control of the discussions of the seminar group and always 'directed the literary material down the interpretative paths *he* wished to follow' (Bishop, 1994, p. 97) implies that Jung too did not have 'real' disciples per se, but mere 'sucklings' and 'bambinos' – those who would merely follow his lead. Jung criticizes Nietzsche's response to his/Zarathustra's dream by deciding to 'seek his lost friends', and return to his 'sucklings', and he sums up this response and Nietzsche's general position in the *first person*, that is, in terms that ironically (and unconsciously) apply to himself:

> So the logic is: Oh, I see I have a very black face, those very bad people have blackened it, they are against my doctrine, therefore I must run away to my friends, to my audience, in order to escape the ugly aspect of my other side. Very human!
>
> (*SNZ*, II, p. 848)

Jung, by stating that 'I must run away to *my audience*', effectively admits that Nietzsche's problem might be his own; for it is Jung, not Nietzsche, who is literally speaking/performing to an 'audience', to his seminar group.

Nietzsche somewhat surprisingly anticipates and supports my accusation and criticism of Jung in his discussion of the 'objective man' (*BGE*, 207). Jung might be thought of as the 'objective man'. He is 'an instrument, let us say a *mirror* – he is not an "end in himself"'. In a passage that supports my speculative argument, Nietzsche writes:

> And the objective man is in fact a mirror: accustomed to submitting to whatever wants to be known . . . Whatever still remains to him of his 'own person' seems to him accidental, often capricious, more often disturbing: so completely has he become a passage and reflection of forms and events not his own. He finds it an effort to think about 'himself', and not infrequently he

thinks about himself mistakenly; he can easily confuse himself with another, he fails to understand his own needs and is in this respect alone unsubtle and negligent. Perhaps he is troubled by his health or by the pettiness and stuffiness of his wife and friends, or by a lack of companions and company – yes, he forces himself to reflect on his troubles: but in vain! Already his thoughts are roaming, off to a *more general* case, and tomorrow he will know as little how to help himself as he did yesterday. He no longer knows how to take himself seriously, nor does he have the time for it: he is cheerful, *not* because he has no troubles but because he has no fingers and facility for dealing with *his troubles*.

(BGE, 207)

In addition to the notion of the mirror, some of the passages of *TSZ* omitted by Jung congregate around the themes of the Will to Power and Eternal Recurrence (see chapters 34, 'Of Self-Overcoming'; 42, 'Of Redemption'; 54, 'Of the Three Evil Things'). This is significant when we note that Jung misunderstood the first of these doctrines, the Will to Power, and admitted that he did not 'quite understand' the second, the Eternal Recurrence (*SNZ*, II, p. 1044). (We shall examine Jung's reception of the doctrine of the Will to Power in detail, and with reference to these omitted passages, in the next section.)

There are also significant isolated points made in *TSZ*. For example, one would have expected Jung to comment on Nietzsche's interesting allusion in chapter 37, 'Of Immaculate Perception', to the conscious recognition of the (collective unconscious): 'The glowing sun [that] wants to suck at the sea and drink the sea's depths up to its height: now the sea's desire rises with a thousand breasts'. We might also have expected Jung to comment on Nietzsche's allusion to the dangers of inflation, which he applies to himself/Zarathustra, when he writes, in this same chapter, of the 'dreadful coiling snake' that crawls into 'the mask of the god': 'Truly, you are deceivers, you "contemplatives!" Even Zarathustra was once the fool of your divine veneer; he did not guess at the serpent-coil with which it was filled'. Nietzsche again alludes to inflation in chapter 39, 'Of Poets', omitted by Jung. This time it is his *Übermensch* whom Nietzsche refers to as a 'motley puppet' who 'draws us ever upward – that is, to cloudland'. Nietzsche even admits here that he is 'weary' of the *Übermensch* as it is 'insubstantial' and 'unattainable', though he is still identified with its divine inflationary aspect for he 'cast' his 'net into the sea [unconscious] and hoped to catch fine fish', but could only catch 'an old god's head'.

Most surprising of all, however, is Jung's decision not to comment on Nietzsche's allusion to the alchemical symbol of the peacock in the same chapter. Nietzsche writes:

Is the sea not the peacock of peacocks? It unfurls its tail even before the ugliest of buffaloes . . . truly their [the poets'] spirit itself is the peacock of peacocks and a sea of vanity.

As we saw earlier, according to Jung, the peacock has great alchemical significance as its tail symbolizes the albedo stage in the alchemical process of uniting opposites, where 'the one white colour contains all colours', and the final stage – the rubedo – is represented by the colour red, or the 'peacock's flesh' (Jung, 1936, par. 334). Furthermore, in order to encourage the transformation to the final stage in which the queen gives (re)birth to the 'new' king, she must consume a special 'pregnancy diet' of 'peacock flesh' (Jung, 1955–1956, pars. 388–401). When Nietzsche refers to the sea as the peacock of peacocks, he is unintentionally alluding to this alchemical process, and the implication is that Nietzsche is advanced in the process of individuation, for his unconscious (the sea) displays 'the unfurling tail' of 'the peacock of peacocks' (the albedo stage).[21]

One other omitted passage that is deemed 'uninteresting' by Jung (*SNZ*, II, p. 1243) is where Nietzsche, in chapter 43, 'Of Manly Prudence', writes: 'You highest men my eyes have encountered! This is my doubt of you and my secret laughter: I think you would call my Superman – a devil!' We could think of Jung as the 'highest man' to whom Nietzsche alludes, for it is Jung who maintains that the *Übermensch* is the product of Nietzsche's insane mind, the devil in his mirror. Jung would certainly not want to be labelled in Nietzschean terms – still less when the label is the 'highest man' for, according to Frey-Rohn, the highest men 'lacked something, were disillusioned in spirit and languished in their own dissatisfaction ... [T]hey demonstrated Nietzsche's pain both at his unfulfilled expectations and the *compensatory reactions of the shadow*' (Frey-Rohn, 1988, p. 148). The identification with Nietzsche's unfulfilment and one-sidedness is, I am arguing, exactly that which Jung most feared. Later in this chapter, Nietzsche writes: 'And I myself will sit among you disguised, so that I may *misunderstand* you and myself: that, in fact, is my last manly prudence'. This might reflect Jung's own position, for I am arguing that Nietzsche is really Jung in disguise; therefore it is Jung who 'misunderstands' *himself*.

The case of Miss Frank Miller

My claim that Jung feared identification with Nietzsche and then projected this into his critique of Nietzsche's model is made more credible when we note that Jung believed his work to be indicative of his psychological make-up. In his seminar on 'Analytical Psychology' on 13 April 1925, Jung admitted that *The Psychology of the Unconscious* (*CW* 5, 1911) was effectively an exercise in self-analysis: '*Psychology of the Unconscious* can be taken as myself and ... an analysis of it leads inevitably into an analysis of my own unconscious processes' (*AP*, p. 27; also see *MDR*, p. 249).[22] Furthermore, in this seminar, Jung gives a case-history of a patient, Miss Frank Miller, which he analyses in order to work out his own problematic relationship with the unconscious. That is, Jung admits that in trying to diagnose another person (through her written confession),[23] he is attempting a self-diagnosis. I believe that Jung is making further attempts at a self-analysis in his reception of Nietzsche.

At the beginning of *The Psychology of the Unconscious* Jung describes two kinds of thinking that can be observed: intellectual or directed thinking, and fantastic or passive automatic thinking. He tells us:

> In the process of directed thinking, thoughts are handled as tools, they are made to serve the purposes of the thinker; while in passive thinking thoughts are like individuals going about on their own as it were. Fantastical thinking knows no hierarchy; the thoughts may even be antagonistic to the ego.
>
> (*AP*, p. 27)

Jung tells us that he 'took Miss Miller's fantasies as such an autonomous form of thinking, but I did not realize that she stood for that form of thinking in myself' (*AP*, p. 27).[24] I think Jung adopted the same form of thinking in his analyses of Nietzsche and Miss Miller. His identifications with both cases are 'guided by unconscious motives' (Jung, 1911–1912/1952, par. 20). The following concession might also apply as much to Nietzsche as to Miss Miller:

> [Miss Miller] took over my fantasy and became stage director to it . . . she became an anima figure, a carrier of an inferior function of which I was very little conscious . . . Passive thinking seemed to me such a weak and perverted thing that I could only handle it through a diseased woman . . . in Miss Miller I was analysing my own fantasy function, which because it was so repressed, like hers, was semi-morbid.
>
> (*AP*, pp. 27–28)

Just as Miller became Jung's anima figure, Nietzsche became his shadow figure, and just as Jung identified with Miller's repressed fantasy function, Jung identified with Nietzsche's encroaching insanity. Jung clearly admits that one of his most important case-histories was in fact carried out in his own self-interest and constituted an act of self-therapy. It thus follows that the ultimate source of fundamental concepts of analytical psychology is Jung himself, and its practical application entails an element of self-projection (i.e. transference).[25] Jung notes:

> I watched the creation of myths going on, and got an insight into the structure of the unconscious . . . I drew all my empirical material from my patients, but the solution of the problem I drew from the inside, from my observations of the unconscious processes.
>
> (*AP*, p. 34)

It is thus not unreasonable to conclude that, being fearful of his identification with the insane Nietzsche, Jung might try, unconsciously or not, to work through his own psychological issues using Nietzsche to carry his complexes. After all, Nietzsche was the most suitable and obvious candidate for this – being the 'archetypal' mad genius, with a similar family background and psychological disposition to Jung (i.e. both being intellectual-intuitive types).[26]

Jung's identifications with the Miller case-history and with Nietzsche are also connected by a significant period of isolation and anxiety in Jung's life (often referred to as his 'mid-life crisis': cf. foreword to the fourth Swiss edition of *The Psychology of the Unconscious*), which was caused by his break with Freud. According to Jung, while he was ordering his thoughts on the Miller fantasies and writing *The Psychology of the Unconscious*, he had dreams 'which presaged the forthcoming break with Freud' (*MDR*, p. 186); its eventual publication (in unrevised form, as *Wandlungen und Symbole der Libido* in 1912) marked the end of his friendship with Freud (*AP*, p. 27; *MDR*, p. 191). This break had been anticipated in their different receptions of Nietzsche. Thus, Jung's shock at Freud's admission that he had never read Nietzsche 'planted in the younger man's mind the seed of suspicion' (Jarrett, introduction to *SNZ*, p. xi) and 'gradually led him to think of the dilemma, "Freud vs. Nietzsche"' (Jarrett, 1990, p. 131). Jarrett continues to note: 'It was just after his break with Freud that Jung returned to Nietzsche'. Therefore Jung's focal preoccupation and identification with Nietzsche began just after the publication of the Miller fantasies. Furthermore, Jung's reacquaintance with Nietzsche occurs at a significant time of self-reflection in Jung's life, during 'a period of inner uncertainty – a state of disorientation' (*MDR*, p. 194): it immediately follows his attempt at self-analysis with the Miller fantasies and 'the loss of so important a friendship' (*MDR*, p. 191) with Freud. Indeed, just as Nietzsche's extreme loneliness and feelings of rejection are thought to have encouraged his mental breakdown, Jung, too, felt 'isolated', with the reception of *Wandlungen und Symbole der Libido*, which was 'declared to be rubbish' (*MDR*, p. 191), and he too suffered from what can only be explained in terms of a mental breakdown, which lasted between 1913 and 1917 (*MDR*, p. 233). Jung notes: 'When I parted from Freud, I knew that I was plunging into the unknown. Beyond Freud, after all, I knew nothing; but I had taken the step into darkness' (*MDR*, p. 225); 'I felt totally suspended in mid-air, for I had not found my own footing' (*MDR*, p. 194); cf. Jung's description of Nietzsche's madness:

> Becoming identical with air . . . he rises like a balloon . . . dancing in the clouds . . . he lived high above the clouds . . . without realizing at all that he had no feet on the earth.
>
> (*SNZ*, I, pp. 506–507)

We can therefore see Jung turn to Nietzsche in his isolation and state of disorder to re-establish a sense of identity independently of Freud; it is here that we find identification of the insane Jung with the insane Nietzsche.

Conclusion

This part of our inquiry has focused upon a misrepresentation of Nietzsche's model of opposites. It has taken the Nietzschean model described in Parts I and II and has subjected it to a Jungian analysis. Nietzsche's model did not become distorted in its translation into the terms of analytical psychology. (This is no surprise to us, when we recall our examination of attribute (7) in Chapter 8: that Nietzsche's model anticipates the central tenets of the individuation process and analytical psychology in general.) Rather, it became distorted because of the personal associations that Jung, its interpreter, had with Nietzsche, its author. Thus, the Nietzschean model of this part of our inquiry is a shadow projection of Jung's personal fear of mental illness (an illness Nietzsche himself suffered). Jung, in his conscious interpretation of Nietzsche's model (which is compensatory to his unconscious identification with it), has denied its essential characteristic: that both opposite elements are inherently equal in the binary pair (attribute (3) in Chapter 8). As we have seen, this has huge implications for his model, for it is this regulative principle that generates the tension between opposites necessary for creation and 'new and more powerful births' (*BT*, 1; cf. *WS*, 53; *WP*, 881, 1027); without it, the personality is doomed to 'stagnation and decay'. Jung (mis)interprets Nietzsche's model in these latter terms, because he incorrectly maintains that Nietzsche's model both promotes the conscious body over the unconscious spirit, and lacks the third unifying element (God, the symbol, or transcendent function: Jung, 1916/1957, par. 189; *MDR*, p. 384), which, in Jung's model, is necessary for the balance and unification of opposites. Although Nietzsche's model does not promote this 'third thing' and instead relies upon the Heraclitean notion where there is 'the diverging of a force into two qualitatively different opposed activities [which subsequently] seek to re-unite' (*PTAG*, 5), this does not mean that a triadic arrangement cannot be found implicit within his model,[27] and in Chapter 10 I argued that the redemptive symbol of God is hidden within Nietzsche's model in his admission of the 'spiritual' realm and collective unconscious. Jung's conscious argument and criticism of Nietzsche's model fail. They cannot survive the fact that Jung is unconsciously in support of Nietzsche's model and that their models share considerable affinity. Here we are reminded of Jung's own words:

> Any structure built over against the unconscious . . . no matter how bold, will always collapse because it has no feet, no roots. Only something that is rooted in the unconscious can live.
>
> (*SNZ*, II, p. 1250)

When translated into the language of analytical psychology, Nietzsche's model remains coherent. The Nietzschean model of parts two and three promotes the healthy whole individual in its binary framework of equal opposites, and this is supplemented by the model of part four, which sees it translated into a triadic framework (in line with Jung's model), in which a third element equalizes the opposites. Both 'Nietzschean' models promote balance and unification of opposites; as I have presented it, Nietzsche is not guilty of one-sidedness (neurosis) in his original model, or in its translation into the terms of analytical psychology. Only Jung's misrepresentation of Nietzsche's model is one-sided; it is Jung's own disposition and misinterpretation of, and projection on to, Nietzsche's model that is neurotic.

Nietzsche demands of his reader that 'one has above all to *hear* correctly the tone that proceeds from this mouth, this halcyon tone, if one is not to do pitiable injustice to the meaning of its wisdom' (*EH*, 'Foreword', 4; cf. *D*, 'Preface', 5: 'learn to read me well'; *BGE*, 260; *EH*, 'Why I Write Such Good Books', 7, 8). Jung fails to do just this; he is one of 'the worst readers', one of 'those who behave like plundering troops: they take away a few things they can use, dirty and confound the remainder, and revile the whole' (*AOM*, 137; cf. the dirty 'parasite' in *TSZ*, n. 15). Jung's mistaken conviction that Nietzsche was a 'pathological personality' due to his 'neurotic one-sidedness' (Jung, 1917/1926/1943, pars. 37, 40) 'dirties', 'confounds' and 'reviles' his interpretation of Nietzsche's model. Jung is guilty of recognizing only *one side* of Nietzsche, at the expense of seeing Nietzsche as he had asked to be seen – 'as a whole'.

Nietzsche and Jung present the same criteria for the diagnosis of mental health/illness – the equilibration and unification of opposites/the promotion of one opposite at the expense of the other. I have argued that Jung's diagnosis of Nietzsche's 'pathological personality' is not only incorrect (Nietzsche does not promote one opposite at the expense of the other) but also really a self-diagnosis. Jung is mentally imbalanced himself, and this materializes in his one-sided interpretation of Nietzsche. In accordance with their common model for the diagnosis of mental illness, Nietzsche is not a mentally ill personality per se, but Jung is. Jung is mentally ill according to his own insights.

Thus far I have concluded that, according to Jung's model, Nietzsche has more potential for attaining Selfhood in the union of opposites than Jung gives him credit for, while the potential for Jung himself is less, for he must still recognize and reclaim his shadow projections (that have been projected on to Nietzsche). I have yet to offer a diagnosis of the two men according to Nietzsche's model. Chapter 12 will attempt to offer a Nietzschean 'diagnosis' of Jung to determine if he can achieve *Übermenschlichkeit* in the union of opposites. In the concluding part of this book I shall comment on the problematics of attempting a Nietzschean self-diagnosis. I shall also comment on whether or not Jung and Nietzsche believed that they themselves had realized the whole self.

Chapter 12

Jung's madness

A Nietzschean critique of Jung's model

In Chapters 10 and 11 I have evaluated Nietzsche's model from a Jungian perspective and concluded that Nietzsche's dyadic framework of opposites remains coherent when translated into the triadic framework proposed by Jung. In this chapter I shall evaluate Jung's model from a Nietzschean perspective to determine if it can function without the third element, the symbol.

I contend that, from a Nietzschean perspective, the Jungian Self fails to unite the opposites satisfactorily because it seeks to unite the opposites in a source external to them and does not directly harness the energy inherent within the opposites themselves. In Chapter 7 we saw that Nietzsche's model does not require a third element or an external medium to encourage the unification of opposites, for Nietzsche maintains that the opposites originate in each other as two elements that have become separated from one original source, and that they have a natural inclination for reunification (*PTAG*, 5). This natural inclination or motivating force in their separation and unification is the Will to Power. The Will to Power is the original underlying force or 'oneness' of which the opposites are part – the 'development of one definite will into many forms' (*WP*, 692; cf. 1050). If the opposites are to reunite they will do so under the 'yoke' of the Will to Power, for it is through this force that '*all* the strong, seemingly contradictory gifts and desires . . . go together' (*WP*, 848). I believe it is Jung's denial of the Will to Power as the *only* 'driving . . . physical, dynamic or psychic force' (*WP*, 688) that prevents him from uniting the opposites of Nietzsche's model, and thereby failing to attain *Übermenschlichkeit*.

Jung cannot unite Nietzsche's opposites without their founding force; by failing to promote the Will to Power Jung is forced to look beyond the dyadic relationship and introduce an external element to try to ground and unite the opposites. Nietzsche would interpret this move as ascetic, for it is effectively devaluing the inherent power and dynamism of the instincts while placing greater value on a 'third element' that is external to them.[1] Indeed, Nietzsche would have been rattled by the metaphysical connotations of the name 'transcendent function' that Jung gives to this external symbolic element.[2] On the other hand, Jung's third element, the symbol, is not external to the individual but is part of his psychological make-up (it is of conscious and unconscious composition: see Chapter 7) and in this sense Nietzsche would not reject it on ascetic grounds. At most, Nietzsche would criticize it for furnishing the opposites with a conceptual sense of order and structure, and an objective sense of meaning. Bishop notes:

> [Although] Nietzsche's view that 'reality' is constituted by the constantly changing disposition of the Will to Power has much in common with Jung's view that 'reality' is constituted by the (archetypal) psychic images within us and, more importantly, the changes which they bring about in us . . . the chief difference between Jung and Nietzsche lies in the question of what it is that is said to structure existence. In Jung's psychic monism, the archetypes function as categories of the imagination, canalizing the libido and, by giving it shape and form, endowing life with meaning . . . Nietzsche's 'volitionary' monism by contrast knows no such structures, and the ceaseless flux of Becoming – the perpetual struggle of the Will to Power – resists attempts to exercise conceptual mastery over it.
>
> (Bishop, 1995, p. 207)

Nietzsche's criticism of a conceptual sense of order and structure

The libido is simply the underlying energetic process through which the opposites unite (Jung, 1921, par. 778). It therefore parallels Nietzsche's Will to Power. However, the parallel dissolves when the nature of their respective energetic processes is examined. Jung expresses the difference thus:

> My first conception of the libido then was not that it was a formless stream so to speak, but that it was archetypal in character. That is to say, libido never comes up from the unconscious in a formless state, but always in images.
>
> (*AP*, p. 4)

In Chapter 7 we saw that Schopenhauer influenced Jung's conception of the libido. For Jung, both Schopenhauer's Will and his own concept of the libido constitute an energetic stream manifesting itself in structures: in archetypes corresponding to Schopenhauer's version of the Platonic Ideas (Bishop, 1995, p. 247), while Nietzsche rejected the Platonic Idea outright.

Because the Jungian framework through which the opposites unite has shape, form, and image, Jung maintained that it could be monitored: the symbol could be traced as an archetypal text that could be read off from dreams and other creative practices. For Nietzsche, this is an absurd notion. According to Nietzsche, the 'basic text *homo natura*' (*BGE*, 230) has been distorted. The task of tracing the Will to Power is compromised since each new configuration erases the meaning of the preceding one (*GM*, II, 12). Nietzsche would reject Jung's claim that the unification of opposites constellates in certain archetypal 'stages', which, although not necessarily forming a definite linear sequence, proceed towards a definite goal, a process that can be monitored within the individual. For Nietzsche, the Jungian model is too rigid: the unification of opposites does not proceed through definite 'stages', and even if it did, such stages would certainly not lend themselves to interpretation. Indeed in Chapter 3 we saw that, according to Nietzsche, individuals can never know the content and character of their sensations; there is no 'meaning' to discover, only the reality of conflicting instincts and 'the judgement of our muscles' (*WP*, 314). Any interpretation must be accompanied by many conflicting interpretations, thereby bringing into play the Will to Power, and disabling the Jungian practice of 'monitoring'.

Contrary to Jung's thought, Nietzsche would deny that the union of opposites is something to be *discovered* rather than *created*. (We saw that this disagreement was also a defining feature of Jung's criticism of Nietzsche.) In Chapter 7 we saw that the Jungian model unites the opposites through an *already existing* union of opposites (that is, through the third element as a pre-established synthesis of the two opposites). For Jung, an a priori union of opposites must already be posited before any further union can take place. This a priori structure designates the 'purposive orientation' of the psyche; it is 'something like a preliminary exercise or sketch, or a plan roughed out in advance' (Jung, 1916/1948, par. 493; cf. par. 456). The Jungian system therefore depends upon the discovery of this a priori regulative and constitutive structure. It is only when the archetypal symbol is realized that experience can be ordered and the creative process started. From a Nietzschean perspective, on the other hand, experience is not something that is controlled or ordered from a predetermined external source. It is to be generated and created from within the opposites themselves. The union of opposites is not an a priori starting point, it is rather an (a posteriori) end-product of the opposites acting alone. The union of opposites is not prior to experience, because it is the opposites themselves that create the relevant experience. For Nietzsche, there can be no pre-designated teleological path of experience (*WP*, 1062, 1064, 1066; *BGE*, 13), only the ceaseless and random flux of becoming. While the Self is an inevitable goal of the healthy psyche, an intrapsychic pre-designated plan, the *Übermensch* is defined by the strength to endure the immediate chaos of existence. It is to create order and form, but in such a way that no shape can be recognized or fully established. As Nietzsche says, simply to 'impose upon becoming the *character* of being – that is the supreme will to power' (*WP*, 617, italics mine; cf. *GS*, 109). To assemble a definite structure out of the chaos of opposites, as Jung has done, is to impose limitations on individual creativity.

Nietzsche's criticism of an objective sense of meaning: Jung's Will to Truth

Nietzsche's doctrine of the Eternal Recurrence is a radical denial of teleology and 'purposive orientation', and an expression of the absence of meaning: 'The most extreme form of nihilism: the nothing ("the meaningless"), eternally!' (*WP*, 55). For Nietzsche, any residual meaning is located within the energetic process of the Will to Power, in the hierarchy of opposites within that disposition to will. Nietzsche would thus be critical of Jung's insistence that archetypal structures are the source of meaning. Nietzsche would criticize Jung's preoccupation with the Will to Truth: the need to discover meaning, to find the 'correct' interpretation (Jung, 1934/1954, pars. 65–67; cf. Jung, 1949, par. 1236) and to posit archetypal structures as universally valid.[3] He would find such structures as detrimental to the creative process, which demands multiple conflicting interpretations. Nietzsche regards those people who are preoccupied with the Will to Truth as decadent. Jung cannot aspire to *Übermenschlichkeit* because he fails to correlate the contrary instincts with the Will to Power, and associates them instead with the motivation of the Will to Truth; ironically, this motivation of decadence is associated with the problem of one-sidedness and the 'inverse cripple' (*TSZ*, II, 'Of Redemption'). It would thus seem that Jung is guilty of the very thing for which he criticized Nietzsche.

Jung's failure to promote the Will to Power and aspire to *Übermenschlichkeit* is demonstrated further when we note that only those who are 'intelligent enough' to understand it can successfully utilize the Will to Power. Nietzsche's *TSZ* insists that the Will to Power can be grasped only by the very few.[4] Thus, Zarathustra addresses his discovery of the Will to Power only to 'you who are wisest' (*TSZ*, II, 'Of Self-Overcoming'). Although the connection may be somewhat presumptuous, we might say that Jung does not have the intellectual vigour necessary to be a disciple of Zarathustra, for he wildly misinterprets the meaning of the Will to Power.

Jung's misunderstanding of the Will to Power is another facet of his failed critique of Nietzsche's model: he rejects the Will to Power, because he believes it is a one-sided doctrine adopted by Nietzsche to hide his feelings of inferiority.[5] He thinks Nietzsche's Will to Power is a theory of power as *domination* (Jung, 1921, par. 625; Jung, 1917/1926/1943, pars. 38–39, 42–43; *JS*, p. 280; *MDR*, p. 153).[6] But this is certainly not the case, if by 'power as domination', Jung means physical power over others. The Will to Power is the unifying force of creativity and, according to Nietzsche, it is this discipline necessary for self-integration that evinces greater power than undisciplined brute strength. Indeed, Nietzsche's envisaged 'order of rank' (see Chapter 8, note 9) makes clear that military power or dominance over others by brute force (the '*cruder* instruments of force': *GS*, 358, italics mine) ranks lowest, and that spiritual power ranks highest: 'The most spiritual men, as the *strongest*' belong to the 'highest caste' (*AC*, 57). And again: 'not in their physical strength, but primarily in their psychical' (*BGE*, 257). The *Übermenschen*, as the most spiritual individuals, are those who demonstrate power in self-discipline: they will be '"masters of the earth"; – a new, tremendous aristocracy, based on the severest self-legislation' (*WP*, 960); they are 'the most moderate' and 'will prove to be the strongest' (*WP*, 55); see also *WP*, 954; *GS*, 290). There is thus a distinction (that Nietzsche makes clear, but Jung fails to note) between victory as 'an overcoming of *oneself*' (which is 'for the benefit of others': *AOM*, 152).

Jung's misunderstanding is compounded by his conflating Nietzsche's Will to Power with Alfred Adler's 'one-sided' (Jung, 1921, par. 92) conception of power as self-preservation. Jung asserts that in claiming the urge for power as the fundamental underlying instinct, Nietzsche overlooked 'that other elemental urge [the sexual instinct . . .] upon which Freud's psychology is built' (Jung, 1917/1926/1943, par. 43; cf. Jung, 1917/1926/1943, pars. 35–55; Jung, 1958, par. 658; *MDR*, pp. 153–154).[7] However, Nietzsche anticipated the importance of the sexual instinct (*BGE*, 189; cf. *GM*, II, 7; *AOM*, 95), though without making it the central instinct.[8] Likewise, Nietzsche anticipated Adlerian psychology by emphasizing the value of the self-preservation instinct. Unlike Adler, however, he did not regard it as the central instinct, and therefore did not equate it with the Will to Power: 'Life . . . is the *will to power* – : self-preservation is only one of the indirect and most frequent consequences of it' (*BGE*, 13).[9]

The Will to Power is not the one-sided doctrine that Jung maintains. It is unlike Adler's conception of power; it is not a doctrine of domination that falls victim to one-sidedness. In a passage of *TSZ* that discusses the Will to Power (and which, notably, Jung chooses to omit from his analysis),[10] Nietzsche equates power with compensation: 'The highest longs to stoop down after power. Truly, there is no sickness and lust in such a longing and descent' ('Of the Three Evil Things', 2). Nietzsche's Will to Power is the energy that unites the opposites. It can be understood as a process of compensation, as it accentuates the weaker instincts in order to increase the tension between opposites, and enhance their creative competition. The Will to Power is identified with both opposites in the binary pair; it is the original form from which they originate and within which they unite. Jung, however, identifies the Will to Power with only one of the opposites, and in doing so, he fails to unleash its unifying power: it has nothing to oppose in its own right. Nietzsche would criticize Jung, not only for reducing the scope of the unifying force, but also for furnishing the Will to Power with content and form. Jung reduces the doctrine to a theory of domination, a move which implements significant restrictions, for the doctrine is set up as one half of a pair, and can now only be understood with reference to its opposite: Eros. ('Freud versus Adler' becomes 'Freud versus Nietzsche', *MDR*, p. 176.)

Although Jung's misinterpretation of the Will to Power leads him to a reductionism that contests the very values expressed by *Übermenschlichkeit*, a less reductive view of Nietzsche's notion of power can be identified in Jung's work. This more acceptable interpretation of Jung's is found in his analysis of *TSZ*, chapter 54, 'Of the Three Evil Things'. Here Nietzsche cites 'voluptuousness, passion for power, and selfishness' as 'the three best cursed things in the world'. According to Jung's analysis, 'These things are powers of life, therefore they are really merits . . . and [Nietzsche] recognizes [this], but . . . comes to the conclusion that of course those ordinary people do *not* recognize these facts, that they discredit these powers of life' (*SNZ*, II, pp. 1459–1460). Jung continues to note that in these powers of life Nietzsche anticipates the three 'main aspects' of psychoanalytic theory:

> Voluptuousness, the lust principle, is Freud; passion for power is Adler; and selfishness – that is myself, perfectly simple . . . my idea really is the individuation process and that is just rank selfishness.
>
> (*SNZ*, II, p. 1451)

It is here that Jung expresses his more 'Nietzsche-friendly' interpretation of power, for he admits that his idea 'peculiarly enough . . . includes the other two, for voluptuousness and passion for power are only two aspects of selfishness' (ibid.). Jung interprets power as that 'which makes things move on' (*SNZ*, II, p. 1460), which, when understood in its wider connotations of 'selfishness', is an all-encompassing 'power of life'. The Will to Power is thus accepted as having much wider significance than Jung previously attributed to it; it is no longer understood in the rigid and 'one-sided' terms of dominance but is now considered a motivating 'all-encompassing' force aimed at the whole self. Thus, 'energy is a concept by which you try to express by analogy all the manifestations of power' (*JS*, p. 316).

By correlating power as selfishness with the individuation process Jung has effectively brought his notion of libido into parallel with Nietzsche's Will to Power. This parallel has been noted by Dixon (1999, pp. 164–166) and argued for by Bishop. Bishop argues that Jung's concept of the libido 'is not as close to Schopenhauer's Will to Life as it is to Nietzsche's Will to Power' (Bishop, 1995, p. 96; cf. pp. 99, 247). Although Jung himself 'did not make the connection . . . Jung's concept of the libido integrates the creativity of instinctuality with the creative and destructive capacities of an energetically conceived Will to Power' (ibid., p. 111).[11] Bishop cites Jung in support of his argument:

> It is not only as if the libido might be an irresistible striving forward, an endless life and will for construction, such as Schopenhauer has formulated in his world will, death and every end being some malignancy or fatality coming from without, but the libido, corresponding to the sun, also wills the destruction of its creation.
>
> (Bishop, 1995, p. 99, n. 29)

Bishop also cites the following from Jung to consolidate the connection: 'That which is valuable in the God-creating idea is not the form but the power, the libido' (Bishop, 1995, p. 96). Although Bishop does not note it, we can see Jung here prioritizing the Nietzschean value of power over that which Nietzsche rejects: the notion of form and structure in the process of uniting the opposites (cf. *AP*, p. 4). In Chapter 7, I argued that Jung arrived at his conception of the libido as having archetypal form through his reading of Schopenhauer. Thus, Jung's prioritization of power over form reinforces Bishop's argument further: it does not merely connect Jung's concept of the libido to Nietzsche's Will, it enhances their correlation over and above that between the libido and Schopenhauer's Will to Life.

Such correlation between Jung's concept of the libido and Nietzsche's Will to Power does not mean that Jung is on the way to *Übermenschlichkeit*: far from it. Jung might well promote the Will to Power as the unifying force by incorporating it within his notion of 'selfishness' as the motivating 'life power', but his notion of 'selfishness' remains subservient to the Will to Truth in its pursuit of archetypal structures, forms and stages. Jung's concept of the libido cannot be simply equated with Nietzsche's Will to Power (a conclusion also reached by Bishop, but not by Dixon). Neither can Jung's model function within Nietzsche's dyadic framework, without the third element (the symbol), for it is this addition that orders and motivates the opposites in accordance with the Will to Truth, and without it the whole practice of analytical psychology – with its 'structured' diagnoses and consequent prescriptions to restore the psychic balance – would collapse. That is, creativity and development, for Jung, must be situated in a source external to the individual, and thus external to the opposites (*SNZ*, I, p. 61; cf. II, p. 723). If one cuts off this source, which he maintained Nietzsche had done, psychic 'stagnation, congestion and ossification' will follow (Jung, 1917/1926/1943, par. 78; *SNZ*, II, p. 1174).

In his preoccupation with form, Jung cannot accommodate the freedom and creativity that chaos initiates and the *Übermensch* demands. Zarathustra teaches that 'one must have chaos in one, to give birth to a dancing star' (*TSZ*, prologue, 5), but this is just what the Jungian model lacks. Certainly the Jungian model shares similarities with that of Nietzsche but, from a Nietzschean perspective, Jung's model is concerned with Being over Becoming.[12]

Part IV

Conclusion

Chapter 13

Whole selves

Nietzsche's influence on Jung revisited

Our inquiry began by locating and analysing the role of opposites in the *whole self* according to Nietzsche and Jung (Chapters 2–6). First, I analysed the change and development in Nietzsche's thought about the validity of opposites and concluded that Nietzsche rejects metaphysical and aesthetic opposites in favour of psychological opposites. This is because psychological opposites fulfil the criteria of 'valuable' opposites for Nietzsche: they are life affirming and capable of experience. Second, I argued that the *Übermensch* is a whole self that seeks to configure psychological opposites into a creative union. I then examined the compensatory role of opposites in the Jungian model of the psyche. I concluded the analysis of the Jungian model by arguing that the Self is, like Nietzsche's *Übermensch*, a whole self that seeks a union of opposites.

Nietzsche and Jung thus present the same criteria for the diagnosis of mental health (illness): the equilibration and unification of opposites (the promotion of one opposite at the expense of the other). The *Übermensch* and the Self are their respective names for the 'healthy' whole self. To those unhealthy individuals who value the opposites unequally, Nietzsche and Jung issue warnings of impending psychological damage, but they do not assign them a name, to which they might consistently refer. For this reason, our inquiry has adopted the Nietzschean term 'inverse cripple' (*TSZ*, II, 'Of Redemption') and the Jungian notion of 'sick animal' (Jung, 1917/1926/1943, par. 32).

Our inquiry then sought to evaluate the Nietzschean and Jungian models of opposites further by examining their similarities and differences (Chapters 7 and 8). I began by identifying the different processes through which their models sought the union of opposites, and I tried to account for this difference by reference to their different philosophical influences. I concluded that both Nietzsche and Jung have roots in Heraclitus. Jung, unsatisfied with Heraclitus' notion of 'one force divided into two opposites that seek reunification', sought to develop his theory of opposites to include a notion of 'triadicy', a notion found in Aristotle. The fact that Jung relies on a third thing external to the opposites to initiate their union, while Nietzsche does not, is a critical theme central to our inquiry. It is because of this that each takes issue with the other's understanding of the whole self. Before I argued this, I sought to identify similarities between the two models according to their conceptions of what the whole self comprises. Here I identified seven affinities between the Nietzschean *Übermensch* and the Jungian Self – the quality of the relationship between opposites; the value of completion over perfection, and its implications for morality; the privilege and exclusivity of the union, and its political implications; the dangerous implications of the union for the personality; the particular opposites that are united; and the notion of the Dionysian. Also, not explicit in Nietzsche's model of opposites but beneath its surface is Nietzsche's anticipation of the fundamental tenets of Jung's individuation process and analytical psychology in general. I examined each of these similarities to determine the extent to which they could be considered a consequence of Nietzsche's influence on Jung. In the course of this examination I identified a resistance and general ambivalence on Jung's part towards Nietzsche's model and the beginnings of a Jungian critique of it.

I then attempted to criticize each model from the perspective of the other, in order to elucidate further Nietzsche's influence on Jung and to consolidate their differences (Chapters 9–12).

First, I examined Jung's criticisms of Nietzsche's model as a 'one-sided failure' to unite the opposites. This culminated in Nietzsche's failure to promote the 'third' external element (the symbol) to enable the mediation between opposites, and caused, according to Jung, the collapse of Nietzsche's mental health (his ego-inflation).

Second, we saw that Jung's critique is flawed and based upon a wild mis-interpretation of Nietzsche's model, for Nietzsche does in fact admit a spiritual realm that constitutes the redeeming, reconciliatory symbol. Thus we saw that the difference between the models of Nietzsche and Jung is not as Jung argues: it is not the case that Jung's model has the unifying symbol while Nietzsche's does not, because the symbol is evident in both models. Rather, the difference between the two models is that Jung interprets the symbol as being external to the opposites (the 'third thing': the transcendent function or Self, which mediates between the opposites by imposing structure and form), while Nietzsche interprets it as inherent within the opposites (as Will to Power, which mediates between the opposites without imposing structure and form). In other words, Jung maintains that creativity must come from outside the individual, so that the whole self is a matter of *discovery* (Jung, 1942/1954, par. 400), while Nietzsche maintains that creativity is found within the individual, so that the whole self is a matter of *creation* (*TSZ*, prologue, 9). I then concluded, somewhat speculatively, that Jung misinterprets Nietzsche and is generally ambivalent towards him due to an unconscious fear that he might be identified with the insane personality of Nietzsche. This, I argued, could be a reason why Jung denies Nietzsche's influence upon his own model despite their significant affinities.

Third, I criticized the Jungian model from a Nietzschean perspective in order to draw out Jung's potential neurosis: Nietzsche, I argued, would arrive at a diagnosis of Jung's personality complimentary to my interpretation. Thus, I concluded that the addition of the third external element in the Jungian model – to order and motivate the opposites to unification – is detrimental to the dynamic creativity that such opposition should occasion. In other words, according to Nietzsche, creativity arises from the *chaotic* interaction of opposites, and the imposition of order and form from the mediating third element compromises this potential for creativity.

In accordance with the insistence of Jung and Nietzsche that the author's personality is identifiable in his work, I attempted to evaluate or 'diagnose' their personalities according to each other's models of health and illness. In other words, I determined whether or not Nietzsche and Jung are themselves *whole* – whether the former could aspire to Selfhood and the latter to *Übermenschlichkeit*. I concluded that Jung would not count Nietzsche as a whole self, and neither would Nietzsche consider Jung to be a whole self; rather in each other's estimation they would warrant the terms 'sick animal' and 'inverse cripple'. What we have yet to confirm is how they regarded themselves in the grand scale of things. Did Jung regard his personality as fully individualized, and did Nietzsche believe he had successfully implemented the Will to Power? Furthermore, could any of us realize their goals of human wholeness?

In this inquiry we have found that neither Nietzsche nor Jung is so integrated as to realize the Jungian 'goal' of the Self. Jung argues that Nietzsche could not be further from its realization with his one-sided ego-inflation. Although we have dismissed Jung's argument, Nietzsche is certainly troubled with his anima (which is exemplified in his many accusations of misogyny: see Chapter 8, note 33); and in some cases Nietzsche wants to subordinate one opposite to the other and incorporate it into the other (for example, the opposition between 'strength' and 'weakness'). Similarly, I have claimed that Jung is troubled by his shadow side, to the extent that he fails to integrate it consciously and instead projects it on to Nietzsche (in his extraordinary misinterpretation and misdiagnosis of Nietzsche). The two thinkers thus demonstrate a neurotic one-sidedness unacceptable to Selfhood.

It is more difficult to determine whether the two thinkers are so integrated as to realize the Nietzschean 'goal' of the *Übermensch*. This is because whereas the process of the Self is structured and marked out in stages (of increasing integration of unconscious contents), the *Übermensch* is shapeless and unstructured. It is thus easier to ascertain Jung's *failure* to realize *Übermenschlichkeit* than it is to determine Nietzsche's potential success. For Jung, unlike Nietzsche, is insistent on imposing form when the *Übermensch* demands constant flux. Jung fails to promote the Will to Power as that which unifies the flux of creativity, and is instead preoccupied with the Will to Truth with its limitations and restrictions on creativity.

It is not clear whether Nietzsche and Jung regarded themselves as whole selves or, indeed, as promoting the process of unification within themselves. Certainly (the 'insane') Nietzsche thought himself to exemplify Dionysian man, since he thought he literally embodied the god (cf. *SNZ*, II, p. 903) while Jung hints at the end of *MDR* that he had reached a high level of personality integration (*MDR*, pp. 391–392) and 'a completed individuation' (*MDR*, pp. 327–328). But there are no explicit confessions from either thinker on where they stand in relation to the 'goal' of their projects. Such acknowledgement would have implications for the practicality of their projects. They do, however, cite Goethe as the most *übermenschlich* and individuated individual to have lived. Goethe was able to sustain the creative process of unification and thus aspire towards the imagined goal of totality (*TI*, 'Expeditions of an Untimely Man', 49; Jung, 1934a, pars. 301–302). We are led to believe that Goethe is the 'living' example that substantiates the projects of Nietzsche and Jung, though neither Nietzsche nor Jung goes to any length in presenting this claim. An attempt to evaluate their claim would certainly prove interesting, but unfortunately cannot be undertaken within the space of our inquiry. Instead I shall raise the question of the validity of their projects. In response to the question above – could any of us realize their goals of human wholeness? – let us ask if the *Übermensch* and Self are realistic, attainable goals. Let us now try to answer these questions, first by re-examining the validity of the general notion of a union of opposites that comprises the whole self, and then by examining, in turn, the reality of the *Übermensch* and Self.

Is the whole self in the union of opposites an attainable goal?

In Chapter 1, I put forward the proto-theory theory that the notion of a union of opposites (and thus the whole self) is a chimera, because it attempts to conflate and reconcile that which is by definition incommensurable and contradictory. However, for Nietzsche and Jung, the *logical* contradiction of a union of opposites does not undermine the validity of their projects.[1]

Jung accepts that 'comparison between incommensurables is impossible' (Jung, 1955–1956, par. 150) and 'the union of opposites is . . . not amenable to scientific explanation' (ibid., par. 542; see also par. 201). The whole self is a totality that is irreducible to intellectual inquiry; it cannot be conceptually realized and its reality cannot be evaluated:

> What the nature is of that unity [i.e. the Self and its parallel – the *Übermensch*] which in some incomprehensible way embraces the antagonistic elements eludes our human judgement, for the simple reason that nobody can say what a being is like that unites the full range of [opposites].
>
> (Jung, 1955–1956, par. 518)

It is thus a futile task to try to determine whether or not the elusive whole self is an attainable goal. Indeed, Jung expounds upon the irrelevance of this task:

> From the point of view of psychology, the names we give to the self are quite irrelevant, and so is the question of whether or not it is 'real'. Its psychological reality is enough for all practical purposes. The intellect is

incapable of knowing anything beyond that anyway, and therefore its Pilate-like questionings are devoid of meaning.

(Jung, 1946, par. 532)

The self is by definition an entity more comprehensive than the conscious personality. Consequently the latter cannot pass any comprehensive judgement on the self; any judgement and any statement about it is incomplete and has to be supplemented (but not nullified) by a conditioned negative. If I assert, 'The self exists', I must supplement this by saying, 'But it seems not to exist'. For the sake of completeness I must also invert the proposition and say, 'The self does not exist, but yet seems to exist'.

(Jung, 1942/1954, par. 399n)[2]

James Hillman, a major proponent of the archetypal school of Jungian thought, expresses the futility of the task by dismissing the psychological validity of the notion of a union of opposites and maintaining that it belongs solely within the realm of metaphysics (Hillman, 1989, p. 215), thus reflecting (the early) Nietzsche's insistence that the union of Apollo and Dionysus is achievable only through 'a metaphysical miracle' (*BT*, 1).

This is not to say, however, that the *Übermensch* and Self are unattainable metaphysical goals. Both (the later) Nietzsche and Jung were determined to ground their theories away from accusations of metaphysics, mysticism, and idealism. Indeed, although the *Übermensch* and Self cannot be subject to rigorous intellectual examination, they are both empirically grounded within personal *experience*. The reality of the whole self can thus be elucidated on a subjective level: its reality is determinable to one individual but not to another according to whether or not he is capable of harnessing the opposites and of enduring the (dangerous – see Chapter 8) affects that the experience of wholeness occasions.[3] One would assume that individuals who have undergone such an affective experience would know, or at least intuit, that they are now *übermenschlich* or individuated, for both Nietzsche and Jung describe the experience in terms of a sudden heightened conversion or 'redemption' of the personality (*EH*, 'TSZ', 1; Jung, 1951, par. 53).

An evaluation of the reality of the whole self is therefore available to the select few that have experience of it. For the rest of us, we can only arrive at an incomplete and ultimately futile evaluation by examining the whole self for internal logical consistency and coherence. To try to understand the nature of the whole self is to subordinate it to reason, a move that denies its essential Dionysian component of irrationality.

The reality of the Übermensch

Commentators on Nietzsche have disagreed over whether the *Übermensch* is an attainable goal. Both J. M. Kennedy and G. A. Morgan, writing in the early years of the twentieth century, maintain that the *Übermensch* can be realized, but only after a lengthy period of disciplined preparation and instruction. According to Kennedy,

> The Superman is a practical aim – not a new race in the Darwinian sense which it would take thousands of years to bring to maturity; not a species of bliss for us to look forward to after death; but a real, tangible personality, who could be formed in a few generations, if we carried out Zarathustra's teaching.

> (Kennedy, 1910, pp. 345–346)

Kennedy, however, does not elaborate on what Zarathustra's 'teaching' entails. Morgan's envisioned route to the realization of the *Übermensch* is more detailed, and requires the 'higher man' as its starting point. Nietzsche writes more extensively about the 'higher man' or 'objective man' than about the *Übermensch*. Though the higher man is not the ultimate goal of humanity, he is its highest achievement to date,[4] and Morgan maintains that the higher man is a developmental stage before 'thousand year training experiments' lead the higher man to the realization of *Übermenschlichkeit* (Morgan, 1943, pp. 373–374; cf. 'the thousand-year empire of Zarathustra': *TSZ*, IV, 'The Honey Offering'). In support of his view Morgan quotes from Nietzsche's notes the different classifications of value that are attributed to the inhabitants of his new and noble culture (Nietzsche formulates a caste system in which individuals are graded according to the standard and value of power they have attained: see *WP*, 784, 855–862; *BGE*, 257). According to Morgan, Nietzsche's caste system does not employ a fixed and rigid framework but allows for mobility and 'will probably make room for promotion and demotion' (Morgan, 1943, p. 371). This clearly depends upon the change in intensity of the individual's Will to Power (*WP*, 784): that is, whether he can sustain his domination over others and secure a higher rank. It also depends upon what Morgan calls 'thousand year training experiments'. Morgan, like Kennedy before, does not elaborate on what this preparation entails. Perhaps promotion to a higher caste depends upon the teachings of the higher men of the middle class, for as well as legislating, the 'philosophers of power' educate the individual (*WP*, 972, 980) and raise and train him for the heights (*WP*, 957, 980). However, Morgan does not allude to this, and neither does he argue his position to a conclusion; rather we are supposed to take him at his word.

Nietzsche does not provide a detailed account of the individual's training to *Übermenschlichkeit* either. Nietzsche's notes suggest that it will be an international task (*WP*, 960), a task that must be rigorously undertaken, for it 'must appear in association with prevailing moral laws' and therefore requires many means of deception to be devised. It will also include all those characteristics that we have argued for in the course of our inquiry. The 'training' will therefore induce within the individual 'the highest spirituality and strength of will' and the cautious unfettering of 'a host of instincts now kept in check and calumniated'

(*WP*, 957). It is also vital that this training will do everything to prevent the individual from succumbing to a single urge, for, as we saw with the lowest caste, specialism equates with mediocrity (*WP*, 864). Instead, the philosopher of power will train every human faculty to its completion in a perfect synthesis of power. This highest caste of *Übermenschen* will be whole and complete, embodying the unification of the noblest human faculties – the *Übermenschen* will bring together the man of justice, the hero, the poet, the scientist, the prophet, the leader.

According to Bernd Magnus, this lack of detail is significant in determining the reality of the *Übermensch*, for '*Übermenschlichkeit* need not be construed as a normative ideal at all – not merely because one would not know how to begin to realize it or because of its banality, but because it seems, on the surface at least, to entail no specifiable behavioural norms at all' (Magnus, 1988, p. 170). Jacob Golomb claims that the *Übermensch* 'cannot be realized completely' for 'it provides only a regulative idea, a suprahistorical model to approximate and emulate' (Golomb et al. 1999, p. 15). Laurence Lampert also discredits the reality of the *Übermensch* and maintains:

> Nietzsche's ambition so far transcends ordinary ambition that it is scarcely recognisable or credible, and when intimations of its scope first dawn on us, we are compelled to regard it as preposterous – or 'Impossible'.
>
> (Lampert, 1986, p. 2)

Indeed, the *Übermensch* is by definition a goal that can never be achieved because it is a *continual* process of creation. Thus, Richard Howey notes:

> From the very beginning we must keep in mind that the Superman is not to be conceived of as a *state* which man can achieve. One never *is* a Superman except in a relative sense. Relative to the rest of society, we might speak of Goethe as a Superman, but even Goethe had not fully overcome himself and so was, in terms of his possibilities, still on the path to the Superman. No matter how fully and richly a man lives, there is still always the possibility for future self-overcoming.
>
> (Howey, 1973, p. 131)

Nietzsche himself argues that

> the overcoming itself is only a *means*, not a goal; if it is not so viewed, all kinds of weeds and devilish nonsense will quickly spring up in this rich soil now unoccupied, and soon there will be more rank confusion than there ever was before.
>
> (*WS*, 53)

See also *WP*, 108, 708; *GS*, 310; *TI*, 'Maxims and Arrows', 42; *TSZ*, II, 'Of Self-Overcoming': 'And life itself told me this secret: "Behold," it said, "I am that *which must overcome itself again and again'*). Notably, according to Nietzsche, 'nobody has yet had the strength' to endure this ceaseless flux of creation (*GS*, 285) – 'the masters of the earth' are 'a species of man that does not yet exist' (*WP*, 958). However, this is not to say that the *Übermensch* is a 'superterrestrial hope' (*TSZ*, prologue, 3). Zarathustra believes that this 'species of man' will materialize in future generations: 'begotten', 'cultivated' and 'sown' from his disciples' generation (*TSZ*, III, 'Of Old and New Law-Tables', 12), they must 'transform' themselves 'into forefathers and ancestors of the Superman' (*TSZ*, II, 'On the Blissful Islands').[5]

According to Nietzsche, there is much work to be done before the *Übermensch* can be realized. 'The greatest man is all-too-human' (*TSZ*, II, 'Of the Priests') and any advancement on this will be 'rare' and 'slow' (*WP*, 987), taking place through those ambiguous 'thousand year training experiments' cited by Morgan (1943) or through the equally ambiguous 'cultivations' of Zarathustra's disciples.

The reality of the Self

The Self as a goal or end-product of the union of opposites cannot be realized:

> Just as the [alchemical] lapis Philosophorum, with its miraculous powers, was never produced, so psychic wholeness will never be attained empirically, as consciousness is too narrow and too one-sided to comprehend the full inventory of the psyche.
>
> (Jung, 1955–1956, par. 759)

And again: 'We know quite well that no man can ever become the self; the self is an entirely different order of things' (*SNZ*, II, p. 925). Consciousness cannot comprehend the contents of the unconscious, but Jolande Jacobi goes a step further and argues that consciousness is itself too narrow to comprehend the unity of its four functions and two attitude types: 'In theory this is conceivable, but in practice only an approximation is possible, this is because the mind can only be dominated by one function at a time' (Jacobi, 1968, p. 17).[6]

However, as we saw in Chapter 6, the Self can be understood both in terms of the end-product of the process of the union of opposites and as that process itself (see my analysis of Fordham's argument in Chapter 6, note 9, and of Colman's argument that finds no contradiction in the different explanations).[7] In terms of the former understanding, the Self 'will always remain a superordinate quantity' (Jung, 1928b, par. 274), a mere transcendental postulate (ibid., par. 405; Jung, 1946, par. 532).[8] This is because (as with the *Übermensch*) the creative process of uniting the opposites in Selfhood does not end (Jung, 1951, par. 44). In Jungian psychology the individual's values must be revalued not just once but ceaselessly; the opposites must be overcome over and over again, so that the dialectic between the unconscious and consciousness is a life's work. However, Jung, like Nietzsche before him, does postulate, though implicitly, a future time in which the whole self

– as an end-product – will become a reality, when the process of unification will reach some kind of 'termination'. Thus, 'the man of today is far from this wholeness' (Jung, 1934a, par. 286), which

> may not set in for hundreds of years, for the spiritual transformation of mankind follows the slow tread of the centuries and cannot be hurried or held up by any rational process of reflection, let alone brought to fruition in one generation.
>
> (Jung, 1957, par. 583)

If we were to regard the Self in terms of the latter understanding (as identifiable with the process itself), then it is immediately experienceable by the individual; the Self is now an empirical reality and finds expression.[9] But this does not mean that the process is more definite than the 'end-product'. It still evades intellectual understanding as it incorporates the unconscious in its development: the 'mysterious third thing', the symbol, is required to unite the opposites and enable the process to advance.

We can conclude that the *Übermensch* and Self as whole selves cannot be realized, but this does not mean that they should not serve as a basis for meaning in human life. This is not, however, recommended by Nehamas, for 'the totally integrated person . . . may well be morally repulsive . . . the uncomfortable feeling persists that someone might achieve . . . [this] ideal life and still be nothing short of repugnant' (Nehamas, 1985, p. 167). Indeed, the whole self, according to Nietzsche and Jung, will embody those shadow-values that are beyond good and evil, those values that we may find unacceptable and directly opposed to our 'traditional' moral code. Nevertheless, according to Nietzsche and Jung, the individual should aspire towards wholeness, despite it being an immoral (or, rather, amoral: see Chapter 8, note 3) and unachievable *state*. The *Übermensch* and Self are the imaginary (and in this sense metaphysical) goals that lie at the end of the never-ending process of unification, but at the same time they are identified with the dynamics of the creative process itself. Individuals are thus displaying the traits of *Übermenschlichkeit* and individuation if they are able to sustain the process of unification within themselves.

How has Nietzsche influenced Jung, and how might he influence Jungian thought further?

At the end of our inquiry we are left with the question of what, if anything, Nietzschean thought can teach analytical psychology. In Chapter 1, I noted that while Nietzschean philosophy and philosophy in general influenced both Freud and Jung in the development of their theories, Freud refused to admit its influence and Jung celebrated it. It would thus be an interesting proposition to determine whether Freud and Jung could separately arrive at a more complete theory had the former not *repressed* the philosophical stimulus in his work, and had the latter not *misrepresented* it. Such an inquiry would, however, be too extensive for us to consider here. It would also be hypothetical. Aside from being highly speculative, it would be difficult to evaluate exactly how 'complete' a theory it is and indeed could be. Instead, I shall draw our inquiry to conclusion by considering how Nietzschean thought might enrich the development of 'post-Jungian' thought, by re-examining where Nietzsche's and Jung's model of the whole self differ. That is, to see if there is an aspect to Nietzsche's model that is not in Jung's, one that might have otherwise enriched it. But before I do this, let us revisit one of the principal aims of our inquiry, which is to determine the extent to which Nietzsche can be considered an influence on Jung.

We have found that Nietzsche's influence upon Jung's project of the whole self is profound: sometimes explicit, sometimes ambivalent. From our inquiry it is clear that Jung did not inadvertently arrive at a similar model to Nietzsche, but expounds Nietzsche's model and develops his psychological anticipations further. Jung tells us that 'the theory of the preconscious primordial ideas is by no means my own invention . . . we find this theory in the works of . . . Nietzsche' (Jung, 1938/1940, par. 89). However, Nietzsche

> simply listened in to that underground process of the collective unconscious and he was not able to realize it – he talked of it, but nobody else noticed it . . . perhaps I am the only one who takes the trouble to go so much into the detail of Zarathustra.
>
> (*SNZ*, II, p. 1518)

In this respect Nietzsche is an influence (conscious) upon Jung's project: the *Übermensch* and the Self are two expressions and formulations of the whole self. However, in our inquiry I have argued for a deeper, more ambiguous, influence of Nietzsche upon Jung – and that is Nietzsche's *unconscious* influence upon Jung's personality.[10] Jung writes: 'In 1888 he [Nietzsche] went mad. That was a tremendous event; it made a deep impression on me' (*JS*, p. 207). This impression, I argued, was a 'fear that I might perhaps be like him' (*MDR*, pp. 122–123): a fear that Jung himself might be going mad. I have contended that Nietzsche represents an unresolved shadow personality of Jung, so that Jung's misdiagnosis of Nietzsche's madness can be considered a self-diagnosis. In my interpretation, the personality of Nietzsche stands in Jung's way, preventing him from (getting closer to) realizing the Self. The shadow projection on to Nietzsche would explain why Jung is reluctant fully to acknowledge Nietzsche's influence when it is deserved, and why he mistakenly criticizes Nietzsche's argument.

As we have seen, Nietzsche and Jung founded their theories in *experience*, and it is only through experience – expressed through the Jungian terms of thinking, intuition, sensation and feeling – that Jungian thought might develop further.[11] The principal difference between the models of Nietzsche and Jung relates to their different interpretations of the character of experience. And it is to Nietzsche's interpretation that we now turn, to determine if Jungian thought could develop according to Nietzsche's interpretation of experience.

For Nietzsche, experience is characterized by constant flux. Unlike Jung, who seeks creativity through a balance of opposites, Nietzsche seeks it through their chaotic interaction. We have seen Nietzsche express this lack of order by explaining his psychological theory in terms of physiology (a move that Jung (incorrectly) criticizes as depersonalizing the psyche).[12] And we have seen that he would interpret Jung's need to give order and form to experience as an aspiration to the Will to Truth. The implication here is that, although they present similar criteria for mental health and illness, Nietzsche would not have as structured a characterization of these terms as Jung. Furthermore, Nietzsche would want to extend the notion of 'health' to include cases that might otherwise be construed as unhealthy. While Jung would construe the 'well-balanced' personality to be healthy, Nietzsche would find health in the 'chaotic' personality that can never be satisfied, and is easily inclined to discord and strife (*PTAG*, 5). Nietzsche insists: 'One is *fruitful* only at the cost of being rich in contradictions; one remains *young* only on condition the soul does not relax, does not long for peace' (*TI*, 'Morality as Anti-Nature', 3). He demands the highest possible tension between opposites at all times – the greatest antagonism – so that the unconscious is kept as if it were about to explode into consciousness. Nietzsche seeks the most creative personality, and this is one that teeters precariously on the edge of madness and self-destruction. (Cf. *HAH*, 260; Jung: 'A person must pay dearly for the divine gift of creative fire': Jung, 1930/1950, par. 158). Earlier we noted that Nietzsche might not have been so creative in his thought had he not been (in Jung's diagnosis) identified with the collective unconscious, but mentally 'healthy' instead (see Chapter 9, note 4). For Nietzsche there is no such thing as a 'pathological' personality (*BGE*, 197), and if there were, it would be something to celebrate and not reject on the mistaken grounds that it is in any way unhealthy. Indeed, according to Nietzsche, personalities that 'are terrifying and considered inhuman may even be the fertile soil out of which alone all humanity can grow in impulse, deed and work' (*Homer's Contest*, 1872, 1; cited in Dixon, 1999, p. 303). Thus, Nietzsche would insist that one's 'pathological symptoms' not be removed, for this inevitably diminishes one's passion and creative resources.[13]

It must be remembered that Nietzsche does not seek the Dionysian personality that equates with the one-sided 'barbarian' and that plunges head-first into the unconscious abyss (*BT*, 9). Rather he seeks, the rope across the abyss where Dionysus meets Apollo, and the 'dithyrambic madness' is 'healed' (*BT*, 25). Nevertheless, Nietzsche insists that the potentially deadly tightrope walk across the abyss must be attempted (but not by everyone), for it is only by crossing the abyss that one can travel from one tower (of mediocrity) to the other (of nobility) (*TSZ*, prologue, 6). It is thus only in keeping a close and careful proximity to the abyss that one can safely draw out its creative energy. The fact that one knows that one might fall makes one stronger (cf. *TI*, 'Maxims and Arrows', 8).

It is perhaps unfair to suggest that Jung might learn from this Nietzschean chaotic characterization. Although Jung does not seek chaos, he does not shy away from its dangers either, for he maintains that it is only through embracing the danger that it no longer poses a threat: 'The unconscious is unfavourable or dangerous only because we are not at one with it and therefore in opposition to it' (Jung, 1917/1926/1943, par. 195). In this sense, we could say that Jung finds balance through the chaotic experience. Jung also agrees with Nietzsche that these supposed 'unfavourable' aspects of the unconscious should not be rejected, but harnessed for their creative worth: 'The repressed tendencies that are made conscious should not be destroyed but, on the contrary, should be developed further' (*JS*, pp. 41–42).[14] Indeed, Jung would not disagree with any of the above. He would celebrate the personality that is strong enough to endure the darker forces of the unconscious. I think there is, however, a subtle difference between Nietzsche and Jung in terms of their reasons for harnessing the creative energy of the unconscious. Both Nietzsche and Jung are adamant that the unconscious finds expression, and both are wary of the need to contain its expressions; but I sense that while Jung wants to incorporate its communication into consciousness, with the intention of giving the ego a more affluent focus (the Self), Nietzsche simply wants the unconscious to express itself, in order to see how much the ego can contain – as if it were an existential experiment. If this is the case, Nietzsche might suggest that the 'well-balanced' personality of Jung's model should take more risks, and live more dangerously.

Nietzsche might also issue Jung with a warning: not to allow the structures he has imposed on the unconscious to impede its expression. That is, by categorizing the unconscious into different archetypal motivations or 'stages', Jungian thought is susceptible to becoming too reliant on them, of regarding them as the definitive interpretation of unconscious energy, when in fact, in Nietzsche's view, there is no definitive explanation: all structures undergo slow dissolution and alteration. Although Jung issues a similar warning, and regards his attempt to structure the unconscious as provisional (Jung, 1951, par. 429; Jung, 1931b, par. 81; cf. Jung, 1921, par. 731; Jung, 1928b, par. 405), one should be concerned that his archetypal categorizations do not become laboured (or too familiar, as it were) to the point of becoming jargon. In my (academic) experience the notion of the 'shadow', for example, has been bandied about to the extent that its precise meaning has often been obscured. (And in some cases extremely so. Occasionally it has been used as an 'umbrella term', referring to all that is 'negative' in the neglected personality; the fact that the shadow also refers to its positive aspects is ignored.) To regard Jung's 'provisional' attempts to structure the unconscious as fixed is equivalent to reducing the symbol to a sign. Both inhibit unconscious expression.

Nietzsche's interpretation of experience does not enrich Jungian thought as such; Nietzsche does not offer insight into how Jungian theory could be improved or developed further. Rather, Nietzsche consolidates Jungian theory, and he does so in a twofold way: in supporting its insistence on harnessing the creative energy of the unconscious, by seeking its affective communication through the symbol, and in reinforcing its warning of not impeding unconscious communication by addressing it through the reductive conscious terms of the sign.

Through our examination of Jung's critique of Nietzsche's model of the whole self, we have seen that Jung failed to listen to his own warning. Through the example of Nietzsche, we see that Jung must learn not to constrict the symbol – not to have preconceptions of what can and cannot count as a symbol. Jung's misunderstanding of Nietzsche rests on the interpretation that Nietzsche's notion of the Will to Power is merely a conscious invention, merely a sign, when in fact it functions as a symbol within Nietzsche's model. Through Nietzsche, Jung is taught a lesson of his own: not to reduce the symbol to theoretical conception, but instead to consider it in its own terms and allow it to work itself out, so that its creative power can be fully – or *wholly* – experienced.

Notes

I Introduction

1   The question that springs to mind here is why Freud vigorously denies having read
Nietzsche and having been influenced by his ideas when evidence suggests the contrary.
In the minutes of the Vienna Psychoanalytic Society meeting of 1908 we read that in
response to Alfred Adler's assertion that Freud's thought was close to that of Nietzsche,
Freud said he 'knew nothing' of Nietzsche's work, and that all attempts he made at
reading him were 'smothered by an excess of interest'. Similarly, Jung recounts that
'Freud himself had told me that he had never read Nietzsche' (*MDR*, p. 153; also, 'He
[*sc*. Freud] once assured me personally that it never occurred to him to read Nietzsche':
Jung, 1939a, par. 61). However, against Freud's insistence we can cite evidence to
suggest the contrary. For example, in this meeting of the Vienna Psychoanalytic
Society, Paul Federn asked: 'where has he [*sc*. Nietzsche] not come close?' (Federn and
Nunberg, 1967, vol. 1, p. 359), to which Freud retorts: 'he failed to recognize
infantilism as well as the mechanisms of displacement' (ibid., p. 361). Similarly, Ernest
Jones recorded that 'Freud several times said of Nietzsche that he had a more
penetrating knowledge of himself than any man who ever lived, or was ever likely to
live' (Jones, 1953–1957, vol. 2, p. 344). Such evaluations presuppose a high degree of
familiarity with Nietzsche's work. Indeed, if we turn to Freud's work itself, we can see
persuasive evidence that he was both directly and indirectly familiar with Nietzsche's
work. For example, in *The Psychopathology of Everyday Life*, Freud refers to the
68th aphorism of *Beyond Good and Evil*, which is rather amusing in light of our
discussion, for it states: '"I have done that", says my memory. "I cannot have done
that" – says my pride, and remains adamant. At last – memory yields'. In his paper
'On an Autobiographically Described Case of Paranoia' (1910), Freud writes that
the situation of the patient in question reminded him of the emotions expressed in
the section of *Thus Spoke Zarathustra* 'Before the Sunrise'. As well as these direct
references to Nietzsche's work we may also assume that Freud gained some familiarity
with Nietzsche through the Vienna Psychoanalytic Society, which heard talks on both
the *Genealogy of Morals* (1 April 1908) and *Ecce Homo* (28 October 1908). Freud did
admit to having some knowledge of Nietzsche in *History of the Psychoanalytic
Movement* (1914), but this admission was not an admission of Nietzsche's influence,
but an acknowledgement that Nietzsche had anticipated his central themes: 'In recent
times I have denied myself the great benefit of Nietzsche's work, with the express intent
that in the gathering of psychoanalytic expressions I not be impeded by any conceptual
anticipations' (Freud, 1914, pp. 14–15).

   The generally agreed explanation of this ambiguity is that Freud needed to dissociate
his thought from philosophy and its speculative assessments in general (see Lehrer,

1995, 1999a; Golomb et al., 1999, pp. 150–151). Freud certainly displayed a remark-able distrust of speculation. (In answer to Ernest Jones' question of how much philosophy he had read, Freud answered, 'Very little. As a young man I felt a strong attraction toward speculation and ruthlessly checked it': Jones, 1953–1957, vol. 1, p. 29). In acknowledging Nietzsche's ideas Freud would have to concede that specula-tion had produced insights equalling those that psychoanalysis achieved only through laborious scientific investigation. Nietzsche promoted imaginative speculation when Freud did not. Freud's antithetical attitude towards Nietzsche and speculation in general was due to his desire to establish psychoanalysis as a scientific discipline at a time when it was generally ostracized by the scientific community. Identification with the writings of Nietzsche under these circumstances would have hindered his cause.

2   Paul Bishop in *The Dionysian Self* (1995) offers an extensive survey and fair evaluation of previous research into the intellectual affinities between Nietzsche and Jung up to the year 1995 (pp. 2–16). Bishop concludes that none of the standard introductions to Jungian psychology discusses the relevance of Nietzsche for Jung, and nor do those books that deal with the more philosophical aspects of his work. Likewise, many works allude to Jung fleetingly in their research into Nietzschean psychology without acknowledging the latter's influence on the former or the affinities between the two thinkers in general. In contrast, however, nearly all the published biographies on Jung do acknowledge, albeit very briefly, the importance which Jung attached to his reading Nietzsche.

Post-1995 there seems to have been a rise in interest in the relationship between the thought of Nietzsche and Jung. But in general these investigations fall short: they either fail to acknowledge the important affinities *and* differences between Nietzsche and Jung, or are not critical enough in their exposition, often ignoring important impli-cations and problems that arise in their argument. For example, Christopher Hauke in 'Jung, Nietzsche and the Roots of the Postmodern' (Hauke, 2000, pp. 145–174) discusses three 'areas of overlap' in the thought of Nietzsche and Jung: the notion of the ego, how Jung incorporates Nietzsche's perspectivism in his ideas of the personality and complexes, and how the *Übermensch* and the individuation process – as cultural projects – describe the overcoming of modernity. Hauke's argument moves at a great rate, jumping from one idea to the next, only to scratch the surface of an argument. Hauke compounds the problem by introducing numerous other thinkers into his argument – including Freud, Foucault, Lacan, Kristeva and Habermas – so that a comparison of the ideas of Jung and Nietzsche becomes side-lined in favour of a discussion of their relationship to 'postmodern' thought in general. Another example is Anthony Storr's (1996) *Nietzsche and Jung* (the J. R. Jones Lecture). Here Storr examines the 'personal' responses of Nietzsche and Jung to their loss of religion and need to find a substitute (they both felt an 'aching void which post-scientific rationalism [was] unable to fill': Storr, 1996, p. 8). Storr makes the significant claims that 'Nietzsche anticipated Jung's idea of individualism and may in fact have been its originator' (p. 15), and that the *Übermensch* and Self are 'archetypes of unity and totality . . . but expressed in different terms' (p. 10). But he does not expound on these ideas; the fact that the *Übermensch* and Self are intended substitutes for their lost religion is barely implied.

I consider there to be three detailed studies on the common thought of Nietzsche and Jung, which will surface in the course of our inquiry, and which I shall briefly address here. These are Paul Bishop's *The Dionysian Self: C. G. Jung's Reception of Friedrich Nietzsche* (1995), Patricia Dixon's *Nietzsche and Jung: Sailing a Deeper Night* (1999) and Graham Parkes' 'Nietzsche and Jung: Ambivalent Appreciation' (1999).

Bishop (1995) is certainly most rigorous as he chronicles the shift in Jung's attitude towards Nietzsche. However, his great attention to detail often means that the philosophical implications of Jung's thought and treatment of Nietzsche are skated over in favour of detailed intellectual-historical contextualization. This is also true of his article 'C. G. Jung and Nietzsche: Dionysus and Analytical Psychology' (Bishop, 1999a). Bishop takes the theme of Dionysus as that which connects the thought of Jung and Nietzsche, and charts the development of this (Nietzschean) notion in Jung's personal letters, his autobiographical sources, lectures, seminars (including those on *TSZ*) and in his Collected Works. Bishop does not, however, acknowledge or argue through how Jung's reception of Dionysus is critical for the validity of Jungian theory itself. For example, Bishop does not analyse the implications of Jung's failure to distinguish between the two different conceptions of Dionysus that Nietzsche presents in his work – something that is, as we shall see, of paramount significance to both Jung's reception of Nietzsche and to the value of Jungian theory itself. If Jung had noted the difference, he would not have diagnosed Nietzsche as a 'pathological personality' and would not have been so critical of Nietzsche's philosophy in general. This has implications for Jungian psychology, because Jung, in effect, used Nietzsche as a model or 'case study' to demonstrate and express the dynamics of his own psychological theories.

The principal aim of Dixon (1999) is similar to mine: to demonstrate that 'the quest for wholeness, the central theme in C. G. Jung's psychology, is [also] the dominant thread that runs through the entire fabric of Nietzsche's writings' (p. 3). However, Dixon's research is purely expositional and descriptive (often expressed in a barrage of quotations, which at times left me wondering *who* was trying to argue a particular point – her subjects, or Dixon herself?). Dixon's argument lacks substantial analysis and evaluation, which means that many critical implications of Jungian and Nietzschean theory are left unexamined. In particular, Dixon fails to take into account the change and development in Nietzsche's thought on opposites. This change is a crucial factor for determining Nietzsche's influence upon Jung, for Nietzsche's thought becomes antagonistic to the affinities they hitherto shared. Dixon's argument depends entirely on Nietzsche's early metaphysical thought and his unpublished works, and does not acknowledge Nietzsche's later work where he explicitly denounces belief in opposites and equates it, *contra* Jung, with the ascetic ideal: the devaluation of life.

In an attempt to offer a needed examination of the affinities between Nietzsche and Jung, Dixon has been overly enthusiastic and has not acknowledged where the affinity ends. When she does imply that the influence of Nietzsche upon Jung was not so straightforward – where Jung, often explicitly, misrepresents the thought of Nietzsche – she does not attempt to give a reason or explanation for why he made, in her words, such 'surprising' errors. The lack of analysis here is critical, for Dixon fails to acknowledge the important implications that Jung's misrepresentation of Nietzsche has for Jungian psychology. Dixon's lack of analysis of the implications is given further expression in the absence of any critical engagement of what the 'wholeness' of man – according to Nietzsche and Jung – actually entails, how it relates to life in practice, and whether such an achievement is possible.

Of all the commentators on Nietzsche and Jung, Parkes (1999) comes closest to anticipating the underlying arguments of my inquiry. Parkes argues that Jung misinterprets Nietzsche's thought and offers a misdiagnosis of Nietzsche (as having an ego-inflation). Parkes explains the former in terms of Jung simply being 'a careless reader' (p. 225), and he explains the latter in terms of Jung having acquired misleading personal information about Nietzsche – that is, of pronouncing 'Nietzsche's character on the basis of gossip gleaned during his time in Basle rather than the biographical information available by the time of the *Zarathustra* seminars' (ibid.). Parkes' explanation for Jung's overall ambivalent reception of Nietzsche is purely on the basis of his misreading of Nietzsche's works, which he considers 'one of the most perverse hermeneutic gestures in the history of textural interpretation' (p. 218). Parkes does briefly mention that Jung's fear of being 'all-too-similar to Nietzsche with respect to morbidity prompts him to distance himself from the mad philosopher' (p. 206), and later he writes of Jung's 'irritation' with Nietzsche's personality, which Parkes considers to be indicative of 'some kind of projection' from Jung. However, Parkes does not consider these to be connected – something that I shall set out to show in my inquiry.

3   Bishop claims: 'Jung's appeal to Nietzsche has an additional highly polemical purpose. For Jung's words of praise for Nietzsche's intuitive insights in the field of psychology served as a means of attacking Freudian psychoanalysis' (Bishop, 1995, p. 193). According to Assoun:

> Nietzsche will thus furnish the dissident disciple the mode of expression for his emancipation! . . . Nietzsche intervenes between Freud and Jung to mark the assertion of the disciple [Jung], which is met by the master's [sc. Freud's] silence, as the gospel of the revolt of the disciple against the master, and finally as a reference to his own dissident work – as an indication of Nietzschean ideas in Jung's work . . . Freud . . . discovers Nietzsche's name as the stake in the conflict' between his ideas and those of Jung.
>
> (Assoun, 2000, p. 25)

Lehrer notes that: 'a number of analysts who were associated with Freud . . . [and Jung would be included] appear to have utilized Nietzsche in their attempts to liberate themselves from Freud' (Lehrer, 1999b, p. 241). Jarrett in his introduction to *SNZ* claims that Jung's shock at Freud's admission of never having read Nietzsche 'planted in the younger man's mind the seed of suspicion' (Jarrett, introduction to *SNZ*, p. xi), and 'gradually led him to think of the dilemma, "Freud vs. Nietzsche"' (Jarrett, 1990, p. 131). Jarrett notes: 'It was just after his break with Freud that Jung returned to Nietzsche' (ibid.). Later in this inquiry, at the end of Chapter 11, we shall see that Jung's attraction to Nietzschean philosophy (and the personality of Nietzsche) occurs at a significant time of self-reflection in Jung's life, at 'a period of inner uncertainty . . . a state of disorientation' (*MDR*, p. 194), which immediately followed his 'loss of so important a friendship' (*MDR*, p. 191) with Freud. I shall argue that Jung turns to Nietzschean philosophy not only to establish a psychological theory distinct from Freudian psychoanalysis (something that is notably expressed by Jung in a letter to Freud of 3 March 1912, in his quoting of Nietzsche's *Zarathustra*: 'One repays a teacher badly if one remains only a pupil': McGuire, 1974, p. 491), but also in order to re-establish a sense of personal identity independent of Freud.

4   For clarification see Jung (1928b, pars. 202–220). However, some commentators have noted that Freud's theory does postulate an autonomous collective unconscious. See Paul Bishop's (1996) article 'The Use of Kant in Jung's Early Psychological Works' (Appendix, pp. 139–140). However, Freud was certainly an extreme rationalist who upheld objective value and proof at the expense of emotion and subjective experience. While both Nietzsche and Jung wanted psychology to be grounded in empirical observation, neither was as insistent as Freud on founding a rational 'science'. Nietzsche would have condemned such preoccupation with rationality as ascetic. Nietzsche and Jung were certainly more speculative, and Jung believed Freud was wrong to shun philosophical speculative inquiry, and for reducing mental processes to a biological understanding.

5   Of course, the same applies to the inquiry that follows.

6   I have decided to use the term *Übermensch* in our inquiry, rather than 'superman' or 'overman', simply because I find these two translations unsatisfactory. The word 'Self'

is not capitalized in the *Collected Works* of Jung, but I have capitalized it in our inquiry in order to convey its transcendent nature, and to distinguish it from the concept of self in other psychologies where Jung would ordinarily refer to 'ego'.

7 Bishop also applies the distinction between discovery and creation to Jung and Nietzsche (Bishop, 1995, pp. 353, 365–366; 1999, p. 229).

8 For further clarification of the problem of defining the Jungian Self see Huskinson (2002).

9 Whether the *Übermensch* or Self can be considered 'end-products' of a process is debatable; I shall assess this claim later.

10 See *PTAG*, preface; *BGE*, 6; cf. 3; *AOM*, prologue, 1; Jung, 1938/1954, par. 150; *MDR*, p. 249.

11 From now on, works of Nietzsche and Jung that I shall frequently cite will be referred to in their abbreviated form as explained in the list of abbreviations at the beginning of the book.

12 Elsewhere I have discussed the problem of a unification of opposites at length. See Huskinson (2000).

13 The 'mutual repulsion of warring opposites' is grounded in the early thought of Anaximander (*c.*610 BC to *c.*546 BC), the earliest thinker for whom a detailed cosmology is attested). Anaximander claimed that 'the ring of the sun is furthest from the earth, and the rings of the stars are closest', for the 'ring of the sun obviously contains the greatest mass of fire, and given the opposition between fire and earth, it is not implausible that in the course of the process of cosmology such a mass of fire should have been flung furthest from the centre' (Long, 1999, pp. 55–56).

14 Unless one were to accept a metaphysical model in which opposites can merge and interact on a transcendental level. Later we shall see that Jung compares the union of opposites to God. This idea is expressed in the thought of Nicholas of Cusa (1401–1464).

> God is, for Nicholas, the *coincidentia oppositorum*, the synthesis of opposites in a unique and absolutely infinite being. Finite things are multiple and distinct, possessing their different natures and qualities while God transcends all distinctions and opposition which are found in creatures. But God transcends these distinctions in an incomprehensible manner . . . If we say that God is the *complicatio et eorum coincidentia*, we must realize that we cannot have a positive understanding of what this means.
>
> (Copleston, 1964, p. 41)

This suggests that the union of opposites is not a logical question per se. Indeed, as Jung notes, 'That the opposites must cancel each other is *logically* correct, but *practically* it is not so' (Jung, 1921, par. 178). I address this issue throughout the following pages and, particularly, in Chapter 13.

15 Our inquiry concerns dynamic opposites, I am not concerned with the abstract notion of the opposites of presence and absence.

16 According to Emmanuel Levinas (1906–1995), two polar extremes can never exist by themselves within a dyadic relationship, because the terms 'opposition' or 'difference' in themselves presuppose a higher spectrum of meaning, which the two polar extremes are measured against (so that they can indeed be compared against one another and be deemed 'opposite'). Levinas therefore writes: 'Thesis and antithesis, in repelling one another, call for one another. They appear in opposition to a synoptic gaze that encompasses them' (Levinas, 1969, p. 38). An implied third thing is required in the relationship. (It must be noted, however, that Levinas regards the third thing to be a fallacy of ontology; the above quotation is intended to be a critique of ontology.) 'In

alchemy we often come across the image of a pair linked together by a third' (Von Franz, 2000, p. 396; see also: 'Three and one, moreover, are well-known alchemical formulae for the wholeness of the central symbol', ibid., p. 275).

17 Thus, the methods of Jungian psychology can be useful when applied to philosophical theory, as it is able to expose that which theoretical reflection is unable to access. For example, it is able to get behind the motivations of the author. Indeed, by analysing the role of opposites in Nietzsche's model of the self, in comparison with that of Jung, we shall be given new interpretation and resolution to particular problems of inconsistency and obscurity in Nietzschean philosophy through understanding them in psychological terms. Most notably, the meaning and constitution of the *Übermensch*.

18 While philosophical criticism can *distort* Jungian thought, elsewhere I have argued that the Self is principally a numinous experience that evades and *violates* ego-comprehension. The Self cannot be defined or reduced to an intellectual analysis. Furthermore, it should not be reduced to limited definitions, where it is no more than a transcendental postulate, passive function or derivative from the internal structure of Jungian argument. See Huskinson (2002).

2 Opposites in early Nietzsche: metaphysical, aesthetic and psychological opposites

1 Nietzsche later calls this metaphysical notion of 'primal unity' the 'Will to Power'. However, I believe that the Will to Power is not a metaphysical doctrine. For commentators on Nietzsche that interpret the Will to Power as a non-metaphysical doctrine see Maudmarie Clark (1990), who argues that the Will to Power is a hypothetical argument that, ironically, encourages his reader not to look for metaphysical meaning in life. Sarah Kofman (1972) argues that the Will to Power is a 'superior hypothesis' about interpretation because it promotes the greatest 'enrichment and embellishment of life' (p. 202): it is 'not a revelation but a justification of Being' (p. 201); it affirms the fullness of life by promoting the multiplicity of its possible interpretations (cited in Clark, 1990, p. 15). Walter Kaufmann (1968) argues that the Will to Power is a psychological doctrine: it is 'the one and only interpretation of human behaviour [and reality in general] of which we are capable when we consider the evidence and think about it as clearly as we can' (ibid., p. 206). In other words, the Will to Power is true only because it is the theory that best accounts for our experience. (Nietzsche certainly regarded the Will to Power as the basis of psychology; thus: psychology is the 'morphology and the *development-theory of the will to power*': *BGE*, 23).

2 Nietzsche later remarks that 'in contrast to the animals, man has cultivated an abundance of *contrary* drives and impulses within himself: thanks to this synthesis he is master of the earth' (*WP*, 966).

3 This tragic world view is evident in the philosophy of Heraclitus, who transformed the thought of the world as eternal flux from one of terror 'into its opposite, into sublimity and the feeling of blessed astonishment' (*PTAG*, 5). This transformation occurs with the discovery of a cosmos-creating force, 'Logos', through which 'wonderful order, regularity and certainty manifested themselves in all coming-to-be' (*PTAG*, 9).

4 Nietzsche here anticipates Freud's notion of the manifest and latent content of dreams (see Freud, 1900/1991, vi).

5 Nietzsche later changes his attitude towards tragedy: humans should no longer seek this transcendent realm in order to escape the confrontation with terrible reality, but must learn to find joy in that confrontation. This tragic attitude – a 'pessimism of strength' – will be discussed in Chapter 3.

6 However, in *The Greeks and the Irrational* (1951), Eric Dodds notes: 'Tradition said,

probably with truth, that the original Earth oracle at Delphi had been a dream-oracle' (p. 110).

7 Nietzsche does allude to 'Apollinian music' (*BT*, 2) of a strongly rhythmic character that is associated with the lyre, but he does not expand upon the traditional association of Apollo with music.

8 See William Guthrie (1950, pp. 205–253) for further discussion of this distinction.

9 The association of Apollo with consciousness and of Dionysus with the unconscious will be examined in Chapter 9.

10 The connection between Nietzsche's aesthetics and metaphysics is apparent. It is not simply the case that art is privileged within his metaphysical theory (as it is with Schopenhauer), for his aesthetics is metaphysical. In *Preface to Wagner* (1888d/1967) Nietzsche writes: 'art represents the highest task and the truly metaphysical activity of this life'; that is, art, by serving to protect the individual through its illusions, has a high metaphysical purpose attached to it.

11 This contradiction will be examined in Chapter 3.

12 In Greek tragedy the Dionysian is associated with the chorus, which was composed of satyrs who, through their dance, induced a sense of ecstasy in the spectator, thereby achieving a breakdown of the barrier between spectator and stage, and creating an atmosphere similar to a cultish ceremony. The function of the Apollinian is to shield the spectator against the full impact of the music, at the same time as accentuating it. By itself Dionysian music would be a devastating experience, with its evocation of primordial universality. The Apollinian drama of the tragic myth makes the evocation bearable in its portrayal of the sublime hero, with whom the spectator can empathize and find pleasure. Contrary to the negation of individuality, the spectator is relieved of the burden of the Dionysian by the hero of the play, who struggles to take on the Dionysian world himself.

13 In Chapter 3 we shall see that this consideration is irrelevant, for Nietzsche's dismissal of metaphysics brings with it the need to reinterpret the Dionysian and Apollinian as psychological impulses only.

14 It must be noted that moderation for Nietzsche does not mean the avoidance of strong opposition; it does not find a parallel in the Aristotelian mean (which Nietzsche rejects as 'mediocre': *TSZ*, III, 'Of the Virtue that Makes Small', 2). Rather, it refers to the promotion of the most antagonistic traits in equal measure. Thus, the maintenance of the most intense conflict between elements in a strong binary opposition characterizes the most spiritual of men (*TI*, 'Expeditions of an Untimely Man', 17).

15 Kaufmann in his essay 'Nietzsche and the Death of Tragedy: A Critique' (1976) argues that Nietzsche was wrong to consider Euripides the rationalist among the Greek tragedians, and considers instead Aeschylus (Nietzsche's candidate for the most irrational) as the most rational and closest to Plato. Dodds accepts Kaufmann's reversal of Nietzsche's schema, and argues in 'Euripides the Irrationalist' (Dodds, 1929, pp. 78–92). that the decline of Greek tragedy was caused by irrationalism, and that Socrates and Plato, contrary to Nietzsche's thought, embody true Greek genius.

3 Opposites in Nietzsche post-1878: the denial of metaphysical opposites

1 As we shall see in the course of our inquiry, Nietzsche does not reject aestheticism completely in his model of opposites. See note 9.

2 The metaphysician therefore denies the Heraclitean notion of polarity that Nietzsche himself endorses: 'The diverging of a force into two qualitatively different opposed activities that seek to reunite' (*PTAG*, 5).

3 The distinction between 'true' and 'apparent' worlds is his most frequent target for the

refutation of opposites. See the end of 'History of an Error', 'How the World at Last Became a Myth' (*TI*), where Nietzsche identifies the abolition of this dualism as his personal mission. This is because Nietzsche believes the idea of a true world beyond time to have lost its purpose and to be wholly irrelevant to our 'earthly' concerns. With the abolition of the true world also comes the abolition of the apparent world; the whole metaphysical dichotomy is thus dissolved.

4 In *HAH* a difficulty arises for Nietzsche. Nietzsche draws a distinction, an *opposition*, between his 'historical philosophy' and metaphysical philosophy. Perhaps due to the recognition of this danger and failure Nietzsche changes his approach in *BGE* from a direct comparison between his own interpretation and that of the metaphysicians to focusing on the future and the anticipation of 'the arrival of the new species of philosopher' (*BGE*, 2). This change demonstrates a potential awareness on Nietzsche's part of falling into oppositional thinking himself. However, this view is negated in Nietzsche's insistence that we 'have to await the arrival of a new species of philosopher, one which possesses tastes and inclinations *opposite to* and different from those of its predecessors' (ibid., italics mine).

5 Maudemarie Clark argues that the reason for this is that Nietzsche had not yet found a way to deny the conceivability of the thing-in-itself (Clark, 1990, pp. 98–99). Thus in *HAH* Nietzsche refuses to rule out the possibility of a metaphysical world; he insists only that truth or essence might differ radically from its possible appearance to human beings. But by the time Nietzsche writes *BGE* he thinks he has found a way to discard the metaphysical world completely by arguing that the thing-in-itself is an impossible notion that involves a contradiction in terms: 'But I shall reiterate a hundred times that "immediate certainty", like "absolute knowledge" and "thing in itself" contains a *contradictio in adjecto*: we really ought to get free from the seduction of words!' (*BGE*, 16). The rest of this passage, however, does not explicitly argue why the very idea of the thing-in-itself involves a contradiction in terms; this must be sought elsewhere. Thus, in *GS* Nietzsche writes:

> What is 'appearance' for me now? Certainly not the opposite of some essence: what could I say about any essence except to name the attributes of its appearance! Certainly not a dead mask that one could place on an unknown x or remove from it!
>
> (*GS*, 54)

In *TL* Nietzsche writes of this 'mysterious X of the thing-in-itself' and equates it with 'the essence of all things' (*TL*, 83; *WP*, 880). The argument in *GS*, 54 therefore supports the argument of *BGE*, 16: Nietzsche rejects the existence of a metaphysical world for its manifestation must be within a world of appearance, the world that it necessarily negates.

6 The question of Nietzsche and metaphysics is derived from Heidegger's interpretation of Nietzsche. See 'The Word of Nietzsche: "God is Dead"' (Heidegger, 1977).

7 However, the inherent movement itself that is found within Nietzsche's writing can be seen as a denial of the rigid structure of these opposites. Nietzsche insists upon fluidity and playfulness within written texts:

> What a torment books written in German are for him who has a *third* ear! How disgustedly he stands beside the slowly turning swamp of sounds without resonance, of rhythms that do not dance, which the Germans call a book! . . . How many Germans know . . . that there is *art* in every good sentence – art that must be grasped if the sentence is to be understood!
>
> (*BGE*, 246)

Nietzsche is aiming for a Derridian style of writing where 'philosophical criticism' is replaced by something closer to an 'art criticism' that leads the reader to a greater enlightenment and personal depth of feeling through the sheer provocation of its style; the reader is not given 'answers' but is asked actively to seek the themes presented within the text.

8 However, Paul de Man in *Allegories of Reading* (1979) shows that Nietzsche consistently rejects metaphysics by deconstructing it and destabilizing it from within. He maintains that there is a distinction in between what a statement literally asserts and what it does or shows. In Nietzsche there are statements with an obvious meta-physical content, and if we are concerned only with what these statements literally assert then we must conclude that Nietzsche is indeed a metaphysician who contradicts his own criticism of metaphysics. But, if we are concerned instead with what these statements actually do, we see that they undermine their own authority and reveal their own inadequacy. De Man therefore asserts that statements can show what they cannot literally assert without falling into contradiction. He therefore considers language to be metaphorical, that is, grounded in rhetoric rather than logic, and incapable of corresponding to anything non-linguistic, which is contrary to the metaphysical demand. De Man therefore believes that the limitations of rational-discursive thought can be shown when its origin in rhetoric or metaphor is revealed, but that this origin cannot simply be asserted because this assertion would itself presuppose the validity of rational-discursive thought. The apparent contradiction between Nietzsche's theory and practice of metaphysics does not, therefore, reveal any inadequacy and inconsistency in his thought, since it is only by means of such contradictions that the illusions of metaphysics can be exhibited. Nietzsche's thought is therefore not a claim to truth, for if it were, Nietzsche would be wrong when he claims that all truth is illusion, and his thought would remain inconsistent. (When Nietzsche says life is chaotic and stable he does not assert the truth, for this would contradict with his assertion that life cannot be articulated adequately in language.) Therefore, to avoid rendering Nietzsche's thought inconsistent, De Man insists that Nietzsche remains immersed within the errors he sought to expose. According to De Man, the allegory of errors found in Nietzsche's thought is 'the very model of philosophical rigor' (ibid., p. 118).

9 Although art is no longer required in its illusory capacity (that is, to mask the terrors of life in a veil of comfort), it is still endorsed by the later Nietzsche in its *creative* capacity. In Chapter 4 we shall see that Nietzsche's notion of the Will to Power is the 'artistic' power of adaptation that increases one's capacity for creativity through the union of opposites. Later we shall see that the unification of opposites does not lend itself easily to intellectual, scientific examination; it's meaning is better conveyed through symbols. Also, we shall see that Nietzsche's notion of art has religious connotations. In this sense we could say that the psyche still requires 'art' for its expression.

4 The *Übermensch* as a union of opposites

1 Perhaps the most notorious misinterpretation of the *Übermensch*, as a doctrine of the 'Master Race', is made explicit in Nazi distortions (see Heller, 1988; Aschheim, 1992, pp. 232–272, 315–331).

2 Nietzsche writes: 'In art, man takes delight in himself as perfection' (*TI*, 'Expeditions of an Untimely Man', 9; *WP*, 852). 'Art' here does not refer to art in its illusory capacity, but in its creative capacity. For clarification of my interpretation see Chapter 3, note 9.

3 Other commentators on Nietzsche have defined the *Übermensch* in similar terms as

'uniting the instincts', in the pursuit of increased creation, by the 'power of adaptation'. Arthur Danto writes:

> The *Übermensch* is not the blond giant dominating his lesser fellows. He is merely a joyous, guiltless, free human being, *in possession of instinctual drives, and so is in a position to make something of himself rather than being the product of instinctual discharge* and external obstacle.
>
> (Danto, 1965, p. 200, italics mine)

Kaufmann writes: '[The *Übermensch*] has overcome his animal nature, organized the chaos of his passions, sublimated his impulses, and given style to his character' (Kaufmann, 1968, p. 316). Richard Schacht writes: 'The Übermensch is the essence of the "higher man"; he is vital, healthy, self-controlled . . . and he is creative' (Schacht, 1983, p. 340).

4   Zarathustra also takes up this theme:

> Truly, my friends, I walk among men as among the fragments and limbs of men! The terrible thing to my eyes is to find men shattered in pieces and scattered as if over a battle-field of slaughter. And when my eye flees from the present to the past, it always discovers the same thing: fragments and limbs and dreadful chances – but no men!
>
> (*TSZ*, II, 'Of Redemption')

5   Karl Jaspers also maintains that creation is integral to Nietzsche's philosophy and necessary to the 'the highest type' (Jaspers, 1966, p. 152). For

> Creation is *evaluation* . . . Creation is *faith* . . . Creation is *love* . . . In creation is *annihilation*. All creation is *communication* . . . Still, all of creation is great pain and lack of knowledge . . . In creation *authentic being is attained*.
>
> (Jaspers, 1966, pp. 151–152)

The greatest capacity for creation is attained when all instincts are subordinate to the unifying principle: the Will to Power. The Will to Power is the dominating instinct. Nietzsche refers to it as:

> The dominating passion, which even brings with it the supremest form of health; here the co-ordination of the inner systems and their operation in the service of one end is best achieved – but this is almost the definition of health!
>
> (*WP*, 778)

Sickness and weakness are defined by entropy, an absence of creativity; sickness occurs when there is a 'multitude and disgregation [sic] of impulses and the lack of any systematic order among them' (*WP*, 46). Strength and health, on the other hand, are defined by 'their co-ordination under a single predominant impulse' (ibid); that is, when the impulses are coordinated by the Will to Power.

6   This version of the myth is found in Hornblower and Spawford (1999, pp. 479–482). There are variations of the story; for example, in another version the Titans whiten their faces with chalk and attack the infant Dionysus as he looks into a mirror. It is interesting to note the corresponding section at the beginning of *TSZ*, II, entitled 'The Child with the Mirror', in which Zarathustra looks into the child's mirror and sees himself as a Titan-like devil. Zarathustra understood this as a warning that his 'Dionysian' doctrine was in danger (see Chapter 11 for discussion of this).

7 This myth supports the notion that mankind is composed of opposites: the human body is vulgar and evil (since man sprang from the Titans) and the human soul is pure and divine (for the Titans have devoured the god). Thus, in its current state mankind is mediocre, but has within it the potential to be *Übermenschlichkeit*.

8 Nietzsche here is discussing his later notion of the Dionysian, which can be construed as a union of Dionysian and Apollinian elements.

5 Opposites in the Jungian model of the psyche

1 Here I am referring to the realm of the unconscious itself. I am not referring to the contents of the unconscious, which can, according to the intensity of its energetic charge, become conscious and therefore accessible to, and no longer alienated from, the individual.

2 However, according to Hillman (1979), a major proponent of the Archetypal School of Jungian thought, the dream is complete in itself. It must be taken literally and there is no need to talk about the dream compensating consciousness. Hillman writes: 'Theory of compensation appeals to the dayworld perspective of ego and results from its philosophy, not from the dream' (Hillman, 1979, p. 79).

3 According to Jung, this explains

> why people who have unrealistic ideas or too high an opinion of themselves, or who make grandiose plans out of proportion to their real capacities, have dreams of falling. The dream compensates for the deficiencies of their personalities, and at the same time it warns them of the dangers in their present course.
>
> (*MHS*, p. 40)

4 This corresponds to the 'inverse cripples' of Nietzsche, who 'lack everything except one thing, of which they have too much' (*TSZ*, II, 'Of Redemption').

5 From out of this scheme, of implementing the two attitudes and the four functions, it is possible to produce a total of sixteen different personality types. Jung says that there is no a priori basis for these different types. He distinguishes the four functions as the criteria for these types 'because they cannot be related or reduced to one another' (Jung, 1921, par. 731).

6 It is clear that Jung is implementing his theory of opposites in the construction of his system of typology. Jung divides the four functions into opposing categories of rational and irrational, and separates a superior and dominant function from its opposing inferior function, attributing the former to consciousness and the latter to the unconscious. It must be noted that the superior and inferior functions do not each represent one of the opposing categories of rationality and irrationality; rather Jung conceived the superior and inferior functions to come from the same category, that is, to be both rational or irrational. Thus, intuition and sensation are opposites because they both share in irrationality. I think it is more fitting to have intuition and thinking as true opposites, as representing rational and irrational tendencies. However, as we have noted, the rational functions are evaluative and the irrational are perceptive, and two corresponding functions of similar disposition cannot operate at the same time; that is, two evaluative functions or two perceptive functions cannot be simultaneously applied to measure the same thing. In accordance with this, Samuels writes: 'Jung felt that, as a person is more likely to be rational or irrational, the important question typologically would have to be answered from within either the rational or the irrational category' (Samuels, 1985, p. 63).

7 It is inherent because it is part of the individual's natural disposition. Jung writes: 'The type antithesis must have some kind of biological foundation' (Jung, 1921, par. 559).

8 It therefore follows that an individual with a natural disposition towards extraversion should have an easier time than the individual with an introverted disposition in making such adjustment to the environment. This is because the interest of the former lies within the external environment while the latter is more concerned with his inner subjectivity. However, in the second half of life the introvert will probably have an easier time than the extravert, because this phase of life is concerned primarily with the confrontation of the unconscious attitude: that is, with the neglected attitude that remains in opposition to ego-consciousness.

9 According to Jung, the need to confront the unconscious attitude is also a result of the individual's vocation. The individual must change his attitude 'as if it were a daemon whispering to him of new and wonderful things . . . Only the man who can consciously assent to the power of the inner voice becomes a personality' (Jung, 1934a, pars. 300, 308).

10 Although knowledge of the whole personality is contained within the psyche, its realization or discovery occurs over a course of time. Specifically, Jung tells us it is an achievement of the second half of life, an achievement that sees the psyche naturally accept the neglected attitude and functions into consciousness. The 'second half of life' is vague. Jung equates the transition from the first half of life to the second with the 'mid-life crisis', which, in psychoanalytic terms, is considered to be at an approximate age of 35 years for a man (Jaques, 1965, p. 502; Jung, 1929, par. 16). Jaques notes that the mid-life crisis is more difficult to identify in women as it is often obscured by the proximity of the onset of changes connected with the menopause. However, such mid-life crises are not universal. This means that the idea that there are two halves of life with their corresponding characteristics of 'sickness' and 'healthy balance' are not applicable to *all* individuals. Indeed, it is argued by the Developmental School (notably by Fordham) that the activities of the 'second half' of life (that is, of balancing and uniting opposites) is a process that spans the whole of the individual's life and its essential characteristics can be seen within children. The Developmental School therefore dissolves the periodic boundaries in which the individual can be identified either as healthy and wholesome or a 'sick animal'. In other words, the individual may never regard one opposite in the binary pair as primary and may thus always maintain a balance of opposites. But this is not something one should imitate, for a balance of opposites in this case is not necessarily healthy. The individual will have failed to develop a strong conscious attitude and will have difficulties adapting to the social environment; such individuals will be easily disposed to neuroses and the 'sick animal'.

11 Of course, individuals are also required to confront their personal unconscious; the contents of the collective unconscious require the involvement of elements of the personal unconscious in their manifestation. According to M. Williams (1973), the two kinds of unconscious are indivisible. The distinction between personal and collective categories of unconscious is irrelevant because primordial images or archetypal structures remain skeletal without personal experience to give them substance.

12 In Chapter 9 we shall see that Jung's definitive example of an over-inflated personality is that of Nietzsche.

13 It must be noted that there are many more archetypes to be encountered in the individuation process than I have mentioned here. Jung writes:

> Besides these figures there are still a few others, less frequent and less striking, which have likewise undergone poetic as well as mythological formulation. I would mention, for instance, the figure of the hero and of the wise man, to name only two of the best known.
>
> (Jung, 1939b, par. 515)

Jung also talks about encountering figures that represent superior wisdom and personifications of intelligence and knowledge (*MDR*, pp. 174–178). There are also archetypal situations such as death, birth and initiation.

14 According to Jung, the shadow is represented in dreams as a figure of the same sex. 'In the dreams of Europeans [it often appears] as dark-skinned, alien or primitive' (Storr, 1988, p. 87). Jung tells us about a 'small, brown-skinned savage' in a dream he had about Siegfried (*MDR*, par. 174) and he affirms that this figure 'was an embodiment of the primitive shadow' (par. 181). The anima is often represented as a witch or a priestess, 'with women who have links with the "spirit world", i.e. the unconscious' (*MHS*, p. 177), while the animus is often represented as a group of men (for women often focus on one man in their conscious relationships). The Self is often personified in dreams as a superior human figure, as a goddess to women, and a wise old man to men (ibid., p. 197). The manifestation of one of these personifications in a dream indicates that part of the unconscious attitude (i.e. the shadow or anima/animus) is in some way actively compensating the conscious attitude, which further indicates that a particular 'stage' in the individuation process requires further development.

15 However, Jung also notes that the shadow is never fully integrated into consciousness: 'There are certain features [of the shadow] which offer the most obstinate resistance to moral control and prove almost impossible to influence' (Jung, 1951, par. 16). Attention to one's shadow is necessary *throughout* the individuation process.

16 Hupert Hermans describes this phenomenon as 'moving opposites', so that 'when a person attempts to come to a unification of opposites within a certain polarity, there may be a spontaneous movement towards yet another polarity' (Hermans, 1993, p. 438). Edinger distinguishes between a 'lesser *coniunctio*' and a 'greater *coniunctio*' (Edinger, 1994a, pp. 211–231). The lesser union 'must be subjected to further procedures' (p. 212) while the greater union is 'the goal of the *opus*, the supreme accomplishment' (p. 211). Similarly, Von Franz, in her commentary on Aquinas' *Aurora Consurgens*, refers to 'the starting point' of the individuation process as 'the preconscious totality', and 'the end-product' of the process as 'the actualized totality' (Von Franz, 2000, p. 347).

17 These notions are 'derived by the alchemists from the dissolution of the "matter" in acids, from the roasting of ores, the expulsion of sulphur or mercury, the reduction of metallic oxides, and so forth' (Jung, 1945/1954, par. 468).

18 Jung argues that the symbol of the queen drinking blood is further indication of the displacement and overlapping of imagery often found within alchemical texts. When 'we are told that the queen drank blood, this image corresponds in every aspect to the king drinking water . . . to the king drowning in the sea' (Jung, 1955–1956, par. 403).

19 It is interesting to note that the peacock is an early Christian symbol for resurrection (Jung, 1955–1956, par. 395). We could say that the peacock's flesh in the alchemical model initiates the resurrection of the king.

6 The Self as a union of opposites

1 Indeed, *Aion*, the title of Jung's *Researches into the Phenomenology of the Self* (1951), refers to the transcendent aspect of the Self, for it is taken from the ancient religion of Mythraism where 'Aion' is the name of the god that rules over the astrological calendar and over time itself.

2 Levinas' idea that the experience of the Other is violent is similar to that of Otto who, in *The Idea of the Holy* (1917), defines the experience of the numinous as immediate experiences of 'awefulness' (Otto, 1917/1936, IV: 1), 'overpoweringness' (IV: 2) and 'urgency' (IV: 3).

3 The parallel between Jungian 'Self-experience' and the Levinasian experience of the Other is further paralleled in the Kantian notion of the sublime (see Chapter 8, note 16).

4 Jung writes: 'You see, by means of a symbol, such dangers can be accepted: one can submit to them, digest them. Otherwise . . . it is a very dangerous situation: one is exposed without protection to the onslaught of the unconscious' (*SNZ*, II, p. 1249).

5 The features of the Self-symbol will change as the conscious attitude changes.

6 The subjective power of analogies of the Self is aptly demonstrated in the discourse between Redfearn (1990) and Booth (1990a, 1990b) in the *Journal of Analytical Psychology*, vol. 35. The disagreement between the two scholars revolves around the analogy Redfearn uses to describe the notions of the many 'selves' and the many feelings of 'I', implemented across the psychoanalytic traditions, including the Jungian 'Self'. Booth first tries to enlarge Redfearn's analogy to include further connotations of the Self that he thinks have been ignored. Then he offers a different analogy, which he personally feels more appropriately encapsulates the notion of the Self. In *My Self, My Many Selves* (1985) Redfearn uses an analogy of the theatre to provide a general model of the self/Self. He writes:

> This 'I' migrates hither and thither to various locations in the total personality, like the spotlight at a theatre picking out first one actor then another, or, even more pertinently, like a pilgrim on his journey of life visiting one place, then another, in his universe . . . I call these various actors in ourselves 'sub-personalities'.
>
> (Redfearn, 1985, p. xii)

Booth in 'A Suggested Analogy for the Elusive Self' (1990a) argues against this analogy. He states that words such as 'theatre' and 'pilgrim' are 'loaded words' and as such have connotations that 'point our understanding in certain directions' (p. 335). Booth says that it specifically

> leaves open the question of governance: who is providing the integration – is there a 'personality' co-ordinating the activities of the sub-personalities? Or, if the 'feeling of I' as 'pilgrim' merely visits 'places' in the self, what authority does it carry as a visitor, or find there as it 'arrives'?
>
> (Booth, 1990a, p. 336)

Booth proceeds to offer his own analogy of the self/Self, that of a 'committee of the whole', which, like Booth's criticism of Redfearn's analogy, is guilty of using loaded words. Booth's 'committee' has innumerable members who each have equal authority and can 'seize the floor at any time', thereby taking the position of the 'I' with the other parts of the self acting as 'aides or advisers'. Booth regards his own subjective analogy to be more appropriate for expressing the objective self/Self than that of Redfearn. However, Redfearn quickly responds to Booth, maintaining that the analogy of the committee is no better than that of the theatre. He writes:

> His picture . . . strikes me as one way in which the self and the sub-personalities of the self interact. But of course it is only *one* way . . . If we remember that the 'sub-personalities' are meant to denote the archetypal as well as the complex figures, then the notion of a committee seems hardly more adequate than the picture of a company of actors.
>
> (Redfearn, 1990, p. 339, italics mine)

Booth later responds: 'Dr. Redfearn's generous acknowledgement that the committee analogy might show *one* way in which parts of the self interact, gives about as much recognition as one analogist can hope for from another' (Booth, 1990b, p. 341, italics mine). The subjective power of symbolic imagery is at play here. Both scholars are more content to uphold their own analogy, and any attempt to persuade and communicate its authority requires justification; no one symbol can be universally accepted because symbols are subjectively determined.

7 The Ouroboros (the alchemical symbol of the snake/dragon swallowing its tail) is similar to the mandala and would also work as a protective circle. See Goethe's *The Parable* where the serpent wound herself around the Prince's dead body and took her tail in her mouth in order to become 'a protective maternal power, for she preserves the body of the Prince from corruption' (Raphael, 1965, p. 98).

8 This process would be a form of Aristotelian *kinesis*. But the union of opposites does not correspond to Aristotle's notion of *energia* either, where there is no *process* at all, but every 'stage' is complete in itself. For Jung, on the contrary, the Self is the very purpose of the process, as a lifetime project that never terminates.

9 Fordham's analysis of the Self maintains the distinction between the process and the end-product of the process. However, this does not rescue the notion of a union of opposites from its demotion to a subjective symbol, for although he distinguishes between the two, he still maintains that they are both identified with the Self, albeit as different aspects of it. Fordham's discussions on the Self bring to light an apparent contradiction between two definitions of the Self that Jung developed – the Self as totality and the Self as archetype (Fordham, 1985, pp. 20–24). To see how Fordham's discussion contributes to our analysis, we can equate the 'Self as totality' with the notion of the 'Self as process', and the 'Self as archetype' with the notion of the 'Self as final product of the process'. The process in each case refers to the process of the unification of opposites, so that in the former definition the process is directly identified with the Self but in the latter it is not (the Self is merely its end result, not the means by which this result is achieved). The 'Self as totality' is equivalent with the 'Self as process' because both define the Self as the sum of that which determines its manifestation – that is, everything that has gone in to its establishment. The Self is identified with that which leads to its manifestation; it has connotations of movement and transition. Likewise, the 'Self as archetype' is equivalent to the final product in itself: it is complete, the end result.

Fordham begins by examining the concept of Self as a totality, which he maintains first makes an appearance in *Psychological Types* (1921), where Jung discriminates between the ego and the Self and states that the Self is 'the subject of my total psyche which also includes the unconscious. In this sense the self would be an ideal entity which embraces the ego' (Fordham, 1985, p. 20). Fordham notes significant implications of this, for

> if the self is the whole psyche, then it cannot be observed intrapsychically since the ego is contained in it as a part and cannot function as an observer. It is only when some part of the ego stands separate from or only participates up to a point in the rest of the whole that data about the self can be collected.
>
> (Fordham, 1985, p. 21)

Next Fordham examines the concept of the Self as an archetype, which contradicts the totality thesis. Here he quotes Jung as stating that the Self is 'the real organizing principle of the unconscious, the quaternity, or squared circle of the self' (Jung, 1951, par. 318), and again refers to places where Jung defines or implies that the Self is the archetype of order, whose special function is to balance and pattern the other archetypes (*CW* 12; Jung, 1942/1954, par. 433; Jung, 1958, pars. 624, 805). Fordham makes clear that the archetype thesis does not contradict the fundamental notion from the totality thesis – that the Self is unknowable to consciousness – for the archetype itself is purely unconscious. What he does find problematic in the totality thesis is how the Self can be both the totality of the psyche including all the archetypes, and also one of these archetypes. Therefore, in terms of our own use, the question will read: 'If the Self is equivalent to the process of uniting opposites, how can it also be the product of this process?' Fordham notes that, as an archetype, the Self cannot be a totality (for the ego and archetypes must distinguished to avoid inflation) and neither can it ever be experienced (since it stands outside ego-comprehension). Nevertheless, the symbolic images that represent the Self in consciousness are clearly archetypal and are presumably structured by the archetype that they represent: the Self. By way of conclusion to this paradox, Fordham conceives the Self not as an archetype (and thus, not as the 'product' of the process) but as 'beyond' archetypes and ego (which corresponds to our notion of the Self as a synergy – 'beyond' the sum of its parts and process), which are then seen as arising out of or 'deintegrating' from the Self. Furthermore, he suggests that a distinction in terminology be made so that the term 'Self' would be used only to refer to a psychic totality; otherwise the term 'central archetype of order' would be preferred (Fordham, 1973). For the purpose of our analysis, we see that Fordham upholds the definition of the 'Self as totality' only: a totality that is not directly identifiable with the sum of its parts, and therefore with the process itself, but is 'beyond' them, as a synergy. The process of the Self's realization (the unification of opposites) is defined by Fordham not explicitly as the Self, but as the 'central archetype of order'. In accordance with this view, Jung himself rewrote his definition of the Self (Jung, 1921, pars. 789–791), taking into account this apparent contradiction, and emphasizing the Self as a special transcendental concept. This new definition strengthens the notion of the Self as a totality, but its transcendental element also enables the Self to function as the archetype of unity.

10 But is Jung correct to say that the concept of the Self is turned into *fact* simply because it arises out of experience and is elucidated by further experience? Plaut remains uncertain, for 'such understanding drives one to the very edge of sanity. If Jung's vision arose from that very place in his mind (as we have reason to believe), small wonder that it makes us anxious too' (Plaut, 1985, p. 248). However, Plaut is resigned to acknowledge other scientifically 'approved' theories that make use of such 'mad-driving' paradoxes, such as quantum physics where the facts depend ultimately upon the act of observation. Nevertheless, Colman saves Jung from potential flaw and takes the argument of experience a step further by concluding that

> the self is not an experience and it certainly is not a content of experience, but rather it is the taste of experience, its quality. The self is not subjectivity but the condition by which subjectivity is possible. It is not myself, nor the experience of myself but the very possibility of my having self-experience.
>
> (Colman, 2000, p. 15)

The Self provides the grounding upon which the individual can have experiences; it is not merely, in Levinasian terms, the Other that questions the authority of the Same (the ego), but the fundamental grounding which enables the Other to question the Same: it is the very 'encounter' itself between the two elements of Other and Same. Or, in Jungian terms, it is the 'third thing' (Jung, 1916/1957, par. 189) that unites the two elements. The Self is the dangerous 'relation of non-relation' that forces individuals into a more complete understanding of themselves.

7 The disagreement between Nietzsche and Jung: the process of uniting opposites

1 Similarly, Jung writes: 'Opposites can be united . . . *irrationally* [in] some new thing arising between them which, although different from both, yet has the power to take up their energies in equal measures as an expression of both and of neither' (Jung, 1921, par. 169); 'the existence of two mutually antagonistic tendencies . . . demands the existence of a counterweight. This is the "irrational third"' (Jung, 1921, par. 369); 'the coniunctio symbolism is a common motif in alchemy, concerning the problem of opposites . . . uniting to produce a third thing' (Jung, 1909, par. 800); 'thesis is followed by antithesis, and between the two is generated a third factor' (*MDR*, p. 384). Edinger (1994b, p. 44) writes: 'There's a confrontation and that confrontation takes place under the motivation of a third thing', Von Franz (2000, p. 396) writes: 'We have to suppose a third, unifying power which acts as a link between the two'.

2 Which is why we turned to alchemical texts earlier – to examine the 'third thing' through its symbolic interpretation rather than direct intellectual examination.

3 We could argue that those 'inverse cripples', who cannot aspire to *Übermenschlichkeit*, experience no correlation between the Will to Power and their contrary instincts (their instincts will be tied up with other motivations – and origins – such as the will to truth); such correlation is available only to those who profess the Will to Power.

4 The concern of this chapter is an analysis of the differences between the models of opposites of Nietzsche and Jung. Elements (1) and (2) of the proto-theory, where the views of Nietzsche and Jung converge, will not be analysed here.

Schopenhauer, although a great influence on Nietzsche and Jung, disagrees with them on the quality of aspects (1) and (2) of the proto-theory. Unlike Nietzsche and Jung, Schopenhauer does not promote the tension of opposites as a high energy source; he simply acknowledges that opposites illumine one another (Schopenhauer, 1818/ 1969, vol. I, par. 40, p. 207). This does not reduce the significance of opposites for his thought. He was particularly concerned with those opposites fundamental to questions of epistemology, such as 'subject' and 'object' – which 'face each other inseparable and irreconcilable' (ibid., vol. II, p. 6) – 'internal' and 'external', and 'body' and 'Will'. According to Schopenhauer, opposites simply illuminate one another because they are two contrasting aspects and manifestations of the same thing. Schopenhauer writes:

> [The] body is merely the outward appearance of [the] will, in other words, the mode and manner in which [the] will exhibits itself is in [the] perceiving intellect, or [the] will itself under the form of the representation . . . there is actually no causal connexion between the act of will and the action of the body, for they are directly *identical*. Their apparent difference arises solely from the fact that one and the same thing is here apprehended or perceived under two different modes of knowledge, the outer and the inner.
>
> (Schopenhauer, 1818/1969, vol. II, p. 248; cf. p. 36)

This echoes Nietzsche's insistence that '"warm and cold" . . . are not opposites, but differences of degree [or] transitions' (*WS*, 67). They are, to reiterate Nietzsche's claim with reference to Heraclitus, 'The diverging of a force into two qualitatively different opposed activities seek to re-unite' (*PTAG*, 5). Indeed, Schopenhauer himself alludes explicitly to this scenario: 'The sundering of a force into two qualitatively different and opposite activities striving for reunion . . . [as] the fundamental type of almost all the phenomena of nature' (Schopenhauer, 1818/1969, vol. I, par. 27, pp. 143–144). Both Nietzsche and Schopenhauer regard opposites as different modes of an original source, but they disagree on the value of this difference: Nietzsche (like Jung) sees the difference in opposites as a dynamic tension, and Schopenhauer as passive illumination.

5 Nietzsche is often accused of denying the intrinsic value of rationality. (In the next chapter we will see Jung make this accusation against him.) But Nietzsche is not guilty of this; he simply draws our attention to the intrinsic value of the irrational.

6 Jung was influenced by St Augustine's (354–430) definition of the *ideae principales*. Augustine writes:

> For the principal ideas are certain forms, or stable and unchangeable reasons of things, themselves not formed, and so continuing eternal and always after the same manner, which are contained in the divine understanding. And though themselves do not perish, yet after their pattern everything is said to be formed that is able to come into being and to perish, and everything that does come into being and perish. But it is affirmed that the soul is not able to behold them.
>
> *(Liber de diversis quaestionibus, XLVI)*

7 Similarly, in a letter to Arnold Künzli of 4 February 1943, Jung writes: 'If I posited the archetypes, for instance, I would not be a scientist but a Platonist' (Adler and Jaffé, 1973–1975, p. 329).

8 Thus Jung writes: 'The individual may strive after perfection . . . but must suffer from the opposite of his intentions for the sake of completion' (Jung, 1951, par. 123).

9 The Ideas of Plato and Kant are not interchangeable (see note 14). I shall argue that Jung makes the mistake of conflating the two.

10 Jung refers to Kant continually throughout his works, often citing whole passages at a time. In *MDR* Jung writes of Plato, that 'I was attracted' to his thought (*MDR*, p. 87), but Kant impressed him to the extent that he was concerned that he 'was able to study Kant only on Sundays' (ibid., p. 122).

11 Thus pure reason leads us to form the theological Idea, the cosmological Idea and the psychological Idea, and postulates the existence of God, freedom and immortality.

12 According to Paul Bishop, 'The potentially devastating moral deficit at the centre of analytical psychology can thus be seen as, in part, deriving from one of the consequences of Jung's failure to understand Kant' (Bishop, 2000b, p. 163).

13 See Paul Bishop's article 'The Use of Kant in Jung's Early Psychological Works' (1996) for a similar argument. But Bishop does not arrive at this argument through the same reasoning as I employ; he does not acknowledge Jung's mistake of compounding the Kantian category/concept with the Kantian Idea.

14 See, for example, Jung (1921, par. 733) where Jung discusses the Platonic Idea and the Kantian Idea in one breath. Jung should have listened to Schopenhauer's warning that the word 'Idea' must not be used out of its original Platonic context:

> Now I say that the . . . *Will* is nothing but *Plato's Ideas*. I mention this here for the moment, so that in future I can use the word *Idea* in this sense. Therefore with me the word is always to be understood in its genuine and original meaning, given to it by Plato; and in using it we must assuredly not think of those abstract productions of scholastic dogmatizing reason, to describe which Kant used the word wrongly as well as illegitimately, although Plato had already taken possession of it, and used it most appropriately.
>
> (Schopenhauer, 1818/1969, vol. I, par. 25, pp. 129–130)

In his article Paul Bishop (1996) also notes that Jung wrongly correlates Plato's Idea with Kant's, but he does not explain how he does so.

15 Stephanie de Voogd in 'Fantasy versus Fiction: Jung's Kantianism Appraised' rightly

states that Jung's Kantianism is 'both self-contradictory and self-defeating' (Voogd, 1992, p. 79).

16 According to Schopenhauer, an 'Idea' arises directly from out of perceptive experience; it is not abstracted to the level of the concept, and as such cannot be communicated from one individual to another, but it still encapsulates the full affectivity of the experience (Schopenhauer, 1818/1969, vol. I, par. 49, pp. 234–235).

17 It is interesting to note here that Schopenhauer does not always distinguish between willing and feeling (see Schopenhauer, 1818/1969, vol. II, ch. XXXVIII, p. 459 where their correlation is explicit). If we take 'feeling' to parallel 'willing', and if we maintain that 'thinking' is operation of the intellect, we have two of the four conscious functions of Jung's model of the psyche. As we saw in Chapter 5, the functions of 'feeling' and 'thinking', according to Jung, are opposites. On this matter Schopenhauer remarks, 'The true opposite of rational knowledge is feeling' (ibid., vol. I, par. 11, p. 51).

18 Nietzsche writes: 'Plato is a coward in the face of reality – consequently he flees into the ideal' (*TI*, 'What I Owe to the Ancients', 2). Of Kant, Nietzsche notes: 'To say nothing of the 'thing in itself', that *horrendum pudendum* [ugly shameful part] of the metaphysicians!' (*TI*, 'The Four Great Errors', 3). 'Perhaps we shall then recognize that the thing in itself is worthy of Homeric laughter: that it appeared to be so much, indeed everything, and is actually empty, that is to say empty of significance' (*HAH*, 16). 'Schopenhauer, whose great knowledge about the human and all-too-human . . . was not a little dimmed by the motley leopard skin of his metaphysics (which one must first remove from him if one is to discover the real genius beneath it)' (*AOM*, 33). '*Schopenhauer's* basic misunderstanding of the *will* (as if craving, instinct, drive were the *essence* of will) is typical: lowering the value of the will to the point of making a real mistake' (*WP*, 84).

19 Similarly, Nietzsche writes: 'The *conscious* world of feelings, intentions, valuations is a small section', merely 'the surface phenomenon' (*WP*, 707). 'However far a man can go in self-knowledge, nothing may be more incomplete than his image of the totality of his *drives* which constitute his being' (*D*, 119). For further allusions to the unconscious see *UM*, III, 1; *GM*, III, 18; *BGE*, 3; *WP*, 372, 707; *GS*, 8, 11, 333, 357; *TSZ*, I, 'Of the Despisers of the Body'; *HAH*, 13.

20 Compare Nietzsche's description of the 'psychic grounding' as 'an accumulated ancestral estate in which everyone has his share' (*TL*, 173), and human thinking is 'not so much a discovering as a recognizing, a remembering, a return and home-coming to a far-off, primordial total household of the soul out of which those concepts once emerged' (*BGE*, 20; cf. Plato's doctrine of recollection: *Phaedo* 77c–77d, *Meno* 80a–85b).

21 Nietzsche speaks of '*Heraclitus*, in whose vicinity in general I feel warmer and more well than anywhere else' (*EH*, 'BT', 3). This favourable account is expressed in the great emphasis Nietzsche puts on Heraclitus in *PTAG* (sections 5–9), and in his announcement that the fundamental doctrine of Zarathustra, the doctrine of Eternal Recurrence, '*could* possibly already have been taught by Heraclitus' (*EH*, 'BT', 3). Nietzsche also says such things as 'I set apart with high reverence the name of Heraclitus . . . Heraclitus will always be right' (*TI*, iii, 2). 'The world forever needs the truth, hence the world forever needs Heraclitus' (*PTAG*, 8). Jung also makes reference to Heraclitus (he even cites him as the only forerunner in Western philosophical thought of his idea of synchronicity: Jung, 1952a, par. 916), and cites several of his fragments in recognition of significant analogies between his own and Heraclitus' doctrine of the interplay of opposites in general (Jung, 1921, par. 708). Jung writes: 'Old Heraclitus, who was indeed a very great sage, discovered the most marvellous of all psychological laws: the regulative function of opposites' (Jung, 1917/1926/1943, par. 111).

22   It is interesting to note that, in his presentation of the relativism of opposites, Heraclitus starts the sentence emphasizing the 'oneness', the unity, in which the opposites are both manifest. This recurrent pattern helps to draw attention back from the paradoxically related opposites to the unity in which they coexist (Hussey, 1999, pp. 93–94). This implies that Heraclitus held the unity in which the opposites inhere to be more valuable than the opposites themselves (as did Nietzsche and Jung, who saw the goal of human life as the realization of a union of opposites in the guises of the *Übermensch* and Self respectively).

23   It must be noted that in Classical Greek the term translated as 'the warm' can mean either 'warmth' or a 'thing that is warm'. In the latter sense, it is not logically incorrect to say that 'the warm' grows cool.

24   Aristotle is here alluding directly to Empedocles' principal pair of opposites – Love and Strife. According to Empedocles, the four elements or 'roots' of the universe (earth, water, air and fire) are united by the force of Love, and separated by the force of Strife. The four elements can never be completely united or separated; they relate only according to the endless struggle between Love and Strife. The universe thus experiences a ceaseless alternation between the opposite processes of union and division. Jung notes that he was 'attracted' to the thought of Empedocles (*MDR*, p. 87), and Nietzsche saw in Empedocles 'the great potential Reformer that failed' (cited in Cowan, 1962, p. 13).

25   Nietzsche was certainly more exposed to Heraclitus' thought than Jung because of his training in philology; this may account for Nietzsche having been more influenced by his thought.

26   The influence of Aristotle's notion of teleology upon the psychology of Jung has been acknowledged frequently. For example, see Nagy, 'Aristotle's View of Teleology as Act and Potency', in *Philosophical Issues in the Psychology of C. G. Jung* (Nagy, 1991, pp. 221–226). While Aristotle's teleological thinking is implicit within the Jungian model of opposites, Nietzsche's notion of teleology, as the progressive union of opposites towards the goal of complete unification in the *Übermensch*, is distinctly anti-Aristotelian. Therefore, we can see Nietzsche reject the existence of a third thing in the opposites. This aversion to Aristotle is aptly demonstrated in the model of opposites provided by the early Nietzsche, where his *Übermensch* is anticipated in his earlier formulation of the *tragic* being. As we argued in Chapter 2, Nietzsche sought to affirm ultimately the horrors issued by life's eternal and meaningless flux; the individual who promoted the appropriate synthesis of opposing Apollinian and Dionysian drives (as Apollinian illusion and Dionysian bliss) could achieve this affirmation in the tragic experience. The harnessing of these two opposing drives would generate enough strength for the individual to affirm the destruction of life as inherently joyful. The goal of tragedy, for Nietzsche, is thus the affirmation of life through the promotion of the tragic impulses. For Aristotle, however, the emotions aroused in the tragic performance (he calls them pity and fear – *eleos* and *phobos*) are dangerous and are therefore purged (*katharsis*) from the body as soon as they become manifest. Nietzsche is in agreement with Aristotle over the powerful emotions that the tragic spectacle issues, but he is in disagreement with Aristotle over their value:

Affirmation of life even in its strangest and sternest problems . . . *that* is what I call the Dionysian, *that* is what I recognized as the bridge to the psychology of the *tragic* poet. *Not* so as to get rid of pity and terror, not so as to purify oneself of a dangerous emotion through its vehement discharge – it was thus Aristotle understood it – but, beyond pity and terror, *to realize in oneself* the eternal joy of becoming – that joy which also encompasses *joy in destruction*.

(*TI*, 'What I Owe to the Ancients', 5; also see *HAH*, 212; *D*, 240)

This disagreement with Aristotle led Nietzsche to make the contentious claim: '*I have been the first to discover the tragic*' (*WP*, 1029). For Nietzsche, '*the tragic artist* . . . is a question of strength' (*WP*, 852) and the pent-up emotions, which Aristotle regards as a danger and in need of purging, are in fact guarantees of this strength. According to the Nietzschean model, the elimination of these essential emotions would be disastrous, for the strength that is generated from these emotions, which is necessary for life's affirmation, remains out of reach; the individual in Aristotle's model could not proceed along Nietzsche's envisioned teleological path, he would remain weak and overcome by the horrors of life (*WP*, 852). Nietzsche therefore interprets Aristotle's doctrine of *katharsis* as a doctrine of weakness, as antithetical to his notion of the *übermenschlich* tragic being. Indeed, Nietzsche accuses the Aristotelian doctrine of asceticism, in line with the Christian doctrine that he so profoundly abhors (*WP*, 851).

8 The similarities between Nietzsche and Jung: the whole self in the union of opposites

1 In his introduction to Jung's seminars on *Nietzsche's Zarathustra* (1989) James Jarrett refers to eight principal areas where the thought of Nietzsche and Jung converge (p. xviii); six of these are relevant, in varying degrees, to their respective notions of the union of opposites. (i) 'Both were haunted by Christianity.' (This, I believe, is tangential and not crucial to the determination of the *Übermensch* and Self, and I therefore address it implicitly within areas (2), (5) and (6), and throughout this work.) (ii) 'Alike, they were elitists – not on trivial grounds of wealth, family, class, race, but with respect to intelligence, understanding, and consciousness'. (I expound upon this further in (3).) (iii) 'Alike they were contemptuous of hedonism . . . both [believed] that without conflict and suffering, consciousness is doomed to stagnation.' (I expound upon this further in (1).) (iv) 'Theirs alike was a philosophy . . . of the Dionysian spirit.' (This is addressed by (6).) (v) 'Both deplored and regretted . . . what Nietzsche called "the diminished personality".' (This is the antithesis of the union of opposites, and is therefore argued as such throughout this work.) (vi) The notion of 'the *whole* self of the creator'. (This is explored in (2).) The two other areas that are not relevant to this discussion are: (1) both Nietzsche and Jung were of similar psychological type (we examine this claim in Part III); (2) they acknowledge their debt to similar philosophical influences (we examined both their similar and dissimilar philosophical influences in Chapter 7).

2 It is perhaps because the *Übermensch* and Self are in a continual dynamic state of becoming that they cannot be satisfactorily defined. The *Übermensch* and Self are defined by an almost infinite number of configurations of antithetical forces, which are directed by the Will to Power or by compensation from the vast and unknowable depths of the unconscious. This assertion is supported by Fischer, who writes:

> It is part of the determination of the 'Übermensch' not to be determined – that we shall have to experiment, that we shall have to create. Nietzsche puts emphasis on the creativity of the individual and therefore we should accentuate that the conception of the 'Übermensch' is *necessarily not* determined. We cannot ask whether an author has confused the issue, or has presented us with a dangerous alternative.
>
> (cited in Aschheim, 1992, p. 8)

3 Although (or indeed because) the union of good and evil is beyond the structured value-system of conventional morality, Nietzsche's and Jung's formulation of it (the *Übermensch* and Self) have been accused of immorality. Indeed, Nietzsche's insistence

on the equality between good and evil can appear somewhat startling (see *WP*, 881, 98; *TSZ*, II, 'Of Self-Overcoming'; *HAH*, 107; cf. *SNZ*, I, p. 260 where Jung correlates Nietzsche's interpretation of God as Satan). Likewise, Jung is not far from moral controversy. As we saw in Chapters 5 and 6, the Self 'is a God-image, or at least cannot be distinguished from one' (Jung, 1951, par. 42); but when we interpret the Self in terms of completion rather than perfection, we must also regard evil as an inherent attribute of God. Jung consequently reformulates the Holy Trinity (of Father, Son and Holy Ghost) into a Holy Quaternity to include the Devil (Jung, 1951, pars. 79–98; Jung, 1952b, pars. 579–608). 'Completion' entails an amoral union of good and evil.

4   According to Jung, Nietzsche promotes the irrational (Dionysus) over the rational (Apollo), and the body over the spirit. The first inconsistency that Jung highlights is an elaboration of the ambiguity we found in Chapter 7. There I argued that although the rational and the irrational (as the Apollinian and Dionysian impulses respectively) are valued equally in the Nietzschean model, rationality is given secondary status as the 'vehicle' through which irrationality is harnessed. Nietzsche therefore questions the value of rationality and seeks its justification against its opposite – the Dionysian, which is already justified as the goal of Nietzsche's project. Jung saw in Nietzsche a one-sided promotion of the irrational over the rational, and this, according to Liliane Frey, led ultimately to the 'fatal dissociation which ended his intellectual existence' (Frey, 1971, p. 323).

5   Frey writes:

> The Self derives psychic energy (*potentia*) which is the beam of an as yet unknown, redeeming third factor, the symbol. The absence of a symbol [is] disseminated by Nietzsche . . . without the integrating spirit or meaning no reconciliation of what has been torn apart is possible.
>
> (Frey, 1971, p. 319)

6   See *WP*, 1027 where Nietzsche tells us that growth in greatness is directly compensated by growth in *terribleness*: 'The more one radically desires the one, the more radically one achieves precisely the other.' In Jung the assimilation of 'evil' and 'negative' traits occur in the encounter with the shadow (in the 'demonic', 'bloody rampages' of the 'raging monster': Jung, 1917/1926/1943, par. 35).

7   Indeed, Richard Noll (1994) argues that (3) is the principal area of affinity between Nietzsche and Jung, for, according to Noll, analytical psychology is like National Socialism because it is based on '"Nietzscheanism" in the elitist and pseudo-liberational sense'. Furthermore, 'the Jung cult and its present day movement is in fact a "Nietzschean religion"' (p. 137). However, Noll's argument is flawed by his misunderstanding of the 'new nobility' of the *Übermensch*, for he regards the elitism of the *Übermensch* as a product of 'blood-inheritance' and biological evolution (p. 264).

8   Indeed, Nietzsche and Jung strongly insist on exceptional creativity and strength, to the extent that they ask us to abandon their respective teachings in favour of our own. Zarathustra tells his disciples: 'One repays a teacher badly if one remains only a pupil . . . You had not sought yourselves when you found me . . . now I bid you lose me and find yourselves' (*TSZ*, I, 'Of the Bestowing Virtue', 3). (Jung uses this passage from *TSZ* in a letter to Freud to express his break with Freud's thought and influence: McGuire, 1974, p. 491.) Zarathustra also says: 'This is now *my* way: where is yours?' (*TSZ*, III, 'Of the Spirit of Gravity', 2; cf. Samuels, 1985, p. 3).

9   Nietzsche establishes a caste system in which mankind is graded according to the standard and value of power he has attained (*WP*, 784, 854–862; *BGE*, 257). It must be noted that power for Nietzsche does not equate with brute strength and domination, but

refers to a 'spiritual' strength, which can be construed as having power over oneself, or simply 'self-integration' and 'self-control' (see Chapter 12 for clarification). Evolution through time of the practice of the Will to Power means that life can rise higher only by favouring the few at the expense of the many; it is only through competition that the strong are established. The weak are thus required, in their competition and subsequent defeat, to create the strong, and it is in this way that Nietzsche maintains that a high culture requires the lower, weaker classes to support the privileged classes: 'A high culture is a pyramid: it can stand only on a broad base, its very first prerequisite is a strongly and soundly consolidated mediocrity' (*A*, 57; also see *WP*, 864, 901).

Nietzsche's comments on the 'Laws of Manu' (*A*, 57) suggest that the main division of gradation will consist of three castes. The lowest caste will consist of ordinary individuals; these individuals are considered 'mediocre' because their power is directed to one specialism (*A*, 57; *WP*, 864). This caste will thus consist of 'the crafts, trade, agriculture, science . . . in a word the entire compass of professional activity'. Their function is purely instrumental to the higher castes (*WP*, 962). They are therefore slaves; but there is no injustice here for the right of the mediocre is a 'privilege . . . To be a cog, a function, is a natural vocation, it is not society, it is the kind of happiness of which the great majority are alone capable, which makes intelligent machines of them' (*A*, 57).

The middle caste will consist of the 'higher men', the 'philosophers of power' who are 'beyond good and evil' (*WP*, 980) and as such are the legislators of the earth and 'the executives of the most spiritual order' (*A*, 57). The 'higher men' personify the high spirituality – i.e. the refinement and strengthening of the individual's spiritual qualities that expresses itself in the justice of 'letting things be', of *amor fati*.

Nietzsche is opposed to state idolatry (*TSZ*, I, 'Of the New Idol') and regards 'state' and 'culture' to be antagonistic. He therefore places the affairs of government into the hands, not of the highest caste, but into this middle caste. These philosophers are the 'executives' of the highest caste, of the *Übermenschen*, sparing them the coarser part of the work of ruling (*WP*, 998). The purpose of the highest caste is not the exercise of supreme power over society; instead they are the end to which society is a means. They live in detached unconcern towards society like 'Epicurean gods' and are concerned only with representing perfection and beauty on earth (*A*, 57). While they experience the worst sufferings, they give to the lower orders the happiness and comfort which they renounce for themselves (*A*, 57; see also Golomb et al., 1999, p. 8; *D*, 163, 164, 546). For analysis of Nietzsche's caste-system and its political and ethical implications see Morgan, 1943, chapter XIII; also *SNZ*, I, p. 582.

10 According to Jung, Nietzsche decided to call the god 'Dionysus' instead of 'Wotan' due to the influence of Wagner (Jung, 1936b, par. 383). According to Arthur Rudolph, 'Nietzsche called his godlike principle by the name of Dionysus rather than Wotan in deference to his studies of classical philology and the need to utilize classical themes in his defence of Wagner' (Rudolph, 1974, p. 314).

11 See especially *TSZ*, II, 'The Prophet'; *SNZ*, II, pp. 1227–1229.

12 Jung attributes this description to Nietzsche, because he believed Nietzsche was personally identified with his notion of the *Übermensch*, thereby causing him to have an ego-inflation, which led to his psychotic demise (*SNZ*, pp. 133, 137). I shall examine this claim in Part III, and shall thereby determine if Nietzsche's controversial blue-print for an ideal society can in fact be explained psychoanalytically, as a projection of his own inflated ego-consciousness.

13 The notion of the 'dangerous' Dionysian as a significant connecting theme between the projects of Nietzsche and Jung has been addressed by the following: Ross Woodman (1986), remarks:

> The *deus absconditus*, the dark Dionysos who is hidden even from himself under the cloak of his own darkness is everything which appears mindless, causeless, without precedent, unexpected . . . Jung followed Nietzsche in search of the dark God.
>
> (Woodman, 1986, p. 105)

James Jarrett remarks: 'Theirs alike was a philosophy of darkness, no less than light, a celebration of the Dionysian spirit' (see note 1 above); James Hillman (1972, p. 197) remarks: 'The first Dionysos of whom Jung writes . . . is neither a figure of antiquity nor a figure in Jung's own life, but one who is vicariously known to Jung through Nietzsche'; and Bishop (1995, p. 49) remarks: 'The Dionysian is the guiding thread through Jung's (labyrinthine) reception of Nietzsche'.

14 'Death' will also occur if there is an over-identification with the Dionysian creative process. In this case the individual is fixated in the process, and is unable to develop towards rebirth. In Chapter 5 we saw that, according to Jung, if the ego is unable to accept its rebirth, it will be subject to 'destructive mass psychoses'. Furthermore, in the Jungian model Dionysus correlates with the unconscious (*SNZ*, II, p. 1227). Thus, if the conscious ego becomes identified with the unconscious it will attempt to reduce the unconscious to its own terms, but it cannot do this; instead the ego experiences a dangerous inflation. By identifying directly with Dionysus, the ego becomes a 'barbarian' (Jung, 1921, par. 346), which refuses to accept the affectivity of the Dionysian creative process, and thus that which would otherwise secure its rebirth into the Self. According to Jung, this is precisely what happened to Nietzsche; Nietzsche became insane because he over-identified with Dionysus and the dynamic process of creation (Jung, 1938/1940, par. 142; Jung, 1936a, par. 118; Jung, 1917/1926/1943, par. 40; *SNZ*, pp. 144, 1306; cf. 'Nietzsche's insanity, which Jung found the "quintessence of horror", was a stage erected for the soul's performance, the Dionysian theatre in which the soul enacted itself': Woodman, 1986, p. 106). We shall return to this claim in Part III.

15 On rebirth as dangerous see *WS*, 298; *UM*, IV, 6; *GS*, preface, 4.

16 Compare the proclamation of Nietzsche's Zarathustra:

> The Self . . . conquers, destroys. It rules and is also the Ego's ruler . . . Your Self laughs at your Ego and its proud leapings . . . The Self says to the Ego: 'Feel Pain!' Thereupon it suffers and gives thought how to end its suffering.
>
> (*TSZ*, I, 'Of the Despisers of the Body')

Later in this chapter I shall analyse precisely how Nietzsche anticipates Jung's notion of the Self.

The ego's fear of destruction and reformulation of the Self as Other finds many parallels in the history of philosophy. Compare, for example, Levinas' discussion of the encounter of the Other (as discussed in Chapter 6). Also, compare Kant's discussion of the sublime in *The Critique of Judgement* (1790). The sublime is 'an abyss in which the imagination is afraid to lose itself' (258). The imagination fails to encompass the sublime object because the object is infinitely greater. The object is therefore *mathematically sublime*; it is 'unknowable' (244), 'absolutely great' and 'beyond all comparison' and 'measurement' (248). The object is also *dynamically* sublime, so that, it poses a threat to the experiencing subject; it inspires 'fear' (260) and demands 'respect' (256). However, the subject is not actually 'afraid' of it (260); his faculty of reason enables him to comprehend the totality of the infinite object (254), and thereby enables him to regard the dangerous object in a disinterested manner. Kant asks, 'What is admired the most?' and answers, 'It is a man who is undaunted, who knows no fear, and who, therefore, does not give way to danger, but sets manfully to work with full deliberation' (262). This is, indeed, the 'Dionysian man' of Nietzsche and Jung, he who embraces the terror of Dionysian creativity and rebirth.

17 Frey (the aforementioned Liliane Frey-Rohn) writes:

> [Nietzsche's] devotion to the irrational powers of life was destined to be the precipice on which his own life finally foundered . . . Nietzsche's exclusive and unconditional yea-saying to the Dionysiac traits . . . inevitably resulted in destruction, dissolution and death.
>
> (Frey, 1971, p. 309)

Jung's interpretation does not identify 'Dionysus' with Nietzsche's later formulation. According to Jung, Nietzsche's Dionysus is not 'an urge to unity' of Dionysus *and* Apollo, as passion *controlled*, but is that one-sided 'barbarian' (Jung, 1921, par. 346) in *BT* who promotes chaos and intoxication (see Jung, 1936a, par. 118, where Jung asks, 'What did Dionysus mean to Nietzsche?' and answers according to Nietzsche's early formulation of 'impassioned dissolution').

18 Also see Schopenhauer, 1818/1969, vol. II, ch. XX, p. 248.

19 Nietzsche presents the Eternal Recurrence as devoid of meaning, teleology and purpose ('existence as it is, without meaning or aim, yet recurring inevitably without any finale of nothingness: "*the eternal recurrence*"': *WP*, 55, 787). This position is far from the Jungian Self, which expresses the ultimate meaning and telos of life. (For Nietzsche, meaning and purpose are located within the Will to Power (*WP*, 590). In Chapters 9 and 12 I shall argue that Jung rejects Nietzsche's doctrine of the Will to Power, according to Jung's limited understanding of it.)

20 The language Jung uses to describe his notion of totality (the Self) could almost be lifted directly out of those passages where Nietzsche discusses the Eternal Recurrence. Thus, Jung describes the union of opposites in terms of a wedding, the '*hieros gamos*', literally the ritual marriage (Jung, 1955–1956, par. 207; cf. alchemical 'wedding' of King and Queen). Likewise, when Nietzsche announces that the 'high noon' of Eternal Recurrence (which has the union of opposites as its central message) is close at hand, he does so in terms of a wedding: 'Now, sure of victory together, we celebrate the feast of feasts . . . Now the world is laughing, the dread curtain is rent, the wedding day has come for light and darkness' (*BGE*, 'From High Mountains: Epode'). Similarly, we note that Jung describes the process of individuation as a 'rounding out' of the personality, which aims for 'wholeness, and ripeness' and 'perfection' (Jung, 1934a, par. 288; Jung, 1917/1926/1943, par. 186). Nietzsche calls the great noontide of the Eternal Recurrence, when the opposites 'wed', 'the Moment', which is the experience of rebirth. Thus, Zarathustra cries: 'Observe this moment!', 'Time itself is a circle' (*TSZ*, III, 'Of the Vision and the Riddle'). 'Just now my world became *perfect*', exclaims Zarathustra, and in his enlightened attitude he rejoices in the mysterious totality of existence: 'midnight is also noontide, pain is also joy, a curse is also a blessing, the night is also a sun' (*TSZ*, IV, 'The Intoxicated Song', 10, italics mine). Prior to this noon hour experience, Zarathustra requests 'that I may one day be ready and *ripe* in the great noontide: ready and *ripe* like glowing ore, like cloud heavy with lightning, and like swelling milk-udder' (*TSZ*, III, 'Of Old and New Law-Tables', 30, italics mine). Then in the stillness of the 'solemn hour' he discovers that the world is perfect (that is, *whole*, *round* and *ripe*): 'Has the world not just become perfect? Round and ripe? Oh, golden round ring' (*TSZ*, IV, 'At Noontide'). Nietzsche continues to anticipate Jung's description of completeness in the penultimate sentence of *TSZ*, where Zarathustra states: 'Zarathustra has become ripe, my hour has come!' (*TSZ*, IV, 'The Sign').

The 'moment' of the great noon event of Eternal Recurrence occurs when one experiences the unifying force – the Will to Power – in oneself and recognizes it as the underlying force of the universe. One simultaneously experiences one's own totality and the totality of the universe with the recognition that everything shares the same fundamental characteristic – the Will to Power. This experience of wholeness is glimpsed in 'timeless moments' (*WP*, 1038). Here Nietzsche implies the Eternal Recurrence:

> So many strange things have passed before me in those timeless moments that fall into one's life as if from the moon, when one no longer has any idea how old one is or how young one will yet be.

Jung calls this 'a moment of eternity in time' (Jung, 1940/1950, par. 209), when all opposites come together and are seen as parts of the 'great, greatest, incomprehensible fabric of the world, formed in a circle!' (Jung, 1942, par. 198). The similarities of language in the above quotations are also noted in Dixon (1999, pp. 343–344).

21 Also see *SNZ*, I, pp. 18–20, 226–235, where, at the end of the prologue to *TSZ*, Jung identifies a symbol of the union of spirit and body, represented by the eagle and serpent. Jung writes: 'Zarathustra sees [the eagle and the serpent] together, representing pairs of opposites, because spirit is always supposed to be the irreconcilable opponent of the chthonic, eternally fighting against the earth' (p. 19). But in Nietzsche's symbolism, the snake is tied around the neck of the flying eagle (and is not clasped within the eagle's talons, which is a common symbol of strength of spirit over body). Jung (p. 230) exclaims that this

> is surely not quite right . . . the snake might have a fantasy and squeeze his neck so that he couldn't breathe, which would be very bad for them both; it is most risky, it could go wrong in many ways.

The reconciliation between eagle and snake, spirit and body, is thus most precarious for Nietzsche.

22 This supports Frey's statement, cited earlier in this chapter, that unconditional affirmation of Dionysus inevitably results 'in destruction, dissolution and death' (Frey, 1971, p. 309).

23 Goethe, like Nietzsche and Jung, emphasized 'becoming' in the development of the individual. He regarded the individual personality as a multiplicity, which needs to be unified towards a 'middlepoint' (Goethe, *Werke*, 13: 56). Moreover, Goethe applied this notion specifically to himself (ibid., 10: 529). Goethe's concept of the 'whole' individual was underpinned by the notion of opposites (and the related notions of 'systole' and 'diastole'). For Goethe, opposites, together with 'intensification', were the 'two great driving forces of Nature' (ibid., 13: 48, cited in Bishop, 1999b, pp. 426–427). It is also interesting to note that Goethe's poetry is saturated with alchemical symbolism (see Raphael, 1965), which, as we have seen, finds correlation with Jung's process of individuation.

24 Cf. Nietzsche: 'All psychology has hitherto . . . not yet ventured into the depths' (*BGE*, 23). Jung referred to Nietzsche in order to highlight his differences from Freud, who (controversially) claimed he had never read Nietzsche. Indeed, Bishop claims:

> Jung's appeal to Nietzsche has an additional highly polemical purpose. For Jung's words of praise for Nietzsche's intuitive insights in the field of psychology served as a means of attacking Freudian psychoanalysis.
>
> (Bishop, 1995, p. 193)

25 Jung's description of how he discovered the collective unconscious finds remarkable parallel in Nietzsche. Jung tells us that after his break with Freud he experienced a period of mental illness, which he describes as a 'journey' or 'confrontation' with the unconscious (*MDR*, pp. 225, 233). Similarly, in the preface to *AOM* (the second part of *HAH*, the book that immediately followed Nietzsche's break with Wagner) Nietzsche describes his own period of illness as a kind of 'journey to the underworld':

> [S]o I, as physician and patient in one, compelled myself to an opposite and unexplored *climate of the soul*, and especially to a curative journey into strange parts, into *strangeness* itself, to an inquisitiveness regarding every kind of strange thing.
>
> (*AOM*, preface, 5)

Accordingly, Nietzsche maintains that a 'proper' psychology is founded on 'insight' revealed to 'daring travellers and adventurers' (*BGE*, 23).

26 For Jungian commentators who have acknowledged Nietzsche as anticipating Jung's individuation process see Ann Casement (2001, pp. 47–48); Roderick Peters (1991, p. 125); David Thatcher (1977, p. 256); Christopher Hauke (2000, pp. 145–174); Bishop (1995) provides only implicit acknowledgement and argues 'around' the issue. Patricia Dixon (1999) argues for Nietzsche's anticipation of the individuation process at length (pp. 202–224). (Dixon, however, does not examine Nietzsche's influence on Jungian typology, which is integral to the process of individuation.) To my knowledge, only one Nietzschean commentator provides acknowledgement of it: Kaufmann (1968, pp. 82–83). Kaufmann, is, however, rather implicit; noting the existence of a 'strikingly similar' idea in Jung's psychological practice, he claims that problems, for Nietzsche, are not solved but 'outgrown' through the 'attainment of a higher level of consciousness and subsequent broader perspective'.

27 Jung frequently identifies the individuation process at work within Nietzsche's *TSZ*. For example, in *SNZ*, I, pp. 254–272, Jung analyses Nietzsche's chapter 'Of the Three Metamorphoses', and concludes that the transformation of the camel into the lion and then into the child is an expression of the individuation process. For further references of the individuation process in Nietzsche, see *HAH*, 624, 'Traffic with One's Higher Self', where he talks of the rare moments in every individual's life when he discovers his own self; and GS, 270; TSZ, IV, 'The Honey Offering'; *GS*, 335; *WS*, 366; *TSZ*, I, 'Of the Afterworldsmen'.

28 Furthermore, Jung remarks:

> The fact that it is just the psychological functions of intuition on the one hand and sensation and instinct on the other that Nietzsche emphasizes must be characteristic of his own personal psychology.
>
> (Jung, 1921, par. 242)

Thus, Jung deduces that Nietzsche was himself an introverted intuitive type (though we find that he also classified Nietzsche as an introverted thinking type: Jung, 1921, par. 632). In Chapter 9 we shall see that this has further implications for Jung's analysis of Nietzsche's model.

29 However, we later learn that the shadow of Zarathustra's encounter is not equivalent to Jung's, for he has lost his way and has no goal.

30 Jung does make further reference to Nietzsche's theoretical conception of the shadow: but, in the next part of our inquiry we will see that Jung discusses Nietzsche's own shadow-personality at length. Further discussion of their similar conceptions of the shadow is found in very few secondary texts of Jungian commentators. Frey examines

Nietzsche's remarks on the shadow in her article, 'The Shadow Revealed in the Works of Friedrich Nietzsche' (1971), and confirms that Nietzsche was not only 'the first to discover the existence of the Shadow' (p. 317), but, moreover, in describing the Shadow

> as an unconscious tendency which clashes with conscious intention [and] as a concealed and abysmal reverse trend which represents the complement to commonly accepted, historical views [Nietzsche] discovered those backgrounds of life which C. G. Jung called the 'collective shadow'.
>
> (Frey, 1971, p. 301; see also Bishop, 1995, p. 193;
> Dixon, 1999, pp. 210–215)

According to Jung, the '*collective* shadow' represents the experience of those values that are rejected by society as morally evil. Earlier we saw that both Nietzsche and Jung wish to promote the individual above the collective herd; this includes the collective shadow and the *persona* (the 'socially acceptable' personality). Jung calls the persona a 'mask' that hides the true personality ('This mask, i.e., the *ad hoc* adopted attitude, I have called the *persona*, which was the name for the masks worn by actors in antiquity': Jung, 1921, par. 800.) Nietzsche's allusions to the mask can often be read as descriptions of the person. Thus, Nietzsche asks: 'Are you genuine? Or only an actor? A representative? Or that which is represented?' (*TI*, 'Maxims and Arrows', 38).

> Every profound spirit needs a mask: more, around every profound spirit a mask is continually growing, thanks to the constantly false, that is to say *shallow* interpretation of every word he speaks, every step he takes, every sign of life he gives.
>
> (*BGE*, 40; cf. GS, 54, 356, 361)

31 Likewise, just as Jung maintains that we project the characteristics of our anima/animus on to the opposite sex, Nietzsche's proposes the same view:

> If, in the choice of their marriage partner, men seek above all a deep nature full of feeling, while women seek a shrewd, lively minded and brilliant nature, it is clear that at bottom the man is seeking an idealized man, the woman an idealized woman – what they are seeking, that is to say, is not a complement, but a perfecting of their own best qualities.
>
> (*HAH*, 411; cf. *AOM*, 272)

32 Bishop notes that Jung failed to annotate *HAH*, 380 in his own copy (Bishop, 1995, p. 202). If we want further acknowledgement that the anima/animus is evident in Nietzsche's texts, we must turn to secondary texts. Thus, Bishop notes that a 'close reading of "Archetypes of the Collective Unconscious" (Jung, 1951, pars. 3–42), reveals that Jung's description of the anima as early as 1934 has its literary counterpart in another part of Nietzsche'. Bishop argues that Jung's notion of the anima as 'soul' is depicted in *TSZ*, III, 'Of the Great Longing', and actually 'takes form on the basis of deeper influence from the figure of Life in "The Dance Song" and "The Second Dance Song"' (*TSZ*, II, III). He concludes that 'Nietzschean imagery and Jungian psychology are thus brought together to produce the archetype of Anima' (Bishop, 1995, p. 202). Both Kathleen Higgins and Walter Kaufmann acknowledge Nietzsche's prior concern with the anima in connection with his use of the name 'Ariadne'. Higgins (1985), argues that 'Ariadne, when understood as a concept resembling the Jungian anima, is an appropriate response to the Dionysian lament of "The Night Song"' (p. 33), and

Kaufmann (1968), after citing Nietzsche as saying 'A labyrinthine man never seeks the truth but always only his Ariadne – whatever he may tell us', states:

> [Nietzsche's] sister is not entirely wrong when she claims that he is speaking of the human soul, though today we have perhaps a somewhat more accurate term in C. G. Jung's conception of the *Anima*: originally dependent on a 'mother image', it grows into the ideal which a man pursues throughout his life
>
> (Kaufmann, 1968, p. 34)

Dixon supports Kaufmann in equating Nietzsche's Ariadne with Jung's notion of the anima by citing confirmation from Nietzsche himself (Dixon, 1999, pp. 216–217). In *Ecce Homo* Nietzsche writes: 'Who knows except me what *Ariadne* is!' (*EH*, 'TSZ', 8). Dixon then refers to the preceding section where Nietzsche provides an isolated answer: 'Who knows? Perhaps I am the first psychologist of the eternal-womanly?' (*EH*, 'Why I Write Such Good Books', 5).

33 It is odd that Jung ignores Nietzsche's declaration that 'perhaps I am the first psychologist of the eternal-womanly' (*EH*, 'Why I Write Such Good Books', 5). A possible reason for Jung's failure to promote the anima in Nietzsche's writings is the latter's many apparently misogynistic comments (e.g. *TSZ*, I, 'Of Old and Young Women'; *BGE*, 139, 144, 145, 232; *EH*, 'Why I Write Such Good Books', 5) and consequent misunderstanding of female psychology. Hence, at the head of his essay 'Woman in Europe' (1927), Jung curiously cites a passage from *TSZ* in which Nietzsche discusses servitude as the woman's only right (*CW* 10, p. 113), and in *SNZ* he maintains that Nietzsche 'was terribly clumsy and foolish when it came to women' (II, p. 770). However, to label Nietzsche a misogynist is unjust (see *D*, 346; *HAH*, 377; *GS*, 339; for rigorous examination and evaluation of Nietzsche's views see the collection of essays in *Nietzsche and the Feminine* (Burgard, 1994); also see Rochelle L. Millen, 'The Garden of Innocence? Nietzsche's Psychology of Women', in Golomb et al., 1999, pp. 73–89).

34 Also see *GM*, preface; *TSZ*, I, 'Of the Afterworldsmen', 'Of the Way of the Creator', 'Of Marriage and Children'; *TSZ*, II, 'Of the Virtuous', 'Of Redemption'; *TSZ*, III, 'Of Passing By'; cf. *HAH*, 629; *BGE*, 231; *EH*, 'HAH', 4; *D*, 491.

35 This point is given extreme expression by Robin Alice Roth, who in 'Answer to [Kathleen Higgins' article] "The Night Song's Answer"', criticizes such 'reductionistic' comparison:

> Arguing [as Higgins has done] that Nietzsche's 'Ariadne' resembles a Jungian anima is dangerous because Nietzsche never read Jung and therefore could not himself have intended any Jungian notions . . . it is clear that it must have been something other than a Jungian, psychological concept, something philosophical instead.
>
> (Roth, 1985, p. 51)

This point is itself guilty of being too reductionistic in its willingness to separate Nietzsche and Jung by what Roth wrongly considers to be two completely discordant modes of thought, philosophy and psychology. Nevertheless, an attempt to conflate the two models into one is unjust (and is equivalent to promoting one-sidedness).

9 Nietzsche's madness: a Jungian critique of Nietzsche's model

1 Cf. Frey, 1971, p. 318: 'Such opposition tears the person apart into the polarities of the monster and the exalted animal.'

2 It would seem that Jung is here contradicting his deeply held view that Nietzsche was one of the first investigators of the ('Jungian' collective and autonomous) unconscious. However, as we shall see later, there is no contradiction for, although Jung accepts the anticipation of the collective unconscious in Nietzsche, Nietzsche only 'intuits' its existence: he does not grasp its essential meaning, and therefore does not explicitly argue or acknowledge its implications (*SNZ*, II, p. 1147). It is perhaps because of Nietzsche's failure to grasp fully the dynamics of the unconscious beyond mere intuition that Jung is reluctant to promote Nietzsche as a pioneer and explicit influence on his own model.

3 However, Nietzsche does have Zarathustra say that the true image envisaged by all creativity, the 'image of images' (an analogy to God), did not lie in consciousness, but slept as if incarcerated deep down in the soul and its 'hardest, ugliest stone' (*TSZ*, II, 'On the Blissful Islands'). We cannot presume that Nietzsche was aware of the similarity here with the alchemical notion of a 'spirit in matter' (Jung, 1937a, pars. 410, 413, 436). Nevertheless, Frey-Rohn (1988) notes that Nietzsche's

> vision of this image in all probability pointed towards the archetype of the '*lapis philosophorum*' [the Philosopher's Stone] inherent in the collective unconscious and, according to Jung, a symbol of the Self. But Nietzsche did not grasp what 'Zarathustra in himself' knew – namely that it was a *god* which slept in his soul and that the secret of creation lay in bowing down before this divinity.
>
> (Frey-Rohn, 1988, p. 114)

4 Thus, it could be argued that if Nietzsche had acknowledged his unconscious inferior side and maintained a healthy balanced psyche, he would not have produced such creative thought as he does. Indeed, Nietzsche

> saw his loneliness and even his sickness as essential to the creative tasks he had set for himself; as he wrote . . . to Georg Brandes, 'My illness has been my greatest boon: it unblocked me, it gave me the courage to be myself'.
>
> (Jarrett, introduction to *SNZ*, I, p. xiv)

But Jung thought the contrary: 'A creative person is not creative, or more creative, because of a neurosis . . . Against Freud, he maintained with firmness that "art is not a morbidity"' (ibid., p. xii).

5 An illustration of this point can be drawn from a passage in *TSZ* where Zarathustra exclaims: 'Alas, there are so many great ideas that do nothing more than the bellows: they inflate and make emptier than ever' (*TSZ*, I, 'Of the Way of the Creator'). In response to this passage, Jung states: '[Nietzsche] has absolutely the right intuition', and if he had also employed his sensation function and applied 'that thought to his [whole] identification, then things would be right' (*SNZ*, I, p. 709). According to Jung, Nietzsche's sanity could have been saved if he had acknowledged his *whole* identity. If Nietzsche had employed his sensation function he would have been able to 'appreciate things for what they are', and relate to his own teachings. In other words, it is Nietzsche's conscious inflation that prevents him from relating to Zarathustra's teaching, since he has claimed the mantle of the prophet for himself, and it is the unconscious 'sensation' orientation within him (the unknown 'other' that generates creativity for and within him) that would resolve the inflation and restore a healthy psychological balance, if it were consciously acknowledged.

6 This is the Eternal Recurrence: only by accepting the inferior man can one create the 'super' man. The Eternal Recurrence can be regarded as the *enantiodromia* between the inferior man and the *Übermensch*.

7   Graham Parkes (1999) argues that Jung's analysis of the anima in Nietzsche is contradictory. For Jung maintains

> that we have no anima in *Zarathustra*. Only very near the end anima figures appear in the erotic poem 'Unter Töchtern der Wüste' ['the Daughters of the Desert'] . . . It takes the whole development of *Zarathustra* to call Nietzsche's attention to the fact that there is an anima.
>
> (*SNZ*, I, p. 533)

Then we see Nietzsche allude to several feminine figures in the text in addition to the Daughters of the Desert. Jung himself equates several other aspects in the text with the anima (such as when Zarathustra sings his song about his relations with Life (*SNZ*, II, p. 1163); Zarathustra's 'Wild Wisdom' (ibid., p. 1167); and the enigmatic figure of the chapter of *TSZ* entitled 'The Stillest Hour' (ibid., p. 1244); cited in Parkes, 1999, p. 223). Parkes thus concludes: 'So it would seem, contrary to Jung's initial assertion, that by the end of the first half of *Zarathustra* its author is quite aware of "the fact that there is an anima"' (Parkes, 1999, p. 223).

8   Nietzsche tells us that the tightrope walker's fateful fall was instigated by the arrival of an aggressive buffoon upon the rope. The buffoon emits a cry 'like a devil' and 'sprang over the man standing in his path' (*TSZ*, prologue, 6). According to Jung, this buffoon represents Nietzsche's active shadow (*SNZ*, I, pp. 115, 124). This, Jung tells us, 'is the anticipation of Nietzsche's fate. It is as if this whole scene had performed itself in Nietzsche's life . . . [T]he shadow has jumped over him and killed him' (ibid., p. 125).

9   Indeed, Nietzsche himself reveals the almost 'schizophrenic' nature of *EH* in his letter to Peter Gast, 9 December 1888: '*Ecce Homo* so exceeds the term "literature" that even Nature itself cannot provide an image: it veritably blasts the *history* of mankind into two pieces – the highest superlative of dynamite' (Middleton, in Nietzsche, 1969, p. 369).

10   However, one could also interpret this as irony and humour on Nietzsche's part.

11   Jung regarded the Dionysian personality as 'barbaric' (Jung, 1921, par. 230). Nietzsche, in Jung's view, was no exception. According to Jung, the Dionysian man is a barbarian because he is one-sided, with such a massive overbalance on the side of the unconscious that all sense of individuality is lost – the personal unconscious disappears along with the conscious mind, and the individual is entirely swallowed up in the collective unconscious (inflation). However, the Dionysian 'barbarian' must not be confused with the Dionysian man of exceptional 'creation'. Jung understands any confrontation with the unconscious as an encounter with Dionysus, and as we have seen throughout this book, the unconscious is a compensating aspect of the psyche that can be both creative and destructive. (Similarly, Dionysus represents birth and death.) In the words of Paul Bishop:

> It is therefore not inappropriate for Jung to speak of trying to drive out the Devil with Beelzebub: Dionysus, as the source of artistic creativity (unconsciousness), against Dionysus, the one-sidedness of barbarianism. Yet these two different understandings of Dionysus are, in Jungian thought, not so much pitted against each other as reciprocal. In tragedy, according to Nietzsche, Dionysus was both the victim and the murderer. In Jung, Dionysus is both the danger (a repressed archetype returning) and the 'saving thought' (archetypal inspiration from the Collective Unconscious).
>
> (Bishop, 1995, p. 175)

Jung regarded Nietzsche as falling victim to the former aspect of Dionysus; he was identified with Dionysus the barbarian and murderer, and died accordingly. Jung thus notes: 'A person must pay dearly for the divine gift of creative fire' (Jung, 1930/1950, par. 158).

10 Nietzsche's absolution: a metacritique of Jung's critique of Nietzsche's model

1 Thus, Nietzsche insists that the Apollinian and Dionysian impulses are 'artistic powers that burst forth from nature herself, *without mediation of the human artist*' (*BT*, 2). Therefore the *Übermensch*, as promoting the Apollinian and Dionysian impulses within, is not merely 'body' or 'nature' as Jung contends, because he is shaped by 'the true creator' and 'artist of worlds' (cf. Parkes, 1999, pp. 211–212).

It is interesting to note that commentators on Nietzsche often refer to the unconscious body and the conscious spirit. I interpret Nietzsche as associating both body and spirit with consciousness and the unconscious, so that the body, as well as the spirit, is the conscious vehicle through which the unconscious finds expression.

2 For further discussion of Nietzsche and Jung's attack on the 'blasphemy of Christianity's humanitarianism', and of the dangers of Nihilism see 'Nihilism and the Death of God' in Dixon (1999, ch. 6, pp. 101–146).

3 Also see the classicist R. P. Winnington-Ingram (1983) who, in his discussion of how strange it is that philosophers and theologians have not taken a greater interest in tragedy, notes that Nietzsche is the most interesting and influential exception (Winnington-Ingram, 1983, p. 172, n. 60; cited in Dixon, 1999, p. 67). See also the classicist Hugh Lloyd-Jones, who notes: 'Nietzsche's writings show an unprecedented insight into the nature of divinity as the Greeks conceived it' (Lloyd-Jones, 1976, p. 10; cited in Dixon, 1999, p. 67).

4 Indeed, in his early notes for the short book *We Philologists* (1874–1875, never completed), Nietzsche related his view of art directly to that of religion and concluded: 'Religion is "*love beyond ourselves*". The work of art is the image of such *self-transcending love, and a perfect image*' (185; cited in Dixon, 1999, p. 69).

5 Nietzsche's case was 'pathological' because his identification was not with his persona but with an historical and religious figure (*MDR*, p. 415) – Zarathustra (cf. *SNZ*, I, pp. 4–9; II, p. 1306). It is perhaps because Jung regarded Nietzsche's inflation as extreme that it has been accepted by Jungian scholars and analysts (despite their general unfamiliarity with Nietzsche's work) as both the definitive account or case study of inflation and the definitive interpretation of Nietzsche's illness (see Von Franz, 1975, p. 152, cf. p. 44; Jaffé, 1970, p. 81; Jacobi, 1968, p. 204; Moreno, 1974, pp. 232, 235–237; cf. Schlamm, 2000, p. 113; all cited in Dixon, 1999, p. 270, n. 52. While Frey-Rohn has certainly read Nietzsche, she uncritically accepts Jung's analysis; see Frey-Rohn, 1988, pp. 4, 82, 85–88, 254–255, 271, 287–288; and Frey, 1971, pp. 209, 302).

6 This is demonstrated throughout his work. For example, see the preface to *BT* entitled *Attempt at a Self-Criticism* (1886). Also see the preface to *The Case for Wagner*:

I am, no less than Wagner . . . a decadent: but I comprehended this, I resisted it. The philosopher in me resisted . . . For such a task I required a special self-discipline: to take sides against everything sick in me.

Even his formula for the 'revaluation of values' is described by him as 'radical self-examination' (*EH*, 'Why I am a Destiny', 1; *EH*, 'D', 2). Jaspers notes that Nietzsche 'did his thinking in constant self-illumination' (Jaspers, 1966, p. 103). Dixon notes that 'few men, if any, have engaged in war with themselves by way of deliberate and continual self-examination as did Nietzsche' (Dixon, 1999, p. 265). And Chive notes that 'Nietzsche's lot was to argue against himself, to turn himself inside out' (ibid.). Even Freud, according to his biographer Ernest Jones, 'several times said of Nietzsche that he had a more penetrating knowledge of himself than any other man who ever lived or was ever likely to live' (Jones, 1953–1957, vol. II, p. 344). Parkes notes: 'Jung's *idée fixe* about Nietzsche's lack of self-awareness . . . further confounds his understanding of Nietzsche's personal psychology as well as his reading of *Zarathustra*' (Parkes, 1999, p. 221). The extent to which Nietzsche examined and criticized himself suggests that, *contra* Jung's interpretation, Nietzsche would have indeed been aware of his own shadow personality.

7 In 'Schopenhauer as Educator', Nietzsche alludes to Rousseau as the victim of the 'threatening power' and 'dangerous excitations' (*UM*, III, IV; cf. Kaufmann, 1974, p. 169; also cited in Dixon, 1999, pp. 264, 245).

8 Storr supports my assertion: 'I think [his misdiagnosis of Nietzsche] is a betrayal of Jung's training as a doctor, and a piece of unjustifiable boastfulness' (Storr, 1996, p. 11). It could also be argued that Jung is unjustified in using *Thus Spoke Zarathustra* as the definitive text to evaluate not only Nietzsche's psychological disposition but also, and more significantly, his theories. This is because *TSZ* is not a philosophical treatise as such, and therefore does not adequately represent the extent of Nietzsche's philosophical arguments.

9 Jung himself admits that Nietzsche's insanity can be explained in these physiological terms:

> The results are no doubt very interesting and may perhaps have the same kind of scientific value as, for instance, a post-mortem exhibition of the brain of Nietzsche, which might conceivably show us the particular atypical form of paralysis from which he died.
>
> (Jung, 1922, par. 103; cited also in Bishop, 1995, p. 158)

Also, in a letter to Walter Robert Corti of 30 April 1929, Jung writes:

> Nietzsche preached: 'You should make friends with the nearest things'. I would hold his world-negating life responsible for this did I not know that *syphilis lurked in him and that paralysis hung over him like the sword of Damocles.*
>
> (Adler and Jaffé, 1973–1975, p. 65, italics mine; cited also in Bishop, 1995, p. 78)

And on 28 February 1943 Jung writes to Arnold Kunzli:

> In the critical philosophy of the future there will be a chapter on 'The Psychology of Philosophy'. Hegel is fit to burst with presumption and vanity, *Nietzsche drips with outraged sexuality,* and so on.
>
> (Adler and Jaffé, 1973–1975, p. 330, italics mine; cited also in Bishop, 1995, p. 79)

10 Although, aside from Nietzsche's own 'confession', there was no evidence of him having syphilis; also dementia is not compatible with the increasingly high level of creativity that Nietzsche experienced until his sudden collapse.

11 Nietzsche's father's autopsy revealed that a quarter of his father's brain was affected by 'softening'; this condition had also affected his father's father (cited in Cybulska, 2000, p. 571; Dixon, 1999, p. 271, n. 65; also see Storr, 1996, p. 11).

12 Perhaps the most explicit example is his letter to Rohde which he wrote a year before his breakdown, on 11 November 1887: 'Has anyone the faintest notion of the real cause of my long illness? . . . I'm just as alone as I was in my childhood' (Middleton, in Nietzsche, 1969, pp. 275–276). Such evidence can also be found in Nietzsche's work itself; in *Human, All Too Human* Nietzsche notes: 'What I again and again needed most for my cure and self-restoration, however, was the belief that I was *not* thus isolated, not alone in *seeing* as I did' (*HAH*, preface, 1).

11 Jung's shadow: the ambiguities of Jung's reception of Nietzsche resolved

1 Jarrett says that, after reading *TSZ*, Jung

> was even more strongly impressed with how powerfully Nietzsche's case illustrated his own growing understanding that one's most basic beliefs have their roots in personality and in turn one can discover much about an author's own personality from his writings.
>
> (Jarrett, introduction to *SNZ*, p. xi)

This is certainly the case; but what Jarrett does not note is how this has significant implications for Jung's own writings. Indeed, commentators on Jung have not examined or even acknowledged *SNZ* as an exercise of Jungian self-analysis; it is simply taken as a definitive assessment of the personality of Nietzsche. If one accepts that *TSZ* enables a Jungian analysis of Nietzsche's personality, one must also accept that *SNZ* enables a Jungian analysis of Jung himself, and in this chapter we shall attempt to do just that.

2 Indeed, the review of the published seminars by Thomas Kirsch (whose mother, Hilda Kirsch, attended the meetings) opens with the following statement: 'In the lore of analytical psychology Jung's seminar discussions on Nietzsche's *Thus Spake Zarathustra* have long carried a mysterious and numinous quality' (Kirsch, 1989, p. 101; cited in Bishop, 1994, p. 93). Furthermore, Bishop notes:

> Mary Bancroft, who also attended the Seminar, spoke of the 'talisman syndrome' which surrounded not only the warning that the notes were not for circulation but also some of the people who attended the Seminar.
>
> (ibid.)

Richard Noll (1994, 1996) argues that Jungian psychology in general is a 'secret church', a religious cult, centred on the figure of Jung as the cult leader.

3 Those who attended the seminars were certainly in awe of Jung. Professor Dr Tadeus Reichstein, who attended the seminars, notes that such attendance was 'only for the initiated'; and Mary Bancroft, another member of the group, uses a religious image to describe the relationship between the seminar members and Jung: 'I was fascinated by those I thought of as handmaidens or Vestal Virgins, Jung, of course, being the Flame' (Bishop, 1994, p. 94). Surely the 'initiated' would not begin to question their leader.

4 For example see *SNZ*, II, p. 1209, where Jung says: 'I got bored stiff [with *TSZ*] . . . so I came to the conclusion that you have now had enough of this and that we don't need to go further into the detail'. Parkes notes:

> One does not expect from him closely argued readings of texts . . . but it is sad, given the time and energy so many intelligent people expended in the seminar, that

he didn't try to set aside his prejudices and apply his exegetical talents to the rich and complex text of *Zarathustra*.

(Parkes, 1999, p. 214)

Noll takes this argument further to suggest that Jung 'confused' and 'deliberately misled' his followers (Noll, 1996, p. 172).

5 'Nietzsche . . . was the son of a parson . . . I know what *that* means' (*MDR*, p. 123; *SNZ*, I, p. 31).

6 Noll (1996) claims that Jung very seriously believed he had actually been deified in a December 1913 vision, when he suffered as Christ, was worshipped as Christ, and was then transformed into the Mithraic lion-headed god Aion (pp. 121, 143).

7 My surprise extends to the failure of Jungian commentators on this fact too. It must be noted, however, that *MDR* was written twenty-five years after *SNZ* – time for Jung to realize his identification with Nietzsche. Also, *MDR* and *SNZ* were directed at different audiences: the former for the 'public' and the latter for 'initiates'.

8 Indeed, Barbara Hannah (Jung's personal secretary for twenty-five years) adds: 'I think he was doubtful that he could have survived this most difficult of all journeys had he been entirely alone in it' (Hannah, 1981, p. 120).

9 We see that Jung is dismissive of Nietzsche's personality in his autobiography *MDR*:

Among my friends and acquaintances I knew only of two who openly declared themselves adherents of Nietzsche. Both were homosexual; one of them ended by committing suicide, the other ran to seed as a misunderstood genius.

(*MDR*, p. 124)

10 In a letter dated 12 May 1928 to Hermann Graf Keyserling, Jung criticizes the laughter of Nietzsche, which is ultimately, according to Jung, not funny:

I don't believe the 'Last Man' laughs 'heartily', nor 'like a Homeric hero', but, if I may say so, rather like Nietzsche . . . No one can laugh when reading Nietzsche. The laughter of alienation is not infectious.

(Adler and Jaffé, 1973–1975, pp. 50–51; also cited in Bishop, 1995, p. 78)

11 Jung does not discuss the psychological implications of boredom in his *Collected Works*. He does interestingly note, however, that

the sense of boredom which then appears in the analysis is simply an expression of the monotony and poverty of ideas – not of the unconscious, as is sometimes supposed, but of the analyst who does not understand that these fantasies should not be taken merely in a concretistic-reductive sense, but rather in a constructive one. When this is realized, the standstill is often overcome at a single stroke.

(Jung, 1916/1957, par. 146)

The implication here for our argument is that Jung fails, as an analyst, to apply Nietzsche's ideas 'constructively'; he is too rigid in their interpretation and does not see their full significance and application (i.e. that they could also be applied to himself).

12 This is my interpretation. One could interpret the ironic tone (suggested by the exclamation mark) to imply 'of course, I *do not* exclude myself'.

13 However, not every passage in *TSZ* omitted by Jung is an expression of his unconscious fear of being identified with Nietzsche. Jung's reasons for omitting certain passages are justifiable. For example, I have not found anything particularly revealing in Chapter

50, 'On the Mount of Olives', that could undermine Jung's reasons for its omission; it certainly seems that Nietzsche does 'just go on feeling his resentment against the small people and exaggerates it to such an extent that his nature gets sick of it' (*SNZ*, II, p. 1386). Likewise there is nothing notable in the two chapters 'Of the Apostates' and 'The Home Coming', Chapters 52 and 53, which Jung surveys only briefly since 'it is hardly worth while to spend time on these critical remarks because they are so clearly based on his resentment' (*SNZ*, II, p. 1424). Jung again refers to Nietzsche's personal resentment as the reason for omitting Chapters 38 and 39, 'Of Scholars' and 'Of Poets' (*SNZ*, II, p. 1215), and again there is nothing notable in these two chapters to discredit Jung. However, the fact that Jung ignores these chapters because they express Nietzsche's personal resentment could be interpreted as a projection of Jung's own personal resentment and shadow. (Of course the lack of anything revealing in these omitted chapters is a matter of my own interpretation and deduction.)

14   Frey-Rohn (a member of the original seminar group) offers an interpretation of some of these passages, but they are very few, and her analysis only ever extends to a few lines that strike her as interesting. Part four is covered in just twenty-one pages (of a large type-font!): see Frey-Rohn, 1988, pp. 140–169. My concern is not, however, with Frey-Rohn's interpretation and analysis of *TSZ* but with Jung's, and with his own unconscious fear and confession.

15   However, Nietzsche's own response to this section is relevant, for this part 'gave Nietzsche more trouble' than the other parts (*SNZ*, I, p. xv, n. 3). Nietzsche writes: 'the years during and above all *after* Zarathustra were a state of distress without equal' (*EH*, 'TSZ', 5). Previous to this Nietzsche equates physical and general well-being with an abundant flow of creative power (ibid.). We could therefore interpret the difficulties Nietzsche had with part four of *TSZ* as a possible lack of inspiration. In this case, Nietzsche would have been less in possession of the collective unconscious and more in control of his conscious faculties, thereby affording a less conducive and conformative reading of Nietzsche's personality to Jung's diagnosis. Indeed, Frey-Rohn notes that part IV of *TSZ* lacks 'that Dionysian spark which had so enlivened the work before' (Frey-Rohn, 1988, p. 148). Does this mean Nietzsche is no longer identified with Dionysus and therefore no longer mad? Frey-Rohn believes the undertones of the book are now associated with more external issues rather than those of inner personality: with 'resignation and melancholy . . . pessimism . . . [due to the] disappointment at the indifferent reception of the previous three books [of *TSZ*]' (ibid.), and also with issues of doubt surrounding the possibility of his project, for 'hope was also fading in him that a "higher" type of humanity would be born' (ibid.). The implication is that the undertones of part four seem not to be propelled by a personality inflated by the unconscious, but one that is deflated and looking to situate its meaning outside of itself, much in the same way as Jung describes the ego as seeking to establish itself as the predominant part of the psyche in the individual's first half of life.

However, from the unanalysed chapters of part three, one passage at the very end is of interest to us. Here Nietzsche writes:

> But whenever you would climb with me, O my brothers, see to it that no *parasite* climbs with you! Parasite: that is a worm, a creeping, supple worm, that wants to grow fat on your sick, sore places.
>
> ('Of Old and New Law Tables', 19)

According to Jung, to 'climb' with Nietzsche is to follow him into madness, into the 'inflated heights'. Jung could be considered a candidate for this parasite, for, in my reading, Jung wants to look 'fat' in relation to Nietzsche. Nietzsche is the scapegoat to

Jung's own weaknesses, so that Jung puts Nietzsche down in order to make himself appear bigger – Jung 'grows fat' on Nietzsche's 'sick, sore places'. Nietzsche continues to note:

> And it is its art to divine the weary spots in climbing souls: it builds its loathsome nest in your grief and dejection, in your tender modesty. Where the strong man is weak, where the noble man is too gentle, there it builds its loathsome nest: the parasite dwells where the great man possesses little sore places.

To continue our analogy: Jung's 'art', is analytical psychology, and this could be understood as that which 'divines the weary spots in climbing souls [i.e. inflated minds]', and it is Jung himself who creates in his projection a 'loathsome nest' in Nietzsche, when Nietzsche was simply 'grieved and dejected'. Nietzsche then alludes to the great noble man as the mad man with sore places (i.e. himself). In our analogy, Jung is the lowest man: the parasite, whom Nietzsche nourishes. Later, in relation to the Eternal Recurrence, Nietzsche argues that 'the greatest man and the smallest man [are] all too similar to one another' ('The Convalescent', 2) – as, I would argue, are Nietzsche and Jung.

16 Although the chapter 'The Pale Criminal' is included in Jung's analysis, the reaction it produces in Jung is significant to our argument. Jung describes this chapter as 'not particularly engaging – even disagreeable' (*SNZ*, I, p. 457); 'it is exceedingly disgusting to my feeling' (ibid., p. 459). This chapter obviously affects Jung deeply and unconsciously. After Jung claims that Nietzsche 'reaches here one of the prestages of his own madness', Jung immediately feels the need to confirm his own psychological health by stating that one's 'natural feeling function, as well as a natural untwisted mind, will be hurt by the special psychology here'. This chapter is particularly 'pathological' for Jung. However, when Jung appeals to his audience for support by asking how they felt about this chapter, he is met with straightforward intellectual responses; Jung is the only one to respond with feeling. Jung's feeling toward this chapter is immense; he says its influence is 'poisonous' and it leads him to criticize the whole of *TSZ*, claiming it

> should not have been published but should have been concealed and worked over in another form because it can have such an evil influence; it should be reserved for people who have undergone a careful training in the psychology of the unconscious.
>
> (*SNZ*, I, p. 475)

In terms of the content of Jung's analysis, he argues that the community needs the criminal/murderer as a scapegoat upon whom to project their own murderous tendencies, thereby relieving them of the burden of evil (ibid., p. 463). We could say that this corresponds to Jung's need to project his own evil (shadow/madness) on to Nietzsche for personal relief; for according to Jung, if one identifies directly with the criminal (i.e. Nietzsche) one will inevitably/consciously become insane (ibid.). Jung, however, tries to repress the fact to escape its conscious burden. Bishop confirms my suspicions. In response to Jung's reaction to the 'Pale Criminal', Bishop writes:

> It is therefore highly significant that Jung should have chosen to invoke [in the context of his discussion of Nazi Germany] an image which he, personally, had found so disturbing. Unconsciously, Jung is voicing his horror not just of the

Germans, but of the 'shadow-side' of his own personality; and his analysis of the Germans is simultaneously an exercise in Self-analysis.

(Bishop, 1995, pp. 316–317)

17 In Chapter 9 we saw Jung criticize Nietzsche for not acknowledging the meaning of his words when he writes in 'Of the Way of the Creator': 'Alas, there are so many great ideas that do nothing more than the bellows: they inflate and make emptier than ever' (*SNZ*, I, p. 709). According to Jung, Nietzsche admits, though unconsciously, that his 'great idea' of the *Übermensch* is an impossible position in which man is made divine, an empty idea that pertains to mere inflation or a lot of 'hot air'. In this passage in the main text we see Nietzsche again refer to inflation, though this time it is his shadow that is associated with inflation. However, the notable difference is that Nietzsche's shadow is inflated with 'earthly things'. Nietzsche's shadow 'smells of the earth', not of the heavens.

18 Jung briefly alludes to the mirror as a reflection of the intellect in an earlier seminar, though he does so purely in the context of Schopenhauer and does not relate it to Nietzsche. Jung, referring to Schopenhauer, says: 'Then he said it also happened that man developed an intellect which was able to mirror itself. He must hold this mirror before the intellect and it will see its own face' (*SNZ*, I, p. 119). In a later seminar, when referring to the chapter 'The Child with the Mirror', Jung notes: 'The mirror is the intellect or the mind' (*SNZ*, II, p. 845). And he again refers to the mirror as a reflection of the intellect in his *Seminar on Dream Analysis* on 26 June 1929 (Jung, 1928–1930/ 1995, p. 291).

19 Jung briefly alludes to the mirror as a reflection of the unconscious (the final allusion he makes to the mirror in *SNZ*, aside from his analysis of the chapter 'The Child with the Mirror', which I discuss later): 'Whenever somebody speaks directly out of the unconscious, one must always keep in mind that those are mirrored facts and truly prophetic: a true prophet mirrors the flow of potential facts' (*SNZ*, I, p. 553). This is significant for our argument when we note Jung's claim that *TSZ* is a direct expression of Nietzsche's unconscious (*SNZ*, I, p. 461). Nietzsche is the 'true prophet', as it were, of Jung's 'potential' madness.

20 Perhaps Jung should take his own advice on weeding, and not criticize Nietzsche for his own failing. In a passage unrelated to Nietzsche's 'The Child with the Mirror', Jung ironically and amusingly writes:

Ah, that is just Nietzsche's style. He recognizes the thing but other people must practice it. He merely preaches it, but it doesn't concern him. He doesn't realize when he preaches house cleaning that it might be his own house. Everybody has to clean house because his own house is dirty. It is like those people who always talk about the *weeds* in other people's gardens but never weed their own.

(*SNZ*, II, pp. 1459–1460, italics mine)

21 However, it must be noted that the peacock's flesh is also 'an early Christian symbol for resurrection' (Jung, 1955–1956, par. 395). The 'Poets' to whom Nietzsche refers in Chapter 39 are most likely to be Christians, for this chapter is full of other Christian symbols – such as the wine that Nietzsche describes as 'adulterated', those 'fine fish' which are always sought, and the 'god's head' which Nietzsche describes as 'old' to parallel the 'poor in spirit'. If the peacock is given its Christian interpretation here, then Nietzsche cleverly makes fun of it, for he does not allude to its symbolic meaning (of resurrection) but alludes to the peacock's natural tendency towards vanity: which is condemned as sinful in Christianity.

22   My works can be regarded as stations along my life's way, they are the expression
      of my inner development . . . All my writings may be considered tasks imposed
      from within; their source was a fatal compulsion. What I wrote were things that
      assailed me from within myself.

                                                                    (*MDR*, p. 249)

23 Miss Frank Miller was not a patient of Jung's, but an American student at the University
     of Geneva, who wrote a memoir describing her fantasies: *Some Instances of
     Subconscious Creative Imagination*, published (in French) in *Archives de psychologie*
     (Geneva, vol. V, 1906), with an introduction by the psychologist Théodore Flournoy,
     who was treating her.
24 In his chapter 'Two Kinds of Thinking', Jung alludes to Nietzsche's appreciation of this
     autonomous state as 'dream-thinking' (Jung, 1911–1912/1952, par. 27).
25 Bishop makes a similar claim (Bishop, 1995, p. 246). However, that Jung's psychiatric
     basis should be based on his own self-therapy is no surprise; as we have seen, Jung
     himself readily admits this. On a similar note, we know that Jung was one of the first
     psychoanalysts to insist that the analyst should undergo analysis (Storr, 1989, p. 41).
26 As an intuitive type, Jung is encouraged to think passively or fantastically. The final
     paragraph of *Psychological Types* (1921) supports our claim above. Here Jung's
     discussion of Nietzsche can be read as a description of Jung himself:

        In his initial work he unwittingly sets the facts of his own personal psychology in
        the foreground. This is all quite in harmony with the intuitive attitude, which
        characteristically perceives the outer through the medium of the inner, sometimes
        even at the expense of reality. By means of this attitude he also gained deep insight
        into the Dionysian qualities of his unconscious.

                                         (Jung, 1921, par. 242; cited in Bishop, 1999, p. 238)

27 Cf. *AOM*, 126: 'That is neither I nor not – I but some third thing'.

12 Jung's madness: a Nietzschean critique of Jung's model

 1 Thus, as Jung (unjustifiably) criticized Nietzsche's model for promoting the body at the
     expense of spirit, Nietzsche might well criticize Jung for denying the inherent value of
     the body and for hastily turning to its spiritual aspect for needless validation: that is, for
     believing them to be two separate things. If the spiritual realm is not found beyond the
     body but within it, then the symbol is not external to the opposites but is found within
     them. In this reading, the Will to Power can be interpreted as a symbol.
 2 Jung also calls the external symbolic element 'God'. Although 'God' has metaphysical
     connotations, the term might not offend Nietzsche, for he equates God (i.e. the non-
     metaphysical and Christian God) with the Will to Power (cf. *WP*, 639, 1037).
 3 It must be noted, however, that Jung presents his model of psychic structures as
     provisional, and he is aware of the difficulty of grasping truth propositionally – he
     therefore focuses on symbols and images.
 4 Lampert notes: 'Although it is the most comprehensive of truths with respect to its
     applicability to all human beings, with respect to its relevant audience it is a limited
     truth' (Lampert, 1986, p. 246).
 5 Jung writes that when 'one measures things from the standpoint of power . . . [it is
     founded on] the psychology of feelings of inferiority . . . Nietzsche['s] Will to Power
     is created by resentment' (*SNZ*, II, p. 1353.).
 6 Jung's colleague Liliane Frey-Rohn holds a similar view. She wrongly maintains that
     Nietzsche's proposed hierarchy of humankind is founded on an 'appeal for increased

power and violence', which leads to 'the glorification of a dominant class comprising the strong and powerful' (Frey-Rohn, 1988, p. 280). Moreover, she claims that, in taking the 'bloodthirsty tyrant and malicious despot' (Frey, 1971, p. 304) such as Cesare Borgia and Napoleon as 'his heroes', as the future 'Masters of the Earth', 'Nietzsche does not take into consideration that a person must master the act of obedience in order to be able to lead' (p. 308). Then in citing Nietzsche's passage, 'Quanta of power alone determine rank and distinguish rank: nothing else does', Frey claims that 'according to [Nietzsche], whoever embodies the will to power in the purest form holds the highest rank' (pp. 319–320). What Frey does not note, however, is that, for Nietzsche, it is not the 'bloodthirsty tyrant' or 'malicious despot' (*TI*, 'Expeditions of an Untimely Man', 37) but the artist, philosopher and saint who express the Will to Power in its highest and most authentic forms.

7   Thus, Jung maintains that 'where love is, power cannot prevail, and where power prevails, love cannot reign' (Jung, 1921, par. 408; cf. Jung, 1917/1926/1943, par. 43). But Nietzsche, like Jung, views love and power as complementary: in *GS*, 337, Nietzsche describes 'a god full of love and power' as exemplary of 'the *"humaneness" of the future'*.

8   Indeed, Kaufmann writes:

> Nietzsche did not decide to reduce the will to power to a sexual *libido* (for sexuality is that very aspect of the basic drive which is cancelled in sublimation and cannot, for that reason, be considered the essence of the drive). Sexuality is merely a foreground of something else that is more basic and hence preserved in sublimation: the will to power.
>
> (Kaufmann, 1968, p. 222)

9   Perhaps the most crucial difference between Adler's power instinct and Nietzsche's Will to Power is that the latter does not seek to possess power; Nietzsche insists that one

> should think again before positing the 'instinct of preservation' as the cardinal drive in an organic creature. A living thing wants above all to *discharge* its force: 'preservation' is only a consequence of this.
>
> (*WP*, 650)

The Will to Power does not covet power; it is simply 'an insatiable desire to manifest power; or as the employment or exercise of power, as a creative drive' (*WP*, 619). Power in the Adlerian model, however, is linked with 'increased possession . . . and influence, and for the disparagement and cheating of other persons' (Adler, 1956, p. 112).

10 Indeed, Jung omits several passages that discuss the Will to Power (see also Chapter 34, 'Of Self Overcoming'; Chapter 42, 'Of Redemption') and not one of these refers to power in Jung's one-sided conception of power as domination.

11 Bishop does note, however, that Jung made a connection between the libido and the concept of the *Will* in *TSZ*. Thus Jung writes: 'Nothing remains for Mankind but to work in harmony with this Will. Nietzsche's Zarathustra teaches us this impressively' (cited in Bishop, 1995, p. 95).

12 This is aptly expressed in *MDR* where Jung describes his family coat of arms:

> There is a cross azure in chief dexter and in base sinister a blue bunch of grapes in a field d'or; separating these is an etoile d'or in fess azure [a blue cross in the upper right and blue grapes in the lower left in a field of gold; a blue bar with a gold star]

> ... Just as cross and rose represent the Rosicrucian problem of opposites (*'per crucem ad rosam'*), that is, the Christian and Dionysian elements, so cross and grapes are symbols of the heavenly and chthonic spirit. The uniting symbol is the gold star, the *aurum philosophorum*.
>
> (*MDR*, pp. 259–260)

The Nietzschean ingredients are present: Dionysus, as god of wine, is represented by the grapes, and Zarathustra literally means 'gold star'. (On 23 April 1883 Nietzsche wrote in a letter to Peter Gast: 'Today I learnt by chance *what* "Zarathustra" means: it means "Gold Star"': cited in Bishop, 1995, p. 282, n. 47; 1999a, p. 239, n. 10). But these ingredients are firmly contained and positioned in their allotted space; the 'star' does not 'dance' as it does in Nietzsche, it sits motionless under a blue bar in 'the lower left'.

13 Whole selves: Nietzsche's influence on Jung revisited

1 As I have argued elsewhere (Huskinson, 2000), the logical contradiction of a 'union of opposites' can be resolved with the philosophical thought of Emmanuel Levinas.

2 The passage continues: 'Actually, this inversion is superfluous in view of the fact that the self [is] an empirical concept of psychology, and can therefore be hypostatized if the above precautions are taken.'

3 Indeed, Jung insists: 'The superman . . . is only a possibility inasmuch as it can be applied subjectively and symbolically' (Peters, 1991, p. 126; *SNZ*, II, p. 925). Furthermore, the Self 'can be reached only by the symbol' (Jung, 1921, par. 178), which is itself subjectively determined. (The symbol is effective for one individual but merely appears as a sign for another; see Chapter 6.) Jung equates the acceptance of the reality of the symbol with religion (Jung, 1921, par. 202; see also Jung, 1955–1956, par. 515), so that the whole self, for Jung, is a goal attainable only through religion; it is a religious experience. Nietzsche himself was keen to explain the moment when he first *experienced* the force of Eternal Recurrence, as an experience of the redemption of his own life (*EH*, 'TSZ', 1).

4 Indeed, Goethe, both Nietzsche's and Jung's epitome of human excellence, is described by Nietzsche not as an *Übermensch* but as a higher man (*TI*, 'Expeditions of an Untimely Man', 49).

5 Cf. 'through many generations' (*WP*, 996); 'through breeding' (*WP*, 964); 'there is only nobility of birth, only nobility of blood' (*WP*, 942).

6 'However,' Jacobi continues,

> successful differentiation and understanding of all four functions is possible, and when this is achieved the individual (with a dominant function of thinking) will be able to . . . first apprehend an object cognitively, then intuitively 'track down' its hidden potentialities, then palpate it with sensation, and finally – if feeling is the inferior function – evaluate it to a certain degree in regard to pleasantness or unpleasantness.
>
> (Jacobi, 1968, p. 17)

7 Warren Colman (2000) views the Self as both the product realized by the process and the process of realization itself; that is, as both an organizing principle and that which is organized: as both 'a tendency towards organization' (the process of uniting opposites) and 'the structure of that organization' (the Self). 'In other words, the psyche is self-structuring and the name for that process is the self' (Colman, 2000, p. 14). The implication from Colman's reading is that the end-product of the process should not be regarded as separate from the process; rather the end-product is simply the point when

the process ceases to continue. In this reading, the reality of the Self is determined by the process and its termination.

8 Jung writes:

> It seems to me that our psychological inquiry must come to a stop here, for the idea of a self is itself a transcendental postulate which, although justifiable psychologically, does not allow of scientific proof. This step beyond science is an unconditional requirement of the psychological development I have sought to depict, because without this postulate I could give no adequate formulation of the psychic processes that occur empirically. At the very least, therefore, the self can claim the value of a hypothesis analogous to that of the structure of the atom. And even though we should once again be enmeshed in an image, it is none the less powerfully alive, and its interpretation quite exceeds my powers. I have no doubt at all that it is an image, but one in which we are contained.
>
> (Jung, 1928b, par. 405)

9   Indeed, commentators define the Self in terms of its process of becoming and the experience of this. For example, in Chapter 6 we saw Humbert (1980, p. 240) and Samuels (1994, p. 91) refer to the Self as an experience of sensing a teleological purpose and movement towards wholeness (a personal whole with ethical connotations). Hubback refers to the process impersonally in terms of its energetic movement and activity (1998, p. 279).

10 In addition to the argument I have put forward in this inquiry, Jung's ambiguous reception of Nietzsche could be explained by his need to disassociate his ideas from what *he* would regard as adverse political and religious connotations arising from Nietzsche's work: namely its associations with Nazism and its preoccupation with the death of God.

It is held that Jung's thought has not received the full attention it deserves because of his alleged associations with National Socialism (Grossman, 1979, p. 231). A professed allegiance to Nietzsche's thought would be detrimental to Jung and his cause of establishing analytical psychology as an acceptable discipline, for 'Jung consistently regarded Nazism as a kind of Nietzschean project' (Aschheim, 1992, pp. 259–260; Bishop, 1995, p. 129; see *SNZ*, II, pp. 1523–1524). However, Jung was explicitly critical of Nazism and portrayed it as a misapplication of Nietzschean thought, thereby defending both Nietzsche's project and, through association, his own:

> Nietzsche himself would be highly astonished to hear such news. He surely never dreamt that he would be called the father of all this modern political evil. That really comes from the misunderstanding to which Nietzsche is exposed . . . [*Zarathustra*] should be reserved for people who have undergone a very careful training in the psychology of the unconscious . . . If a man reads *Zarathustra* unprepared, with all the presuppositions of our actual civilization, he must necessarily draw the wrong conclusions as to the meaning of the 'Superman', 'the Blond Beast', 'the Pale Criminal', and so on.
>
> (*SNZ*, I, pp. 475–476; see also *SNZ*, I, p. 582)

However, it is interesting to note that Jung is still reluctant to embrace Nietzsche fully even before his 'disciples' – those members of his seminars on *Zarathustra* who had 'undergone a very careful training in the psychology of the unconscious', and who might not be effected by the political presuppositions arising from the German collective unconscious. Thus, I do not think Jung's ambiguous reception of Nietzsche can be reduced to its associations with Nazism.

Jung's resistance to Nietzsche has also been explained in terms of Nietzsche's rejection of God (the 'mysterious third thing'). The projects of both Nietzsche and Jung can be explained as a response to the spiritual death of contemporary man – to Western culture's one-sided overemphasis of reason at the expense of the irrational. Nietzsche and Jung seek a reconciliation of the two in the whole self. However, while such reconciliation for Nietzsche, in Jung's interpretation, entails the death of God, for Jung it entails His resurrection and active participation. 'God is not dead, he is just as alive as ever,' Jung retorts in the Second of *The Seven Sermons to the Dead* (1916a) – though we have noted earlier, elsewhere Jung is not so certain; see, for example, Jung, 1938/1940, par. 148. In Jung's mind, the 'fact' of God would mark a fundamental difference between his project and Nietzsche's, and would thereby prevent him from fully endorsing Nietzsche's project. Whether or not this explains Jung's attitude of resistance towards Nietzsche is not certain. It is clear that Jung does not shy away from Nietzsche's supposed atheism: his seminars on *TSZ* can be read as a response to it, a response that is positive as much as it is negative, for both thinkers would claim that 'the Death of God looks forward to a rebirth of divinity in a new form' (Bishop, 1995, p. 336, pp. 342–356) – that is, the whole self as *Übermensch* and Self.

11 Thus Jung writes:

[Philosophical] criticism has as little effect on the [psychic] object as zoological criticism on a duck-billed platypus. It is not the concept that matters; the concept is only a word, a counter, and it has meaning and use only because it stands for a certain sum of experience.

(Jung, 1951, par. 63)

12 Thus, 'nothing is "given" as real except our world of desires and passions . . . we can rise or sink to no other "reality" than the reality of our drives' (*BGE*, 36; *WP*, 619), and our most valuable convictions are merely the 'judgements of our muscles' (*WP*, 314). It is important to note that Nietzsche does not reduce psychology to physiology, or promote the body at the expense of the spirit, as Jung claims he did. We have to bear in mind the particular context in which Nietzsche refers to physiology. Nietzsche purposely emphasizes the sensory and physiological aspects of the psyche in order to separate his psychology from metaphysical idealism and its investigative methods of abstract speculation (cf. *EH*, 'HAH', 6; *WP*, 408).

13 On a similar note, the poet Rainer Maria Rilke refused Freudian analysis because he feared that in exorcising his devils, his angels might also be eliminated (letter to Lou Andreas-Salomé, 24 January 1912; cited by Stephen Mitchell (ed.) (1984) *The Selected Poetry of Rainer Maria Rilke*, New York: Vintage, p. 312; cited also in Dixon, 1999, p. 321, n. 110)

14 Jung criticizes Freud for wanting to destroy the unfavourable aspects of the psyche. The quotation in full reads as follows:

The doctor curing a neurosis according to Freud's method tries to dig up the wishes and tendencies buried in the subconscious of the patient and to bring them into the clear light of consciousness in order to destroy them. My method is different. The repressed tendencies that are made conscious should not be destroyed but, on the contrary, should be developed further.

(*JS*, pp. 41–42)

Bibliography

Adler, A. (1956) *The Individual Psychology of Alfred Adler: A Systematic Presentation in Selections from his Writings* (ed. H. L. Ansbacher and R. R. Ansbacher), New York: Basic Books.

Adler, G. and Jaffé, A. (1973–1975) *C. G. Jung Letters*, 2 vols 1906–1950 and 1951–1961, London: Routledge and Kegan Paul.

Anthony, M. (1990) *The Valkyries: The Women around Jung*, Shaftesbury: Element Books.

Aristotle (1926a) *Eudemian Ethics* (trans. H. Cooke), Loeb Classical library, Cambridge, MA: Harvard University Press.

—— (1926b) *Politics* (trans. H. Cooke), Loeb Classical library, Cambridge, MA: Harvard University Press.

—— (1961) *Poetics* (trans. S. H. Butcher), New York: Hill and Wang.

—— (1962) *Nichomachean Ethics* (trans. H. Rackman), London: Heinemann.

—— (1970) *Physics*, Bks I–II (trans. W. Charlton), Oxford: Clarendon Press.

—— (1983) *Physics*, Bks III–IV (trans. E. Hussey), Oxford: Clarendon Press.

—— (1985) *Metaphysics* (trans. M. Furth), Indianapolis, IN: Hackett.

Aschheim, S. (1992) *The Nietzsche Legacy in Germany*, Berkeley, CA: University of California Press.

Assoun, P-L. (2000) *Freud and Nietzsche* (trans. R. L. Collier Jr), London: Athlone Press.

Augustine (1846) *Liber de Diversis Quaestionibus LXXXIII*, in *Patrologia Latina* (ed. J. P. Migne), vol. 40, cols 11–100. Reprint of edition published in Paris.

Bär, E. (1976) 'Archetypes and Ideas: Jung and Kant', *Philosophy Today*, 20: 114–123.

Barrack, C. (1974) *Nietzsche Studien*, vol. 3, New York: Walter de Gruyter.

Bauer, K. (1999) *Adorno's Nietzschean Narratives: Critiques of Ideology; Readings of Wagner*, Albany, NY: SUNY Press.

Berkowitz, P. (1995) *Nietzsche: The Ethics of an Immoralist*, London: Harvard University Press.

Bishop, P. (1994) 'The Members of Jung's Seminar on Zarathustra', *Spring: Journal of Archetype and Culture*, 56: 92–121.

—— (1995) *The Dionysian Self: C. G. Jung's Reception of Friedrich Nietzsche*, London: Walter de Gruyter.

—— (1996) 'The Use of Kant in Jung's Early Psychological Works', *Journal of European Studies*, 26: 107–140.

—— (1999a) 'C. G. Jung and Nietzsche: Dionysus and Analytical Psychology', *Jung in Contexts: A Reader* (ed. P. Bishop), London: Routledge.

—— (1999b) 'The Birth of Analytical Psychology from the Spirit of Weimar Classicism', *Journal of European Studies*, 29: 417–440.

—— (1999c) 'Nietzsche and Weimar Aesthetics', *German Life and Letters*, 52: 413–429.

—— (2000a) 'Affinities between Weimar Classicism and Analytical Psychology: Goethe and Jung on the Concept of the Self', *Forum for Modern Language Studies*, 36(1): 74–91.

—— (2000b) *Synchronicity and Intellectual Intuition in Kant, Swedenborg, and Jung*, Problems in Contemporary Philosophy vol. 46, Lampeter: Edwin Mellen Press.

Booth, T. (1990a) 'A Suggested Analogy for the Elusive Self', *Journal of Analytical Psychology*, 35: 335–337.

—— (1990b) 'Response to J. W. T. Redfearn's Comment', *Journal of Analytical Psychology*, 35: 341–342.

Brandes, G. (1895) *Menschen und Werke, cap. Nietzsche*, Frankfurt: Literarische Austalt.

Burgard, P. (ed.) (1994) *Nietzsche and the Feminine*, Charlottesville, VA: University of Virginia Press.

Casement, A. (2001) *Cark Gustav Jung*, London: Sage.

Cauchi, F. (1974) 'Figures of *Funambule*: Nietzsche's Parable of the Ropedancer', *Nietzsche-Studien*, 23: 42–64.

—— (1998) *Zarathustra Contra Zarathustra*, Avebury Series in Philosophy, Aldershot, Hants: Ashgate.

Caurus, C. (1846/1989) *Psyche: On the Development of the Soul*, Part 1, 'The Unconscious', Dunquin series No. 3, Dallas: Spring Publications.

Clark, J. J. (1992) *In Search of Jung: Historical and Philosophical Enquiries*, London: Routledge.

Clark, M. (1990) *Nietzsche on Truth and Philosophy*, Cambridge: Cambridge University Press.

Colman, W. (2000) 'Models of the Self', in *Jungian Thought in the Modern World* (ed. E. Christopher and H. Solomon), London: Free Association Books.

Conway, D. (1997) *Nietzsche and the Political*, Thinking the Political Series, London: Routledge.

Copleston, F. (1964) *A History of Philosophy: Late Mediaeval and Renaissance Philosophy*, vol. 3, part II (in two parts), Westminster, MD: Image Books, Newman Press.

Cowan, M. (trans.) (1962) *Philosophy in the Tragic Age of the Greeks*, South Bend, IN: Gateway.

Cybulska, E. (2000) 'The Madness of Nietzsche: A Misdiagnosis of the Millennium?' *Hospital Medicine*, 61(8): 571–575.

Danto, A. (1965) *Nietzsche as Philosopher*, New York: Macmillan Press.

Del Caro, A. (1989) *Nietzsche Contra Nietzsche*, Baton Rouge, LA and London: Louisiana State University Press.

Deleuze, G. (1983) *Nietzsche and Philosophy* (trans. H. Tomlinson), London: Athlone Press.

De Man, P. (1979) *Allegories of Reading*, New Haven, CT: Yale University Press.

Derrida, J. (1978) *Writing and Difference* (trans. A. Bass), Chicago: University of Chicago Press.

Dixon, P. (1999) *Nietzsche and Jung: Sailing a Deeper Night*, Contemporary Existentialism, vol. 3, New York: Peter Lang.

Dodds, E. (1929) 'Euripides the irrationalist', in *The Ancient Concept of Progress and Other Essays on Greek Literature and Belief*, Oxford: Clarendon Press, 1986, pp. 78–92.

—— (1951) *The Greeks and the Irrational*, Berkeley, CA: University of California Press.

Edinger, E. (1972) *Ego and Archetype*, London: Shambhala.

—— (1994a) *Anatomy of the Psyche: Alchemical Symbolism in Psychotherapy*, Chicago: Open Court.

—— (1994b) *The Mystery of the Coniunctio: Alchemical Image of Individuation*, Lectures transcribed and edited by Joan Dexter Blackner, Toronto: Inner City Books.

Ellenberger, H. (1970) *The Discovery of the Unconscious: The History and Evolution of Dynamic Psychiatry*, London: Allen Lane, The Penguin Press.

Emlyn-Jones, C. (1976) 'Heraclitus and the Identity of Opposites', *Phronesis*, 21: 89–114.

Federn, E. and Nunberg, H. (eds) (1967) *Minutes of the Vienna Psychoanalytic Society*, vols I and II, New York: International Universities Press.

Fordham, M. (1957) *New Development in Analytical Psychology*, London: Routledge and Kegan Paul.

—— (1973) 'The Empirical Foundation and Theories of the Self in Jung's works', in *Analytical Psychology: A Modern Science*, London: Library of Analytical Psychology.

—— (1976) *The Self and Autism*, London: Heinemann.

—— (1985) *Explorations into the Self*, Library of Analytical Psychology, Karnac Books, London: Academic Press.

Franz, M-L. Von (1975) *C. G. Jung: His Myth in our Time* (trans. W. H. Kennedy), New York: G. P. Putnam's Sons.

—— (2000) (Commentary) *Aurora Consurgens, On the Problem of Opposites, A Document Attributed to Thomas Aquinas* (trans. R. F. C. Hull and A. S. B. Glover; ed. M-L. von Franz), Toronto: Inner City Books.

Freud, S. (1900/1991) *The Interpretation of Dreams*, Penguin Freud Library, vol. 4, London: Penguin.

—— (1901/1991) 'The psychopathology of everyday life,' *The Standard Edition of the Complete Psychological Works of Sigmund Freud* (eds J. Strachey and A. Freud) vol. 6, pp. 1–290, London: Hogarth Press, 1960.

—— (1910) 'On an autobiographically described case of paranoia', *The Standard Edition of the Complete Psychological Works of Sigmund Freud* (eds J. Strachey and A. Freud) vol. 12, pp. 9–82, London: Hogarth Press.

—— (1914) 'On the history of the psychoanalytic movement', *The Standard Edition of the Complete Psychological Works of Sigmund Freud* (eds J. Strachey and A. Freud) vol. 14, pp. 7–66, London: Hogarth Press.

—— (1922/1991) *Group Psychology and the Analysis of the Ego* (trans. J. Strachey) International Psychoanalytic Library, vol. 6, London: International Psychoanalytic Press.

Frey, L. (1971) 'The Shadow Revealed in the Works of Friedrich Nietzsche', in H. Kirsh (ed.) *The Well-Tended Tree: Essays on the Spirit of our Time*, New York: G. P. Putnam's Sons.

Frey-Rohn, L. (1988) *Friedrich Nietzsche: A Psychological Approach to his Life and Work* (eds R. Hinshaw and Lela Fischilli, trans. G. Massey), Zurich: Daimon Press.

Golomb, J., Santaniello, W. and Lehrer, R. (eds) (1999) *Nietzsche and Depth Psychology*, Albany, NY: SUNY Press.

Grossman, S. (1979) 'C. G. Jung and National Socialism', *Journal of European Studies*, 9: 231–251.

Guthrie, W. (1950) *The Greeks and their Gods*, London: Beacon Press.

Hannah, B. (1981) *Jung, his Life and Work: A Biographical Memoir*, New York: G. P. Putnam's Sons, Pedigree Books.

Hartmann, E. Von (1869) *Philosophy of the Unconscious* (trans. W. Chatterton Coupland), London: Kegan Paul.

Hauke, C. (2000) *Jung and the Postmodern: The Interpretation of Realities*, London: Routledge.

Heidegger, M. (1961/1982) *Nietzsche*, in two vols (trans. D. Krell.), vol. 4, New York: Harper and Row.

—— (1962) *Being and Time* (trans. J. Macquarrie and E. Robinson), New York: Harper and Row.

—— (1977) 'The Word of Nietzsche "God is Dead"', in *The Question Concerning Technology and Other Essays* (trans. W. Lovitt), New York: Harper and Row.

Heller, E. (1988) *The Importance of Nietzsche*, London: University of Chicago Press.

Heller, P. (1984) 'Concerning the Nietzsche Cult and Literary Cults in Generally', in *Nietzsche, Literature, and Values* (eds V. Durr, R. Grimm and K. Harms), Monatshefte occasional vols, no. 6, Madison, WI: University of Wisconsin Press.

Henderson, J. (1985) 'The Self in Review', *Journal of Analytical Psychology*, 30: 234–246.

Heraclitus (1959) *Fragments* (trans. P. Wheelwright), in P. Wheelwright, *Heraclitus*, Oxford: Oxford University Press.

Hermans, H. (1993) 'Moving Opposites in the Self: A Heraclitean Approach', *Journal of Analytical Psychology*, 30: 437–462.

Higgins, K. (1985) 'The Night Song's Answer', *International Studies in Philosophy*, 17: 33–50.

—— (1987) *Nietzsche's Zarathustra*, Philadelphia, PA: Temple University Press.

Hillman, J. (1972) 'Dionysus in Jung's Writings', *Spring: Journal of Archetype and Culture*, 33: 191–205.

—— (1979) *The Dream and the Underworld*, New York: Harper and Row.

—— (1989) 'Back to Beyond: On Cosmology', in *Archetypal Process* (ed. D. Griffin), Evanston, IL: Northwestern University Press.

Homans, P. (1979) *Jung in Context: Modernity and the Making of a Psychology*, Chicago: University of Chicago Press.

Hornblower, S. and Spawford, A. (1999) *The Oxford Classical Dictionary*, 3rd edn, Oxford: Oxford University Press.

Houlgate, S. (1986) *Hegel, Nietzsche, and the Criticism of Metaphysics*, Cambridge: Cambridge University Press.

Howey, R. L. (1973) *Heidegger and Jaspers on Nietzsche: A Critical Examination of Heidegge's and Jaspers' Interpretations of Nietzsche*, The Hague: Nijhoff.

Hubback, J. (1985) 'Concepts of the Self', *Journal of Analytical Psychology*, 30: 229–231.

—— (1998) 'The Dynamic Self', *Journal of Analytical Psychology*, 43: 277–285.

Humbert, E. (1980) 'The Self and Narcissism', *Journal of Analytical Psychology*, 25: 237–246.

Huskinson, L. (2000) 'The Relation of Non-Relation: The Interaction of Opposites, Compensation, and Teleology in C. G. Jung's Model of the Psyche', *Harvest: Journal for Jungian Studies*, 46: 7–25.

—— (2001) (Book review) Patricia Dixon, *Nietzsche and Jung: Sailing a Deeper Night*, *Journal of Analytical Psychology*, 46: 388–390.

—— (2002) 'The Self as Violent Other: The Problem of Defining the Self', *Journal of Analytical Psychology*, 47: 439–460.

Hussey, E. (1999) 'Heraclitus', in *The Cambridge Companion to Early Greek Philosophy*, ch. 5, pp. 88–112.

Jacobi, J. (1968) *The Psychology of C. G. Jung* (trans. K. W. Bash), London: Routledge.

Jacoby, M. (1981) 'Reflections on Heinz Kohut's Concept of Narcissism', *Journal of Analytical Psychology*, 26: 19–32.

Jaffé, A. (1970) *The Myth of Meaning in the Work of C. G. Jung* (trans. R. F. C. Hull), London: Hodder and Stoughton.

Jaques, E. (1965) 'Death and the Mid-Life Crisis', *International Journal of Psychoanalysis*, 10: 502–514.

Jarrett, J. (1979) 'The Logic of Psychological Opposition: Or How Opposite is Opposite?', *Journal of Analytical Psychology*, 24: 318–325.

—— (1990) 'Jung and Nietzsche', *Harvest: Journal for Jungian Studies*, 36: 130–148.

Jaspers, K. (1966) *Nietzsche: An Introduction to the Understanding of his Philosophical Activity* (trans. C. F. Wallraff and F. J. Schmitz), Tucson, AZ: University of Arizona Press.

Jones, E. (1953–1957) *Sigmund Freud: Life and Work*, 3 vols, London: Hogarth Press.

Jung, C. G. (1953–1983) *Collected Works* (eds H. Read, M. Fordham, G. Adler and W. McGuire, trans. R. F. C. Hull), 20 vols, London: Routledge and Kegan Paul.

—— (1907) 'The psychology of dementia praecox', CW 3, pars. 1–316.

—— (1909) 'Review of Waldstein: "Das Unbewusste ich"', *CW* 18, pars. 797–800.

—— (1911–1912/1952) *Symbols of Transformation*, *CW* 5.

—— (1913) 'A Contribution to the Study of Psychological Types', *CW* 6, Appendix, pars. 858–882.

—— (1916a) *The Seven Sermons to the Dead Written by Basilides in Alexandria, the City Where the East Toucheth the West*, in *The Gnostic Jung* (ed. R. A. Segal), London: Routledge, ch. 10, pp. 181–196.

—— (1916b) 'Appendix: The structure of the unconcious', *CW* 7, pars. 437–507.

—— (1916/1948) 'General Aspects of Dream Psychology', *CW* 8, pars. 443–529.

—— (1916/1957) 'The Transcendent Function', *CW* 8, pars. 131–193.

—— (1917/1926/1943) 'On the Psychology of the Unconscious', *CW* 7, pars. 1–201.

—— (1918) 'The Role of the Unconscious', *CW* 10, pars. 1–48.

—— (1919) 'Instinct and the Unconscious', *CW* 8, pars. 263–282.

—— (1920/1948) 'The Psychological Foundations of Belief in Spirits', *CW* 8, pars. 531–600.

—— (1921) *Psychological Types*, *CW* 6, pars. 1–987.

—— (1922) 'On the Relation of Analytical Psychology to Poetry', *CW* 15, pars. 97–132.

—— (1925a) 'Marriage as a Psychological Relationship', *CW* 17, pars. 324–345.

—— (1925b/1991) *Analytical Psychology: Notes of the Seminar Given in 1925* (ed. W. McGuire), Princeton, NJ: Princeton University Press.

—— (1927/1931) 'The Structure of the Psyche', *CW* 8, pars. 283–342.

—— (1928a) 'On Psychic Energy', *CW* 8, pars. 1–130.

—— (1928b) 'The Relations between the Ego and the Unconscious', *CW* 7, pars. 202–406.

—— (1928–1930/1995) *Dream Analysis: Notes on the Seminar Given in 1928–1930* (ed. W. McGuire), 2 vols, London: Routledge.

—— (1928/1931) 'The Spiritual Problem of Modern Man', *CW* 10, pars. 148–196.

—— (1929) 'Commentary on "The Secret of the Golden Flower"', *CW* 13, pars. 1–84.

—— (1930/1950) 'Psychology and Literature', *CW* 15, pars. 133–162.

—— (1931a) 'Basic Postulates of Analytical Psychology', *CW* 8, pars. 649–688.

—— (1931b) 'The Aims of Psychotherapy', *CW* 16, pars. 66–113.

—— (1931c) 'Forewords to Jung: *Seelenprobleme Der Gegenwart*', 1st edn, *CW* 18, pars. 1292–1293.

—— (1932) 'Psychotherapists of the Clergy', *CW* 11, pars. 488–538.

—— (1933/1934) 'The Meaning of Psychology for Modern Man', *CW* 10, pars. 276–332.

—— (1934a) 'The Development of Personality', *CW* 17, pars. 284–323.

—— (1934b) 'The Practical Use of Dream-analysis', *CW* 16, pars. 294–352.

—— (1934–1939/1989) *Seminars on Nietzsche's Zarathustra*, 2 vols (ed. J. Jarrett), London: Routledge.

—— (1934/1950) 'A Study in the Process of Individuation', *CW* 9i, pars. 489–626.

—— (1934/1954) 'Archetypes of the Collective Unconscious', *CW* 9i, pars. 1–86.

—— (1935/1953) 'Psychological Commentaries on "The Tibetan Book of the Dead"', *CW* 11, pars. 831–858.

—— (1936a) 'Individual Dream Symbolism in Relation to Alchemy', *CW* 12, pars. 44–331.

—— (1936b) 'Wotan', *CW* 10, pars. 371–399.

—— (1937a) 'Religious Ideas in Alchemy', *CW* 12, pars. 332–554.

—— (1937b) 'Psychological Factors Determining Human Behaviour', *CW* 8, pars. 232–262.

—— (1938/1940) 'Psychology and Religion' (The Terry Lectures), *CW* 11, pars. 1–168.

—— (1938/1954) 'Psychological Aspects of the Mother Archetype', *CW* 9i, pars. 148–198.

—— (1939a) 'In Memory of Sigmund Freud', *CW* 15, pars. 60–73.

—— (1939b) 'Conscious, Unconscious, and Individuation', *CW* 9i, pars. 489–524.

—— (1940) 'The Psychology of the Child Archetype', *CW* 9i, pars. 259–305.

—— (1940/1950) 'Concerning Rebirth', *CW* 9i, pars. 199–258.

—— (1942) 'Paracelsus as a Spiritual Phenomenon', *CW* 13, pars. 145–236.

—— (1942/1948) 'A Psychological Approach to the Dogma of the Trinity', *CW* 11, pars. 169–295.

—— (1942/1954) 'Transformation Symbolism in the Mass', *CW* 11, pars. 296–448.

—— (1943) 'The Gifted Child', *CW* 17, pars. 230–252.

—— (1943/1948) 'The Spirit Mercurius', *CW* 13, pars. 239–303.

—— (1944a) 'Introduction to the Religious and Psychological Problems of Alchemy', *CW* 12, pars. 1–43.

—— (1944b) 'Epilogue', *CW* 12, pars. 555–565.

—— (1945/1948) 'On the Nature of Dreams', *CW* 8, pars. 530–569.

—— (1945/1954) 'The Philosophical Tree', *CW* 13, pars. 304–482.

—— (1946) 'The Psychology of the Transference', *CW* 16, pars. 353–539.

—— (1947/1954) 'On the Nature of the Psyche', *CW* 8, pars. 343–442.

—— (1949) 'Foreword to Neumann: "The Origins and History of Consciousness"', *CW* 18, pars. 1234–1237.

—— (1950) 'Concerning Mandala Symbolism', *CW* 9i, pars. 627–712.

—— (1951) *Aion: Researches into the Phenomenology of the Self*, *CW* 9ii.

—— (1952a) 'Synchronicity: An Acausal Connecting Principle', *CW* 8, pars. 816–968.

—— (1952b) 'Answer to Job', *CW* 11, pars. 553–758.

—— (1954) 'On the Psychology of the Trickster-Figure', *CW* 9i, pars. 456–488.

—— (1955–1956) *Mysterium Coniunctionis: An Inquiry into the Separation and Synthesis of Psychic Opposites in Alchemy*, *CW* 14.

—— (1957) 'The Undiscovered Self (Present and Future)', *CW* 10, pars. 488–588.

—— (1958) 'Flying Saucers: A Modern Myth', *CW* 10, pars. 589–824.

—— (1964) *Man and his Symbols* (*MHS*), London: Arkana Penguin.

—— (1967) *Memories, Dreams, Reflection* (trans. R. Winston and C. Winston), London: Fontana.

—— (1973–1975) *C. G. Jung Letters* (ed. G. Adler and A. Jaffé), 2 vols: 1906–1950 and 1951–1961, London: Routledge and Kegan Paul.

—— (1974) *The Freud/Jung Letters* (ed. W. McGuire; trans. R. Manheim and R. F. C. Hull), London: Hogarth Press.

—— (1977) *Jung Speaking: Interviews and Encounters 1912–61* (eds W. McGuire and R. F. C. Hull), Princeton, NJ: Princeton University Press.

Kant, I. (1781/1997) *Critique of Pure Reason* (trans. P. Guyer and A. W. Wood), Cambridge Edition of the Works of Immanuel Kant, Cambridge: Cambridge University Press.

—— (1785/1964) *Groundwork for the Metaphysics of Morals* (trans. H. G. Paton), New York: Harper and Row.

—— (1790/1952) *Critique of Judgement* (trans. J. Creed Meredith), Oxford: Clarendon Press.

Kaufmann, W. (1967) 'Nietzsche' entry in *Encyclopedia of Philosophy* (ed. P. Edwards), vol. 5, New York: Macmillan.

—— (1968) *Nietzsche, Philosopher, Psychologist, Antichrist*, 3rd edn, Princeton, NJ: Princeton University Press.

—— (1976) 'Nietzsche and the Death of Tragedy: A Critique', in *Studies in Nietzsche and the Classical Tradition* (eds J. O'Flaherty, F. Timothy and R. Helm), Chapel Hill: North Carolina University Press, pp. 234–255.

—— (1992) *Tragedy and Philosophy*, Princeton, NJ: Princeton University Press.

Kennedy, J. M. (1910) *The Quintessence of Nietzsche*, London: Clifford's Inn.

Kirsch, T. (1989) (Book review) C. G. Jung, *Nietzsche's Zarathustra*, 'Notes of the Seminar Given in 1934–1939', *Quadrant*, 22(2): 101–102.

Kofman, S. (1972) *Nietzsche et la Metaphore*, Paris: Peyot.

—— (1993) *Nietzsche and Metaphor* (trans. D. Large), London: Athlone Press.

Lampert, L. (1986) *Nietzsche's Teaching: An Interpretation of Thus Spoke Zarathustra*, London: Yale University Press.

Lavrin, J. (1971) *Nietzsche: A Biographical Introduction*, New York: Charles Scribner's Sons.

Lehrer, R. (1995) *Nietzsche's Presence in Freud's Life and Thought*, Albany, NY: SUNY Press.

—— (1999a) 'Freud and Nietzsche, 1892–1895', in J. Golomb, W. Santaniello and R. Lehrer (eds) *Nietzsche and Depth Psychology*, Albany, NY: SUNY Press.

—— (1999b) 'Adler and Nietzsche', in J. Golomb, W. Santaniello and R. Lehrer (eds) *Nietzsche and Depth Psychology*, Albany, NY: SUNY Press.

Levinas, E. (1969) *Totality and Infinity: An Essay on Exteriority* (trans. A. Lingis), Pittsburgh, PA: Duquesne University Press.

Lichtenberger, H. (1910) *The Gospel of the Superman* (trans. J. M. Kennedy), London: Foulis.

Lindsay, J. (1970) *The Origins of Alchemy in Graeco-Roman Egypt*, London: Frank Muller.

Lloyd-Jones, H. (1976) 'Nietzsche and the Study of the Ancient World', in J. O'Flaherty, F. Timothy and R. Helm (eds) *Studies in Nietzsche and the Classical Tradition*, Chapel Hill, NC: North Carolina University Press.

Long, A. (ed.) (1999) *The Cambridge Companion to Early Greek Philosophy*, Cambridge: Cambridge University Press.

McGuire, W. (1974) (ed.) *The Freud/Jung Letters: The Correspondence between Sigmund Freud and C. G. Jung* (trans. R. Manheim and R. F. C. Hull), Princeton University Press.

Magnus, B. (1978) *Nietzsche's Existential Imperative*, Bloomington, IN: Indiana University Press.

—— (1983) 'Perfectibility and Attitude in Nietzsche's *Ubermensch*', *Review of Metaphysics*, 36(3): 633–659.

—— (1988) 'The Deification of the Common Place: "Twilight of the Idols"', in R. Solomon and K. Higgins (eds) *Reading Nietzsche*, Oxford: Oxford University Press.

May, K. (1990) *Nietzsche and the Spirit of Tragedy*, London: Macmillan.

Moreno, A. (1974) *Jung, Gods, and Modern Man*, Notre Dame, IN: University of Notre Dame Press.

Morgan, G. A. (1943) *What Nietzsche Means*, Cambridge, MA: Harvard University Press.

Nagy, M. (1991) *Philosophical Issues in the Psychology of C. G. Jung*, Albany, NY: SUNY Press.

Nehamas, A. (1985) *Nietzsche: Life as Literature*, London: Harvard University Press.

Nietzsche, F. (1872/1967) *The Birth of Tragedy* (trans. W. Kaufmann), New York: Vintage.

—— (1873a/1962) *Philosophy in the Tragic Age of the Greeks* (trans. M. Cowan), Washington, DC: Regnery, Gateway.

—— (1873b/1979) *On Truth and Lie in the Extra-Moral Sense* (ed. and trans. D. Breazeale), Atlantic Highlands, NJ: Humanities Press.

—— (1873–1876/1983) *Untimely Meditations* (trans. R. J. Hollingdale), Cambridge: Cambridge University Press.

—— (1878/1996) *Human, All Too Human* (trans. R. J. Hollingdale), Cambridge: Cambridge University Press.

—— (1879/1996) *Assorted Opinions and Maxims* (trans. R. J. Hollingdale), Cambridge: Cambridge University Press.

—— (1880/1996) *The Wanderer and his Shadow* (trans. R. J. Hollingdale), Cambridge: Cambridge University Press.

—— (1881/1997) *Daybreak* (eds M. Clark and B. Leiter, trans. R. J. Hollingdale), Cambridge: Cambridge University Press.

—— (1882/1974) *The Gay Science* (trans. W. Kaufmann), New York: Vintage.

—— (1883–1885/1969) *Thus Spoke Zarathustra* (trans. R. J. Hollingdale), Harmondsworth: Penguin.

—— (1883–1888/1967) *The Will to Power* (ed. W. Kaufmann, trans. W. Kaufmann and R. J. Hollingdale), New York: Vintage.

—— (1886/1990) *Beyond Good and Evil* (trans. R. J. Hollingdale), Harmondsworth: Penguin.

—— (1887/1968) *The Genealogy of Morals* (trans. W. Kaufmann), New York: Random House.

—— (1888a/1990) *Twilight of the Idols* (trans. R. J. Hollingdale), Harmondsworth: Penguin.

—— (1888b/1990) *The Anti-Christ* (trans. R. J. Hollingdale), Harmondsworth: Penguin.

—— (1888c/1990) *Ecce Homo* (trans. R. J. Hollingdale), Harmondsworth: Penguin.

—— (1888d/1967) *The Case of Wagner*, in *The Birth of Tragedy* (trans. W. Kaufmann), New York: Vintage.

—— (1969) *Selected Letters of Nietzsche* (ed. and trans. C. Middleton), Chicago: University of Chicago Press.

—— (1977) *A Nietzsche Reader* (selected and trans. R. J. Hollingdale), Harmondsworth: Penguin.

Noll, R. (1994) *The Jung Cult: Origins of a Charismatic Movement*, Princeton, NJ: Princeton University Press.

—— (1996) *The Aryan Christ: The Secret Life of Carl Jung*, New York: Random House.

O'Flaherty, J., Timothy, F. and Helm, R. (eds) (1976) *Studies in Nietzsche and the Classical Tradition*, Chapel Hill, NC: North Carolina University Press.

Otto, R. (1917/1936) *The Idea of the Holy* (trans. J. W. Harvey), Oxford: Oxford University Press.

Parkes, G. (1994) *Composing the Soul: Reaches of Nietzsche's Psychology*, Chicago: University of Chicago Press.

—— (1999) 'Nietzsche and Jung: Ambivalent Appreciation', in J. Golomb, W. Santaniello and R. Lehrer (eds) *Nietzsche and Depth Psychology*, Albany, NY: SUNY Press.

Peters, R. (1991) (Book review) 'Nietzsche's Zarathustra', *Journal of Analytical Psychology*, 36: 125–127.

Pfeffer, R. (1972) *Nietzsche: Disciple of Dionysus*, Lewisburg, PA: Bucknell University Press.

Plato (1997a) *Cratylus* (trans. C. D. C. Reeve), in *Plato: The Complete Works* (ed. John M. Cooper), Indianapolis, IN: Hackett.

—— (1997b) *Meno* (trans. G. M. A. Grube), in *Plato: The Complete Works* (ed. John M. Cooper), Indianapolis, IN: Hackett.

—— (1997c) *Laws* (trans. Trevor J. Saunders), in *Plato: The Complete Works* (ed. John M. Cooper), Indianapolis, IN: Hackett.

—— (1997d) *Republic* (trans. G. M. A. Grube), in *Plato: The Complete Works* (ed. John M. Cooper), Indianapolis, IN: Hackett.

Plaut, A. (1985) 'The Self: Concept and Fact', *Journal of Analytical Psychology*, 30: 247–250.

Poellner, P. (1995) *Nietzsche and Metaphysics*, Oxford: Clarendon Press.

Pugmire, D. (1981) 'Understanding the Psyche: Some Philosophical Roots and Affinities of Analytical Psychology', *Harvest: Journal for Jungian Studies*, 27: 90–102.

Raphael, A. (1965) *Goethe and the Philosopher's Stone*, London: Routledge and Kegan Paul.

Rapp, R. (1974) 'Nietzsche's Concept of Dionysus', *Philosophy Today*, 18: 319–329.

Redfearn, J. W. T (1977) 'The Self and Individuation', *Journal of Analytical Psychology*, 22: 125–141.

—— (1985) *My Self, My Many Selves*, Library of Analytical Psychology, vol. 6, London: Karnac Books, Academic Press.

—— (1990) 'Comment on "A Suggested Analogy for the Elusive Self"', *Journal of Analytical Psychology*, 35: 339–340.

Robinson, J. (1968) 'Answer to "The Night's Song's Answer"' in *An Introduction to Early Greek Philosophy*, Boston, MA: Houghton Mifflin.

Roth, R. (1985) *International Studies in Philosophy*, 17: 51–54.

Rudolph, A. (1974) 'Jung and Zarathustra: An Analytic Interpretation', *Philosophy Today*, 18: 312–317.

Samuels, A. (1985) *Jung and the Post-Jungians*, London and New York: Routledge and Kegan Paul.

—— (1994) *Jung and the Post-Jungians*, London: Routledge.

Sartre, J- P. (1969) *Being and Nothingness* (trans. H. Barnes), London: Routledge.

Schacht, R. (1983) *Nietzsche*, London: Routledge.

Schlamm, L. (2000) 'C. G. Jung, Mystical Experience and Inflation', *Harvest: Journal for Jungian Studies*, 46(2): 108–128.

Schopenhauer, A. (1818/1969) *The World as Will and Representation*, II vols (trans. E. F. J. Payne), New York: Dover.

—— (1988–1999) *Manuscript Remains*, vols 1–4 (ed. A. Hübscher; trans. E. J .F. Payne), Oxford: Berg.

Schrift, A. (1995) *Nietzsche and the Question of Interpretation: Between Hermeneutics and Deconstruction*, London: Routledge.

Schwartz-Salant, N. (ed.) (1995) *C. G. Jung on Alchemy*, London: Routledge.

Segal, R. (1992) *The Gnostic Jung*, London: Routledge.

—— (1995) 'Jung's Fascination with Gnosticism', in *The Allure of Gnosticism: The Gnostic Experience in Jungian Psychology and Contemporary Culture* (ed. R. Segal), Chicago and La Salle, IL: Open Court.

Shamdasani, S. (1998) *C. G. Jung and the Founding of Analytical Psychology*, London: Routledge.

Silk, M. and Stern, J. (1981) *Nietzsche on Tragedy*, Cambridge: Cambridge University Press.

Simmel, G. (1986) *Schopenhauer and Nietzsche* (trans. H. Loiskandle, D. Weinstein and M. Weinstein), Boston, MA: University of Massachusetts Press.

Sloterdijk, P. (1989) *Nietzsche's Materialism*, Theory and History of Literature vol. 56, Minneapolis, MN: University of Minnesota Press.

Soll, I. (1973) 'Reflections on Recurrence: A Re-examination of Nietzsche's Doctrine', in R. Solomon and K. Higgins (eds) *Reading Nietzsche*, Oxford: Oxford University Press.

Solomon, R. (ed.) (1973) *Nietzsche: A Collection of Critical Essays*, New York: Garden City Press.

Solomon, R. and Higgins, K. (eds) (1988) *Reading Nietzsche*, Oxford: Oxford University Press.

Stein, M. (1998) *Jung's Map of the Soul*, Chicago and La Salle, IL: Open Court.

Stern, J. P. (1978) *Nietzsche*, Cornwall: Fontana.

Storr, A. (1973) *C. G. Jung*, New York: Viking.

—— (ed.) (1988) *The Essential Jung: Selected Writings*, London: Fontana.

—— (1989) *Freud*, Oxford: Oxford University Press.

—— (1996) *Nietzsche and Jung*, J. R. Jones Lecture, University of Swansea, Wales, 20 November 1996, Swansea: University of Wales Press.

Strong, T. B. (1975) *Friedrich Nietzsche and the Politics of Transformation*, Berkeley, CA: University of California Press.

Thatcher, D. (1977) 'Eagle and Serpent in *Zarathustra*', *Nietzsche-Studien*, 6: 240–260.

Voogd, S. De (1977) 'C. G. Jung, Psychologist of the Future "Philosopher" of the Past', *Spring: Journal of Archetype and Culture*, 22: 152–182.

—— (1992) 'Fantasy Versus Fiction: Jung's Kantianism Appraised', in R. Papadopoulous (ed.) *Carl Gustav Jung: Critical Assessments*, vol. 1, London: Routledge.

Waugaman, R. (1973) 'The Intellectual Relationship between Nietzsche and Freud', *Psychiatry*, 36: 458–467.

Wheelwright, P. (1959) *Heraclitus*, Oxford: Oxford University Press.

Williams, H. (1989) *Hegel, Heraclitus, and Marx's Dialectic*, London: Harvester Wheatsheaf.

Williams, M. (1973) 'The Indivisibility of the Personal and Collective Unconscious', in M. Fordham (ed.) *Analytical Psychology: A Modern Science*, London: Heinemann.

Winnington-Ingram, R. (1983) *Studies in Aeschylus*, Cambridge: Cambridge University Press.

Woodman, R. (1986) 'Nietzsche's Madness as Soul-Making: A View Contra Jung's', *Spring: Journal of Archetype and Culture*, 22: 101–118.

Zinkin, L. (1985) 'Paradoxes of the Self', *Journal of Analytical Psychology*, 30: 1–17.

Index